AN INTRODUCTION TO
CHINA'S TAXATION

AN INTRODUCTION TO
CHINA'S
TAXATION

Edited by Yang Hong

Enrich Professional Publishing

Published by

Enrich Professional Publishing (S) Private Limited
16L, Enterprise Road,
Singapore 627660
Website: www.enrichprofessional.com
A Member of Enrich Culture Group Limited

Hong Kong Head Office:
2/F, Rays Industrial Building, 71 Hung To Road, Kwun Tong, Kowloon, Hong Kong, China

Beijing Office:
Rm 1800, Building C, Central Valley, 16 Hai Dian Zhong Jie, Haidian District, Beijing, China

English edition © 2013 by Enrich Professional Publishing (S) Private Limited
Chinese original edition © 2010 China Renmin University Press

Translated by Wang Jinhui and Shao Qinghua
Edited by Simon Sui and Jane Elliott

ISBN (Hardback)   978-981-4332-01-9
ISBN (ebook)   978-981-4332-00-2 (pdf)
                   978-981-4339-88-9 (epub)

This publication is designed to provide accurate and authoritative information in regard to the subject matter covered. It is sold with the understanding that the publisher is not engaged in rendering legal, accounting, or other professional service. If legal advice or other expert assistance is required, the services of a competent professional person should be sought.

Enrich Professional Publishing is an independent globally minded publisher focusing on the economic and financial developments that have revolutionized new China. We aim to serve the needs of advanced degree students, researchers, and business professionals who are looking for authoritative, accurate and engaging information on China.

Contents

Preface

Taxation is a historical and fiscal concept, an important component of a nation's financial and economic system, and a norm for a nation to handle tax distribution. It is not only the legal basis and regulations for a nation to levy taxes upon taxpayers, but also the statutory criteria for the taxpayers to fulfill their obligation.

In a broad sense, taxation refers to various legal systems on taxation such as national tax laws and regulations, taxation administration system, administration system of tax collection, and management system of the tax department; in a narrow sense, taxation refers to tax laws and regulations, analyzed mainly from the angle of taxation administration.

Since the founding of new China, China's taxation has been reformed several times. The current taxation has been gradually improved and established since the reform of industrial and commercial taxation in 1994. Due to the gradual development of China's socialist market economic system, the impact of taxation as an important strategic tool for bringing in revenue and adjusting the economy will be more and more significant.

The book in ten chapters introduces China's taxation structures and nine types of tax, namely, Value-Added Tax, Consumption Tax, Enterprise Income Tax, Customs Duty, Business Tax, Individual Income Tax, Resource Tax, Property Tax, and other taxes such as Stamp Duty. Aspects including scope of tax collection, taxpayers, tax rate, calculation of the taxable amount, tax preferences, and administration of tax collection are covered.

The contributors to the book are a team of experts from the School of Taxation of the Central University of Finance and Economics, who have been teaching taxation for over 20 years, including Professor Yang Hong, Professor Liang Junjiao, Associate Professor Zhang Guangtong and Associate Professor Huang Yun. This book helps readers quickly grasp the basic ideas of China's taxation.

1 Chapter

An Overview of Taxation

Concept of Taxation

Basic concepts

Taxation is a historical and fiscal concept, an important component of a national financial and economic system and a national norm for handling tax distribution relations. It aims to impose a financial charge or other levy upon taxpayers (individuals or legal entities) by the state or its functional equivalent legislative authorities. It also involves the regulations on the taxation, and the statutory criteria for taxpayers to fulfill their obligations to pay taxes.

The concept of the taxation can be looked at from both broad sense and narrow sense.

Broad-sense and narrow-sense taxation

Broad-sense taxation refers to the generic term of various legal systems on taxation, including national tax laws and regulations, systems of taxation administration, institutions of tax collection and administration, and systems of tax authorities' internal management.

1) Legal systems on taxation i.e. normative legal documents regulating the relationship between tax levy and payment, including various tax laws, ordinances, implementing rules, provisions, measures, agreements and so on.
2) Systems of taxation administration i.e. the system specifying the division of jurisdiction over tax revenue legislation, taxation law enforcement and taxation administration between the central and local governments.
3) Institutions of tax collection and administration.
4) Systems of tax authorities and staff i.e. systems of establishment, division of labor and relationship of administrative subordination of relevant authorities and tax staff's responsibilities, jurisdictions etc.
5) Systems of taxation planning, accounting and statistics.

Narrow-sense taxation refers to various national tax laws and regulations as well as tax collection and administration systems, including tax laws, ordinances, implementing rules, measures for tax collection administration and other relevant taxation rules.

The taxation also refers to the structural system of a country's taxation formed under certain historical conditions i.e. the taxation composed of various tax categories on the basis of mutual cooperation and coordination. It studies the configuration, design the tax categories, items and rates in accordance with a country's development level of productive force and economic structure, and provides theoretical foundation for taxation reform and tax revenue legislation.

The abovementioned two concepts, though overlapping in some aspects, are mutually distincted. The former is the legal form of taxation and the legal norm on tax allocation activities; while the latter refers to the structural taxation adopted by a country in accordance with its economic conditions and financial needs.

Four hierarchies of the broad-sense taxation

In the broad sense, the taxation can be classified into four categories, namely tax laws, tax regulations, tax rules and tax administration norms.

Tax laws

Tax laws refer to the fundamental systems of relevant tax allocation activities formulated by the national highest organization or functional equivalents with legislative power. Under the provisions of *Article 31* of the *Constitution of the People's Republic of China* (hereinafter refers to "the constitution"), only the NPC and its Standing Committee are entitled to make laws. China's tax laws are also formulated by the NPC and its Standing Committee, and their legal status and force are inferior only to the constitution but superior to those of tax regulations and rules. Under the existing taxation, tax laws approved by the NPC and its Standing Committee include the *Individual Income Tax Law of the People's Republic of China*, the *Law of the People's Republic of China on Tax Collection and Administration* etc.

Tax regulations

Tax regulations refer to operative provisions or measures on relevant taxation activities formulated through certain legal procedures and pursuant to the constitution and tax laws by the highest organization of state administration or functional equivalents. The power of tax regulations is inferior to the constitution and tax laws but superior to tax rules. Under China's existing tax system, implementing rules for most tax categories are formulated in the form of tax administrative regulations by the State Council. For example, the *Provisional Regulations on Value-Added Tax of the People's Republic of China* and *Regulations for the Implementation of the Individual Income Tax Law of the People's Republic of China*.

Tax rules

Tax rules refer to normative documents that are formulated in accordance with laws or the State Council's administrative regulations, and within the scope of functions and powers of the State Administration of Taxation, and have a general binding force for nationwide tax authorities, taxpayers, withholding agents and the parties concerned. For example, the *Measures for Formulation and Implementation of Rules of Tax Authorities.*

Tax administration norms

Tax administration norms refer to the general designation of other administrative and normative documents on taxation other than the tax rules formulated and issued by tax authorities. Most tax administration norms interpret and explain laws, administrative regulations and rules of tax authorities and interpret meanings and boundaries of laws, administrative regulations and rules, and relevant legal norms as applied in detailed tax administration. For example, the *Circular on Issues of Tax Policies on Value Added Tax*, the *Circular on Some Questions Concerning the Levy of Consumption Tax* and the *Supplementary Circular on Issues Concerning the Income Tax of Financial and Insurance Enterprises* Taxation is relevant to every aspect of economic and social life, and all complicated and special circumstances should be specified accordingly for tax purposes, but not all issues can be reflected through fundamental laws, and it is inconvenient for some aspects to be covered in fundamental laws due to the complicacy of economic and social life and for legislative reasons. Therefore separate documents are issued for specifying these issues and aspects, which not only helps to maintain the stability and integrity of tax laws but also facilitates adaptation of the taxation to the constantly changing economy. However, this method is adoptable only to a certain extent in that frequent adoption indicates that there is inadequate knowledge and cognition of economic conditions and more defects in laws promulgated, and separate specifications on specific issues become means for remedying defects of tax laws, which will be both detrimental to the effectiveness and adverse to maintaining the relative stability of the taxation.

The taxation and the tax law

The tax law

The tax law is the legal form of the taxation and the generic term of legal norms for regulating the relationship between rights and obligations concerning tax levy and payment between the state and taxpayers. During the state's participation in distribution of national income and organization of fiscal revenue, there will be inevitable transfer of social wealth ownership between the state and taxpayers, which is regarded as tax levy and payment activities; and the tax laws are the legal norms regulating these activities. It is the code of conduct for the state to levy and the taxpayers to pay in accordance with the law, which on the one hand can maintain normal taxation order and guarantee state financial revenue, and can safeguard legitimate rights and interests of taxpayers on the other hand.

As a legal norm, the tax law has same generality as other legal branches under the state legal system. Since it regulates a different object of legal relationship, it is an independent legal branch with characteristics distinct from those of other legal branches.

1) Co-existence of tax and law. Tax is generated along with the formation of the state, while the law coexists with the state which has to depend on its own political power and participates in national income distribution in a legal form to acquire tax revenue. On the one hand, the state's acquisition of income from taxpayers without compensation must be guaranteed by the coercive power of the law; on the other hand, the tax levy must conform to the legal standards and specified procedures so as to safeguard the legitimate rights of taxpayers.

2) Fixity of one party in the legal relation of taxation. Any legal relation involves subjects, and so does the legal relation of taxation. But the subjects of this relation are different from those in other legal relations i.e. one of the two parties in the legal relation of taxation is always the tax authorities exercising the right of taxation on behalf of the state of functional equivalents, while the other party is taxpayers (individuals or legal entities). In other words, tax authorities are one party fixed while taxpayers are the other party subject to change under different circumstances.

3) Unequal arrangement of rights and obligations of subjects in the legal relation of taxation. Equity between rights and obligations is a fundamental rule of law. However this conclusion is based on the investigation of all rights and obligations of the subjects involved in a legal relation; under certain laws or regulations, their realistic designations of rights and obligations may not necessarily be equal. Regarding the tax law, taxpayers mainly fulfill their obligations because the levy-payment activities established by tax law is an enforced relation not being subject to principles such as negotiation, equivalence

and compensation, and is exacted pursuant to the legislative authority. Yet in a financial perspective, taxpayers can obtain their rights from the arrangement of national financial expenditure. Therefore the unity of rights and obligations of taxpayers is reflected by the financial arrangement, and there is no equivalence between the rights of obligations of taxpayers in terms of the tax law.

4) Structural integrity of the tax law. The tax law is an integrated law system composed of substantive law, adjective law and procedural law etc. The tax law is a kind of law structure formed by combining substantive law with adjective law. Structural integrity of tax law is manifested in the fact that the tax law plays a very important role in the national law system, and only an integral tax law structure can guarantee the country's exercising of the taxation and full-amount acquisition of fiscal revenue, and safeguard the legitimate rights of taxpayers.

The relationship between the taxation and the tax law

From the economic perspective, taxation is essentially an economic benefit relationship formed during the state's participation in the national revenue allocation, including the tax allocation relationship between the state and taxpayers and the tax benefit allocation relationship within government at various levels. The realization of these tax allocation relationships needs the implementation of a specific and extrinsic taxation.

Tax law is a juristic concept and its subject matter is the right-obligation relationship formed in the course of taxation allocation. Both the taxation benefit allocation relationship between the state and taxpayers and that among government at various levels is realized by means of law i.e. by means of designing taxation rights and obligations. Thus what the tax law regulates is the relationship between taxation rights and obligations but the direct taxation allocation relationship.

The taxation is inseparable from tax law and they have both similarities and differences. The similarities are that 1) the subject matter of both the taxation and tax law is the levy-payment relationship; 2) both the taxation and tax law involve factors such as taxpayers, object of taxation and tax rate. The taxation is only different from tax law in two aspects i.e. the scope of legislation for the fundamental taxation and implementation rules, and the legal force thus generated. Regarding the scope of legislation, tax laws are approved and promulgated by the highest organizations of state power or functional equivalents (in China, they refer to the NPC and its Standing Committee); while taxation administrative regulations and rules are formulated and promulgated by administrative organizations (highest administrative organizations and local administrative departments) authorized by organizations of state power. In terms of the potency, the tax law is superior to the administrative regulations and rules.

To sum up, the taxation and tax law are related to different scopes. Generally, all legal norms on taxation can be called the taxation, which specifically consists of the tax law, tax regulations and tax rules. For example, the *Enterprise Income Tax Law of the People's Republic of China* is both a tax law and a tax system while the *Provisional Regulations on Value-Added Tax of the People's Republic of China* is only a tax regulation but not a tax law.

The legal relationship of taxation

The concepts of taxation and tax law usually accompany the concept of the legal relationship of taxation. Legal relationship of taxation refers to the rights-obligation relationship between the state and taxpayers which is regulated under legal norms on taxation. The tax levy is a relationship of benefit distribution between taxpayers, and this relationship will be escalated to a special legal relationship after the rights and obligations of both sides are defined in legal terms. This legal relationship mainly includes three aspects:

Subject of rights

Subject of rights refers to the party enjoying rights and fulfilling obligations in the legal relationship of taxation. Subject of rights can be classified as the subject of tax levy and the subject of tax payment according to the different situations of the parties involved.

In China, the subject of tax levy is the state tax authorities, which exercise the duty of taxation on behalf of the state. Those authorities include tax authorities, the Customs and financial authorities at all levels. The subject of tax payment refers to entities and individuals fulfilling obligation to pay tax, including individuals and legal entities. In China, entities and individuals bearing obligations of withholding and remitting tax or collecting and remitting tax specified in taxation laws and regulations may also be categorized as the subjects of tax payment.

As aforementioned, the rights and obligations of both sides of the legal relationship of taxation are unequal. This is different from what is described in a general civil law relationship.

Object of rights

Object of rights in the legal relationship of taxation refers to the object aimed at by both rights and obligations of a subject of rights, and specifically refers to the object of taxation among key elements of tax law.

The object of the legal relationship of turnover tax is the goods sales revenue or service income; that of the legal relationship of income tax is the income obtained from production and operation; that of the legal relationship of property tax is the property.

Meanwhile, the object of the legal relationship of taxation is the goal of adjusting and controlling the economy by employing the tax leverage. For example, the state adjusts the taxation object by expanding or decreasing the incidence of taxation according to the macro-economic development in a specific period, thus to a balanced growth of the national economy.

The legal relationship of taxation

The legal relationship of taxation refers to rights enjoyed and obligations undertaken by the subject of rights in accordance with the law, and this is the most substantial element of this relationship and also the core of the tax law.

Rights of the subject of tax levy are mainly to collect tax, practice taxation inspection and punish the violators by law; obligations are mainly to provide propaganda, consultation and guidance about the tax law for taxpayers, timely transfer the levied tax to the state treasury and tackle the tax disputes.

Rights of the subject of tax payment are mainly to apply for refund of excessive tax paid, to postpone tax payment, to apply for tax relief by law, to apply for reconsideration and to institute an action; obligations are mainly to complete taxation registration and to practice tax declaration, and to pay tax and receive tax inspection.

Components of Taxation

Components of taxation refer to essential constituent elements forming each specific tax category, including three basic elements: the taxpayer, the object of taxation and the tax rate; and others: such as intermediate links of taxation, the assessable period, the tax preference, and the violation handling.

Taxpayers

The taxpayers refer to legal entities and individuals directly responsible for paying tax as specified by the tax law. The provision on taxpayer solves the issue of on whom the tax is levied, or who shall pay tax. The taxpayer is the object of tax payment.

Natural person and legal person

The taxpayer includes natural persons and legal persons as described in legal terms. The taxpayer may be a natural person or a legal person. The natural person refers to an ordinary person legally becoming the subject of rights and obligations and individually undertaking tax-paying obligations specified legally, for example, the individual with taxable income. The legal person refers to an organization that has the capacity for civil rights and civil conducts, and independently enjoys civil rights and assumes civil obligations in accordance with the law. Compared with the natural person, the legal person is the legal personification of a social organization and shall meet four conditions as follows:

1) The legal person shall be registered and recorded officially with the industrial and commercial administrative departments.

2) The legal person shall have requisite assets and funds. "Asset" is generally used for business entities, while "fund" is used for government agencies, government-sponsored institutions and social organizations. The legal person must possess a certain amount of assets or funds as the backup for liquidating debts and assuming risks so as to secure the socioeconomic order and the safety of business transactions.

3) The legal person shall possess its own name, organization and premises. This provision is to prevent legitimization of any "bogus company."

4) The legal person shall have the ability to independently bear civil liability and to instigate a prosecution and respond to prosecutions. For example, a company with limited liability conducts taxable acts specified by tax law and acquires corresponding taxable income.

Withholding agent

The withholding agent refers to an entity or individual specified in tax law shouldering the obligations of tax withholding and paying tax to the state during business operations. The tax law specifies that tax authorities shall pay the withholding agent a commission of a certain proportion of tax payment withheld or collected. At the same time, the withholding agent must fulfill tax withholding and collecting obligations in accordance with law. Otherwise, the withholding agent shall bear corresponding legal liabilities. Taking the *Law of the People's Republic of China on the Administration of Tax Collection* for example, it specifies that a withholding agent failing to execute its obligations shall be requested to withhold or collect the amount that should be withheld but not has not been withheld, or should be collected but has not been collected within a designated period of time.

Tax bearer refers to the legal entity or individual ultimately bearing the tax. Tax bearer and taxpayer are two different concepts. For some tax categories such as income taxes, the taxpayer is the tax bearer since these taxes cannot be transferred. For other categories such as value added tax (VAT), consumption tax and business tax, the taxpayer is not the tax bearer since these taxes transferrable. There is no provision on tax bearer in tax law, but policy-makers should consider and study the tax bearer's tax burden when making taxation policies and designing the tax system.

Object of taxation

The object of taxation refers to the basis of taxation i.e. the object of paying taxes. Object of taxation of each tax category specifies its tax incidence; in other words, that listed as object of taxation falls into the tax incidence. Therefore the difference of various tax categories is mainly determined by different objects of taxation (such as commodities, incomes, properties and certain conducts). Object of taxation is the outstanding feature differentiating one tax category from another. The state may select the object of taxation at the right moment according to objective economic conditions at different periods in order to achieve the purpose of organizing fiscal revenue and regulating the economy. There are two concepts relevant to the object of taxation, namely the tax item and the basis of tax calculation.

Tax item shows specific tax incidence and the scope of taxation. Provision on tax item among the components of the taxation is to meet the technical requirements of tax collection, and is a criterion for dividing the boundary between levy and exemption and that between high and low taxation. There are two objectives by setting tax items: first, it is to put the principle of tax equitability into practice and to regulate tax by setting different tax rates for different tax items according to profit levels of different taxable items and the requirements of national economic policies; second, it is to put the convenience of taxation into practice and to set tax for taxable items of the same category, the same profit level and the same path of macroscopic re-adjustment, and to set tax rates according to categories of taxable items. There are two basic methods for establishing tax items, one is the enumeration method i.e. tax items are designed respectively for each kind of commodity or business. Specific sub-items may be divided under a tax item when needed. The enumeration method has advantages such as clear-cut boundaries and easy-to-master mechanism, and disadvantages such as too many tax items and inconvenient to look up. The other is the summarization method i.e. tax items are designed according to categories or industries of commodities. This method has its advantages such as fewer tax items and convenient to look up and disadvantages such as rough tax items arrangement and difficult to practice a reasonable distribution of tax burden. These two methods should be used dependently and flexibly according to the production and operation conditions of different tax categories and commodities and state policy requirements in different periods. Tax is levied at the same tax rate uniformly according to the taxable amount of the object of taxation for some tax categories despite the nature of the object. Tax items should be divided specifically for some tax categories with complicated objects of taxation, for example the consumption tax.

Base for tax calculation is the measuring unit and the levy standard of the object of taxation. Some tax categories are of basically consistent object of taxation and base for tax calculation. For example, the object of taxation of various income taxes is income and its base for tax calculation is taxable income. But some categories of taxes are basically of different objects of taxation and basis for tax calculation, for example, the object of taxation of business tax is taxable services and its base for tax calculation is business turnover acquired from providing taxable services.

In addition, another concept related to the object of taxation is the source of taxation. It is the ultimate source of tax payment. The object of taxation is closely related to source of taxation. Generally, source of taxation is the national income created by laborers in material production sectors, but each category of tax has its own source of finance. Source of taxation and object of taxation are consistent for some taxes such as enterprise income tax, where both are income on profit of the taxpaying entity, and different for some taxes such as property tax, with the object of taxation being the quantity or value of property while source of taxation is the profit on property or the income of the property owner. Generally, wielding the national taxation to regulate of the overall economic development starts with the object of taxation but does not directly interfere with the source of taxation. However the object of taxation is the core for analysis of tax burden by analyzing its relationship with the source of taxation, and this is an important way of comprehending tax burden.

Tax rates

Tax rate is the proportion of the amount of tax to the object of taxation, and it reflects the depth of taxation and is the key linkage of the taxation. Tax rate directly influences the national revenue income and taxpayer's burden and is the main basis for economic entities to infer whether the future economic activities are reasonable. It can be seen that tax rate is a very important means of influencing economic activities of enterprises and individuals. Tax rate includes three basic forms:

Flat tax rate

Flat rate sets a fixed tax rate regardless of the amount of object of taxation. There are the following forms for specific application of flat rate: 1) Uniform tax rate i.e. one tax rate for one tax category, such as vehicle purchase tax and enterprise income tax. 2) Industrial flat rate i.e. the same tax rate for the same industry. This form of tax rate is generally applicable when imposing the business tax. 3) Product flat rate i.e. one flat rate for one kind of product. Objectively, there is no fixed standard on the tax rate and it is mainly subject to the scale of source of taxation of various products and the state levy purposes. For commodities of a kind but with large differences in variety, specification, quality or profit level, respective or graded flat rates may be designed. 4) Regionally different flat rate. High and low flat rates may be adopted for different regions considering their differences in natural resources, production levels and income distributions. 5) Adjustable flat rate i.e. both ceilings and floors are set, the applicable regional tax rate may be determined within this range by the people's governments of provinces, autonomous regions and municipalities directly under the central government.

Flat rate has two advantages. One is that different taxpayers of a same object of taxation are laid with the same incidence of taxation, which favors fair competition; the other is that the calculation is simple, which helps the management of tax levy. Its limitation lies in the inability to embody the principle of levying more from those with more capability and less from those with less capability.

Progressive tax rate

Progressive tax rate specifies different grades of tax rate according to the amount of object of taxation and it increases with the increase of the amount of object of taxation. This kind of tax rate system is generally applicable to income tax because of its relatively direct and obvious effect on regulation of taxpayer's income, good adaptability and flexibility.

Progressive tax rate is classified into four forms according to progressive bases and methods.

Full amount progressive tax rate. This refers to the total amount of object of taxation being levied according to progressive rates of corresponding grades.

Multi-level progressive tax rate (based on the amount). This means that taxable amounts are respectively calculated by categorizing the objects of taxation into levels according to their amounts and specifying corresponding tax rates for each grade from high to low, and the sum of tax amounts of all levels is equal to the taxable amount.

A simplified tax calculating method is employed in practice i.e. "quick calculation deduction" is used in case of complicated calculation of multi-level progressive tax rate. "Quick calculation deduction" refers to the balance by deducting the tax amount calculated based on multi-level progressive tax rate from the tax amount calculated based on the full amount progressive tax rate.

Full rate progressive tax rate. This is of the same progressive method as that of total progress tax rate, but its progressive basis is relative numbers such as sales profit rate, profit rate on funds and profit rate on wages.

Multi-level progressive tax rate (based on the rate). This uses the same progressive method as that of progressive tax rate in excess of a specific amount, but its progressive basis is relative numbers such as sales profit rate, profit rate on funds and profit rate on wages. Existing land value increment tax in China employs land value increment rate as the progressive basis and the applicable tax rate increases with the increase of the amount of this rate.

Full amount progressive tax rate and full rate progressive tax rate are of simple calculation, but the incidence of taxation around the critical point of the progressive grade interval is unreasonable. Two multi-level progressive tax rates are of relatively moderate progressive degree and reasonable tax incidence, but the complexity in calculation increases the tax levy and payment costs.

Norm quota tax rate

This means that a certain amount of tax is directly specified for the object of taxation but not in the form of a proportion, so it is also called fixed tax. This is a special form of tax rate and it is generally applicable to the incidence of taxation based on specific duties. Norm quota tax rate has the following forms: 1) Regional tax amount. For example, a higher tax amount for salt tax is applicable for the places with low production cost and high profit as opposed to a lower amount in some low-profit yet high-production locations. 2) Adjustable tax amount. The tax law only specifies ceilings and floors of the tax amount; each region may autonomously determine the tax amount applicable to the actual regional conditions within the range specified by the tax law, for example, existing land use tax in China. 3) Multi-level tax amount. Objects of taxation are classified into many categories and levels and tax amounts are designed in a low-to-high approach.

Norm quota tax rate has three advantages. The first is that tax is levied based on specific duties but not by means of ad valorem, which helps taxpayers improve product quality and better the packaging; the second is that the calculation is simple and convenient; the third is that the tax amount is not influenced by the price fluctuations of objects of taxation and the tax incidence is relatively stable. The limitations of the norm quota tax rate are manifested in its limited capacity in helping the national fiscal revenue to grow synchronously with people's income level; in other words, the limitations mainly come from its deficient income regulation and scope of application.

Links of taxation

Intermediate links of taxation refer to the links with payable taxes during commodity circulation. There are many circulation links from commodity production to consumption. For example, industrial products go through links such as industrial production, and commercial wholesale and retail. The determination of intermediate links of taxation is an important issue in turnover tax, and it mainly solves the issue of whether one, two or all taxes are to be levied and on which links. It is related to the tax structure, the composition of tax categories, timely and full handover to the state treasury, and tax income distribution among regions. It is also related to issues such as enterprise's economic accounting and taxpayer's convenience of payment. Therefore intermediate links of taxation become an element of the taxation.

During the whole process of commodity circulation, the selection of intermediate links of taxation on commodity circulation amount are generally classified into three scenarios according to the number of links of tax payment: 1) One-link tax system, in which tax is levied only on one link with one kind of tax. 2) Two-link tax system, in which the same kind of tax is levied on two links. 3) Multi-link tax system, in which the same kind of tax is levied on each circulation link.

Assessable period

Assessable period refers to the period for taxpayers to pay taxes. Assessable period shall be specified for each tax category and this is determined by the characteristics of taxation i.e. enforceability and fixity.

The following three aspects should be considered when determining assessable period: 1) It shall be determined according to the different characteristics of production operation of various sectors of the national economy and the different objects of taxation. 2) It shall be determined according to the taxable amount. Generally, assessable period is shorter for larger taxable amounts and longer for shorter taxable amounts. 3) Successive levy may be practiced for some tax categories according to the occurrence of taxable acts.

Tax preference

Tax preference is the generic term for various preferential treatments, reduction or exemption from tax burden granted to specific taxpayers and taxation objects by the state in taxation laws and regulations by means of taxation policies in accordance with the general objectives of politics, economy and social development within a given period.

As an indispensable component of the taxation, tax preference is classified into narrow-sense tax preference and broad-sense tax preference. Narrow-sense tax preference refers to tax reduction and tax exemption which are a special specification encouraging and giving consideration to some taxpayers or taxation objects; tax reduction means that a portion of the taxable amount is reduced and tax exemption means that the entire taxable amount is exempted. Broad-sense tax preference refers to preferential treatments to taxpayers or taxation objects for reducing or exempting their tax burdens, such as tax reduction, exemption of tax item, preferential tax rate, export rebates, accelerated depreciation, tax item deduction, investment credit, make-up of loss, exemption of tax amount, tax credit and tax sparing.

It appears that preferential treatments such as tax reduction, tax exemption, preferential tax rate, export rebates and accelerated depreciation are specific expressions of preferential taxation policies and fall into the category of fiscal revenue, but they are similar to governmental fiscal expenditure since these preferential treatment policies reduce government revenue. Therefore tax preference is also regarded as a kind of government expenditure.

Tax preference is mainly used to better implement state taxation policies in accordance with the principle of local conditions and circumstances. Since the measures for collecting taxes and the design of tax rates are determined according to the general conditions of economic development and the average social burden capacity, they are able to adapt to universal and general requirements but not individual and special ones. Therefore a means of flexible regulation is needed as a supplement on the basis of the unified taxation, so tax preference is a necessary and indispensable element of the taxation. Taxation laws and regulations of other countries have provisions on tax reduction and exemption, and so has the taxation of China. For example, China's provisions cover reduction and exemption for difficulties, for encouragement and for investment etc.

There are three types of tax preferences according to their preferential modes i.e. tax base preference, tax rate preference and tax amount preference.

Tax base preference

Tax base preference is mainly implemented by directly lessening the base for tax calculation, including threshold, exemption volume, tax item deduction and make-up of loss etc. 1) Threshold. This is a boundary where the taxation object reaches the amount liable for tax. No tax is levied if the amount of taxation object does not reach the threshold; tax is levied based on the whole amount, not only the part exceeding the threshold, if the threshold is reached or exceeded. 2) Exemption volume. This is a volume exempted from levy from the total amount of the taxation object i.e. the volume deducted in advance from the total amount according to a certain standard, with tax not levied on the exemption volume but only on the part exceeding the exemption volume. 3) Tax item deduction. This refers to deduction of the amount of some items from the taxation object and calculation of tax amount based on the balance. 4) Make-up of loss. This refers to deduction of the operational loss in previous tax years from the operating profit of the current tax year and calculation of the tax amount based on the balance.

Tax rate preference

This refers to implementation of tax preference directly by reducing the tax rate, for example by redefining the tax rate, selecting other low tax rates, zero rate, and provisional customs duty rate.

Tax amount preference

This refers to implementation of tax preference directly by reducing the taxable amount, such as through tax reduction, tax exemption, export rebates, investment credit, tax credit and tax sparing.

It should be noted that tax preference is a policy-oriented measure. Its proper application will promote the development of enterprises and the economy; if not applied properly it will not only directly reduce fiscal revenue but also become a means of "protecting the laggard."

Violation handling

This refers to the education and punishment measures adopted against taxpayer's acts in violation of tax law. It is a necessary measure for maintaining the effectiveness of the tax law.

Acts in violation of tax laws and decrees generally include tax evasion, tax arrears, refusal to pay and tax fraud. These acts and the penalties for them are specified in detail as follows:

Tax evasion. This refers to a taxpayer's violation through failing to pay tax as specified by tax law by intentional illegal means such as falsification or alteration of vouchers, account books and statements, and transfer of assets or income, concealment of taxable items, number and amount, unjustified allotment of cost and expenses, or unauthorized increase of spending standards. *Article 63* of the *Law of the People's Republic of China on the Administration of Tax Collection* (herein after referred to as the *Law of Administration of Tax Collection*) specifies that in the case of tax evasion by a taxpayer, the tax authorities shall pursue the payment of the amount of tax and overdue payment fine that the taxpayer has failed to pay or has underpaid, and impose a fine of not more than five times the amount of tax which has not been paid or underpaid but more than 50% of this amount; if the act constitutes a crime, the criminal liability shall be investigated in accordance with the relevant laws. *Article 64* of the *Law of Administration of Tax Collection* specifies that a taxpayer or withholding agent fabricating a tax basis shall be ordered by the tax authority to turn over the tax within the set period of time and concurrently be fined an amount not exceeding RMB50,000.

Tax arrears. This refers to a taxpayer's act of violation of failing to pay tax within the specified period of time. *Article 65* of the *Law of Administration of Tax Collection* specifies that in the case of evasion of payment demand, the tax authorities shall pursue the payment of the amount of tax and overdue payment fine that the taxpayer has underpaid, and impose a fine of not more than five times the amount of tax which has been underpaid but more than 50% of the unpaid amount.

Tax refusal. This refers to a taxpayer acting against state tax law and refusing to pay tax in accordance with law. *Article 67* of the *Law of Administration of Tax*

Collection specifies that if the taxpayer's refusal circumstances are not so serious as to constitute a crime, the tax authorities shall pursue the payment of the tax and overdue payment fine the taxpayer has refused to pay and impose a fine of not less than one time but not more than five times the amount of tax which has been refused for payment.

Tax fraud. This refers to the act of fraudulently obtaining a tax reimbursement (exemption) or reduction by means of practicing fraud and deception. *Article 66* of the *Law of Administration of Tax Collection* specifies that the taxpayer obtaining a tax refund for export from the state shall be fined not less than one time but not more than five times the amount of tax obtained by practicing fraud. The tax authorities may suspend refunds for export within the specified period of time.

Classification of Taxation

This refers to classification of numerous tax categories according to different objectives and certain standards. In modern society, a multiple tax system is universally practiced and the taxation of a state consists of many categories of taxes. Scientific and reasonable tax classification either in theory or in practice is helpful for recognizing and comprehending the characteristics of different tax systems and the properties and effects of different categories of taxes, accordingly providing a reliable basis for formulating scientific and reasonable tax policies and an effective tax collection and administration system. Frequently-used classification methods are as follows:

Classification according to the nature of taxation objects

There are five categories of taxes according to the properties of taxation objects, namely commodity and service tax (also called turnover tax), income tax, property taxes, resource taxes and taxes for special purposes. This method is the main tax classification method used in China.

Commodity and service taxes

This is a category of tax whose taxation objects are commodities and services. The tax is calculated based on commodity sales amount, amount paid for purchasing commodities, and income from business, generally in the form of a flat rate. Under the existing taxation in China, commodity and service taxes mainly include value added tax, consumption tax, business tax and customs duty.

Income taxes

This is a category of tax whose taxation object is the amount of income. The tax is levied mainly according to taxpayer's income from production and operation, individual income, and other incomes. Under the existing taxation in China, income taxes mainly include enterprise income tax and individual income tax.

Property taxes

This is a category of tax whose taxation object is property value. Property taxes can be further classified into general property tax, tax on transfer of property and property increment tax etc. according to different objects of taxation. Under the existing taxation in China, property taxes mainly include house tax, vehicle and vessel usage tax, and deed tax.

Resource taxes

This is a category of tax in which the taxation objects are the absolute income and differential income of resources. Taxation object of the absolute income is the development and utilization of certain state-owned resources; that of the differential income is the difference between the quantity and the quality of resources possessed by the taxpayer, which aims at regulating differential income. China's resource tax mainly includes urban and township land use tax, land value increment tax and farmland occupation tax.

Taxes for special purposes

This is a category of tax in which the taxation object is certain behaviors or actions. Levy of the tax for special purposes is to regulate and restrict some specific acts in the socioeconomic domain by using tax leverage to bring about cooperation with the state's macroeconomic policies. China's tax on behavior mainly includes city maintenance and construction tax, stamp tax, vehicle purchase tax, fixed assets investment orientation tax, livestock slaughter tax, banquet tax etc.

Classification according to the transferability of taxes

Taxes are classified into two categories, namely direct tax and indirect tax, based on the transferability.

Direct taxes refer to various taxes the taxpayer directly bears. Income tax and property tax belong to direct taxes. In terms of direct taxes, the taxpayer is the tax bearer since they are not transferable.

Indirect taxes refer to various taxes that the taxpayer can transfer to others. Commodity tax belongs to indirect tax. In terms of indirect taxes, the taxpayer is not necessarily the tax bearer and the tax burden may be finally borne by consumers.

Classification according to the relationship between tax and price

There are two categories i.e. tax included in the calculated price and tax excluded from the price.

Tax included in price refers to a category of tax which is a component part of the price of commodities or services. Its taxable value is the price including tax. Since the tax is a part of price, the tax is realized with the realization of price, which is helpful for the state to obtain fiscal revenue in a timely way. China's current consumption tax and business tax are taxes included in price.

Tax excluded from price refers to a category of tax that is not included in the price of commodity or service. Taxable value of tax excluded from price is the price excluding tax.

Currently, value added tax in China is a tax excluded from price.

Classification according to the measuring standards of taxes

There are ad valorem tax and specific tax according to tax measuring standards.

Ad valorem tax is a category of tax whose basis is the price of taxation object. Existing categories of taxes such as VAT and enterprise income tax in China are ad valorem taxes.

Specific tax is a category of tax whose basis is the taxation object's natural units such as quantity, weight and volume. Existing taxes such as resource tax and vehicle and vessel usage tax in China are specific taxes.

Tax payable of ad valorem tax changes with the change of commodity price or service charge, and ad valorem tax is able to embody tax policies of reasonable burden and also ensure same proportional change of fiscal revenue and taxable value; therefore most categories of taxes adopt this kind of tax calculation method. The amount of specific tax changes with the change of number of taxation objects, and although the calculation is simple, tax burden and fiscal revenue cannot increase or decrease with the increase or decrease of price; therefore the tax burden is unreasonable and this tax calculation method is only adopted for a small number of tax categories.

Classification according to the revenue ownership of taxes

All countries practicing the system of tax allocation adopt two types of system of tax allocation, namely the exhaustive system of tax allocation and the non-exhaustive one.

Countries adopting the exhaustive tax allocation system classify taxes into two categories, namely central tax and local tax; the central government and local governments have respectively independent authority over tax revenue legislation, collection and administration.

Countries adopting non-exhaustive tax allocation system classify taxes into three categories, namely central tax, local tax and shared tax; the legislative power belongs to the central government while local governments have no legislative power; revenues of central tax and local tax respectively belong to the central government and local governments while the shared tax is administered in the form of respective collection and joint division arrangements.

China's existing tax system uses the non-exhaustive tax allocation arrangement.

Central tax

This is a category of tax that is collected and administered by the State Administration of Taxation and the tax revenue is disposed by the central government, such as consumption tax and customs duty under the existing tax system in China.

Local tax

This is a category of tax that is collected and administered by local governments which also dispose the tax revenue, such as business tax, urban maintenance and construction tax, and urban and township land use tax under the existing tax system in China.

Shared tax

This is a category of tax that is collected and administered by the State Administration of Taxation and the tax revenue is disposed by both central and local governments, such as value added tax, enterprise income tax and personal income tax under the existing tax system in China.

Other classification methods

There are four kinds of tax classification methods: 1) Taxes are classified into labor tax, tax in kind and money tax according to the forms of taxation; 2) taxes are classified into ordinary tax and temporary tax according to their duration; 3) taxes are classified into personal tax and objective tax according to the taxation conditions and capacities of taxpayers; 4) taxes are classified into proportional tax, progressive tax and quota tax according to the characteristics of the forms of tax rates.

Tax Structure

Concept of tax structure

Tax structure means that a state sets a combination of taxes of different functions according to specific conditions during formulating the taxation and forms a tax structure with clear main taxes and auxiliary taxes of individual advantages, effects and complementary functions. Tax structure mainly relates to the issue of the structural form of taxation, so it called tax structure.

As for the abovementioned taxes, some can be main taxes in the taxation of a state and some can only be auxiliary taxes. Main taxes are those universally levied, and the income represents a larger proportion of the total tax revenue, so they play the predominant role in the tax structure. Moreover a state's objectives of tax policies are mainly realized through setting and operating main taxes. Auxiliary taxes are supplements to main taxes and are usually set in order to realize a state's objectives of its social and economic policies under specific conditions, and they play a role of special regulation.

The setting of the tax structure determines the realization of the functions and objectives of a state's taxation policies to a considerable extent; therefore how to define a tax structure relatively suitable for national conditions is a matter of general concern for all countries. Generally speaking, the tax structure of a state is adjusted constantly with the changes in social and economic environment. Under normal circumstances, this process is also the process of increasing optimization of a state's taxation.

Different types of tax structures

Generally there are five types of tax structures i.e. the turnover tax–based tax structure, income tax–based tax structure, resource tax–based tax structure, "tax haven" tax structure featuring low–tax policies, and turnover tax and income tax–based tax structure.

Turnover tax–based tax structure

This type of tax structure features the turnover tax as the fundamental component, while other taxes are subordinate to it and play an auxiliary role. Since the object of the turnover tax is typically on a turnover amount basis of commodities and services, so there is tax levied as long as there is occurrence of such a turnover amount. Therefore the turnover tax is characterized by its extensive incidence of taxation, immunity from influence of production and operation cost and expense fluctuation, and rich tax revenue sources; the tax revenue guarantees a timely and stable fiscal revenue and features convenient tax collection and administration. When implementing the tax included in price, tax of this type is a part of the price and it can be used in cooperation with price leverage to control production and consumption, and to regulate the profit level of enterprises. This type of tax structure has some shortcomings since the turnover tax regulates national income only during the process of income formation in the production and circulation domain, so its regulation is relatively weak and thus may trigger tax transfer, which hides some problems such as regressive taxes, duplicate taxation etc.

Income tax–based tax structure

In this tax structure, the income tax plays the dominant role. This type of tax structure adopts taxpayer's amount of income as the tax basis and universally levies tax from all members of society. In other words, tax is levied not only on producers and business operators but also on persons not obtaining income from production or business operations. Income tax can also be used in cooperation with progressive tax rate and is levied according to bearing capacity, thus achieving an automatic regulation of the economy and an equitable distribution. However this type of tax structure features shortcomings such as unstable income, complicated calculation, higher degree of social accounting, and difficulty in collection and administration.

Resource tax–based tax structure

As the name suggests, the resource tax is the building block of this tax structure. Resource tax is levied on resources such as land, minerals, hydropower and forests, thus protecting resources, promoting appropriate resource allocation, and regulating differential income of resources. It is generally immune from variation of cost and expense. Most countries are facing non-uniform resource allocation, so this tax structure is only adopted in a small number of Middle Eastern countries with rich petroleum resources.

"Tax haven"

Countries adopting this type of tax structure usually practice a low tax-exemption system; in other words, people in these countries possess property or obtain income without any tax incidence, or merely pay a rather small amount of tax. This type of tax structure is manifested in three specific forms: the first form features no income tax, no property tax, and no inheritance tax or gift tax. The second form is composed of direct taxes bearing a low tax burden, such as income tax and property tax; moreover, many foreign-related tax preferences are practiced. The third form practices a normal tax system, with flexible tax preference measures. The "tax haven" structure has three main characteristics: 1) low-tax structure; 2) income tax as the main body, and turnover tax including customs duties are generally less levied or not levied; 3) there is a clearly delineated boundary "tax haven." This type of structure is usually favored by island countries or nations with a relatively stable political environment, comfortable fiscal budget expenditure, and which are geographically close to countries with high taxation and developed economies.

Dual-tax structure

The turnover tax and income tax collectively support this structure with relatively equal effects. This type of tax structure is not only adopted in rapidly developing countries but also in some developed countries where income tax is the main source of tax revenue.

Main factors influencing formulation of tax structure

The systems of taxation vary among nations, and the main factors influencing the tax structure can be broadly classified into the following aspects.

Socioeconomic development

Socioeconomic development level is the most fundamental factor influencing and determining the tax structure. Socioeconomic development level mainly refers to social productivity development level and the economic structure. Historical development of the tax structure of major nations demonstrates that tax structure roughly goes through a process from traditional direct tax system to indirect tax system, and then to the modern direct tax system. This development process is basically in line with the process of socioeconomic development. In the period of natural economy with the agricultural economy as the mainstay, agricultural income is definitely the main source of taxation, and agricultural production's non-commodity characteristics determine the land and population as the necessary taxation objects, so we call this tax category, which features indiscriminate taxation based on external identifiers of land and population without consideration of taxpayer's tax-bearing capacity, the traditional direct tax. In the wake of the development of industry and commerce, there emerged an economic structure dominated by the industrial and commercial economy; at the same time, agricultural production was affected by the commercial economy, and thus under such circumstances the income obtained from industrial and commercial businesses became the main taxation object and consequently forged the indirect tax–based tax structure. However the development of social productivity in modern capitalist society, the ever-strengthening government's functions in economic and social affairs, and the increasing fiscal expenditure collectively necessitated the increase of fiscal revenue. Income tax has relative favorable elasticity and less intervention in the economic activities and behavior of enterprises and individuals, and is able to stabilize the economy, so this tax category developed rapidly in this period and contributed to the modern direct tax–based tax structure.

National policy orientation

Detailed setting of tax structure should both embody fundamental taxation principles and serve to realize the objectives of national taxation policies. As one of major tools of state macroeconomic policy, taxation should wield its regulatory power to regulate socioeconomic activities by means of setting specific taxes. In recent years, China has levied the deposit interest tax (a kind of personal income tax) to coordinate with fiscal and monetary policies and to stimulate effective demand. A securities exchange tax is to be levied to regulate the stock market and securities exchange behavior. Inheritance tax and gift tax are to be levied in order to alleviate the unfair social allocation and narrow the rich-poor gap.

Tax administration

Tax administrations will influence the design of the national tax structure. Generally, the collection and administration of turnover tax are relatively simple since the levy is based on the income obtained from commodity sales or labor services. However the collection and administration of income tax are relatively complicated since the levy is based on the various incomes obtained by the taxpayer and is related to many specific issues such as pre-tax deduction, and difference from and coordination with the accounting system. Therefore national implementation of the income tax–based structure requires a high tax administrative level.

China's tax structure

China's tax structure has experienced a process of regulation and reform from the planned economy to the planned commodity economy and then to the socialist market economy; and the taxation reform in 1994 is the one with most extensive scope since the emerging of new China. This taxation reform complied with the requirements of building a socialist market economic system, with guidelines clarifying a "unified and simplified taxation, fair tax burden, rational decentralization of authority, clear distribution relationships, and sound fiscal revenue." The reform focused on the turnover tax system and income tax system and established a composite system of taxation featuring multi-taxes, multi-levying.

China has gradually set up a system of taxation applicable to the socialist market economy system since the reform in 1994. Currently there are 20 kinds of taxes under the existing tax system and they are basically classified into five types according to their properties and effects.

Turnover taxes, including VAT, consumption tax, business tax and customs duty. These taxes are levied according to sales income or business income obtained by the taxpayer from production, circulation or services.

Income taxes, including enterprise income tax and personal income tax, which are levied according to the profit obtained from production and operation, and from personal income.

Resource taxes, including resource tax, urban and township land use tax, land value increment tax and farmland occupation tax. They are levied from those engaged in resource or land development.

Property taxes, including house property tax, vehicle and vessel usage tax, and deed tax.

Taxes for special purposes, including stamp tax, city maintenance and construction tax, and vehicle acquisition tax. Fixed assets investment orientation tax has been suspended, and levy of animal slaughter tax and banquet tax are empowered to local governments for administration (in reality, most local governments have stopped the levy). These taxes are levied on specific objects and purposes.

Moreover, there is tobacco tax that belongs to the category of agricultural taxes.

So far there have been 20 kinds of taxes, of which 17 taxes are levied currently.

2

Chapter

Value Added Tax

An Overview

Value added tax (VAT) is the largest tax category at present in China and it was formally put into a nationwide levy as of January 1, 1994. Currently, the fundamental norm on VAT is the *Provisional Regulations on Value-Added Tax of the People's Republic of China* which was amended and adopted at the 34th Session of the Standing Committee of the State Council on November 5, 2008, and was put into force as of January 1, 2009.

Some concepts

VAT is a kind of tax levying on the statutory value added, and the value added and statutory value added should be clearly defined before expounding the VAT.

What is the value added?

The value added refers to the value created by the producers or business operators during production and business operations. Marx's labor value theory demonstrated that the value added is equivalent to the balance *(v+m)* of total commodity value *(c+v+m)* deducting the transferred value *c* of capital goods consumed by the production process i.e. *v+m=(c+v+m)–c* where *c* includes fixed assets (land, premises, machinery, equipment etc.) and non-fixed assets (raw material, fuel, power, low-value consumables, etc). Value added mainly includes wages, profits, interest and other expenses featuring value-adding.

Table 2.1.   The demonstration of the levy of the VAT

	Production of raw material	Production of semi-finished products	Production of finished products	Wholesale	Retail	
Sales amount	30	50	80	90	100	
Value added	30	20	30	10	10	100

What is the statutory value added?

Statutory value added refers to the value added determined in legal form and it is relative to theoretical value added.

Practices in different countries verify that the value added is not necessarily the theoretical value added. The significance of statutory value added are as follows: It embodies a state's economic policies. Some countries specify that purchased fixed assets may be deducted once and for all no matter whether they are consumed or not for the purpose of encouraging expansion of investment; some specify that no purchased fixed assets are may be deducted for fiscal revenue purposes. It meets the requirements for unifying calculation of tax amount. Only a value added amount specified legally can guarantee the unitary and consistency of calculation of the VAT amount.

What is VAT?

VAT is a kind of tax where the taxation object is the statutory value added of the commodity.

When countries levying VAT calculate this tax, they do not calculate directly based on the value added but calculate tax payable by multiplying sales amount by an applicable tax rate and deducting tax amount paid for purchased items. This method is called the creditable tax method. This method is used for VAT because the value added is difficult to calculate due to various production and operation links in actual collection and administration, thus would otherwise increase the tax authority's cost of levying tax and the taxpayer's tax-paying cost.

Emergence of the VAT

VAT originated between the late 1940s and early 1950s in France. Before the practice of VAT, France implemented a "business tax" according to the total value of all production links of a commodity. The obvious flaw of this method of tax was the duplicate taxation, which undermined the development of specialized production. In 1948, France practiced "production tax" in production links which was levied based on the balance of total value of the commodity deducting money paid for purchase of raw materials, components and parts or semi-finished products. In 1954, the deduction scope was expanded to fixed assets purchased and the incidence of taxation to the commercial wholesale link, and it was renamed as VAT. Later on, the incidence of taxation was again expanded to links such as commercial retail, agriculture and service industries.

VAT successfully addresses the problem of duplicate taxation resulting from full tax on all links of conventional turnover tax and favors development toward specialization and collaboration, so it rapidly became into vogue worldwide. There are over 140 countries and regions practicing VAT, which has gradually become an international tax category.

China has gradually introduced and popularized VAT since its reform and opening to the outside world. In 1979, China first piloted on two industries with serious contradictions of duplicate taxation i.e. the machine industry and the machinery and agricultural equipment industry; then in 1983, VAT was uniformly implemented nationwide for these two industries and for three products, namely sewing machines, bicycles and electric fans; in 1984, regulations on VAT were formally promulgated and the incidence of taxation was expanded to 12 categories of products, which marked the beginning of the formal practice of VAT in China. Since then, the incidence of taxation has continued to expand. In 1994, new regulations on VAT were promulgated and the incidence of taxation included links of industrial production and manufacture, links of commercial wholesale and retail, processing, repair and replacement service of the service industry. VAT has now become the largest tax in China (see Table 2.2).

Table 2.2. China's VAT revenue and its proportion in the total tax revenue, 1994–2007 (RMB100 million)

Year	Domestic VAT	Total tax revenue	Proportion of domestic VAT to total tax revenue (%)
1994	2,338.60	5,070.80	46.12
1995	2,653.70	5,973.70	44.42
1996	3,024.10	7,050.60	42.89
1997	3,343.80	8,225.50	40.65
1998	3,729.00	9,093.00	41.01
1999	4,000.90	10,315.00	38.79
2000	4,667.50	12,665.80	36.85
2001	5,452.50	15,165.50	35.95
2002	6,275.40	16,996.60	36.92
2003	7,341.40	20,466.10	35.87
2004	8,930.10	25,718.00	34.72
2005	10,698.29	30,865.83	34.66
2006	12,894.60	37,636.27	34.26
2007	15,609.91	49,449.29	31.57

Source: Website of the State Administration of Taxation, http://www.chinatax.gov.cn.

Types of VAT

When countries use VAT to calculate tax payable, they allow deduction of the amount of tax that has been paid by taxpayers for current assets such as raw materials purchased, auxiliary materials, semi-finished products, components and parts, and fuel and power consumed during production and business operations. In other words, the amount of tax that has been paid for current assets purchased is allowed to be deducted when statutory value added is calculated, but laws on VAT in different countries have different provisions on whether to deduct tax that has been paid for fixed assets such as purchased machine, equipment and factory building. Therefore three types of VAT are formed as follows:

Consumption-type VAT. This means that the amount of tax that has been paid for fixed assets purchased during the tax-paying period is allowed to be deducted once and for all when VAT is levied. In other words, no tax is levied for all capital goods purchased for production by tax-paying enterprises. As far as the whole society is concerned, tax is levied only for consumption goods, so it is called consumption-type VAT.

Income-type VAT. This type of VAT allows the once-and-for-all deduction of the amount of tax equivalent to that which has been paid for the depreciated part of fixed assets purchased during the current period. As far as the whole society is concerned, the tax base is equivalent to national income, so it is called income-type VAT.

Production-type VAT. Unlike the previous two types, this type of tax forbids the deduction of the amount of tax that has been paid for fixed assets purchased. As far as the whole society is concerned, the tax base includes not only consumption goods but also capital goods, and the incidence of taxation is basically consistent with gross national product (GNP), so it is called production-type VAT.

VAT of different types may produce different income effects and motivation effects since the three types abovementioned have different tax bases. Production-type VAT produces greatest effect in terms of fiscal revenue because it has a larger tax base, thus may collecting more VAT under the same tax rate. While in terms of the investment incentive, consumption-type VAT generates greatest effect. Consumption-type VAT allows the amount of tax that has been paid for fixed assets purchased during the tax-paying period to be deducted once and for all when it is levied, which is helpful in encouraging the production, eliminating the drawbacks caused by double taxation to a large extent, minimizing most adverse influence of VAT on investment, speeding up equipment replacement, and promoting technological progress. Moreover compared with the other two types, consumption-type VAT features simple calculation and deducts tax according to invoices, and it not only facilitates taxpayer's operation but also realizes cross audit of taxpayers, which makes collection and administration by the tax authorities easy.

China practiced production-type VAT before 2009 and enterprises bore a heavier tax burden for purchasing machine and equipment under this type of tax. In order to reduce the burden on enterprises, regulations on VAT amended on November 5, 2008, deleted the provision that input tax for credit against fixed assets purchased was banned, thus permitting taxpayer's credit against fixed assets purchased. In doing so, the transition of VAT from production type to consumption type was achieved.

Characteristics

First, tax is levied only for the value added part of the sales amount and thus avoids duplicate taxation (aka double taxation). VAT is levied only for the part of value for which no tax has been levied and that is created by the enterprise and covered in the enterprise's sales amount, the part of value for which tax has been levied on other enterprises and covered by sales amount is no longer levied. This is the most fundamental characteristic of the VAT and also the characteristic distinguishing it from other indirect taxes.

Second, commodities of the same price bear a consistent tax burden. For VAT, change of production and circulation links does not affect tax burden which is consistent for different commodities as long as the final total sales amount remains the same, no matter how many links of production and business operation involve.

Third, it is universally and continuously levied. The universality means that tax is levied for enterprises engaged in production and business operations as long as there is value added seen from the horizontal relationship of production and business operations, regardless of the enterprise's nature of business, mode of business operation, business scale and business results. The continuity means that VAT extends to every link of production and circulation and levy is implemented for the value added of each link seen from the vertical relationship of production and business operation.

Effects

The characteristics of VAT mentioned above enables it to play an active role in aspects such as promoting specialized collaborative production, guaranteeing stable growth of fiscal revenue, and boosting foreign trade development. The details are as follows.

The promotion of a rational structure of enterprise production and business operation

In the commodity economy, the development of social productivity itself demands specialized and collaborative enterprise production organization forms. Production specialization and collaboration are centralization of the same kinds of production established on the basis of an ever-finer division of labor. This is a scientific, reasonable and advanced production organization form. The most important characteristic is very fine division of labor during the production process, and the same production object is often finished by many different production departments and enterprises; the product characteristics are many production links and a large proportion of purchased components and parts within the product structure, so the turnover tax levied based on total value of the commodity shows that the tax burden of the commodity increases with the increase in turnover links and proportion of purchased components and parts. In other words, the tax category levied based on total amount of turnover hinders the development of a specialized and collaborative production model. However VAT is levied based on the value added and the tax burden is consistent as long as the final sale price of the commodity is the same no matter how many links in turnover, which enables VAT to promote the development of a specialized and collaborative production model.

The stable growth of fiscal revenue

Under the tax system based on total amount of turnover, the enterprise often sets up both "large and comprehensive" and "small and comprehensive" plants so as to reduce sales links, thus less tax is paid due to the reduced tax-paying links. Therefore tax revenue from levy based on total amount of turnover is affected by turnover: the more links of turnover, the more tax revenue, and vice versa. VAT is levied based on the value added and $(v+m)$ is the value added for the enterprise and the national income of a state during a specific period of time for the whole society, therefore income from VAT increases with the growth of national income and is not affected by the number of turnover links, and leads to a steady tax revenue.

The development of foreign trade

It is an international practice that export commodities do not include tax. Tax refund for export products is an important measure for a country to develop foreign trade, which will enable export commodities to enter the international market at the price excluding tax, thus enhancing international competitiveness, and expanding the export scale of the country. VAT is levied based on the value added and the sum of value added from all links equal to the product's final sales amount. Calculation of refund tax according to final sales amount enables a correct and thorough refund of the entire tax amount paid during the whole process of production and circulation to the enterprise, which will facilitate the commodity to enter the international market at the price excluding tax and so enhance commodity competitiveness of the exporting country.

Levy of VAT for import commodities is used to balance the tax burden between domestic commodities and import commodities, and avoid the problem of a relatively lighter tax burden of import commodities compared with that of domestic commodities and the potential loss of competitiveness of domestic commodities. The amount of VAT is calculated according to the total money amount of import commodities and the VAT rate is equivalent to the entire amount of VAT paid for links of production and circulation of the same kinds of domestic commodities, which balances the tax burden between import commodities and domestic commodities and facilitates development of the national economy.

Incidence of Taxation

According to the *Provisional Regulations on Value-Added Tax of the People's Republic of China,* the incidence of taxation covers sales of goods, provision of processing, repair and replacement service or import of goods within the territory of China.

General provisions

Sales or import of goods

Those goods refer to tangible personal property, including electric power, heat and gas.

Sales of good refer to compensatory transfer of ownership of goods.

Import goods refer to goods directly imported from overseas, including those transported from bonded factories, bonded warehouses and bonded areas to other regions.

Provisions of processing, repair and replacement services

Processing refers to a service of consigned goods processing; in other words, the consigner provides raw materials and main materials and the consignee manufactures goods according to consigner's requirements and receives a processing fee. For example, a cigarette factory consigns a cut tobacco processing plant to process cut tobacco.

Repair and replacement refer to the consigned services for restoring goods with damaged or lost functions to their original status and functions. For example, automobile repair plant repair of automobiles.

Provisions of processing, repair and replacement services mentioned above is on a compensation basis. It does not include the services provided for entities or individual businesses by their employees.

The compensation here refers to money, goods or other economic benefits acquired from the purchaser.

Special provisions

Special items included in the incidence of taxation

1) Futures (including commodity futures and precious metal futures) are levied for VAT, which shall be paid in the link of physical delivery of futures.
2) Bank business of sales of gold and silver are levied for VAT.
3) Sales of dead pawns of pawn broking and consignment agent's sales should be levied for VAT.
4) Production of philately commodities (stamps, first-day covers, stamp holders etc.) and sales of them by other entities and individuals except postal sectors should be levied for VAT.

Activities treated as sales of goods

The following activities of entities or individual businesses are treated as sales of goods:
1) Handing over goods to other entities or individuals for sales on a commission basis.
2) Selling goods directly or on a commission basis.
3) Taxpayers setting up at least two organizations and practicing unified accounting transferring goods from one organization to others for sales, excluding the case of relevant organizations in the same county (city).
4) Using goods self produced or processed on a commission basis for taxable items not for VAT.
5) Using goods self produced or processed on a commission basis for collective welfare or individual consumption.

6) Using goods self produced or processed on a commission basis or purchased for investment and providing them to other entities or individual businesses.

7) Using goods self produced or processed on a commission basis or purchased for distribution to shareholders or investors.

8) Using goods self produced or processed on a commission basis or purchased for donation to other entities or individual businesses.

The Provisions of the tax law mentioned above have two objectives: the first is to guarantee the implementation of the VAT credit system to avoid suspension of tax credit links due to taxpayer's acts mentioned above. VAT practices a tax credit system on the basis of invoices which connect producers and business operators of all circulation links of taxable commodities and form an inseparable tax credit chain. In other words, a VAT invoice issued by goods sellers is the evidence for sellers to calculate the output value and for purchasers to credit against input tax. The second is to avoid the problem of unbalanced tax burden of sales of goods resulted from taxpayers' acts mentioned above.

Mixed sales mode

Once a sales activity involves both goods and non-VAT taxable services, it is called a mixed sales mode. "sales mode" means that sales of goods and provision of non-taxable service synchronize, associate closely and get payment from the same assignee. "Non-taxable services" refer to the services for paying business tax and these services must be provided for direct sales of this batch of goods.

The tax law specifies that mixed sales mode of enterprises, enterprise units and individual businesses engaged in goods production, wholesale or retail, are treated as sales of goods and VAT shall be paid; mixed sales mode of other entities and individuals are treated as sales of non-VAT taxable services and no VAT needs to be paid.

The "non-VAT taxable services" refer to the services covered in the incidence of taxation of business tax items, including the transportation industry, construction industry, financial and insurance industries, postal and telecommunication industries, culture and sports industries, entertainment industry and service industry.

The "enterprises, enterprise units and individual businesses engaged in goods production, wholesale or retail" as mentioned include units and individual businesses engaged in goods production, wholesale or retail, providing non-VAT taxable services.

For mixed sales mode of taxpayers mentioned below, the goods sales amount and business turnover of non-VAT taxable services shall be accounted separately and the VAT to be paid shall be calculated based on goods sales amount with no VAT required for business turnover of non-VAT taxable services. The competent tax authorities should appraise and decide goods sales amount if they are not accounted separately:

1) Acts of sales of self-produced goods and provision of construction services.
2) Other scenarios specified by the Ministry of Finance and the State Administration for Taxation.

For mixed sales covered in the levy of VAT, the sales amount should be the sum of goods sales amount and non-taxable service turnover. The input tax on goods purchased for non-VAT taxable services conforming to provisions on VAT (i.e. goods purchased for these non-VAT taxable services are with a VAT amount indicated on the VAT credit document) can be credited against the output tax when VAT is calculated.

Sideline activities

The sideline activity refers to a VAT payer who is also engaged in non-VAT taxable items while engaging in taxable goods sales or providing auxiliary taxable services; and the non-VAT taxable items are not of direct link and affiliation with a certain item of sales of goods or provision of taxable services.

The tax law has provisions on sideline activities, which state that for taxpayers engaged in auxiliary non-VAT taxable services, sales amounts of goods or taxable services and business turnover of non-VAT taxable services shall be accounted separately, and VAT shall be levied for sales amounts of goods or taxable services according to their respective tax rates and that business tax shall be levied for business turnover of non-VAT taxable services. The competent tax authorities shall appraise and decide sales amounts of goods or taxable services if sales amount of goods or taxable services and non-VAT taxable services are not separately accounted or not able to be correctly accounted.

Other provisions on the incidence of taxation

1) Provisions on comprehensive utilization of resources and renewable resources are as follows. VAT is exempted for regenerated water, rubber powder and recapped tires produced out of materials completely from waste tires, and for sewage treatment; the policy of refund upon collection of VAT is practiced for sales of self-produced goods such as

high-purity carbon dioxide produced out of raw material of industrial waste gas, electric power or heat produced out of raw material of garbage, and shale oil produced out of raw material of oil shale in the coal mining process.

2) Provisions on professional cooperatives of farmers are as follows. The cooperative's sales of agricultural products produced by its own members is regarded as sales of agriculturalists' self-produced products and the VAT is exempted; a cooperative's sales of agricultural film, seed, germchit, chemical fertilizer, agricultural chemicals and agricultural machinery to its own members bear no tax.

3) Provisions on duty-free shop's sales of duty-free goods are as follows. No VAT is levied for acts of sales of duty-free goods by duty-free shops in customs isolation zone and sales of duty-free goods by duty-free shops in the city if the goods are picked up as duty-free goods from within the customs isolation zone. The "customs isolation zone" refers to a special zone especially delimited by Customs and frontier inspection authorities for the departure of people going abroad. The duty-free goods as mentioned refer to imported commodities with exemption of customs duty and import links, and domestic goods sold in duty-free shops with refund (exemption) of VAT and consumption tax.

4) Except for financial lease business carried out by entities approved to operate financial lease business by the People's Bank of China (PBOC) and the then Ministry of Foreign Trade and Economic Cooperation (the current Ministry of Commerce), VAT is levied on financial lease business carried out by other entities if the ownership of leased goods is transferred to the lessee, and the VAT is not levied if the ownership of leased goods is not transferred to the lessee.

5) For the non-recurring charge levied from VAT payers engaged in public utilities such as heat, electric power, fuel gas and running water, VAT is levied if this charge is directly related to the sales quantity of goods; VAT is not levied if this charge is not directly related to the sales quantity of goods.

6) Expenses collected by taxpayers on behalf of relevant administrative departments do not belong to other charges and no VAT is levied if all of the following conditions are met.
   • Approval has been obtained from the State Council, the relevant departments of the State Council or provincial governments.
   • Dedicated bills for administrative charges approved by the financial

authorities have been issued.

- The total amount of all money levied has been turned over to the state treasury or is under government supervision though not turned over, and the money may only be used as designated.

7) Insurance premium collected from the purchaser on his behalf by the taxpayer selling goods, and vehicle purchase tax and license fee collected from the purchaser on his behalf by the taxpayer engaged in automobile sales, are not treated as other expenses for the levying of VAT.

8) VAT shall be levied according to the relevant provisions on mixed sales for the income from sales of software products and software installation fees, maintenance fees and training fees charged together with the sales and enjoy the policy of refund upon collection of VAT for software products.

No VAT is levied for maintenance fees, technical service fees and training fees collected on schedule or in time after the software product is put into service.

For taxpayers consigned with the development of software products, VAT is levied if the copyright belongs to the consignee and VAT is not levied if the copyright belongs to the consigner or to both parties.

9) Books, newspapers and magazines printed by printing enterprises consigned by publishing organizations and which buy the paper themselves, print with a unified edition number (CN) and are serialized by an International Standard Book Number (ISBN), are treated as goods sales for levying VAT.

10) VAT is not levied for membership fees charged for VAT payers.

11) Transfer of taxable goods involved in the transfer of the enterprise's all the property is not covered in the incidence of taxation of VAT.

Taxpayers

General provisions

Value added taxpayers refer to entities and individuals selling goods, providing processing, repair or replacement services, or importing goods within the territory of China.

The selling of goods and the provision of processing, repair and replacement services within the territory of China means that 1) the location or place of dispatch of goods for sale is within the territory of China; and 2) the taxable services provided occur within the territory of China.

The entities as mentioned refer to enterprises, administrative units, government-sponsored institutions, military units, social groups and other organizations.

The individuals as mentioned refer to individual businesses or others.

Special provisions

Lessee or contractor. The taxpayer is the lessee or contractor if one entity is leased or contracted to other entities or individuals for operation.

Withholding agent. For entities or individual outside the territory of China who provide a taxable service within the territory of China but establish no operating agency, the withholding agent is their agent within the territory of China or their purchasers if there is no agent within the territory of China.

Taxpayer for imported goods is the consignee of imported goods, or the entity or individual handling Customs entry.

Determination and administration of small-scale taxpayers and ordinary taxpayers

Since VAT practices the system of tax deduction according to special VAT invoices, VAT paid by the taxpayer in the previous link can be credited against when taxpayer pays VAT in the next link. This requires that the VAT payer have perfect accounting and be able to correct account VAT's output tax, input tax and tax payable, otherwise, more tax credited against the taxpayer in the next link will lessen state tax revenue. However, VAT payers in China are of different accounting levels and there are big gaps. Some taxpayers of a small business scale and with imperfect accounting are not able to correctly account VAT's output tax, input tax and tax payable, therefore the *Provisional Regulations of the People's Republic of China on Value-Added Tax* classifies them into ordinary taxpayers and small-scale taxpayers according to the imperfect degree of their accounting and the scale of their business.

In terms of the small-scale taxpayers

Determination

Small-scale taxpayer refers to the value added taxpayer which is unable to submit the relevant tax data as specified and is of an annual taxable sales amount below the standard specified by tax law, and has of imperfect accounting.

The imperfect accounting as mentioned means that the VAT's output tax, input tax and tax payable cannot be correctly accounted.

Standards for recognition of the small-scale taxpayer are as follows: 1) taxpayers producing goods or providing taxable services and taxpayers mainly producing goods or providing taxable services and partially wholesaling or retailing goods, with an annual chargeable VAT sales amount of not more than RMB500,000; 2) taxpayers beyond the scope mentioned above, with an annual chargeable VAT sales amount of not more than RMB800,000.

Taxpayers mainly producing goods or providing taxable services as mentioned mean that the annual amount of sales of produced goods or taxable services provided by the taxpayer accounts for more than 50% of annual taxable sales amount.

Other individuals whose annual taxable sales amount exceeds the standard for small-scale taxpayers should pay tax as small-scale taxpayers do; entities other than enterprises and enterprises with seldom taxable acts may choose to pay tax as small-scale taxpayers.

Administration

Small-scale taxpayers with perfect accounting which are able to provide correct tax data may apply to the competent tax authorities for recognition for not being treated as small-scale taxpayers, and their taxes payable are calculated according to relevant provisions designated for ordinary taxpayers. The perfect accounting as mentioned means that account books are kept in accordance with the uniform state accounting system and accounting is performed based on lawful and effective evidence.

Although simple taxation measures are practiced for small-scale taxpayers and special VAT invoices are usually not used, the State Administration of Taxation specially formulated and implemented the *Measures for Collection and Administration of Value-Added Tax on Small-scale Taxpayers* considering that there is objective economic transaction between ordinary taxpayers and small-scale taxpayers during VAT collection and administration. The specifications of these measures are as follows:

1) Local tax authorities should strengthen the training of accountants of small-scale productive enterprises and help them to keep books of accounts. As long as small-scale enterprises use accountants, keep books of accounts, are able to correctly calculate output tax, input tax and tax payable, and are able to submit relevant tax data as specified, and the annual taxable sales amount is not less than RMB300,000, they may be

determined as general VAT payers.

2) Small-scale enterprises unable to employ full-time accountants may take the following measures voluntarily to enable part-time accountants to independently work and practice financial accounting as soon as possible on condition that there are part-time accountants.

Tax authorities help small-scale enterprises to employ accountants from tax consultancy companies and certified accountant offices to keep accounts and practice accounting.

Tax authorities organize retired accountants who have been engaged in finance and accounting business, and have the related experience and observe discipline and obey laws, to help small-scale enterprises to keep accounts and practice accounting.

On-site accountants may hold a concurrent post as part-time accountants in small-scale enterprises upon the consent of their own organizations and the approval of the competent tax authorities.

3) Small-scale enterprises may independently employ accountants and jointly employ accountants with several other enterprises.

Furthermore, tax law specified that as of July 1, 1998, no small-scale commercial enterprise or enterprise unit with annual taxable sales reaching RMB1.8 million (currently specified as RMB0.8 million), or enterprises or enterprise units mainly wholesaling or retailing goods and partially producing goods or providing taxable services, would be determined as general payers of VAT, regardless of their financial accounting.

In terms of the ordinary taxpayers

Determination

Ordinary taxpayers refer to enterprises and enterprise units whose annual taxable sales amounts are more than the specified standard for small-scale taxpayers.

The following taxpayers are not ordinary taxpayers:

1) Enterprises whose annual taxable sales amounts are more than the standard for small-scale taxpayers.

2) Other individuals whose annual taxable sales amounts are more than the standard for small-scale taxpayers.

Administration

General VAT payers must transact recognition procedures with the tax authorities to acquire the statutory qualifications. The *Measures for Recognizing the Application Filed by Ordinary Value-Added Taxpayer* formulated and implemented in 1994 by the State Administration for Taxation specifies as follows.

1) Ordinary VAT payers shall apply to the local competent tax authorities for transacting procedures for recognizing ordinary taxpayer in accordance with these measures. Unless otherwise specified by the State Administration for Taxation, the status of the taxpayer shall not be changed to small-scale taxpayer once it is recognized as an ordinary taxpayer.

2) Head office and branches of ordinary taxpayer that are not in the same county (city) shall respectively apply to local competent tax authorities for transacting recognizing procedures.

3) Enterprises applying for ordinary taxpayer recognition shall submit an application report and provide the following related certificates and data: business license, relevant contracts, regulations and agreements, bank account confirmation, and other relevant certificates and data required by tax authorities.

4) The competent tax authorities will issue the *Form for Recognizing the Application Filed by an Ordinary Value-Added Taxpayer* after preliminary examination of the enterprise's application report and relevant records. The enterprise shall truthfully fill in the form and submit one form to the grass-roots tax collection authority after approval, and keep one form for reference in the enterprise.

5) Tax authorities at the county level or above responsible for the approval of the *Form for Recognizing the Application Filed by Ordinary Value-Added Taxpayer* shall complete the approval procedure within 30 days from the date of receipt of the application. For those who meet the conditions of ordinary taxpayer, the first page of copies of their tax registration certificates shall be stamped with a special recognition seal "Ordinary VAT Payer" as the certificate for purchase and use of special VAT invoices.

   The color of the special recognition seal "Ordinary VAT Payer" is uniformly red and the red mould is specified and made by the State Administration of Taxation.

6) Newly-opened enterprises conforming to the conditions of an ordinary taxpayer shall apply for recognition procedures while dealing with tax registration. For those (not commercial and trading enterprises) with an expected annual sales amount more than the standard for a small-scale

enterprise, the tax authorities shall provisionally recognize them as ordinary taxpayers. Once the actual annual sales amount after opening is not more than the standard for a small-scale enterprise, procedures for recognizing ordinary taxpayers shall be applied again.

7) Unless otherwise specified by the State Administration for Taxation, the status of a taxpayer shall not be changed to that of a small-scale taxpayer once it is recognized as an ordinary taxpayer.

Tax Rates and Levy Rates

The practices of VAT in different countries show that the design of the VAT rate generally follows the principle of reduction of tax rate level, and this is mainly because VAT is a neutral and creditable tax, has universal regulating effect.

Existing VAT in China specifies a basic tax rate as 17%, a low tax rate as 13% and a zero tax rate for export; it specifies a 3% levy rate for small-scale taxpayers.

Tax rates

General provisions

Basic tax rate at 17%

A basic tax rate 17% is uniformly applied to ordinary VAT payers selling or importing goods and providing processing, repair and replacement services, except those applicable to the low tax rate scope and individuals selling second-hand goods.

Low tax rate at 13%

A low tax rate 13% is used for calculating and levying VAT for ordinary taxpayers selling or importing goods listed below.

1) Grains, foods, edible vegetable oils and fresh milk.
2) Tap water, heating, air conditioning, hot water, coal gas, liquefied petroleum gas, natural gas, methane gas, coal/charcoal products for household use.
3) Books, newspapers, magazines.
4) Feeds, chemical fertilizers, agricultural chemicals, agricultural machinery and plastic film for farming.
5) Other goods specified by the State Council and other related departments.

"Agricultural products" refer to primary products of various plants and animals from crop farming, fish breeding and poultry raising, forestry, animal husbandry and aquaculture. The detailed catalogue of products was in accordance with the *Circular of the State Administration of Taxation on Printing and Distributing the Annotations on Incidence of Taxation of Agricultural Products*, and tax should be levied according to the specified tax rate on all entities and individuals selling or purchasing agricultural products or selling agricultural products produced and processed out from purchased agricultural goods within the scope of products noted.

Since January 1, 2009, the VAT rate on selected products from of metal mining and non-metallic mining was restored from 13% to 17%. Edible salt is a kind of mineral product, but the VAT rate 13% remained applicable to this type of product closely related to people's life.

Zero tax rate

Taxpayer's export of goods is liable to the zero tax rate unless otherwise specified by the State Council.

This specification by the State Council means that the zero tax rate is not applicable to crude oil (both the planned and the unplanned), foreign aid export goods, export of goods forbidden by the state such as natural sulfur, musk, copper and copper alloy (VAT had been refunded at a rebate rate 17% for exported electrolytic copper since January 1, 2001) and silver, and that VAT is still levied according to the specified tax rate.

Special provisions

The tax law has special provisions on the applicable rates for dealing in goods or providing taxable services with different tax rates.

Dealing in goods or providing taxable services with different tax rates means that the taxpayer produces or sell goods of different tax rates or both sells goods and provides taxable services. For example, an agricultural machinery factory produces and sells agricultural machinery and repairs it.

Tax law specifies that taxpayers dealing in goods or providing taxable services with different tax rates shall be accounted separately. If the sales amounts have not been accounted separately, the higher tax rate shall apply.

Separate accounting mentioned means that separate accounts should be kept for income obtained from dealing in goods or providing taxable services with different tax rates and their sales amounts should be separately accounted for and taxes payable separately calculated according to the different tax rates.

For example, the low tax rate of 13% is applicable to production and sales of agricultural machinery of the abovementioned agricultural machinery factory, and the basic tax rate 17% is applicable to repair of agricultural machinery. If two sales amounts are separately accounted, taxes payable should be calculated according to the respective tax rates i.e. 13% and 17%. If the two sales amounts are not separately accounted, taxes payable should be calculated according to the same tax rate of 17%.

Levy rates

General provisions

VAT specifies a uniform levy rate of 3% for small-scale taxpayers due to the small scale of business operation with imperfect financial accounting, and the difficulty to use special VAT invoices to deduct or credit against input tax according to the basic tax rates. According to the relevant regulations, small-scale taxpayers may generally adopt the tax rate of 3%.

Special provisions

The following preferential policies on VAT levy following the simple methods should continue to apply and the input tax should not be credited when:

1) An ordinary taxpayer's sales of good is under any of the following circumstances, VAT should be provisionally calculated and paid based on the levy rate of 4% according to the simple methods:
   • Consignment shop's commissioned and consigned sales of goods.
   • Pawn-broking sales of dead pawns.
   • Duty-free stores' retail of duty-free goods under approval by the competent authorities.
2) Taxpayers' sales of goods used by themselves should conform to the following provisions:
   • For an ordinary taxpayer selling self-used fixed assets that should not be credited against and input tax has not been credited against as specified by the *Provisional Regulations on Value-Added Tax*, VAT shall be levied at half of the general rate of 4%.
   • VAT was levied according to different cases from January 1, 2009 for the ordinary taxpayer selling other fixed assets as self-used: VAT was levied according to the applicable tax rate for selling self-used fixed assets purchased or self-produced after January 1, 2009; VAT was levied at half of the rate of 4% for taxpayers selling self-used fixed assets purchased

or self-produced after December 31, 2008 which were not included in the expanded pilot scope of creditable VAT before December 31, 2008; VAT was levied at half of the rate of 4% for taxpayers selling self-used fixed assets purchased or self-produced before the expansion of pilot scope of creditable VAT in their region who were included in the expanded pilot scope of creditable VAT before December 31, 2008, and VAT was levied according to the applicable tax rate for selling self-used fixed assets purchased or self-produced after the expansion of pilot scope of creditable VAT in their region.

- For ordinary taxpayers selling self-used goods and second-hand goods, VAT should be levied at half of the rate of 4% according to simple methods and the amount of sales and the tax payable should be determined according to the following formula:

$$\textit{Amount of sales} = \textit{(Amount of sales including tax)} / \textit{(1 + 4\%)}$$
$$\textit{Tax payable} = \textit{(Amount of sales} \times \textit{4\%)} / \textit{2}$$

- For small-scale taxpayers selling self-used goods and second-hand goods, the amount of sales and the tax payable should be determined according to the following formula:

$$\textit{Amount of sales} = \textit{(Amount of sales including tax)} / \textit{(1+3\%)}$$
$$\textit{Tax payable} = \textit{Amount of sales} \times \textit{2\%}$$

Calculation of Tax Payable

VAT payers are classified according to their accounting level and business scale into two categories, namely ordinary taxpayers and small-scale taxpayers, and their taxes payable should be calculated by different methods.

For ordinary taxpayers

For ordinary taxpayers selling goods or providing taxable services, their tax payable is the balance of current-period output tax after deduction of current-period input tax Therefore, the amount of VAT payable for the current period for ordinary taxpayers is mainly determined by two factors, namely the current output tax and the current input tax.

Calculation of the output tax

Output tax refers to the VAT collected from purchasers by taxpayers selling goods or providing taxable services according to the amount of sales and the specified applicable tax rate. The formula for calculating output tax is as follows:

Output tax = Amount of sales × Applicable tax rate

Determination of the amount of sales under general sales models

The amount of sales refers to the total consideration and all other charges receivable from the purchasers by the taxpayer selling goods or taxable services. Other charges include service charges, subsidies, funds, fund raising charges, profits returned, damages for breach of contract (interest on deferred payment), handling charges, packaging fees, contingency charges, quality service charges, freight and loading and unloading charges, commission received, commissioned payments, and charges of any other nature which are in addition to the price charged. But the following should not be included:

1) Consumption tax collected and remitted for consumer goods that are of consigned processing and liable for consumption tax.

2) Advanced payment for transport costs meeting all the following conditions: transport department invoices for transport costs are issued to the purchasers; taxpayers transfer these invoices to the purchasers.

3) Governmental funds and administrative fees meeting the following conditions and collected on behalf: governmental funds approved to be established by the State Council or the Ministry of Finance and administrative fees approved to be established by the State Council or provincial people's governments and their finance and price departments in charge; financing notes printed by financial departments above provincial level which are issued upon payment; where the total amount of collection is turned over to central finance.

4) Insurance premiums collected from the purchaser on its behalf while selling goods, and vehicle purchase tax and license fees collected from the purchaser on its behalf.

Determination of the amount of sales under special sales models

Taxpayers will employ various modes of sales during selling activities. Tax law specifies in detail how to determine the amount of sales for calculating and levying VAT under different models of sales:

The discount in goods sales. Discount in sales means that the sellers offer price preference for the purchasers for reasons of larger quantities of purchases while selling goods or providing taxable services.

Tax law specifies that the sellers may issue red-letter special invoices according to the existing *Provisions for the Use of Special Invoices of Value-Added Tax* if the sellers offer the purchasers relevant discounts and allowances such as price preference or compensation because the goods purchased during a specific period of time accumulate to a certain number or the market price decreases after taxpayers sell the goods and issue special VAT invoices for the sellers.

Attentions should be paid to the following aspects: discounted sales are equivalent to sales discount. Sales discount is a discount preference offered to encourage the purchasers to pay off money for goods and it occurs after sales and is a kind of money management expense (i.e. financial expense), so it shall not be deducted from the amount of sales; discounted sales are not equivalent to sales allowance. Sales allowance refers to the reduction of the amount of sales due to reasons related to goods variety or quality; in other words, the allowance given to the purchasers by the sellers under the condition of no goods return, and the sales allowance can be deducted from the amount of sales; discounted sales are limited to discount of goods price. If the sellers goods are self-produced, processed on a consigned basis, and purchased to the discount of physical objects, the money for these physical goods cannot be deducted from the amount of goods sales, and their VAT shall be calculated according to the description of "gift to other people" in the part about "to be treated as sales of goods" in the *Regulations on VAT*.

The "trading new for old" model. Trading the old goods for the new ones is a sales model in which the taxpayer reclaims old goods with compensation and offsets the goods price by the discounted part. Tax law specifies that the amount of sales shall be determined according to the current-period sales price of new goods and the acquisition price of used good shall not be deducted if this model is adopted. Moreover, for special cases of trading in the old goods and for silver jewelries, VAT can be levied according to the entire price excluding VAT that is actually charged by the sellers.

The sales model of "principal repayment." Selling with repayment of principal is a method of sales whereby the sellers fully or partially refund the purchase charges to the purchasers in one repayment or in installments according to the stipulated time limit. Tax law specifies that the amount of sales is the sales price of goods, and expenses for repayment of principal shall not be deducted from the amount of sales if taxpayers adopt this model to sell goods.

The "exchange and barter" model. Sales by exchange and barter is a sales model for the purchasers and the sellers to achieve purchases and sales of goods in the form of settlement in goods of equivalent price rather than in currency.

The tax law specifies that both parities under the model of exchange and barter shall conduct purchases and sales, account the amount of sales and calculate output taxes according to respectively shipped goods, and account the amount of purchases and calculate input taxes according to respectively received goods. The abovementioned provisions in the tax law are to ensure the uninterrupted chain of VAT deduction. It should be highlighted that both parties in purchase and sales under the model of exchange and barter issue legal bills for calculating output taxes, and credit against input taxes, by respectively obtained special VAT invoices or other legal invoices. Input taxes should not be credited against if the relevant special VAT invoices or other legal invoices are not obtained after receipt of the goods.

The tax settlement of guarantee deposit of packaging material. Tax law specifies that guarantee deposit collected by taxpayers for wrappers they have leased or lent keep separate accounts and those accounted with one year and unexpired are not included into the amount of sales for taxation; but for guarantee deposits not refunded due to failure of withdrawal of wrappers beyond the time limit, output taxes shall be calculated according to tax rates applicable to wrapped goods. Attention should be paid to the following issues: "beyond the time limit" means that guarantee deposit is collected for more than one year according to the actual overdue time limit specified in the contract or the time limit of one year shall be included in the amount of sales for levy regardless of refund or not; if the wrapper guarantee deposit is included in the amount of sales for levy, the deposit shall be converted into the price excluding tax and included in the amount of sales for levy; applicable rate for wrapper is according to the rate applicable to the goods wrapped.

From June 1, 1995, the guarantee deposit of wrapper charged for alcoholic products excluding beer and millet wine shall be included in the amount of sales for levy regardless of whether it is refunded and how it is accounted.

Taxpayers' irrational low price setting without any justified reason. Where this condition is met, the amount of sales should be determined according to the following procedures: determined according to the average sales price of the same kind of goods by taxpayers in the most recent period; determined according to the average sales price of same kind of goods by other taxpayers in the most recent period; determined according to the composite assessable price.

The formula of composite assessable price is as follows:

Composite assessable price = Cost × (1 + Cost-profit ratio)

For goods with VAT and consumption tax levied, the formula of composite assessable price is as follows:

Composite assessable price = Cost × (1 + Cost-profit ratio) + Consumption tax;

Or, Composite assessable price = Cost × (1 + cost-profit ratio) + (1 – Consumption tax rate)

Here the cost refers to the actual production cost in the case of sales of self-produced goods, and the actual purchase cost in the case of sales of purchased goods. The cost-profit ratio is determined by the State Administration of Taxation, but for goods on which consumption tax is levied based on the rate on value, the cost-profit ratio shall be the ratio specified in the *Notice on Stipulations Concerning Some Specific Issues Related to Consumption Tax.*

Conversion of the tax-included sales amount

VAT is a tax excluded in price, so the amount of sales for calculating tax is the amount of sales excluding tax. But in the real world, there are often the cases of combination of sales amount and output tax for ordinary taxpayers' selling goods or providing taxable services, and their sales amounts include taxes. Therefore ordinary taxpayers' tax-included sales amount obtained by selling goods or providing taxable services must be converted into the tax-excluded sales amount when calculating the output tax.

In the case of the price setting adopting the combination of sales amount and output tax for ordinary taxpayers' selling goods or providing taxable services, the sales amount is calculated according to the formula as follows:

Sales amount excluding tax = Sales amount including tax / (1 + VAT rate)

The amount of sales of combined selling acts is the sum of the sales amount of goods and the turnover amount of non-VAT taxable services.

Calculation of input tax

The input tax refers to VAT paid by taxpayers for purchasing goods or receiving taxable services; in other words, the output tax collected by the sellers is the input tax paid by the purchasers. This is because the sellers recover output tax at the same as receiving the payment for goods and the purchasers pay input tax at the same of paying for goods during purchasing and selling business. Input tax and output tax are two mutually corresponding concepts. For any VAT payer, there will be both goods selling or taxable services providing and receiving, therefore every ordinary VAT payer will have both output tax received and input tax paid.

Input tax approved to be credited against output tax

Input tax approved to be offset covers the tax indicated in the special VAT invoices, the tax indicated on the payment receipts obtained from the Customs office, and exceptional circumstances approving input tax offset. Input tax approved for exceptional circumstances is calculated based on the amount of goods purchased or taxable services received and at the legal deduction rate, but is not directly based on the tax indicated in the special VAT invoices issued by the sellers and the tax indicated on the payment receipts issued by the Customs office, including:

1) VAT indicated in the special VAT invoices obtained from the sellers,

2) VAT indicated on the special payment warrant for customs import VAT obtained from the Customs office, and

3) The input tax calculated according to a deduction rate of 13% and the purchase price indicated on agricultural products purchasing or selling invoices, except for acquisition of special VAT invoices or special payment warrants for customs import VAT in the case of purchase of agricultural products. The formula for calculating the input tax is as follows:

Input tax = Purchasing price × Deduction rate

Where the buying price covers the price marked by taxpayers of agricultural products on purchasing or selling invoices and the tobacco tax paid as specified.

Other explanations necessary:

"Agricultural products" refer to self-produced agricultural products sold by entities and individuals directly engaged in cultivation, harvesting, animal husbandry and fishing; the detailed catalogue of agricultural products shall be in accordance with the *Annotations on Incidence of Taxation of Agricultural Products* printed and released by the Ministry of Finance and the State Administration of Taxation of the People's Republic of China in June 1995.

"Buying price" refers to the price marked by taxpayers of agricultural products on purchasing or selling invoices and the tobacco tax paid as specified.

Tobacco tax paid and afforded as specified beyond procurement price by agricultural products purchasing entities is approved to be incorporated into the buying price of agricultural products for calculating input tax and is deducted during calculation of VAT to be paid. The deducted amount is calculated based on the specified tobacco purchasing amount, tobacco tax and legal deduction rate. Tobacco purchasing price includes tobacco procurement price and out-of-the-money subsidy which is uniformly and temporarily calculated as 10% of tobacco purchasing money.

Creditable input tax for tobacco purchasing = (Tobacco procurement cost + Tobacco tax payable) × 13%

Where,

Tobacco purchasing price = Tobacco procurement price × (1 + 10%)

Tobacco tax payable = Tobacco procurement price × Tax rate (20%)

The deduction rate of 13% can be used for calculating deducted VAT of tax-free agricultural products purchased by ordinary VAT payers from farmers' specialized cooperatives.

4) Determination of input tax on transportation expenses. In the case of payment of transportation expenses in the course of goods purchasing or selling, and production and operation, input tax is calculated according to the transportation expenses amount indicated on the delivery expense settlement note and the deduction rate of 7%. The formula for calculating the input tax is as follows:

Input tax = Transportation expenses × Deduction rate

Other explanations necessary:

The transportation expenses mentioned refer to the transportation expenses (including transportation expenses for railway lines administered by the Railway Administration and special railway lines) indicated on the document of settlement and the construction funds, excluding other incidental expenses such as loading and unloading expenses and insurance premiums.

Transportation expenses settlement documents (ordinary invoices) approved to be credit certificates refer to freight invoices issued by state-owned organizations related to railway, civil aviation, highway and water transportation and invoices that are issued by non-state-owned transportation organizations with the chromatograph of a nationwide uniform stamp for supervision of the printing.

Fixed assets personally consumed such as passenger cars, motorcycles and yachts shall not be credited against input tax.

Transportation expenses resulting from purchase or sales of duty-free goods (excluding purchase of duty-free agricultural products) shall not be credited against input tax.

From November 1, 2003, taxpayers providing freight services are not allowed to issue freight invoices unless approved by the local competent tax authorities; the State Administration of Taxation will compare all freight invoices applied to be credited by ordinary VAT payers with freight invoices issued by payers of business tax, and all discrepant invoices will not be credited against.

From December 1, 2003, the State Administration of Taxation will compare all freight invoices applied to be credited by ordinary VAT payers with freight invoices issued by payers of business tax. All discrepant invoices will not be credited against. The comparison is to inspect abnormal situations and punish organizations issuing or obtaining freight invoices by violating related laws and regulations.

Ordinary VAT payers declaring credit against VAT input tax for freight invoices obtained since November 1, 2003 should fill in a paper document *Creditable List of VAT Freight Invoices* and provide the relevant electronic information, and report them to the competent state tax authorities. Those not reported shall not be credited against input tax.

Freight invoices obtained by taxpayers after October 31, 2003 shall be declared for credit against to the competent state tax authorities within 90 days of the invoice issuing date, and those not declared within 90 days shall not be credited against.

For ordinary taxpayers purchasing or selling goods by railway transportation and obtaining freight invoices issued by railway departments, if there is a discrepancy in the names of consignors or consignees indicated on the issued invoices but the column of consignor or the column of remark bears the name of the taxpayer (handwriting is invalid), this invoice may be used as a certificate for credit against input tax and is allowed for calculating credit against input tax.

Transportation expenses paid by ordinary taxpayers during production and business operations are allowed for calculating credit against input tax.

Two aspects should be explained as follows. First, input tax should not be credited against output tax if the taxpayer's tax-deduction certificates such as special VAT invoices, special pay-in warrants of VAT for customs import, invoices for purchasing agricultural products, invoices for selling agricultural products, and transportation expenses settlement documents obtained by purchasing goods or taxable services, do not conform to laws, regulations or the relevant provisions of the competent state tax authorities. Second, for acts of combined sales where VAT should be paid according to the fifth item of this detailed rule, input tax of goods purchased for non-VAT taxable services involved in the combined sales acts are approved to be credited against output tax if they conform to the provisions.

Input tax not creditable against output tax

The tax law specifies that input tax on the following items shall not be credited against the output tax:

1) Taxable items used for non-VAT, items exempt from VAT, goods or taxable services purchased for collective welfare or individual consumption.
2) Goods purchased or relevant taxable services which suffer abnormal losses.
3) Goods purchased or taxable services consumed in the production of work-in-progress or finished goods which suffer abnormal losses.
4) Consumption goods used by taxpayers and specified by the competent finance and tax authorities of the State Council.
5) Transportation expenses of goods where input tax shall not be credited against and transportation expenses for selling duty-free goods that are specified in above four items.

Goods purchased as mentioned in the first item do not include fixed assets used for both VAT taxable items (excluding items exempt from VAT) and non-VAT taxable items, items exempt from VAT, and items for collective welfare or individual consumption (fixed assets refer to machines, machinery and transport tools with a service life of more than 12 months and other equipment, tools and appliances related to production and business operation). Personal consumption refers to taxpayers' consumption for social entertainment. Non-VAT taxable items refer to provision of non-VAT taxable services, transfer of intangible assets, sales of real properties (assets that are immobile or will have a change of characteristic and shape after movement, including buildings, structures and other things immovably attached to the land) and construction-in-progress real properties. Real properties newly built, rebuilt, extended, renovated and decorated by taxpayers belong to construction-in-progress real properties.

Abnormal losses as mentioned in the second and third items refer to losses due to theft, loss, mildew, rot and deterioration caused by poor management.

Consumption goods used by taxpayers refer to motorcycles, cars and yachts used by themselves and on which consumption tax should be levied.

In the case of any of the following scenarios, tax shall be calculated according to the amount of sales and VAT rate, and input tax shall not be credited against nor shall special VAT invoices be used: ordinary taxpayers have imperfect accounting or are not able to provide the correct tax data; taxpayers have an amount of sales larger than the standard of small-scale taxpayers but do not apply to undertake the recognition procedures for ordinary taxpayers.

Determination of input tax that cannot be classified as not creditable due to combined operation of duty-free items or non-VAT taxable services

If input tax cannot be classified as not creditable due to taxpayers' combined operation of duty-free items or non-VAT taxable services, current-month input tax that shall not be creditable is calculated by the following formula:

Input tax not creditable = Total input tax unable to be classified × The sum of sales amount of duty-free items of that month and turnover amount of non-VAT taxable services / The sum of total sales amount and turnover amount of that month

In case of violation of the provisions on no credit against output tax (excluding duty-free items and non-VAT taxable services) for purchased goods or taxable services where input tax has been credited against, input tax of this item of purchased goods or taxable services shall be deducted from the current period's input tax; if it is not possible to determine this item of input tax, the deducted input tax shall be calculated according to the current period's actual cost.

Calculation of tax payable

For ordinary taxpayers selling goods or providing taxable services, their tax payable is the balance of the current period's output tax after deducting the current period's input tax. The calculation formula is as follows:

Tax payable = Current period's output tax payable – Current period's input tax

Determination of when to calculate output tax

When to determine output tax after a VAT payer's selling of goods or providing taxable services is related to the taxable amount for the period, so the tax law contains strict provisions. The general principle for determining the time of output tax is that the determination of output tax should not lag behind. See the contents of occurrence time of VAT payment obligations covered in Section 8 (collection and administration) of this chapter for details.

Calculation of creditable time limit of input tax

VAT payers shall bear VAT i.e. input tax while purchasing goods or accepting taxable services, so the determination of creditable time limit for input tax of taxpayers directly affects the amount of tax payable for the period, and therefore the tax law imposes strict regulations. The general principle for determining the creditable time limit of input tax is that the input tax shall not be credited against in advance.

1) Creditable time limit of input tax of special VAT invoices issued by the anti-counterfeit and tax-control system

    Special VAT invoices issued by the anti-counterfeit and tax-control system and applied for credit against by the ordinary VAT payer must be authenticated at the tax authorities within 90 days of the issuing date; otherwise input tax will not be credited against.

    For authenticated special VAT invoices of the ordinary VAT payer issued by the anti-counterfeit and tax-control system, input tax for the period shall be accounted according to the relevant VAT regulations and the credit against shall be declared within the month of acquirement of authentication, or input tax will not be credited against.

    After the ordinary VAT payer's receipt of a special invoice issued by the tax authorities, the tax amount entered on the special invoice shall be treated as input tax; in other words, creditable input tax shall be tax payable calculated according to the sales amount indicated on the invoice and the levy rate.

2) Creditable time limit of input tax of payment receipts obtained from the Customs office

    Ordinary VAT payer obtaining payment receipts from the Customs office after February 1, 2004, shall declare these to the competent tax authorities for credit against before the end of the first tax declaration period, and no tax will be credited against after the specified time limit.

3) Creditable time limit of input tax of freight invoices

    Freight invoices obtained by VAT payers after October 31, 2003, shall be declared for credit against to the competent state tax authorities within 90 days of the invoice issuing date, and those not declared within the 90 days shall not be credited against. A list of creditable invoices shall be attached when the credit for freight input tax is handled.

4) The amount of VAT returned to the purchasers by ordinary taxpayers due to return or allowance of goods sold shall be deducted from the current period's output tax of occurrence of return or allowance; the amount of VAT recovered due to withdrawal or allowance of goods purchased shall be deducted from the current period's input tax of occurrence of withdrawal or allowance.

Insufficient credit of input tax

The amount of the current period's output tax greater than the current period's input tax is the tax due. When the current period's output tax is less than the current period's input tax, the insufficient part for credit may be carried forward to the next period for credit.

Provisions on input tax during the occurrence period of deduction

VAT practices the "purchase tax deduction method" i.e. credit of the current period's input tax against the current period's output tax. If goods or taxable services purchased for the period are not determined in advance for items not related to production and business operation, the input tax should be deducted from the current period's output tax. However, if the purposes of purchased goods or taxable services that have been credited against output tax are changed afterward, for example, they are used for non-taxable items, collective welfare or individual consumption, and in the case of abnormal losses of purchased goods, abnormal losses of work-in-progress or finished goods, the input tax of the purchased goods or taxable services should be deducted from the input tax incurred in the period.

For small-scale taxpayers

For small-scale taxpayers selling goods or taxable services, the tax payable should be calculated according to the sales amount and the specified levy rate, and the input tax should not be credited. The calculation formula is as follows:

Tax payable = Sales amount × Levy rate (3%)

Attention should be paid to the following four issues for the calculation of tax payable by small-scale taxpayers.

Input tax not creditable

The small-scale taxpayer is of imperfect accounting and is not able to correctly account for output tax and input tax, so the tax credit system is not practiced but a simple tax calculation method is practiced for calculating tax payable. Meanwhile, special VAT invoices should not be issued for the selling of goods.

Determination of sales amount

Provisions on sales amount of small-scale taxpayers are the same as those for ordinary taxpayers; in other words, the amount of sales is the total consideration plus all other charges receivable from the purchasers by the taxpayer selling goods or taxable services, excluding the amount of VAT collected according to the levy rate of 3%.

The sales amount returned to the purchasers by small-scale taxpayers due to return or allowance of goods sold should be deducted from the sales amount for the occurrence period of return or allowance of goods sold.

Conversion of the sales amount including tax

Since VAT is a tax-excluded price, the sales amount of small-scale taxpayers does not include their tax payable.

If the method of combination of sales amount and tax payable is used for small-scale taxpayers selling goods or taxable services, the tax-included sales amount must be converted into the tax-excluded amount before calculation of tax payable. The conversion formula of tax-excluded sales amount for small-scale taxpayers is as follows:

Sales amount = (Sales amount including tax) / (1 + 3%)

Calculation of tax payable for invoices issued to small-scale taxpayers by the competent tax authorities on their behalf

Small-scale taxpayers selling goods or taxable services may apply to the competent tax authorities to issue invoices on their behalf. Competent tax authorities issuing invoices on behalf of small-scale taxpayers shall fill in the unit price and VAT-excluded sales amount respectively in the columns of "unit price" and "amount" on the special invoice. The tax payable shall be calculated according to sales amount and levy rate.

For imported goods

It is an international practice to levy tax for imported goods in most countries so as to balance the tax burden between imported commodities and domestic ones. In accordance with the *Provisional Regulations on Value-Added Tax of the People's Republic of China*, entities and individuals importing goods within the territory of the People's Republic of China shall pay VAT as specified.

Tax payable on taxpayers' imported goods is calculated according to the composite assessable price and VAT rate.

Determination of composite assessable price

According to the *Customs Law of the People's Republic of China* and the *Regulations of the People's Republic of China on Import and Export Duties,* the price for duty assessment of import goods under general trade item refers to the cost, insurance and freight (CIF) price on the basis of the knock-down price recognized by the Customs. Knock-down price refers to the price that the purchaser of import goods under general trade items actually pays to or shall pay to the seller. CIF price refers to the sum of the goods price plus packing expenses, freight and insurance premium before transport to the unloading spot within China and other charges for services. Goods imported under special trade have no knock-down price to use as a base when imported, so the *Regulations of the People's Republic of China on Import and Export Duties* formulates detailed methods for determining the price for duty assessment for these import goods.

Composite assessable price of VAT for import goods includes customs duty paid. If the import goods are taxable consumption goods as specified by the regulations on consumption tax, the composite assessable price shall also include the consumption tax that has been paid in the import link.

The calculation formula for composite assessable price is as follows:

Composite assessable price = Price for duty assessment + Customs duty

If imported goods are taxable consumption goods as specified by the regulations on consumption tax, the composite assessable price shall also include the consumption tax that has been paid in the import link. The calculation formula for composite assessable price is as follows:

Composite assessable price = Price for duty assessment + Customs duty + Consumption tax

Calculation of tax payable

Tax payable on taxpayer's import goods should be calculated according to composite assessable price and tax rate as specified by the *Regulations of the People's Republic of China on Import and Export Duties,* and any tax shall not be credited i.e. the various taxes and duties incurred within China shall not be credited.

Tax payable = Composite assessable price × Tax rate

Tax Refund (Exemption) on Export Goods

Tax refund (exemption) on export goods is a taxation measure for refunding or exempting indirect tax generally used in international trade so as to encourage fair competition among countries exporting goods.

China's tax refund (exemption) on export goods refers to the refund or exemption of VAT and consumption tax paid as specified by the tax law or the exemption of VAT and consumption tax payable in all domestic production and circulation links of goods declared at Customs for export.

General policies

China practices the policy of tax refund (exemption) for export goods under existing VAT provisions in order to improve international competitiveness of export goods and encourage and enlarge export of products. At present, China's taxation policies on export goods are classified into three forms as follows.

Tax exemption and refund for export goods. Tax exemption means that VAT is not levied for goods in the export sales link; tax refund means that the tax actually paid on goods before export is refunded according to the specified refund rate.

Tax exemption but no refund for export goods. Tax exemption means that VAT is not levied for goods in the export sales link; no tax refund means that the price of goods does not include tax since it is duty-free before export sales of goods for the links such as production, sales or import.

Neither tax exemption nor refund for export goods. No tax exemption means that the export link of some goods restricted or forbidden by the state to be exported is regarded as the domestic sales link and tax is levied as usual. No tax refund means that tax paid before the export sales link is not refunded.

Applicable scope of export goods with tax refund (exemption)

The scope of export goods qualifying for tax refund currently in China mainly covers goods declared and exported with taxable VAT. However tax refund is practiced for some special goods out of consideration of the requirements of state macro-control and international practice.

Applicable scope of goods with general tax refund (exemption)

The scope of goods qualifying for general tax refund (exemption) covers an enterprise's export goods on which VAT and consumption tax have been levied or shall be levied, except for goods on which tax is not refunded (exempted) as clearly specified by the state.

General goods enjoying tax refund (exemption) must conform to four conditions as follows:

1) They must be goods on which VAT is levied.

2) They must be goods declared at Customs for departure. Declaration at Customs for departure refers to export of goods out of the Customs and it is one of the major methods of differentiating whether the goods qualify for tax refund (exemption) or not. Goods declared but not leaving the country shall not be regarded as export goods for tax refund (exemption) regardless of settlement in foreign exchange or RMB and whatever financial transaction of the enterprise.

3) They must be goods to be sold from the financial perspective.

4) They must be goods verified for export earnings.

Applicable scope of goods with specially authorized tax refund (exemption)

Goods with specially authorized tax refund (exemption) refers to goods which do not conform with the abovementioned four conditions but for which the state specially authorizes the refund or exemption of their VAT and consumption tax due to the special characteristics of their sales modes, consumption links and settlement methods, and to international special circumstances. These goods include:

1) Goods shipped out of the country for use in contracted projects by companies contracting for foreign engineering projects;

2) Goods shipped out of the country for use in repair projects by enterprises undertaking the repairs;

3) Goods sold by ocean shipping supply companies and ocean transportation supply companies to foreign vessels and Chinese ocean-going vessels for foreign currencies; and

4) Goods bought in China and shipped out of the country by enterprises as their shares in investment abroad.

Applicable scope of goods with tax exemption for export yet without tax refund

Goods with tax exemption for export are export goods qualified for tax exemption but not tax refund as specified by tax law. Tax is exempted but not refunded on the following:

1) Self-produced goods exported by small-scale taxpayers belonging to

manufacturer or by their entrusted foreign trade enterprises.

2) Export goods purchased by foreign trade enterprises from small-scale taxpayers and attached with plain invoices. However tax refund is specially authorized for 12 categories of export goods listed as specified with consideration to their larger export proportion and special factors of production and procurement.

3) State specified duty-free goods (including duty-free agricultural products) directly purchased by foreign trade enterprises for export purposes.

The following export goods fall within the applicable scope of goods with tax exemption but without tax refund

1) For goods produced by processing of materials provided by foreign clients and exported again, tax is exempted for import of raw materials but tax is not refunded for export of self-produced goods.

2) Tax is exempted for both domestic sales and export of contraceptive drugs and devices, and for ancient and old books.

3) For enterprises with export rights for cigarettes included in national plan for cigarette export, VAT and consumption are exempted in the production link but tax is not refunded in the export link. For other, unscheduled cigarette exports, VAT and consumption tax are levied in accordance with the regulations and tax is not refunded for export.

4) Tax is exempted for goods produced by military supply manufacturers or allocated and transferred by military supply sectors and exported by military production enterprises and enterprises of the military system.

5) Other duty-free goods as specified by the state, such as agricultural products, feeds and agricultural plastic sheeting produced and sold by producers (farmers) themselves.

For goods enjoying VAT exemption for export, input tax paid for the consumed raw materials, components and parts, including the input tax included in the creditable transportation expenses, shall not be credited against the output tax of domestically sold goods but included in the production costs.

Applicable scope of goods with neither tax exemption nor refund

1) Unplanned crude oil exports.

2) Foreign aid export goods (from January 1, 1999, the policy of no tax refund for export was still practiced for export goods under the item of general material aid; for goods exported using Chinese government

preferential loans for foreign aid and the funds of cooperation projects, the policy of tax refund for export was practiced by reference to those for general trade and export).

3) Goods prohibited by the state for export, including natural ox gallstone, musk, copper and copper-base alloy (VAT was refunded at the rebate rate 17% for exported electrolytic copper from January 1, 2001).

Applicable scope of enterprises with tax refund (exemption) for export goods

Scope of the enterprises with tax refund (exemption) for export goods refers to enterprises entitled to the right to conduct import and export business approved by the state administrative departments of commerce and their authorized organizations and to enterprises entrusting export enterprises to export their self-produced goods on their behalf. These include:

1) Foreign trade enterprises entitled to the right to conduct import and export business approved by state administrative departments of commerce and their authorized organizations;

2) Self-supporting manufacturing enterprises entitled to the right to conduct import and export business approved by state administrative departments of commerce and their authorized organizations,

3) Enterprises with foreign investment;

4) Manufacturing enterprises entrusting foreign trade enterprises to export on their behalf; and

5) Special enterprises with tax refund (exemption).

Tax refund rates on export goods

Tax refund rate on export goods refers to the ratio between the tax that shall be returned for export goods and the taxation basis.

There are nine grades of tax refund rates for export goods i.e. 17%, 15%, 14%, 13%, 11%, 9%, 8%, 6% and 5%.

After the State Council decided to reform the system of refunding taxes on export goods on October 13, 2003, the Ministry of Finance and the State Administration of Taxation jointly issued a document on January 1, 2004, to make structural adjustment to the VAT refund rate on export goods, and the tax refund rate after adjustment was reduced by 3% on average. The Ministry of Finance and the State Administration of Taxation successively promulgated the *Circular on Reducing Tax Refund Rates of Some Export Commodities*, the *Circular* on *Raising Tax Refund Rates of Some Export Commodities* and the *Circular on Raising the Export VAT Refund Rates of Commodities Such as Labor-intensive Products* respectively on June 19, 2007, October 21, 2008, and November 17, 2008.

Calculation of export tax refund (exemption)

The *Measures for the Administration of Export Tax Refund (Exemption)* specifies two tax refund calculation methods in order to correspond with the accounting method of export enterprises. The first method is "exemption, credit and refund," which is mainly applicable to manufacturing enterprises' independent or entrusted export of self-produced goods to others; the second method is "refund after collection," which is mainly applicable to foreign (industrial) trade enterprises exporting purchased goods.

The calculation methods of exemption, credit and refund (applicable to manufacturing enterprises' independent or entrusted export)

From January 1, 2002, the administrative regulations on tax exemption, credit and refund were uniformly practiced for VAT on manufacturing enterprises' independent or entrusted export of self-produced goods unless otherwise specified. Manufacturing enterprises are enterprises and enterprise units recognized by the competent tax authorities as ordinary VAT payers with independent financial accounting and actual productive power. The regulations on VAT exemption were continuously implemented for ordinary VAT payers' export of self-produced goods.

This tax exemption refers to the exemption of VAT in enterprise production and sales links for manufacturing enterprises exporting self-produced goods; the tax credit means that the refundable input tax included in raw materials, components and parts, and power consumed by the manufacturing enterprise's exported self-produced goods is credited against the tax payable on domestically sold goods; the tax refund means that when the current-month creditable input tax of a manufacturing enterprise's exported self-produced goods is more than the tax payable, tax shall be refunded for the part not completely credited.

The calculation methods as follows:

Current period's tax payable = Current period's output tax of domestically sold goods – (Current period's input tax – Current period's tax with no exemption or credit) – Overpaid tax of last period

Where:

1) Current period's input tax includes two parts; one part is domestic sales that can be credited and the other part is export sales that can be credited but have a poor tax refund rate.

2) *Tax with no exemption or credit of current period = Free on board (FOB) price of current-period export goods × (Levy rate – Tax refund rate)*

   Tax of exemption, credit and refund = FOB price of export goods × Posted rate of the RMB × Tax refund rate

   Current period's refundable tax = the lower one between the current period's tax payable and the tax of exemption, credit and refund

   Current period's tax exemption and credit = Current period's tax of exemption, credit and refund – Current period's refundable tax

The calculation methods of refund after collection (applicable to foreign-trade export enterprises)

VAT is exempted for the export sales link of foreign-trade enterprises; input tax of export goods is refunded. Foreign-trade enterprises also paid the VAT that had been paid by enterprises producing and operating such goods when they paid the procurement price, so it should be refunded to foreign-trade enterprises and the difference between the levy and the refund shall be counted into enterprise costs.

1) VAT is exempted for the export sales link of foreign-trade enterprises and industry-and-trade enterprises practicing foreign-trade enterprises' financial system and purchasing goods for export; for the cost of goods procurement, since foreign-trade enterprises have also paid VAT that has been paid by enterprises producing and operating such goods when they paid the procurement price, tax refundable shall be calculated according to procurement cost and tax refund rate after export of goods and refunded to foreign-trade enterprises, and the difference between the levy and the refund shall be counted into enterprise costs.

   VAT on goods exported by foreign-trade enterprises should be calculated according to the input tax indicated on the special VAT invoices for goods purchased for export and the tax refund rate.

   Tax refundable = Foreign-trade enterprise's VAT-excluded purchase cost × Tax refund rate

2) Provisions on refund of VAT on export goods procured by foreign-trade enterprises from small-scale taxpayers are as follows.

First, for 12 categories of export goods such as drawn-works and art wares purchased from small-scale taxpayers, attached with ordinary invoices and specially authorized for tax refund, the tax is exempted for the income from sales of export goods and the input tax of export goods is refunded. Small-scale taxpayers use ordinary invoices and their sales amount and tax payable are not separately measured, while their VAT payable is levied out of cash, therefore the sales amount of consolidated price must be converted into the tax-excluded sales amount according to the following formula when the tax refund amount is calculated.

Tax refundable = Sales amount listed on ordinary invoices × 6% (or 5%) / (1 + Levy rate)

Second, for export goods purchased from small-scale taxpayers and attached with special VAT invoices issued by the tax authorities on their behalf, the tax refundable is calculated according to the following formula:

Tax refundable = Amount indicated on special VAT invoices × 6% (or 5%)

Tax Preference

Tax reduction or exemption

Currently, VAT is mainly exempted for the following items:
1) Self-produced agricultural products sold by agricultural producers;
2) Contraceptive drugs and devices;
3) Old books;
4) Imported instruments and equipment directly used in scientific research, experiments and education;
5) Imported materials and equipment from foreign governments and international organizations as assistance free of charge;
6) Articles imported directly by organizations for the disabled for special use by the disabled; and
7) Sales of used articles.

Agriculture mentioned in *1)* refers to crop farming, fish breeding and poultry raising, forestry, livestock husbandry and aquaculture. Agricultural producers include entities and individuals engaged in agricultural production.

Agricultural products refers to primary agricultural products and the detailed scope is determined by the Ministry of Finance and the State Administration of Taxation.

Old books mentioned in *3)* refers to ancient books and old books purchased privately.

Used articles mentioned in *7)* refer to articles used by others themselves.

Except as stipulated in the above paragraphs, the VAT exemption and reduction items shall be regulated by the State Council. Local governments or departments shall not regulate any tax exemption or reduction items.

Taxable threshold

According to VAT regulations, the VAT threshold is regulated by the competent financial and tax authorities of the State Council. Detailed rules on implementation of VAT specify that the VAT threshold is applicable to individuals.

The range of the VAT threshold is specified as follows:

1) For sales of goods, monthly sales amounting to RMB2,000–5,000.
2) For sales of taxable services, monthly sales amounting to RMB1,500–3,000.
3) For tax payment on a transaction-by-transaction basis, sales amounting each time to RMB150–200.

Sales amount refers to the small-scale taxpayer's sales amount i.e. the VAT-excluded sales amount.

The taxation bureau directly under the State Administration of Taxation shall determine the locally applicable threshold within a specified range and report it to the Ministry of Finance and the State Administration of Taxation for filing.

Administration of Tax Collection

The occurrence time of tax liability

The time at which a liability to VAT arises refers to the starting time when the VAT payer conducts taxable acts and shall bear tax liability. Once the time at which a liability to tax arises is determined, the taxpayer must calculate tax payable according to this time. This regulation on VAT is very important for administration of VAT collection.

Occurrence of VAT taxable acts and acquirement of income happen at different times, so the clear definition of the time at which a liability for VAT arises will help to determine the levy-payment relation between tax authorities and taxpayers and their due responsibilities, reasonably determine the time limit for tax payment, supervise the taxpayer's effective fulfillment of obligation to pay, and guarantee state fiscal revenue.

The time at which a liability to VAT payment arises is specified in detail as follows:

1)   For sales of goods or taxable services, it is the date on which the sales payment is received or the documented evidence of the sales payment is obtained; or it is the date on which the invoices are issued if they are issued in advance.

    According to different models of sales settlement, it is determined in details as follows:

    - For sales of goods through direct payment mode, it is the date on which the sales payment is received or the documented evidence of the sales payment is obtained no matter whether the goods are delivered or not.
    - For sales of goods through the mode of collection and acceptance and entrusted bank payment receipt, it is the date on which the goods are delivered and the collection procedures are finished.
    - For sales of goods through the mode of credit sale and installment sale, it is the date on which the collection date is specified in the written contract, or the date on which the goods are delivered if there is no written contract or the collection date is not specified in the written contract.
    - For sales of goods through the mode of advances on sales, it is the date on which the goods are delivered, but for goods where production and sales duration is more than 12 months, such as large-scale mechanical equipment, ships and airplanes, it is the date on which the advances are received or the collection date specified in the written contract.
    - For goods sold by other taxpayers on a commission basis, it is the date on which the list of commission is received from the commissioned organization or the date on which all or part of the sales payment is received. If the list of consigned goods or sales payment is not received, it is the date on which the period of 180 days after the delivery of the commissioned goods expires.
    - For sales of taxable services, it is the date on which the sales sum is received or the documented evidence of the sales payment is obtained.

- For taxpayer's acts (items 3–8) regarded as acts of sales of goods, it is the date on which the goods are transferred.

2) For importation of goods, it is the date of import declaration.
3) For VAT withholding, it is the date on which the taxpayer's VAT obligation occurs.

Assessable period

Assessable periods for VAT payment are 1 day, 3 days, 5 days, 10 days, 15 days, 1 month or 1 quarter. The actual assessable period of taxpayers shall be determined by the competent tax authorities according to the magnitude of the tax payable; tax that cannot be assessed in regular periods may be assessed on a transaction-by-transaction basis.

Taxpayers that adopt one month or one quarter as an assessable period shall report and pay tax within 15 days following the end of the period. If an assessable period of 1 day, 3 days, 5 days, 10 days or 15 days is adopted, the tax shall be prepaid within 5 days following the end of the period and a monthly return shall be filled with any balance of tax due settled within 15 days from the first day of the following month.

The tax payment deadlines for withholding agents shall be determined with reference to the stipulations of the above paragraphs.

Taxpayers who import goods shall pay tax within 15 days after the issue of the tax payment certificates by the Customs office.

Place of payment

The place of VAT payment is the stipulated place where taxpayers report and pay VAT.

1) Businesses with a fixed establishment shall report and pay tax to the local competent tax authorities where their establishment is located. If the head office and branch are not situated in the same county (or city), they shall report and pay tax separately to their respective local competent tax authorities; the head office may, upon the approval of the State Administration of Taxation or its authorized tax authorities, report and pay tax on a consolidated basis to the local competent tax authorities where the head office is located.

2) Businesses with a fixed establishment selling goods in a different county (or city) shall apply for the issue of an outbound business activities tax administration certificate from the local competent tax authorities where the establishment is located and shall report and pay tax to the local

competent tax authorities where the establishment is located; businesses without a certificate shall report and pay tax to the local competent tax authorities where the sales or services activities take place; the local competent tax authorities where the establishment is located shall collect overdue tax which has not been reported and paid to the local competent tax authorities where the sales or services activities take place.

3) Businesses without a fixed base selling goods or taxable services shall report and pay tax to the local competent tax authorities where the sales or services activities take place; the local competent tax authorities where the establishment is located shall collect overdue tax which has not been reported and paid to the local competent tax authorities where the sales or services activities take place.

4) In terms of import of goods, tax shall be reported and paid to the Customs office where the imports are declared.

5) Tax withheld by withholding agents shall be reported and paid to the competent tax authorities where the establishment is located or where the withholding agents reside.

Tax declaration

The State Administration of Taxation has formulated the following tax declaration methods for ordinary VAT payers in accordance with the relevant provisions of the *Law of the People's Republic of China on Tax Collection and Administration*, the *Provisional Regulations of the People's Republic of China on Value-Added Tax* and the *Methods of the People's Republic of China on Invoice Management*.

1) Ordinary VAT payers (hereinafter referred to as taxpayers) shall make a tax declaration in accordance with this method.

2) Tax declaration materials include the *VAT Declaration Table* and its two annexed tables i.e. *Details of Current-period Sales* and *Details of Current-period Input Tax*.

Administration of Special VAT Invoices

Scope of receipt, purchase and use of special invoices

Receipt, purchase and use of special VAT invoices are limited to ordinary VAT payers. Small-scale taxpayers and non-VAT payers are not entitled to their receipt, purchase or use. In any of the following circumstances, special VAT invoices may not be received, purchased or used by an ordinary taxpayer.

1) Financial accounting is imperfect; in other words, output tax, input tax and tax payable for VAT cannot be correctly accounted for in accordance with the requirements of the financial accounting system and tax authorities.

2) The ordinary taxpayer acts in violation of the *Law on the Administration of Tax Collection of the People's Republic of China* and refuses to accept the disposition from the tax authorities.

3) The ordinary taxpayer conducts any of the following acts and does not make corrections after being ordered by the tax authorities to take remedial action within a specific period:
   - Printing special invoices without authorization.
   - Buying special invoices from entities other than individuals or tax authorities.
   - Borrowing special invoices from others.
   - Providing special invoices to others.
   - Failing to issue special invoices as specified.
   - Failing to keep special invoices as specified.
   - Failing to declare purchase, use and keeping of special invoices as specified.
   - Failing to accept inspection by the tax authorities as specified.

4) Goods sold totally as duty-free items.

Scope of issue of special invoices

Ordinary taxpayers selling goods or providing taxable services should issue special invoices to the purchasers.

Small-scale taxpayers wanting issue of special taxable invoices as the competent tax authorities for issue on their behalf.

Special invoices should not be issued for sales of duty-free goods except those otherwise specified by laws, regulations, and the State Administration of Taxation.

Requirements on issue of special invoices

Special invoices must be issued in accordance with the following requirements

1) The contents are completely filled in and agree with the actual

transaction.

2) The writing is legible, without writing over lines or in the wrong columns.

3) The invoice copy and the deduction copy are stamped with the special financial seal or special nationwide invoice seal.

4) Invoices shall be issued in accordance with the time at which a liability to VAT occurs.

Requirements on issue of special invoices by computer

Use of computers for issuing special invoices must be reported to the competent tax authorities for approval and invoices printed by enterprises appointed by the tax authorities must be used. Ordinary taxpayers meeting the following conditions may apply to the competent tax authorities to use computers to issue special invoices.

1) Technicians and operators having professional computer qualifications.

2) Having the ability to issue special invoices and to print lists of monthly purchases, sales and inventory by computer.

3) Other conditions specified by the taxation bureau directly under the State Administration of Taxation.

An application report and the following data must be provided to the competent tax authorities when applying to use a computer for issuing special invoices:

1) A simulated specimen sheet made by computer according to the format of special invoices (invoices printed by enterprises appointed by the tax authorities).

2) Lists of purchases, sales and inventory for the latest month made by computer based on accounting procedures.

3) Configuration of computer equipment.

4) Information about technicians and operators having professional computer qualifications.

5) Other data to be provided as required by the taxation bureau directly under the State Administration of Taxation.

Provisions on special invoices and non-creditable input tax

In case of any of the following circumstances, the special invoices shall not be used as the evidence for credit of input tax for VAT. The tax authorities shall return the original documents, and the purchasers may request the sellers to issue new special invoices.

1) Certification is not possible.
2) Taxpayer's identification number authentication does not match.
3) Allocation code and number authentication do not match.

If any of the following circumstances are certified, the special invoices shall not be used as the evidence for credit of input tax of VAT temporarily, and the tax authorities shall retain the original documents, find out the causes, and dispose accordingly.

1) Repeated authentication.
2) Wrong cipher text.
3) Unmatched authentication.
4) Listed as uncontrolled special invoices.

Administration of special VAT invoices

Administration of special VAT invoices by the anti-counterfeit and tax-control system

1) When special invoices administration departments of tax authorities use an anti-counterfeit and tax-control system for managing invoice records or issuing special invoices to taxpayers, they shall carefully type in the invoice code and number and attentively check them with the paper special invoices, so as to guarantee that the electronic information on invoice code and number match with those of the paper invoice.

2) When taxpayers issue special invoices through the anti-counterfeit and tax-control system, they shall attentively check that whether the code and number of the electronic invoice in the system match with those on the paper invoice. Any taxpayer finding that the tax authorities have filled in the wrong code or the number of the electronic invoice shall take the paper invoice and IC card for tax control to the tax authorities to deal with the refund.

3) Special invoices issued to taxpayers if tax authorities enter the wrong code or number shall be dealt with according to the following methods:
   - If taxpayers found the problems mentioned above in the current month, the paper special invoices and the electronic information in the anti-counterfeit and tax-control issuing system should be invalidated synchronously and reported to the competent tax authorities. If taxpayers found them in later months, negative special invoices should be issued in accordance with the relevant provisions.
   - If a large number of invoices are involved and the influence widespread, the State Administration of Taxation would modify

the National Database of Invalid Invoices in accordance with the stipulated procedures.

4) The seller shall not invalidate special invoices issued if the deduction form and the invoice form of the special invoice are not recovered or if the seller has sent the deduction form to the tax authorities for authentication although they have been recovered.

5) Since July 2003, the State Administration of Taxation has been appraising the "invalid invoices" resulted from the mal-operation of computer audit systems for special VAT invoices in all areas and publishing the appraisal results on a monthly basis. For regions with serious problems, the State Administration of Taxation will mobilize forces for spot checks and the problems may be publicized.

Administration of special VAT invoices issued on behalf of taxpayers

1) From June 1, 2004, tax authorities issuing invoices on behalf of taxpayers should fill in the *List of Invoices Issued on Behalf* one by one for the invoices issued in the current month, and use the software for collecting invoices issued on behalf from the reporting period in July to form an electronic document, namely the *List of Issue*.

2) *Creditable Invoices*. From the reporting period in June 2004, ordinary VAT payers using invoices issued on their behalf for crediting against the input tax should fill in the *List of Creditable Invoices Issued on Behalf* one by one and submit these together with the tax return during VAT declaration. Taxpayers could submit only a paper copy of the *List of Creditable Invoices* for declarations in the reporting period in June, but they should also submit a floppy disk (or other memory medium) containing the electronic data of this list from the reporting period in July. In case of failure to submit separately or fill in as specified the paper copy of the List of and the electronic data, input tax would not be credited.

3) From July 2004, the electronic data of the List of Issue collected in all regions in each month should be reported via file transfer protocol (FTP) to the State Administration of Taxation before the 20th day of each month. The FTP server of the State Administration of Taxation uses the FTP server uploaded for freight invoices. Tax authorities at all levels should check and summarize upload methods and processes.

4) The State Administration of Taxation is responsible for developing the software collecting information for the *List of Issue and the List of*

Creditable Invoices and the software for summarizing these for use by tax authorities and taxpayers free of charge. Taxpayers may consign the collection to intermediary agencies such as tax agents if they do not have the conditions for using information collection software.

5) Taxpayers who have not use invoices issued on behalf for credit against input tax in the current period may not submit the *List of Creditable Invoices* to the competent tax authorities.

Dealing with special VAT invoices stolen or lost

Taxpayers must keep and use special invoices in strict accordance with the *Provisions for the Use of Special Invoices of Value-Added Tax.* Taxpayers whose special invoices are stolen or lost due to violation of provisions may be fined not more than RMB10,000. Taxpayers losing special invoices may be banned from receipt and purchase of special invoices for a specific period of time (not longer than half a year). Taxpayers declaring special invoices lost shall assume joint liability of tax evasion or fraud if illegal issue on behalf or false issue is found.

Taxpayers losing special invoices must report the loss to the local competent tax authorities and the public security organizations in accordance with the stipulated procedures. Local tax authorities will charge for the loss report and publication fee on behalf of the taxpayer while penalizing the taxpayer which has lost the special invoices according to the stipulated procedures, and will transfer (send) information on the name of the taxpayer which has lost the special invoices, the number of invoices, the track and the number of words, and whether they were sealed or not to the *China Taxation News* for publishing an Announcement of Loss. The *Announcement of Loss* transferred (sent) to the *China Taxation News* must be checked, stamped and signed for approval by the tax authorities at county (city) level.

Special VAT invoices issued on behalf or falsely issued

Issue of invoices on behalf refers to the act of issuing invoices to others without a direct purchase and sales relationship. False issue of invoices refers to the act of issuing invoices for others or oneself, or letting others issue invoices for oneself, or leading others to issue invoices, when there is in fact no purchase and sale. Issuing on behalf and false issue are illegal acts. Those who issue special invoices on behalf or falsely shall be fined the total overdue tax according to the applicable tax rate to the goods listed on the invoices and be punished for tax evasion in accordance with provisions of the *Law on Tax Collection and Administration of the People's Republic of China.* Taxpayers' special

VAT invoices issued on behalf or falsely shall not be used as legal evidence for credit of input tax. Where a crime has been committed by issuing invoices on behalf or falsely, the punishment shall be imposed in accordance with the *Decision on the Suppression of Falsification Counterfeiting and Illegal Sale of Value-Added Tax Invoices* promulgated by the Standing Committee of the NPC.

Falsified special VAT invoices obtained by taxpayers in good faith

The purchase shall not be treated as evasion of tax or fraud of export rebate if there is a real transaction between the purchaser and the seller and the seller uses the special invoices of the province (or autonomous region, municipality directly under the central government and city directly under the state planning) where the seller is located, and all contents indicated on special invoices such as the seller's name, seal, quantity of goods, invoice value and tax amount agree with the reality, and there is no evidence proving that the purchaser knows that the special invoices provided by the seller are obtained by illegal means. However there is no creditable input tax or export rebate as per the relevant provisions; the purchaser's input tax that has been credited or export rebate that has been obtained shall be recovered in accordance with the law.

Tax authorities shall approve the credit against input tax or the export rebate if the purchaser is able to regain from the seller legal and effective special invoices issued by the anti-counterfeit and tax-control system, or to obtain legal and effective special invoices issued manually and the certificate proving that the tax authorities where the seller is located have investigated and prosecuted or are investigating and prosecuting the seller's acts of falsification of special invoices.

3

Chapter

Consumption Tax

An Overview

Some concepts

Consumption tax is a category of tax where the taxation object is the turnover amount of special consumables and consumption behavior. Consumption tax is levied worldwide. There are more than 120 countries and regions levying consumption tax.

China's consumption tax is a category of tax levied by the state on entities and individuals producing, processing on a commission basis or importing taxable consumables in order to reflect consumption policies. Consumption tax was a new category of tax established during the taxation reform in 1994 and together with VAT it forms the bi-level regulation structure of China's turnover taxes. Some of the commodity taxes levied in the early stages of the founding of the new China, the commodity circulation tax levied in the 1950s, the consolidated industrial and commercial tax levied from 1958 to 1973, the part equivalent to commodity tax covered in industrial and commercial tax levied from 1973 to 1983, and the VAT and product tax levied from 1983 to 1993, are of the nature of a consumption tax, but no such independent tax had been established. The State Council promulgated the *Provisional Regulations of the People's Republic of China on Consumption Tax* on December 13, 1993, which came into effect from January 1, 1994. Fundamental norms of current consumption tax are the *Provisional Regulations of the People's Republic of China on Consumption Tax* which was amended and adopted at the 34th Session of the Standing Committee of the State Council of the People's Republic of China on November 5, 2008, and was put into force as of January 1, 2009, and the *Detailed Rules for the Implementation of the Provisional Regulations of the People's Republic of China on Consumption Tax* promulgated by Decree No. 51 of the Ministry of Finance and the State Administration of Taxation on December 15, 2008, which came into force as of January 1, 2009.

Characteristics

Consumption tax levied currently worldwide is a category of tax for commodities or services which has not only a fiscal revenue function but also an economic regulatory function. Correspondingly, modern consumption tax generally has the following characteristics:

Special regulatory effects

Consumption tax is a category of tax through which the state employs tax leverage to have special regulation over special consumables and consumption behaviors. In other words, consumption tax coordinates with VAT to perform a special regulation on specially selected taxable consumables and consuming behaviors on the basis of a universal levy of VAT on goods in accordance with state policy on industry and consumption. High or low tax rates are established for selected special taxable consumables and consuming behavior, and a heavier tax burden is applied to consumables and consumption behaviors that should be restricted and controlled.

Stronger money gathering function

Although the incidence of taxation of consumption tax is smaller, the amount of consumables included in the incidence of taxation is generally larger and the range of application is extensive, so there are abundant sources of taxation. Moreover some consumables included in the incidence of taxation are products of considerable financial significance, so consumption tax is of stronger money gathering function.

Imposed on selective taxable items

Consumables liable to consumption tax in China are selected in accordance with the state policies on industries and consumption, and include high-grade consumables, luxury goods, consumables of high energy consumption, consumables of non-renewable resources and consumables of restricted consumption. Levy on these consumables will not only have no influence on people's living standards, it will also restrict use of harmful consumables, inhibit undesirable consumption behavior, promote effective utilization of resources, and relieve unfair distribution of social wealth.

Single link taxation

Consumption tax is a one-time taxation on a certain selected link of production, circulation or consumption, and there is no levy on other links. Sources of taxation are relatively concentrated, which can prevent tax loss on the one hand and save levy cost and improve levy administration efficiency on the other hand.

Effects

Current consumption tax in China is a tax category levied on the sales amount and quantity of taxable consumables of entities and individuals producing, processing on a commission basis or importing taxable consumables within the territory of China. Currently, the levy of consumption tax in China has three effects:

Implementing state policies on industries and consumption, regulating the structure of consumption, and guiding consumer behavior

Consumption tax is levied for special consumables usually at a relatively high tax rate and the tax is finally borne by consumers, which enables consumption tax to regulate consumption to a certain extent. Levy on the consumption link is limited to a small number of commodities selected by the state, and these commodities are of a certain financial significance or are special commodities restricted or limited by the state. The state may adjust the scope of these products according to changes in the economic situation in a specific period and respectively define high and low tax rates so as to embody regulation purposes. The size of the tax burden directly affects the price, consumers' immediate interests and their decisions on consumption, so the regulation of taxation incidence and tax rate within a specific period can regulate taxpayers' economic benefit, guide consumption directions and structure, and reflect state policies on consumption. Since consumption is the counteraction of production, a change of consumption structure will directly affect production structure and accordingly guide the adjustment of industrial structure and product structure. By regulating taxpayers' economic benefit, consumption tax affects the direction and contents of their operating activities and accordingly regulates consumption structure of the whole society and implements state policies on consumption.

Guaranteeing stable growth of state fiscal revenue

Consumption tax was promulgated against the background of taxation reform in 1994, while the turnover taxes before then were mainly VAT and product tax with their income concentrated on products related to tobacco, alcohol, and the petrochemical and chemical industries. These taxes were of high rates with many grades and strong financing effect. After the taxation reform, many products of with high tax rates were subject to VAT, which was a neutral tax category with a basic tax rate of 17% and a low tax rate 13%, which greatly lessened the tax burden and influenced state fiscal revenue. It was necessary to levy consumption tax in order to ensure that taxation reform did not lessen fiscal revenue nor weaken taxation's regulating effect on production and consumption of some products. Levy of consumption tax guarantees state fiscal revenue on the one hand, and exerts the regulating effect of taxation on the other hand.

Although consumption tax is of a small incidence in taxation, it is of great significance for obtaining fiscal revenue. Consumption tax helps to gather the full amount of fiscal funds stably and in a timely way for reasons such as the wide source of taxation, higher average tax rate, tax base of total turnover amount, and independence from enterprise operating cost.

Relieving the contradiction of unfair distribution of social wealth

At present there is a big objective difference between income level of residents in China and this will continue for quite a long time. Thus the income gap may be regulated by consumption tax other than taxes such as personal income tax. At the present stage, it is not possible to completely achieve fair allocation of tax only by personal income tax due to restriction of many factors. Consumption tax is levied on some luxury goods and high-consumption behavior, so as to add to the tax burden of some consumers from the perspective of regulation of personal payment capacity and achieve the objective of regulating high consumption by those of high income and relieving the contradiction of unfair distribution of social wealth.

Scope of Collection and the Taxpayers

Scope of collection

Scope of collection of consumption tax shall be determined by factors such as economic development level, state policies on consumption and industries within a certain period, urban and rural residents' living standards, consumption level and structure and stable growth of fiscal revenue, and the dual-level regulation structure of turnover tax at the present stage; in other words, consumption tax is levied for consumables included in the scope of collection of consumption tax on the basis of universal levy.

Scope of collection of consumption tax is selective and only some consumables and consuming behaviors are selected for tax collection. By selecting scope of collection, consumption tax can fully embody its strong flexibility and guidance function.

Scope of collection of consumption tax is taxable consumables specified by regulations on consumption tax. Among various consumables, few taxable consumables are included in the scope of collection of consumption tax. They are summarized in the following five categories:

The first is consumables whose excessive consumption damages people's health, ecological environment and social order, such as tobacco, alcohol, fireworks and firecrackers.

The second is non-daily necessities such as cosmetics, valuable jewelry, pearls and jades.

The third is consumables of non-renewable resources or slowly-renewable resources, such as petroleum products, wooden throwaway chopsticks and solid wood flooring.

The fourth is high-consumption or high-grade consumables such as cars, motorcycles, golf balls and clubs, high-grade watches, and yachts.

The fifth is consumables of a certain financial significance such as automobile tires.

Scope of collection of consumption tax is not rigid and it will be adjusted in accordance with the change of state macro-economic policies and consumption structure with the economic development of China.

Scope of collection of consumption tax currently in China is taxable consumables produced, processed on a commissioned basis, and imported within the territory of China.

For taxable consumables produced by taxpayers, tax shall be paid when taxpayers sell them. The sales herein refer to remunerative transfer of the ownership of taxable consumables. The compensation here refers to money, goods or other economic benefits acquired from the purchaser.

Retail businesses of gold and silver jewelry within the territory of China are also within the scope of collection of consumption tax. Retail businesses of gold and silver jewelry refer to businesses selling gold and silver jewelry to entities or individuals other than entities approved by the PBOC to produce, process, wholesale and retail gold and silver jewelry. Levy of consumption tax on gold and silver jewelry was approved by the State Council from January 1, 1995, to be changed from the production and sales link to the retail link. Levy in the retail link was only limited to gold-base and silver-base alloy jewelry and inlaid jewelry of gold, silver, gold-base and silver-base. The tax rate of 5% is applicable to the retail link of gold and silver jewelry and the tax base is the sales amount excluding VAT. Levy is still on the production and sales link for jewelry beyond the above scope and with consumption tax, such as jewelry with gold (silver) plating or gold (silver) covering, and inlaid jewelry with gold (silver) plating or gold (silver) covering. From May 1, 2003, consumption tax for platinum jewelry was changed to the retail link.

Taxpayers

Consumption taxpayers refer to entities and individuals producing, processing on a commissioned basis, or importing taxable consumables within the territory of China, and other entities and individuals defined by the State Council and selling taxable consumables.

Within the territory of China means that the shipping points or locations of consumables produced, processed on a commissioned basis, or imported that shall bear consumption tax shall be within China.

The entities as mentioned refer to enterprises, administrative units, government-sponsored institutions, military units, social groups and other organizations.

Individuals refer to individual businesses or other individuals.

Consumption taxpayers include:

1) Entities and individuals producing taxable consumables;
2) Entities and individuals importing taxable consumables;
3) Entities and individuals processing taxable consumables on a commissioned basis, where consumption tax of taxable consumables processed on a commissioned basis is withheld and remitted by the consignee when the consigner collects the goods (except when the consignee is an individual); for taxable consumables self-produced and self-used, consumption tax is paid when entities and individuals self-producing and using them transfer them for use; and
4) Other entities and individuals as defined by the State Council engaging in selling taxable consumables.

Tax Items and Tax Rates

Tax items

Items of consumption tax shall be determined mainly in accordance with factors such as state policies on consumption and industries, economic development level, people's living standards, consumption level, and structure and stable growth of fiscal revenue.

Regulations on consumption tax specify 14 items for levy of consumption tax, namely tobacco, alcohol, cosmetics, valuable jewelry, pearls and jades, fireworks and firecrackers, petroleum products, tires, passenger cars, motorcycles, golf balls and clubs, high-grade watches, yachts, wooden throwaway chopsticks, and solid wood flooring.

Tax rates

Since consumption tax is levied on special consumables and consumption behavior to implement state policies on industries and consumption, tax rate as a fundamental element and the key link of the taxation which helps to better implement policies on consumption tax. The formulation of consumption tax rate mainly includes two aspects: one is to correctly define a reasonable level of tax burden and the other is to select a reasonable form of tax rate.

Therefore, high and low tax rates should be formulated. China's turnover tax structure consists of VAT and consumption tax, which exerts the universal regulating effect of VAT on goods and gives play to the special regulating effect of consumption tax on special consumables. Consumption tax arranges different tax rates for different tax items and different taxable consumables under the same tax item so as to implement state policies on industries and consumption, for example, a high tax rate is designed for taxable consumables with restricted production and consumption (such as tobacco, alcohol, cosmetics, fireworks and firecrackers) and low tax rate is designed for taxable consumables with restriction only on consumption but not on production (automobile tires). Meanwhile, consumption tax is duly adjusted in accordance with state economic development level, people's living standards, consumption level and structure. The provisions on consumption tax in 1994 specified a tax rate of 17% for skin and hair care products; on July 1, 1999, this tax rate was reduced to 8%; on April 1, 2006, the tax item on skin and hair care products was cancelled and high-grade skin and hair care cosmetic products originally included in the item of taxation were listed into the item of cosmetics. Moreover, from April 1, 2006, for the sub-item of passenger cars under the tax item of sedan cars, the tax rate was specified as 3% for cars with a cylinder capacity (air displacement, the same for the following cases) of no more than 1.5 liters (including 1.5 liter, the same for the following cases); 5% for those with a cylinder capacity of more than 1.5 liters and less than 2.0 liters; 9% for those with a cylinder capacity of more than 2.0 liters and less than 2.5 liters; 12% for those with a cylinder capacity of more than 2.5 liters and less than 3.0 liters; 15% for those with a cylinder capacity of more than 3.0 liters and less than 4.0 liters; and 20% for those with a cylinder capacity of more than 4.0 liters. Moreover, from January 1, 2009, for the sub-item of passenger cars under the tax item of sedan cars, the tax rate was specified at

1% for cars with a cylinder capacity (air displacement, the same for the following cases) of no more than 1.5 liters (including 1.5 liters, same for the following cases); 3% for those with a cylinder capacity of more than 1.0 liters and less than 1.5 liters; 5% for those with a cylinder capacity of more than 1.5 liters and less than 2.0 liters; 9% for those with a cylinder capacity of more than 2.0 liters and less than 2.5 liters; 12% for those with a cylinder capacity of more than 2.5 liters and less than 3.0 liters; 25% for those with a cylinder capacity of more than 3.0 liters and less than 4.0 liters; and 40% for those with a cylinder capacity of more than 4.0 liters.

There are different forms of tax rate. Generally, the forms of consumption tax rate are proportional tax rate and quota tax rate. The form of consumption tax rate for taxable consumables shall be determined according to the specific situation of the taxable consumables. Generally, a proportional tax rate is used for taxable consumables with acute contradiction between supply and demand and relatively large price variance; a quota tax rate is used for taxable consumables with balanced contradiction between supply and demand and relatively small price variance.

Current consumption tax is of two tax rate forms namely proportional tax rate and quota tax rate that are applicable to different taxable consumables; both proportional tax rate and quota tax rate are applicable to two taxable consumables, namely tobacco and white spirits.

There are 14 grades of tax rates (tax amounts) for consumption tax and there are 12 grades for proportional tax rate with minimum tax rate and maximum tax rate of 1% and 45% respectively. Quota tax rates are of 8 grades and the minimum unit tax amount and the maximum one are RMB0.003 and RMB250 respectively (see Table 3.1).

Table 3.1. Tax rates of the consumption tax

Tax item	Tax rate
Tobacco	
Cigarette	
Class-A cigarette	45% plus RMB0.003/piece
Class-B cigarette	30% plus RMB0.003/piece
Cigar	25%
Cut tobacco	30%
Wine and alcohol	20% plus RMB0.5/500 ml

(Cont'd)

Tax item	Tax rate
White wine	RMB250/ton
Yellow rice or millet wine	—
Beer	—
Class-A beer	RMB250/ton
Class-B beer	RMB250/ton
Other spirits	10%
Alcohol	5%
Cosmetic	30%
Valuable jewelry, pearl and jade	
Gold, silver and platinum jewelry, diamond and diamond ornament	5%
Other valuable jewelry, pearl and jade	10%
Firework, firecracker	15%
Petroleum product	
Gasoline	
Leaded gasoline	RMB1.40/liter
Unleaded gasoline	RMB1.00/liter
Diesel oil	RMB0.80/liter
Aviation kerosene	RMB0.80/liter
Naphtha	RMB1.00/liter
Solvent oil	RMB1.00/liter
Lubricant oil	RMB1.00/liter
Fuel oil	RMB0.80/liter
Automobile tire	3%
Motorcycle	
Cylinder capacity (air displacement, same for the following cases) no more than 250ml (including 250ml)	3%
Cylinder capacity more than 250ml	10%

(Cont'd)

Tax item	Tax rate
Sedan	
Passenger car	
Cylinder capacity (air displacement, same for the following cases) no more than 1.0L (including 1.0L)	1%
Cylinder capacity more than 1.0L and less than 1.5L (including 1.5L)	3%
Cylinder capacity more than 1.5L and less than 2.0L (including 2.0L)	5%
Cylinder capacity more than 2.0L and less than 2.5L (including 2.5L)	9%
Cylinder capacity more than 2.5L and less than 3.0L (including 3.0L)	12%
Cylinder capacity more than 3.0L and less than 4.0L (including 4.0L)	25%
Cylinder capacity more than 4.0L	40%
Medium-size and light-weight commercial passenger car	5%
Golf balls and clubs	10%
High-grade watch	20%
Yacht	10%
Wooden throwaway chopsticks	5%
Solid wood flooring	5%

Tax Base

Tax base of consumption tax shall be considered from the perspectives of price variance of taxable consumables and convenience of collection and administration. Three methods are respectively adopted, i.e. rate on value, amount on volume and a combination of the two.

Tax base for the method of rate on value

Tax base is the sales amount

Proportional tax rate is practiced for consumption tax on cigars, cut tobacco, other spirits, alcohol, cosmetics, valuable jewelry, pearl and jade, fireworks, firecrackers, petroleum products, automobile tires, motorcycles, sedan cars, golf balls and clubs, high-grade watches, yachts, wooden throwaway chopsticks and solid wood flooring. Under the method of tax rate on value, the tax base is the sales amount of taxable consumables.

Cross collection is practiced for both VAT and consumption tax, in other words, consumables liable for consumption tax are also liable for VAT, while VAT is based on the price excluding tax and consumption tax is based on the price including tax, so the sales amount for taxation of consumption tax of taxable consumables practicing the method of rate on value is consistent with the sales amount for taxation of VAT, that is to say, the two taxes are of consistent tax base, including consumption tax but not VAT.

Determination of sales amount

General provisions on sales amount

Sales amount refers to the total consideration and all other charges received from the purchasers by the taxpayers selling taxable consumables, excluding the amount of VAT collected from the sellers. Other charges as mentioned include service charge, subsidy, fund, financing cost, returned profit, incentive fee, penalty, surcharge for overdue tax payment, interest on deferred payment, compensation, collection made on behalf, payment made on behalf, packing charge, packaging rent, reserve fee, quality fee, transport handling cost and other charges of various natures. However the following items are excluded:

First, advanced money for transport costs meeting all the following conditions:

1) The transport department's invoices for transport costs are issued to the purchasers;
2) The taxpayers transfer these invoices to the purchasers.

Second, governmental funds and administrative fees meeting the following conditions and collected on behalf:

1) Governmental funds approved to be established by the State Council or the Ministry of Finance and administrative fees approved to be established by the State Council or provincial people's governments and their finance and price departments in charge;
2) Financing notes printed by financial departments above provincial level issued upon payment;
3) The total amount collected is turned over to central finance.

For taxable consumables sold together with wrappers no matter whether they are independently priced or how accounting is achieved, they shall be included into the sales amount of taxable consumables and liable for consumption tax. If wrappers are not priced or sold together with products but a guarantee deposit is charged, this deposit shall not be included into the sales amount of taxable consumables for levy. But for guarantee deposits not refunded due to failure of withdrawal of wrappers beyond the time limit or for the deposits collected for more than 12 months, the deposit shall be included into the sales amount of taxable consumables and consumption tax shall be levied according to the applicable tax rates.

If wrappers are sold together with taxable consumables and a guarantee deposit charged, with their prices included in those of the consumables, the deposit shall be included in the sales amount of taxable consumables and consumption tax shall be levied according to the applicable tax rates if wrappers are not returned within the specified period of time.

Conversion of the amount of sales including tax

If the amount of VAT is not deducted from the sales amount of taxpayers' taxable consumables or the price and VAT are charged together due to prohibition of issue of special VAT invoices, the sales amount shall be converted into that excluding VAT when consumption tax is calculated. The conversion formula is as follows:

Sales amount of taxable consumables = Sales amount including VAT /
(1 + VAT rate or levy rate)

A VAT rate of 17% is applicable if the consumption taxpayer is an ordinary taxpayer of VAT; a levy rate 3% is applicable if the consumption taxpayer is a small-scale taxpayer of VAT.

If taxable price of taxpayer's taxable consumables is obviously low without proper justification, the taxable price shall be determined by the competent tax authorities

The extent of authority for determining taxable price of taxable consumables is specified as follows:

1) Taxable price of cigarette, white spirits and sedan cars is determined by the State Administration of Taxation and reported to the Ministry of Finance for filing.

2) Taxable price of other taxable consumables is determined by the state tax authorities of provinces, autonomous regions and municipalities directly under the Central Government.

3) Taxable price of imported taxable consumables is determined by the Customs.

For taxable consumables sold by taxpayers and settled in currency other than the RMB for sales amount, the RMB conversion rate for sales amount may choose the national foreign exchange rate on the date of settlement or the first day of the month (the middle rate in principle). Taxpayers shall determine the conversion rate in advance and shall not change it within one year once it is determined.

Tax base for the method of amount on volume

The tax base is sales quantity

Quota tax rate is practiced for consumption tax on yellow rice or millet wine, beer and petroleum products. Under the method of amount on volume, the tax base is sales quantity of taxable consumables.

Determination of sales quantity

The tax base is sales quantity of taxable consumables. Details are as follows:
1) It shall be sales quantity of taxable consumables in the case of sales of taxable consumables.
2) It shall be quantity of taxable consumables transferred for use in the case of self production and use of taxable consumables.
3) It shall be quantity of taxable consumables recovered by taxpayers in the case of consigned processing of taxable consumables.
4) It shall be quantity of imported taxable consumables determined by the Customs for levy in the case of import of taxable consumables.

Conversion of measuring unit

It is specified that the tax unit for yellow rice or millet wine and beer is the ton and that for gasoline and diesel oil is the liter. However some taxpayers may use these measuring units together in the actual sales process, so their conversion criteria are specified as follows to normalize measuring units of different products and correctly calculate the tax payable:

Yellow rice or millet wine: 1 ton = 962 liters

Beer: 1 ton = 988 liters

Gasoline: 1 ton = 1,388 liters

Diesel oil: 1 ton = 1,176 liters

Aviation kerosene: 1 ton = 1,246 liters

Naphtha: 1 ton = 1,385 liters

Solvent oil: 1 ton = 1,282 liters

Lubricant oil: 1 ton = 1,126 liters

Fuel oil: 1 ton = 1,015 liters

Tax base for the composite taxation

Within the scope of current consumption tax, only two taxable consumables namely cigarettes and white spirits liable to the combination method of tax calculation and collection. The tax base includes two aspects namely sales amount and sales quantity, and the methods for determining sales amount and sales quantity are consistent with the methods for determining sales amount and sales quantity when the method of rate on value and the method of amount on volume are used.

Special provisions on tax base

Tax base of cigarette tax according to the method of rate on value is transfer price or approved price

Tax base of cigarette tax according to the method of rate on value is transfer price or approved price. Transfer price refers to the cigarette transaction price agreed and signed by cigarette manufacturers and the purchasers on the trading market. The taxable transfer price is determined by the State Administration of Taxation in accordance with the transfer prices of cigarettes of various trademarks and specifications obtained from data of the China Tobacco Trade Center and all provincial tobacco trade (procurement) fairs in 2000. The approved price refers to the taxable price approved by tax authorities according to the method of seizing back the retail price by a certain proportion. The calculation formula of approved price is as follows:

Taxable price of consumption tax of the cigarette of a certain trademark and specification = Retail price of this cigarette / (1 + 45%)

For the cigarette that is not sold at trade markets at or above the provincial level and has no transfer price, taxable price of consumption tax shall be checked and approved by the State Administration of Taxation according to the following formula:

Taxable price of consumption tax of the cigarette of a certain trademark and specification but without a price = Market retail price of this cigarette / (1 + 35%)

For cigarettes with an actual sales price higher than taxable price and approved price, consumption tax is levied according to actual sales price; for cigarettes with an actual sales price lower than taxable price and approved price, consumption tax is levied according to taxable price or approved price.

For cigarettes not of standard strip packaging, their quantity shall be converted into the quantity of cigarettes of standard strip packaging, and the actual sales price after conversion and applicable proportional tax rate shall be determined according to the actual sales price.

Provisions on calculation of tax of self-established sales department with non-independent financial accounting

For self-produced taxable consumables sold by the taxpayer's self-established department with non-independent financial accounting, consumption tax shall be calculated according to the sales department's sales amount or sales quantity.

Provisions on other uses of taxable consumables

For taxpayer's taxable consumables used for exchange for means of production or consumption, investment in capital and liability offset, tax basis shall be the maximum sales price of similar taxable consumables.

Provisions on dealing in taxable consumables with different tax rates

For taxpayers dealing in taxable consumables with different tax rates, these shall be separately accounted for sales amount and quantity. If they have not been accounted for separately or consumables with different rates are formed into a complete set and sold, the higher tax rates shall apply.

Taxpayers' dealing in taxable consumables with different tax rates means that taxpayers produce and sell taxable consumables with more than two tax rates. The higher tax rates shall apply means that if sales amount and quantity of taxable consumables with different tax rates are not accounted separately or taxable consumables with different tax rates are formed into a complete set and sold, the consumption tax payable shall be obtained by multiplying the higher tax rates applicable to taxable consumables by the sales amount and quantity mixed together.

Calculation of Tax Payable

For production and sales of taxable consumables

In terms of taxable consumables directly sold abroad

Calculation according to the method of rate on value

Tax payable equals to sales amount multiplied by the applicable proportional tax rate. The calculation formula is as follows:

Tax payable = Amount of sales × Proportional tax rate

Calculation according to the method of amount on volume

Tax payable equals to sales amount multiplied by the applicable quota tax rate. The calculation formula is as follows:

Tax payable = Sales amount × Quota tax rate

Calculation according to the combination of the two methods

Within the scope of current consumption tax, only cigarette and white spirits are liable to the combination method. The calculation formula is as follows:

Tax payable = Sales amount × Proportional tax rate + Sales quantity × Quota tax rate

In terms of self-produced and self-used taxable consumables

Self-produced and self-used means that taxable consumables after being produced by taxpayers are not directly sold but used for continuous self-production of taxable consumables or for other purposes.

Provisions on tax for continuous production of taxable consumables

There is no tax for taxpayer's self-produced and self-used taxable consumables for continuous production of taxable consumables. Taxpayer's self-produced and self-used taxable consumables for continuous production of taxable consumables refer to taxable consumables that are used as direct materials for producing final taxable consumables and to form final products. For example, a cigarette factory produces cut tobacco which is a taxable consumable itself. The cigarette factory uses the produced cut tobacco for continuous production of cigarettes, therefore cut tobacco used for continuous production of cigarettes is not liable for consumption tax and consumption tax is only levied for the produced cigarettes. Of course consumption tax will be levied for cut tobacco produced if it is directly sold. The tax law's provisions on no tax for self-produced and self-used taxable consumables for continuous production of taxable consumables embody the principles of simple tax calculation.

Provisions on tax for other uses

Tax shall be levied for taxpayer's self-produced and self-used taxable consumables when they are transferred for other uses not for continuous production of taxable consumables. Other uses refer to producing non-taxable consumables and works in progress by taxpayers, providing services by administrative departments and non-productive organizations, and using taxable consumables as gifts, for sponsorship, fund raising or advertising, as samples, for employees' welfare, reward and so on. Use for producing non-taxable consumables means that self-produced taxable consumables are used for producing products beyond the 14 categories of products listed in the table of tax rates for consumption tax items. Use for works in progress means that self-produced taxable consumables are used for various construction projects of the producers themselves. Use for administrative departments and non-productive organizations means that self-produced taxable consumables are used by administrative departments and non-productive organizations in a relationship of administrative subordination. Use for as gifts, for sponsorship, fund raising or advertising, as samples, for employees' welfare or reward means that self-produced taxable consumables are used as free gifts to others or investment funds to other organizations or in commercial advertising, sample distribution or employee's welfare or reward. All in all, consumption tax should be paid in accordance with the laws on enterprises' self-produced taxable consumables although they are not used for sales or continuous production of taxable consumables as long as they are regarded as sales due to use within the scope specified by the tax law.

Calculation of tax payable

For taxpayers' self-produced and self-used taxable consumables, tax payable shall be calculated according to the sales price of similar consumables produced by them; tax payable shall be calculated according to the composite assessable price if there is no sales price of similar consumables.

The calculation formula for composite assessable price for the method of value on rate is as follows:

Composite assessable price = (Cost + Profit) / (1 – Proportional tax rate)

The calculation formula for composite assessable price for the combination method is as follows:

Composite assessable price = (Cost + Profit + Self-produced and self-used quantity × Quota tax rate) / (1 – Proportional tax rate)

The sales price of similar consumables refers to the sales price of similar consumables sold by the taxpayer and the withholding and collecting agent of the month; if sales prices of similar consumables are different, the price shall be the weighted average based on sales quantities. However in any of the following circumstances, taxable consumables shall not be listed into the weighted average calculation:

1) The sales price is obviously low without any justified reason.

2) The taxable consumable has no sales price.

If there is no sale or the sales are not finished in the current month, tax payable shall be calculated according to the sales price of similar consumables of the previous month or recent months.

Cost as mentioned in the above formulas refers to the production cost of taxable consumables. Profit as mentioned in above formulas refers to the profit calculated according to national average profit rates on costs of taxable consumables. The national average profit rates on costs of taxable consumables are determined by the State Administration of Taxation.

On December 28, 1993, and in March 2006, the State Administration of Taxation promulgated the *Stipulations Concerning Some Specific Issues Related to Consumption Tax* and determined the national average profit rates on costs of taxable consumables as shown in Table 3.2.

Table 3.2. National average profit rates on costs of taxable consumables

Name of goods	Profit rate (%)	Name of goods	Profit rate (%)
Class-a cigarette	10	Other valuable jewelry, pearl and jade	6
Class-b cigarette	5	Automobile tire	5
Cigar	5	Motorcycle	6
Cut tobacco	5	Golf balls and clubs	10
White spirits made from grains	10	Luxury watch	20
White spirits made from potato	5	Yacht	10
Other wines	5	Wooden throwaway chopsticks	5
Alcohol	5	Solid wood flooring	5
Cosmetic	5	Passenger car	8
Firecracker, firework	5	Medium-size and light-weight commercial passenger car	5

In terms of consumables processed on a commission basis

Provisions on taxable consumables processed on a commission basis

Taxable consumables processed on a commission basis refers to taxable consumables where the raw materials and main materials are provided by the consigner while the consignee only charges processing fees and pays for some of the auxiliary materials on behalf. Taxable consumables produced out of raw materials provided by the consignee, or those processed by the consignee after the raw materials of the consignee are sold to the consigner, or those produced out of raw materials purchased by the consignee in the name of the consigner, shall not be regarded as taxable consumables processed on a commission basis no matter whether taxpayers treat them as sales from the financial perspective or not, and the consumption tax shall be paid in accordance with sales of self-produced taxable consumables.

It can be seen that taxable consumables processed on a commission basis fulfill two conditions: firstly, raw materials and main materials are provided by the consigner; secondly, the consignee only charges processing fees and pays for some auxiliary materials on behalf. If either the consigner or the consignee fails to meet the above conditions, consumption tax shall not be treated as the tax based on taxable consumables and processed on a commission basis but shall only be paid according to sales of self-produced taxable consumables. The abovementioned provisions are to control sources of taxation and to avoid loss of tax payments.

Provisions on tax collection and payment on behalf

For taxable consumables processed on a commission basis, consumption tax has been collected and paid by the consignee on behalf during delivery, so consumption tax does not need to be paid for those directly sold by the consigner retaking them.

For taxable consumables processed by commissioned individuals, the consigner shall pay consumption tax after retaking them.

For taxable consumables processed by consignees except individuals, the consignees shall pay consumption tax to the competent tax authorities where their establishments are located or where they reside.

Calculation of tax payable

For taxable consumables processed on a commission basis, tax payable shall be calculated according to the sales price of similar consumables of the consignee;

tax payable shall be calculated according to the composite assessable price if there is no sales price of similar consumables.

The calculation formula for composite assessable price for the method of value on rate is as follows:

Composite assessable price = (Cost of materials + Processing fee) /
(1 – Proportional tax rate)

The calculation formula for composite assessable price for the combination method is as follows:

Composite assessable price = (Cost of materials + Processing fee + Quantity of commissioned processing × Quota tax rate) / (1 – Proportional tax rate)

The sales price of similar consumables refers to the sales price of similar consumables sold by the taxpayer and the withholding and collecting agent of the month; if sales prices of similar consumables are different, the price shall be the weighted average based on sales quantities. However in any of the following circumstances taxable consumables shall not be listed into the weighted average calculation:

1)   The sales price is obviously low without any justified reason.
2)   The taxable consumable has no sales price.

If there is no sale or the sales are not finished in the current month, tax payable shall be calculated according to the sales price of similar consumables of the previous month or recent months.

Cost of materials in the above formulas refers to the actual cost of materials provided by the consigner for processing. Taxpayers consigning the processing of taxable consumables must truthfully indicate (or provide in other forms) cost of materials in the contract of consigned processing and the consignee's competent tax authorities are entitled to assess and decide the cost of materials if the cost is not provided.

Processing fee in the above formulas refers to all expenses (including the actual cost of auxiliary materials paid on behalf) charged by the consignee for processing taxable consumables.

In terms of taxable consumables imported

For taxable consumables imported

Consumption tax of taxable consumables imported shall be paid during import declaration and it is levied by the Customs on behalf.

Consumption tax of taxable consumables taken or posted into China by individuals is levied together with customs duty. Specific measures should be worked out by the Customs Tariff Commission of the State Council jointly with other organizations.

For importation of taxable consumables, tax shall be reported and paid to the Customs office where the imports are declared.

Calculation of tax payable for taxable consumables imported

Tax payable for taxable consumables imported shall be calculated according to the composite assessable price.

Calculation of tax payable for the method of rate on value:

Composite assessable price = (Customs dutiable value + Customs Duty) / (1 – Proportional tax rate of consumption tax)

Tax payable = Composite assessable price × Proportional tax rate

Calculation of tax payable for the method of amount on volume:

Tax payable = Import amount × Quota tax rate

Calculation of tax payable for the combination method:

Composite assessable price = Customs dutiable value + Customs Duty + Import amount × Quota tax rate of consumption tax / (1 – Proportional tax rate of consumption tax)

Customs dutiable value in above formulas refers to the customs dutiable value determined by the Customs.

Calculation of deduction of consumption tax paid

Provisions on consumption tax paid of purchased taxed consumables

Since some taxable consumables are continuously produced out of purchased taxable consumables on which consumption tax has been paid, the tax law specifies that consumption tax that has been paid for these purchased taxable consumables shall be calculated according to the quantity received for production in the current period, in order to avoid double taxation.

Taxable consumables permitted to be deducted

For levy of consumption tax on taxable consumables, consumption tax paid for purchased taxed consumables is permitted to be deducted for the following taxable consumables:

1) Cigarettes produced out of purchased taxed cut tobacco
2) Cosmetics produced out of purchased taxed cosmetics
3) Valuable jewelry, pearl and jade produced out of purchased taxed jewelry, pearl and jade
4) Firecrackers and fireworks produced out of purchased taxed firecrackers and fireworks
5) Automobile tires produced out of purchased taxed automobile tires
6) Motorcycles produced out of purchased taxed motorcycles
7) Golf clubs produced out of purchased raw materials for head, body and grip.
8) Wooden throwaway chopsticks produced out of purchased wooden throwaway chopsticks
9) Solid wood flooring produced out of purchased solid wood flooring
10) Lubricant oil produced out of purchased raw material for lubricant oil

Calculation of tax permitted to be deducted in the current period

Paid tax of purchased taxable consumables permitted to be deducted in the current period shall be calculated according to the quantity received for production in the current period.

Paid tax of purchased taxable consumables permitted to be deducted in current period = Buying price of purchased taxable consumables permitted to be deducted in current period × Applicable tax rate of purchased taxable consumables

Buying price of purchased taxable consumables permitted to be deducted in current period = Buying price of purchased taxable consumables of the inventory at the beginning of current period + Buying price of taxable consumables purchased in current period – Buying price of purchased taxable consumables of the inventory at the end of current period

Provisions on taxable consumables continuously produced out of recovered taxed consumables processed on a commission basis

Since some taxable consumables are continuously produced out of taxable consumables processed on a commission basis on which consumption tax has been paid, the tax law specifies that the paid consumption tax on taxable consumables processed on a commission basis permitted to be deducted shall be calculated according to the quantity received for production in the current period when tax is calculated for these taxable consumables produced continuously, in order to avoid double taxation.

Taxable consumables permitted to be deducted

Taxable consumables permitted to be deducted are as follows:

1) Cigarettes produced out of taxed cut tobacco recovered from consigned processing
2) Cosmetics produced out of taxed cosmetics recovered from consigned processing
3) Valuable jewelry, pearl and jade produced out of taxed jewelry, pearl and jade recovered from consigned processing
4) Firecrackers and fireworks produced out of taxed firecrackers and fireworks recovered from consigned processing
5) Automobile tires produced out of taxed automobile tires recovered from consigned processing
6) Motorcycles produced out of taxed motorcycles recovered from consigned processing
7) Golf clubs produced out of raw materials for head, body and grip recovered from consigned processing
8) Wooden throwaway chopsticks produced out of raw materials for wooden throwaway chopsticks recovered from consigned processing
9) Solid wood flooring produced out of raw materials for solid wood flooring recovered from consigned processing
10) Taxable consumable produced out of raw materials of naphtha recovered from consigned processing

Calculation of tax permitted to be deducted in current period

Paid tax of taxable consumables processed on a consigned basis that is permitted to be deducted in the current period shall be calculated according to the quantity received for production in the current period.

Paid tax of taxable consumables processed on a consigned basis that is permitted to be deducted in current period = Paid tax of taxable consumables processed on a consigned basis of the inventory at the beginning of current period + Paid tax of taxable consumables processed on a consigned basis and recovered in current period – Paid tax of taxable consumables processed on a consigned basis of the inventory at the end of current periods

Tax Refund (Exemption) on Exported Taxable Consumables

The state grants tax preferences of refund (exemption) for taxpayers' exported taxable consumables in accordance with policies basically identical to the provisions on VAT refund (exemption) for exported goods. The only provisions different from those on VAT refund (exemption) for exported goods are given below.

General policies

There are three scenarios of basic policies on tax refund (exemption) for exported taxable consumables.

Tax exemption and refund for export goods

This policy is applicable to directly exported taxable consumables purchased by foreign-trade enterprises with authority to export and exported taxable consumables of foreign-trade enterprises consigned by other foreign-trade enterprises.

It should be noted that tax is only refunded on taxable consumables of foreign-trade enterprises consigned by other foreign-trade enterprises and the tax is not refunded (exempted) for exported taxable consumables of foreign-trade enterprises consigned by other enterprises (mainly non-productive commercial enterprises).

Tax exemption but no refund on export goods

This policy is applicable to self-produced taxable consumables exported by producing enterprises with authority to export by themselves or by their consigned foreign trade enterprises with authority to export, and consumption tax is levied according to actual export quantity but it is not refunded. The exemption of consumption tax herein means that consumption tax in the production link is levied according to the production enterprise's actual export quantity. Consumption tax is not refunded means that since consumption tax in the production link is levied and the taxable consumable does not include consumption tax when it is exported, there is no need for refund of consumption tax.

Neither tax exemption nor refund for exports

This policy is applicable to other enterprises other than production enterprises and foreign-trade enterprises; in other words, tax is not refunded (exempted) for exported taxable consumables consigned by ordinary commercial enterprises to foreign-trade enterprises.

Tax refund rate on export goods

Tax rate or unit tax of refundable consumption tax on exported taxable consumables shall be calculated according to the *Table of Tax Rates (Amounts) of Items of Consumption Tax attached to the Provisional Regulations of the People's Republic of China on Consumption Tax*.

Enterprises shall separately account and declare exported taxable consumables with different consumption tax rates, and refundable consumption tax shall be calculated according to the lower tax rate applicable if no applicable tax rate is differentiated.

Calculation of tax refund on export goods

Refundable amount of consumption tax for goods directly exported by foreign-trade enterprises buying them from production enterprises or for taxable consumables exported as consigned by other foreign-trade enterprises shall be calculated according to two scenarios.

Refundable amount of consumption tax of taxable consumables with the levy of consumption tax based on the method of rate on value shall be calculated according to the consumption tax levied when foreign-trade enterprises purchase goods from factories. The calculation formula is as follows:

Refundable amount of consumption tax = Factory sales amount of exported goods × Tax rate

Factory sales amount of exported goods in above formula does not include VAT and the price including VAT shall be converted into sales amount excluding VAT.

Refundable amount of consumption tax of taxable consumables with the levy of consumption tax based on the method of amount on volume shall be calculated according to the quantity of goods purchased and declared at Customs for export. The calculation formula is as follows:

Refundable amount of consumption tax = Quantity of export × Unit tax

Administration after tax refund (exemption) on exported taxable consumables

Where the return of goods or the withdrawal of the customs declaration occurs after the completion of the tax refund on the export goods, the exporter shall in a timely way repay the tax refunded to the competent tax authorities where the exporter's establishment is located or the exporter resides.

Where the return of goods or the withdrawal of the customs declaration occurs after the completion of the tax exemption on goods directly exported by taxpayers and on tax exempted during import, taxpayers may not repay tax temporarily after being approved by the competent tax authorities where the taxpayers' establishments are located or the taxpayers reside and may report to repay consumption tax after the goods are transferred for sale domestically.

Where the return of goods or the withdrawal of the customs declaration occurs after the completion of the tax refund on the export goods, the exporter shall in a timely way repay the tax refunded to the competent tax authorities where the exporter's establishment is located or the exporter resides.

Administration of Tax Collection

The occurrence time of tax liability

The time at which a liability to tax arises includes four scenarios:

1) For taxpayers selling taxable consumables, the effective date of tax liability is elaborated as follows:
   - For the mode of credit sale and collection and settlement by installments, it is the date on which the collection date is specified in the written contract, or the date on which the taxable consumables are delivered if there is no collection date specified in the written contract or there is no written contract.
   - For taxpayers' settlement under the mode of advances on sales, it is the date on which the taxable consumables are delivered.
   - For sales of taxable consumables under the mode of collection and acceptance and entrusted bank payment receipt, it is the date on which taxable consumables are delivered and the collection procedures are finished.
   - For other settlement modes, it is the date on which the sales sum is received or the documented evidence of right to collect the sales sum is obtained.

2) For taxpayer's self-produced and self-used taxable consumables, it is the date on which they are transferred for use.
3) For taxpayers' taxable consumables processed on a commissioned basis, it is the date on which the taxpayers pick up the goods.
4) For taxpayer's imported taxable consumables, it is the date on which the taxpayer declares at Customs for import.

Assessable period

Assessable periods for consumption tax payment are 1 day, 3 days, 5 days, 10 days, 15 days, 1 month or 1 quarter. The actual assessable period of taxpayers shall be determined by the competent tax authorities according to the magnitude of the tax payable of the taxpayers; tax that cannot be assessed at regular periods may be assessed on a transaction-by-transaction basis.

Taxpayers that adopt one month or one quarter as an assessable period shall report and pay tax within 15 days following the end of the period. If an assessable period of 1 day, 3 days, 5 days, 10 days or 15 days is adopted, the tax shall be prepaid within 5 days following the end of the period and a monthly return shall be filed with any balance of tax due settled within 15 days from the first day of the following month.

Taxpayers importing taxable consumables shall pay tax within 15 days after the issue of the tax payment certificates by the Customs office.

Place of payment

Consumption taxpayer's place of payment includes five scenarios as follows:
1) For taxable consumables sold by taxpayers and those produced and used by taxpayers themselves, tax payment shall be declared to competent tax authorities where taxpayers' establishments are located or where they reside unless otherwise specified by the competent financial and tax authorities of the State Council.
2) For taxable consumables processed by consignees except individuals, the consignees shall pay consumption to the competent tax authorities where their establishments are located or where they reside. For taxable consumables processed by consigned individuals, the consigner shall declare tax payment to the competent tax authorities where his establishments are located or where he resides.
3) For imported taxable consumables, the importer or his agent shall report and pay tax to the Customs office where the imports are declared.
4) For taxpayers selling self-produced taxable consumables in a different

county (or city), or consigning agents in a different county (or city) for sales on behalf, tax payment shall be declared to the competent tax authorities where taxpayers' establishments are located or they reside after the sales of taxable consumables.

If the taxpayer's head office and branches are not situated in the same county (or city), they shall report and pay tax separately to their respective local competent tax authorities; the head office may, upon the approval of the State Administration of Taxation or its authorized tax authorities, report and pay tax on a consolidated basis with the local competent tax authorities where the head office is located.

5) If taxable consumables sold by taxpayers are returned by the purchasers due to reasons related to quality etc., consumption tax that has been paid may be refunded after inspection and approval by the competent tax authorities where taxpayers' establishments are located or where they reside.

4

Chapter

Business Tax

An Overview

Some concepts

Business tax is a kind of tax levied on business turnover obtained by entities and individuals providing taxable services, transferring intangible assets, and selling real estate within the territory of China.

Business tax is an old category of tax practiced in the early years of new China. As early as in 1950, there was business tax in China's industrial and commercial tax system. Business tax was incorporated into industrial and commercial tax during the taxation reform in 1958. In 1973, consolidated industrial and commercial tax was incorporated with salt tax, animal slaughter tax, urban real estate tax and vehicle and vessel license tax into industrial and commercial tax. During the substitution of tax payment for profit delivery implemented in the second step of reform in October 1984, the part of industrial and commercial tax that was levied according to turnover amount of wholesale and retail commodities and the part of services that was levied according to business income were divided and improved to establishing business tax so as to adapt to the needs of economic development and change the situation of an over-simplified tax system, which made business tax a kind of tax levied on the turnover of commodities in the link of commercial wholesale and retail and on the business income obtained from providing services. Together with product tax and VAT it became one of the three major tax categories of China's original turnover tax system.

The reform of turnover tax focusing on full implementation of VAT was critical to the whole reform of the tax system in 1994 and the business tax was formed based on the original business tax and consolidated industrial and commercial tax. Therefore the establishment of business tax implemented the principles of adding no tax burden, unifying tax policies, and simplifying the tax system. Business tax made important adjustments and corrections to aspects such as the taxpayer, incidence of taxation, tax item and tax rate. The *Provisional Regulations of the People's Republic of China on Business Tax* promulgated by the State Council on December 13, 1993, is the fundamental statute of business tax, and the Ministry of Finance promulgated the *Detailed Rules for the Implementation of the Provisional Regulations on Business Tax of the People's Republic of China* on December 25, 1993. The fundamental norms of current business tax are the *Provisional Regulations of the People's Republic of China on Business Tax* which was amended and adopted at the 34th Session of the Standing Committee of the State Council on November 5, 2008, and came into force as of January 1, 2009, and the *Detailed Rules for the Implementation of the Provisional Regulations on Business Tax of the People's Republic of China* promulgated by Decree No. 52 of the Ministry of Finance and the State Administration of Taxation on December 15, 2008, which came into force as of January 1, 2009.

Characteristics

Compared with other taxes on commodities and services, business tax has the following characteristics:

Its main tax base is business turnover

Business tax belongs to conventional taxes on commodities and services, but the division of incidence of taxation between it and VAT and consumption tax results in the levy of business tax on both non-commodity business turnover and commodity sales amount, with the levy for non-commodity business turnover playing a dominant role. Generally, the tax base of business tax is the total amount of business turnover and the tax amount is not affected by costs and expenses, which is very important in guaranteeing the steady growth of fiscal revenue.

Tax items and rates are designed according to industries

Tax items and rates of current business tax are designed for different industries and the overall level of tax rates is relatively low, which embodies the universal levy of business tax. Since various businesses are of different levels of profitability, a flat tax rate is practiced for business tax in the same industry and differential tax rates are practiced for different industries to embody policies on equitable tax burden and encouraging fair competition.

Simple and convenient calculation, collection and administration

Business tax is usually levied based on the total amount of business turnover, with tax items and rates designed according to industry categories and proportional tax rate practiced, so it is a simple and convenient method for calculating tax amount, has relatively low cost of collection, and easy calculation and administration for tax authorities.

Effects

Business tax is one of major taxes in China's current turnover tax system and a main tax of the local tax system. Business tax features not only effective money gathering but also powerful economic regulation.

Organizing the fiscal revenue

Incidence of taxation of current business tax covers the majority of tertiary industry, so the taxation domain is extensive. Business tax specifies that entities and individuals providing compensable taxable services, transferring intangible assets and selling real estate shall pay tax based on their business turnover obtained, which embodies the principle of universal levy of business tax. Moreover business tax is not affected by the cost and profit of the business operator, so tax shall be paid for the obtained proceeds of business in the case of occurrence of taxable behaviors. Therefore business tax is an extensive and steady source of taxation and helps the state to obtain fiscal revenue in a timely and reliable way. In particular with the further development of tertiary industry, business tax will play a more powerful role as far as organizing fiscal revenue is concerned.

Promoting coordinated development of the main tax categories

Business tax practices differential tax rates which are designed according to different industries' degrees of effect and profit levels in the national economy. Low tax rates are practiced for some industries related to the national economy and the people's livelihood, such as transportation, post and telecommunications, culture and sports; high rates are adopted for some singing halls, dance halls and golf courses of high-profit and high-grade consumption. This not only gives consideration to those industries closely related to people's livelihood but also guarantees fiscal revenue, regulates and controls socioeconomic activities, and guides various industries to develop in a sound and healthy way.

Supervising socioeconomic activities

Business tax has the characteristic of an extensive levy, so routine administration of collection of business tax helps understanding of the development and changes of related industries, guides this to develop healthily in accordance with the requirements of the national economy, creates an equitable external environment, and promotes fair competition for taxpayers under equal conditions.

Scope of Collection and the Taxpayers

Scope of collection

General provisions on the scope of collection

Scope of collection of business tax is specified by nine tax items listed in the regulations on business tax. Current business tax has nine items respectively established for different industries and categories.

Transportation industry

Transportation industry refers to the business of delivering cargoes or passengers to the destination by means of transport or manpower or animal power, including overland transportation, water transportation, air transportation, pipeline transportation and loading, unloading and carrying.

Overland transportation refers to the transportation business of carrying cargoes or passengers overland (over ground or underground), including railway transportation, highway transportation, cable-car transportation, cableway transportation and other overland transportation.

Water transportation refers to the transportation business of carrying cargoes or passengers through rivers, lakes and streams and other natural and artificial watercourses or through sea-lanes. Although salvage is not a transportation business it is closely related to water transportation, so tax for salvage may be levied with reference to that of water transportation.

Air transportation refers to the transportation business of carrying cargoes or passengers through airlines. Tax for general aviation business and aviation ground services that are directly related to aviation is also levied in accordance with air transportation business.

Pipeline transportation refers to the transportation business of carrying gas, liquid and solid materials through pipeline facilities.

Loading, unloading and carrying refer to the business of loading, unloading and carrying cargoes between transportation tools, loading and unloading spots by means of loading and unloading tools or manpower or animal power.

Construction industry

Construction industry refers to engineering works of construction and installation, including construction, installation, repair and maintenance, decoration and other engineering operations.

Construction refers to new construction, reconstruction and extension.

Engineering operations of various buildings and structures include engineering operations of installation of various devices or props and operating platforms connected with buildings and engineering operations of various kilns and metal structures. However self-built and self-used buildings do not fall within the incidence of taxation of tax items of construction industry. Self-built buildings that are leased or invested as shares also do not fall within the incidence of taxation of construction industry.

Installation refers to engineering operations of assembly and installation of production equipment, power equipment, hoisting equipment, transportation equipment, medical and laboratory equipment and other equipment, including installation operations of working platforms, ladders and handrails connected with equipment and works of insulation, corrosion prevention, thermal insulation and painting of installed equipment.

Repair and maintenance refer to engineering operations of repair, reinforcement, restoration and improvement of buildings and structures to restore their original service value or to extend their service life.

Decoration refers to engineering operations of ornamenting buildings and structures to make them beautiful or useful for special purposes.

Other engineering operations refer to various engineering operations other than construction, installation, repair and maintenance, and decoration, for example, commissioned telecommunications engineering, hydraulic engineering, and road construction, dredging, well drilling (digging), demolition of buildings, land clearance, erection of scaffold, and blasting.

Business of pipelined gas fund-raising fee (installation fee). This refers to the one-time charge collected from users during the application of installation for engineering construction and technical innovation of pipelined gas.

Financial and insurance industry

Financial and industrial industry deals with finance and insurance. Finance here refers to businesses dealing with accommodation activities of monetary funds, including loans, financial leases, transfer of financial products, financial brokerage and other financial transactions. Insurance refers to businesses dealing with compensating the insurant's economic benefit by funds collectively raised in contractual forms.

Finance refers to businesses dealing with accommodation activities of monetary funds, including loans, financial leases, transfer of financial products, financial brokerage and other financial transactions.

1) Loans refer to the businesses of lending funds to others for onerous uses (including forms of discount and bills of exchange). Acts of monetary capital investment but with collection of fixed profit or minimum guarantee profit also belong to the loan business. Loans are classified into two types, namely foreign exchange loans and ordinary loans, according to different capital sources. Foreign exchange loans mean that financial enterprises directly remit capital to foreign borrowers and then loan to domestic enterprises or other entities and individuals. Bank headquarters' loans to entities or individuals by their bank branches after remitting foreign exchange to foreign borrowers also belong to the business of foreign exchange loans. Ordinary loans refer to various loans other than foreign exchange loans.

2) Financing lease refers to the equipment lease business with a financing nature and ownership transfer characteristics carried out by entities engaged in financing lease businesses approved by the PBOC or the Ministry of Foreign Trade and Economic Cooperation (now the Ministry of Commerce).

3) Transfer of financial products refers to the acts of transfer of foreign exchange, valuable securities or ownership of non-commodity futures, including transfer of shares, bonds, foreign exchange and other financial products.

4) Financial brokerage businesses and other financial transaction refers to intermediate financial activities operated under the commission of others, including commission business, agency business, consultancy business etc.

Insurance refers to activities dealing with compensating the insurant's economic benefit by funds collectively raised in contractual forms.

Post and telecommunications industry

Post and telecommunications industry refers to the businesses dedicated to information transfer, including post and telecommunications.

1) Post refers to the business of transfer of materials and information, including letters or parcels (including express delivery), remittances by post, newspapers and publications, sales of postal items, postal savings and other post services.

2) Telecommunications refer to the business of information transfer by various telecommunications devices' transmission signals, including

telegram, telex, telephone, telephone installation, sales of telecom items and other telecom services.

Telecommunications businesses include basic telecommunications businesses and value-added telecommunications businesses. Basic telecommunication businesses refer to businesses providing public network infrastructure, public data transfer and basic voice communication services, including fixed network domestic long-distance call and local call businesses, mobile communication businesses, satellite communication businesses, Internet and other data transfer businesses, network element lease and sales businesses, lease businesses of telecommunications devices and circuits, businesses of network access and hoisting, businesses of international communications infrastructure and international telecommunications, businesses of radio calls, and businesses of re-sales of basic telecommunications reselling. Value-added telecommunications businesses refer to businesses utilizing telecommunications and information services provided by the public network infrastructure, including value-added telecommunications businesses of the fixed telephone network, those of the mobile telephone network, those of the satellite network, those of the Internet, and those of other data transfer networks.

Culture and sports industry

Culture and sports industry refers to businesses related to culture and sports activities, including the culture industry and sports industry. The culture industry refers to businesses related to cultural activities, including performance, broadcast on television, operation of tour sites, various exhibition and training activities, lectures, speeches and reports on literature, arts, science and technology, and borrowing of books and reference materials from libraries. The sports industry refers to businesses holding various competitions and providing sites for sports competitions or activities.

Entertainment industry

Entertainment industry refers to businesses providing sites and services for entertainment activities, including operating entertainment sites such as singing halls, dancing halls, karaoke singing and dancing halls, music cafés, billiard halls, golf courses, bowling alleys, cyber cafés and amusement parks, and providing services for customers' entertainment activities at entertainment sites. Foods and other services provided to customers at entertainment sites are levied in accordance with taxation on the entertainment industry.

Service industry

Service industry refers to businesses providing social services by means of devices, tools, sites, information or skills, including the agency industry, hotel industry, catering industry, tourist industry, warehousing industry, leasing industry, advertising industry and other service industries.

1) Income of entities and individuals obtained from operating cableways at tourist attractions is liable for business tax according to the item "tourist industry" under the tax item "service industry."

2) Transport authorities' acts of compensatory transfer of rights of highway toll collection are within the incidence of taxation of business tax and business tax shall be levied according to the item "lease" under the tax item "service industry."

3) From January 1, 2002, business tax was cancelled for income obtained by welfare lottery agencies by selling welfare lotteries. Business tax is levied on the income from service charges for welfare lotteries sold by consigned entities other than welfare lottery agencies. Welfare lottery agencies include administration agencies of welfare lottery sales and computer-based welfare lottery stations that sign sales agency agreements with sales administration agencies and accept their supervision and administration.

4) Business tax is levied according to the provisions of the tax law on the income obtained by social security fund investment managers and social security fund trustees from social security fund management activities.

5) If both parties sign contracts (agreements, the same for the following cases) for contracting and leasing the enterprise or some assets of the enterprise, business tax shall be levied for the contracting fee and leasing fee charged by the leaser from the contractor and the lessee according to the tax item "service industry." The contracting fee charged by the leaser belongs to the internal distribution of the enterprise and no business tax is levied if it meets three conditions as follows: The contractor operates in the name of the leaser who assumes the relevant legal liabilities; the contractor's full business income and expenses are included into the leaser's financial accounting; profit distribution between the leaser and the contractor is based on the profit of the leaser.

Transfer of intangible assets

Transfer of intangible assets refers to the acts of transferring ownership or right of use of intangible assets, including transfer of land use right, trademark right, patent right, non-patented technology, copyright and commercial goodwill and lease of film copy.

Since January 1, 2003, business tax has been cancelled for acts of becoming a shareholder by investment in form of intangible assets, participating in profit distribution of the party accepting investment and sharing investment risks. Business tax is not levied even if the stock right is transferred after investment.

Sales of real estate

Sales of real estate refer to the acts of compensatory transfer of ownership of real estate, including sales of buildings or structures and other things immovably attached to the land.

Since January 1, 2003, business tax has been cancelled for acts of becoming a shareholder by investment in the form of real estate, participating in profit distribution of the party accepting investment, and sharing investment risks. Business tax is not levied even if the stock right is transferred after investment.

Special provisions on the incidence of taxation

Mixed sale activities

Once a sales activity involves both taxable services and goods, it is seen as a mixed sales activity. Enterprises, enterprise units and individual businesses engaged in the mixed sales of goods production, wholesale or retail, are regarded as sales of goods and no business tax is paid; mixed sales of other entities and individuals are regarded as provision of taxable services and business tax shall be paid. The enterprises, enterprise units and individual businesses engaged in goods production, wholesale or retail as mentioned include enterprises, enterprise units and individual businesses engaged in goods production, wholesale or retail, that also provide taxable services.

For taxpayers' mixed sales activities mentioned below, business turnover of taxable services and sales amount of goods shall be accounted separately, and business tax shall be paid for the business turnover of taxable services while business tax need not to be paid for the sales amount of goods; if they are not accounted separately, the competent tax authorities shall appraise and determine the business turnover of taxable services:

1) Sales of self-produced goods during provision of construction services.
2) Other situations specified by the Ministry of Finance and the State Administration for Taxation.

Whether taxpayers' acts belong to acts of hybrid sales is determined by the tax collection authorities subordinate to the State Administration of Taxation.

Engagement in both taxable services and goods or non-taxable labor services

For taxpayers dealing in both taxable services and goods or non-taxable services, the business turnover of taxable services and the sales amount of goods or non-taxable services shall be accounted separately and business tax shall be paid for the business turnover of taxable acts while business tax need not to be paid for the sales amount of goods or non-taxable services; if they are not accounted separately, the competent tax authorities shall appraise and determine the business turnover of taxable acts.

Situations deemed to be occurrence of taxable events

1) Entities or individuals donate ownership of real estate or land to other entities or individuals free of charge.
2) Acts of self-construction by entities or individuals after they sell self-constructed buildings.
3) Other scenarios specified by the Ministry of Finance and the State Administration for Taxation.

Taxpayers

General provisions

Business taxpayers are entities and individuals providing taxable services, transferring intangible assets, or selling real estate within the territory of China.

"Within the territory of China" refers to regions with administrative jurisdiction over taxation administration. There are varying situations as follows:

1) Entities or individuals providing or accepting services specified by the regulations are within the territory of China.
2) Entities or individuals accepting the transferred intangible assets (excluding land use rights) are within the territory of China.
3) Land of which the use right is transferred or leased is within the territory of China.
4) Real estate sold or leased is within the territory of China.

Providing taxable services, transferring intangible assets or selling real estate refers to the acts of compensatory provision of taxable services, compensatory transfer of intangible assets or compensatory sales of real estate. The compensation refers to the obtainment of currency, goods or other economic benefits by acts of provision, transfer or sale.

The entities as mentioned refer to enterprises, administrative units, government-sponsored institutions, military units, social groups and other organizations. The individuals as mentioned refer to individual businesses or others.

Special provisions

The *Detailed Rules for the Implementation of the Provisional Regulations of the People's Republic of China on Business Tax* has some special provisions on business taxpayers as follows:

1) Taxpayers engaged in railway transportation: The Ministry of Railways is the taxpayer for railway operation business of the central government; the joint railway company is the taxpayer for operating business of jointly owned railway; the local railway administration authorities are the taxpayers for operating business of local railways; the administration authority of a railway line temporarily administered by the railway administration is the taxpayer for operating business of a railway line temporarily administered by the railway administration.

2) For entities operated in forms of contracting, leasing and subordinating, if the contractor, lessee or subordinate (hereinafter referred to in general as the contractor) conducts taxable acts and the lessee operates in the name of the party issuing the contract, lease or the delegation (hereinafter referred to in general as the party issuing the contract), the party issuing the contract is the taxpayer if it assumes the relevant legal liabilities, other the contractor is the taxpayer.

3) If construction and installation works are subcontracted, the subcontractor is the taxpayer.

Provisions on withholding agents

The *Provisional Regulations on Business Tax of the People's Republic of China* formulates provisions on withholding agents to ensure the timeliness and full amount of state revenue since it is difficult to determine taxpayers under some specific circumstances in the practice of tax collection administration:

1) For entities or individuals that are out of the territory of China and provide taxable services, transfer intangible assets, or sell real estate within the territory of China but establish no operating agency, the

withholding agent is their agent within the territory of China. It is their assignee or purchaser if there is no agent within the territory of China.

2) For financial institutions entrusted to grant loans, the financial institutions issuing loans according to tax payable shall be the withholding agents.

3) For general contracting and sub-contracting of construction business, the general contractor shall be the withholding agent.

4) For entities or individuals performing but letting others sell tickets, the withholding agent for tax payable is the ticket seller, if performance broker is an individual, the withholding agent for tax payable for performance business is also the ticket seller.

5) For cede insurance businesses, the withholding agent for tax payable is the initial insurer.

6) For individuals transferring patent rights, non-patented technology, trademark rights, copyrights and commercial goodwill, the withholding agent for tax payable is the transferee.

Tax Rates

General provisions

Current business tax practices proportional tax rates for different industries, and the two lower proportional tax rates of 3% and 5% are usually practiced for the majority of taxable services provided, intangible assets transferred and real estate sold to embody the business tax's characteristic as a universal levy.

Proportional rates ranging from 5% to 20% are practiced for the entertainment industry, and the people's governments of provinces, autonomous regions or municipalities directly under the central government may decide a locally applicable tax rate within this range according to local conditions. The entertainment industry's practice of proportional tax rates within a range is mainly out of consideration of the large gap in local economic development levels and consumption levels, so it is inappropriate to practice a uniform proportional tax rate nationwide. This helps local governments to flexibly employ the taxation lever for proper regulation of consumption according to actual conditions of the development of local entertainment industry (See Table 4.1 for tax rates applicable to various tax items).

Table 4.1.   Rates and items of business tax

Tax item	Tax rate
Transportation industry	3%
Construction industry	3%
Finance and insurance industry	5%
Post and communications industry	3%
Culture and sports industry	3%
Entertainment industry	5%–20%
Service industry	5%
Transfer of intangible assets	5%
Sales of real estate	5%

Any adjustments to business tax items and rates shall be determined by the State Council. The detailed scope is specified by the Ministry of Finance and the State Administration of Taxation. Current provisions on the incidence of taxation are as follows:

1)   Tax rate is 3% for the transportation industry, construction industry, post and communications industry, culture and sports industry.

2)   Tax rate is 5% for the service industry, sales of real estate, and transfer of intangible assets.

3)   Tax rate of 8% was uniformly implemented for the finance and insurance industry from January 1, 1997, to December 31, 2000. From 2001, the tax rate was lowered by one percentage point every year and reduced to 5% in three years; in other words, a tax rate of 5% was put into force from January 1, 2003. Since October 1, 2001, a tax rate of 5% has been used for levying business tax on rural credit cooperatives.

4)   Tax rates ranging from 5% to 20% are practiced for the entertainment industry, and the municipal governments of provinces, autonomous regions or municipalities directly under the central government may decide applicable tax rates within the range specified by tax law according to local conditions.

From May 1, 2001, a tax rate of 20% was used for levying business tax on entertainment acts covering nightclubs, singing halls, dancing halls, shooting, hunting, horse races, games, golf, recreation and electronic games halls. From July 1, 2004, a tax rate of 5% was used for levying business tax on bowling and billiard halls under the tax item "entertainment industry."

Special provisions

Regulations on business tax specify that taxpayers of taxable acts under different tax items shall account separately for their business turnover, transfer amount and sales amount of different tax items and taxes payable shall be calculated according to respective tax rates; taxes payable shall be calculated according to higher tax rates if they are not accounted separately.

Business turnover refers to business income obtained from transportation industry, construction industry, finance and insurance industry, post and telecommunications industry, culture and sports industry, entertainment industry and service industry; transfer amount refers to the income obtained from transfer of intangible assets; sales amount refers to the income obtained from sales of real estate.

For example, if a transportation enterprise leasing idle storehouses while providing transportation services is able to separately account the business turnover of provision of transportation services and that of lease of storehouses, their respective taxes will be calculated according to tax rates 3% and 5%; if it is unable to separately account these two business turnovers, they shall be merged and the tax payable shall be calculated according to the tax rate 5%.

Tax Base

General provisions

Tax base of business tax is business turnover, which is the total consideration and all other charges receivable from the purchasers by the taxpayer providing taxable services, transferring intangible assets or selling real estate. Other charges include service charges, subsidies, funding, financing costs, returned profit, incentive fees, penalties, surcharge for overdue tax payment, interest on deferred payment, compensation, collection made on behalf, payment made on behalf, packing charges, default interest and other charges of various natures, but exclude governmental funds or administrative fees that meet the following conditions and are collected on behalf:

1) Governmental funds approved to be established by the State Council or the Ministry of Finance and administrative fees approved to be established by the State Council or provincial people's governments and their finance and price departments in charge;
2) Financing notes printed by financial departments above provincial level issued upon payment;

3) Total amount of collections which are turned over to central finance.

Any other charge shall be incorporated into business turnover for calculating tax payable regardless of the provisions of the accounting system.

Special provisions

Besides the general provisions mentioned above, the regulations on business tax and the detailed implementation rules have some specific provisions on business turnover for calculating business tax to take the business operating characteristics of some industries into consideration and reasonably determine the tax base of business tax.

Transportation industry

1) For a taxpayer sub-contracting the undertaken transportation business to other entities or individuals, the business turnover is the balance of total consideration and all other charges obtained after deducting transportation expenses paid to other entities or individuals.

2) For transportation enterprises which carry passengers or cargo from the territory of China to overseas locations and transship passengers or cargo to other transportation enterprises overseas, the turnover shall be the balance of transport charges for the whole journey less the transport charges paid to the subcontracted transportation enterprises.

3) For transportation enterprises engaged in combined transport businesses, the tax base is the business turnover actually obtained. Combined transport businesses refer to transportation businesses finished by at least two transportation enterprises in transporting passengers or cargo from the delivery location to the place of arrival. Combined transport businesses are have the characteristics of one ticket and one charge from beginning to end.

Construction industry

1) For the general contractor in the construction industry who subcontracts work to others, the business turnover shall be the balance of the total contract sum less the payment made to the subcontractor.

2) For taxpayers engaged in construction labor services (excluding decoration labor services), the business turnover shall include money paid for raw materials, devices, other materials and power yet excluding money paid for devices provided by the construction party. If the value

of erecting equipment used for installation works is treated as output value of installation works, the business turnover includes money paid for devices.

3) For acts of self-construction and donation of real estate to others by entities or individuals free of charge, the competent tax authorities shall appraise and decide the business turnover in a specified sequence. Acts of self-construction refer to taxpayer's self-construction of houses. No tax is levied for taxpayer's self-constructed and self-used houses; if taxpayers sell self-constructed houses (excluding sales of self-constructed and self-used houses), business tax shall be paid for the self-construction acts according to tax on construction industry firstly, and then business tax is levied according to sales of real estate.

4) For taxpayers using decoration labor services provided in the form of package workers, taxable business turnover should be confirmed according to incomes such as labor cost actually charged from customers, administration costs and auxiliary material fees (excluding money for materials and equipment procured by customers themselves). Decoration labor services provided in the form of package workers mean that the main raw materials and equipment required for works are procured by customers themselves and the taxpayer only charges labor costs, administration costs and auxiliary material fees to customers.

Financial and insurance industry

1) Business turnover of general loan businesses is loan interest (including various raises of interest rates, default interest etc.)

2) Business turnover of foreign exchange loans include the following:
   • For foreign exchange loan business within the system of the PBOC, if the superior bank transfers the borrowed foreign exchange funds to subordinate banks for loans to domestic users, the business turnover (including interest and various raised interest rates and default interest calculated based on the benchmark interest rate) is the total interest income charged from the loan borrowers of subordinate banks. For a superior bank borrowing foreign exchange, the business turnover is the balance of the sum of income from loan interest and income from other taxable business taxes less expenditure of loan interest paid overseas.
   • For foreign exchange loan business of other banks, if the superior bank transfers the borrowed foreign exchange funds to subordinate banks for

loans to domestic users, the business turnover is the balance of the total interest income charged from the loan borrowers less expenditure of loan interest appraised and ratified by the superior bank. In case of any discrepancy between the expenditure of loan interest appraised and ratified by the superior bank and the actual expenditure, the superior bank shall make this up from through business tax.

3) For entities approved to operate financial lease business by the PBOC, the Ministry of Commerce and the State Economic and Trade Commission, the current-period business turnover of financial lease business is converted by the straight-line method based on the total consideration and all other charges (including residual value) receivable from the purchasers less the actual cost of leased goods assumed by the leaser. The calculation method is as follows:

Current-period business turnover =
(Total consideration and all other charges receivable – Actual cost) ×
(Number of days of current period / Total number of days)

Actual cost = Goods buying cost + Customs duty + VAT + Consumption tax + Freight and miscellaneous charges + Installation fee + Insurance expense + Interest for foreign loan and RMB loan paid overseas

4) For buying and selling operations of financial products such as foreign exchange, valuable securities and futures, the business turnover is the balance of selling price less buying price i.e. Business turnover = Selling price – Buying price.

The selling price should include various expenses and taxes paid during selling process. The buying price should exclude various expenses and taxes paid during the buying process. However buying price shall be the buying price of stock and security less dividend income from them during the holding period as specified by financial and accounting rules.

For buying and selling of financial products (including shares, bonds, foreign exchange and other financial products), business tax may be calculated and paid at the end of the same accounting year by summarizing positive balances and negative balances occurring in different tax payment periods. If the payable amount of business tax summarized and calculated is less than the amount of business tax paid that year, a tax refund may be applied for to the tax authorities, but the portion still negative after summarizing within one accounting year shall not be carried over to next accounting year.

5) Business turnover of financial brokerage business and other financial businesses (intermediate businesses) is total income of service charges (commission charges).

Business turnover of financial enterprises engaged in consigned collection for telephone charges, charges for water, electricity and gas, information fees, tuition and incidental fees, paging fees, overall social security fees, traffic violation fines and taxes is the balance of total income less the money paid to the consigner.

6) Business turnover of insurance businesses includes the following aspects:

- Transaction of initial insurance business. Business turnover is the total insurance premium charged by the taxpayer dealing in insurance businesses to the other party i.e. total insurance premium charged from the insurant.

- Savings business. If the insurance company obtains economic benefit by collecting savings (in other words, the premium income is the income from interest of insurance funds paid by the insurant and the principal of insurance premium is returned to the insurant after expiry of the insurance period), the business turnover of "savings business" is the taxpayer's average balance of savings within the period of tax payment multiplied by the monthly interest rate on one-year deposits announced by the PBOC. The average balance of savings is the sum of the balance of savings at the beginning of tax payment period and that at the end of the period multiplied by 50%.

- For insurance enterprises on which business tax has been levied, insurance premium uncollected shall be collected, and that uncollected within the accounting period specified by financial and accounting rules is allowed to be deducted from business turnover. Written-off accrued insurance premium that is collected after the accounting period is incorporated into current-period business turnover.

- For insurance enterprises dealing in business giving rewards for no claims bonus, the business turnover is the insurance premium actually charged from the insurant.

- If insurers within the territory of China transact reinsurance business of accepted insurance subjects in China with overseas reinsurers, the business turnover is the balance of total insurance premium less reinsurance fee. Overseas reinsurers shall assume business tax payment obligations for their reinsurance income and the business tax amount payable shall be withheld by the insurers within China.

Post and telecommunications industry

For telecommunications departments providing trans-provincial circuit lease business for group customers in the form of a centralized transaction, business tax is levied according to the business turnover which is the balance of total amount obtained by local telecommunications departments less the amount divided between telecommunications departments participating in provision of trans-provincial telecommunications business; for telecommunications departments participating in provision of trans-provincial telecommunications business, the business turnover on which business tax is levied is their respective total amount of business.

Centralized transaction means that telecommunications departments provide leasing business of trans-regional telecommunications lines for many customers of some groups according to the requirements of these groups to help their customers maintain special communications nationwide.

The business turnover is the balance of total income less the money paid to partners if post and telecommunications organizations cooperate with other organizations to provide customers with post and telecommunications businesses and other services, and the money is uniformly collected by post and telecommunications organizations.

Culture and sports industry

Tax base of culture and sports industry is the business income obtained by entities and individuals engaged in the culture and sports industry. For entities and individuals carrying out performances, the business turnover is the balance of income of total tickets or block-booking less the money paid to entities providing places, performance companies, or brokers.

Entertainment industry

The business turnover is various fees charged from customers, including admission fee, position fee, song request fee, fees for cigarettes, liquor and beverages, and other charges.

Service industry

1)   For travel enterprises that organize tourist groups to travel outside the

territory of China and sub-contract to other travel enterprises overseas, the turnover shall be the balance of the tourist charges for the whole journey less the payments made to the sub-contracted travel enterprises.

2) For travel enterprises that organize tourists to travel within the territory of China, the turnover shall be the balance of the tourist charges less the payments for rooms, meals, transport, admission tickets and other expenses paid on behalf of tourists to other entities. In case of sub-contracting to other travel enterprises, the business turnover shall be determined according to measures used for overseas tours.

3) The business turnover of the advertising agency industry is the balance of the total consideration and all other charges received by the agent from the consigners less the advertising fee paid to advertisement publishers.

4) For the agency industry, the business turnover shall be the actual remuneration charged from the consigner by the taxpayer engaged in agency business.

5) For any income of service charges obtained by computer-aided welfare lottery stations from selling welfare lottery on a commission basis, business tax shall be levied in accordance with the regulations.

6) Business tax is levied for computer software that is registered with the National Copyright Administration and sold with the copyright and proprietary rights transferred. Computer software products refer to storage media recording computer programs and relevant documents (including floppy disks, hard disks, optical disks etc.).

7) For entities within the territory of China that organize their employees to go abroad and provide labor services for overseas enterprises, their services are not taxable services provided within China. Business tax is not levied for various incomes obtained from labor services provided by employees sent abroad by enterprises within China.

Sales of real estate or transfer of land use rights

1) For entities and individuals selling or transferring their purchased real estate or transferring land use rights, the business turnover shall be the balance of total income less the original price for purchasing or transferring real estate or land use rights.

2) For entities and individuals selling or transferring real estate or transferring land use rights obtained from debt paying, the business turnover shall be the balance of total income less the evaluated price of

real estate or transferred land use rights used for paying the debt.

3) The Ministry of Finance and the State Administration of Taxation jointly promulgated the *Circular on Business Tax Policy on Individual Residential House Transfer* and specified that business tax should be levied for the total income obtained by individuals from sales of non-ordinary housing bought for less than 2 years from January 1, 2009, to December 31, 2009; business tax should be levied for the balance of the sales income obtained by individuals from sales of non-ordinary housing bought for at least 2 years or ordinary housing bought for less than 2 years less the price for purchasing the housing; no business tax should be levied for individuals selling ordinary housing bought for at least 2 years.

Standards of the above-mentioned ordinary housing and non-ordinary housing, specific procedures for transacting tax exemption, housing purchase time, issue of invoices, evidence of deduction of tax difference, acts obtaining housing by non-purchase forms and other relevant taxation administration provisions shall be conducted in accordance with the relevant regulations of the *Reissue by the State Council Office of the Circular of the Ministry of Construction and other Ministries on Opinions on Stabilizing the Price of Residential Houses,* the *Circular of the State Administration of Taxation the Ministry of Finance and the Ministry of Construction on Strengthening the Administration of Real Estate Tax Collection* and the *Circular of the State Administration of Taxation on Several Specific Issues during Implementation of Real Estate Tax Policies.*

Determination of special business turnover

If a taxpayer's price for providing taxable services, transferring intangible assets or selling real estate is obviously low without proper justification or these acts are regarded as taxable acts, the business turnover shall be determined by the competent tax authorities in the following sequences:

1) It shall be determined according to the average price of the taxpayer's similar taxable acts in the recent period.

2) It shall be determined according to the average price of other taxpayers' similar taxable acts in the recent period.

3) It shall be determined according to the following formula:

Business turnover = Business cost or project cost × (1 + Profit rate on cost) / (1 – Rate of Business tax)

The profit rate on cost in the formula is determined by the administrations of taxation in various provinces, autonomous regions and municipalities directly under the central government.

Other provisions on business turnover

1) In the case of refund by entities and individuals providing taxable services, transferring intangible assets and selling real estate, if this refund has been levied for business tax, the levied amount is allowed to be refunded or deducted from the taxpayer's future business turnover.

2) For entities and individuals providing taxable services, transferring intangible assets and selling real estate where the price and discount are issued on one invoice, the business turnover shall be the price after discount; if the discount is issued on another invoice, the discount shall not be deducted from the business turnover regardless of any financial disposal.

3) For entities and individuals providing taxable services, transferring intangible assets and selling real estate who obtain compensation income from the assignee due to his default, business tax shall be levied from business turnover.

4) From December 1, 2004, business taxpayers purchasing tax-control cash registers may credit current-period taxable business tax dependent on special VAT invoices obtained from purchase of tax-control cash registers in accordance with the tax amount indicated on the invoices after being checked and approved by the competent tax authorities, or calculate the creditable tax in accordance with the price indicated on ordinary invoices obtained from purchase of tax-control cash registers according to the following formula:

Creditable tax = Price / (1 + 17%) × 17%

5) For the total consideration and all other charges receivable from the purchasers by the taxpayer providing taxable services, if the business turnover can be determined after deduction of part of the sum according to the relevant regulations, relevant legal and effective evidence shall be provided for the deducted part:

- For the sums of money paid to entities or individuals within the territory of China whose acts are within the incidence of taxation of business tax or VAT, the legal and effective evidence shall be invoices issued by these entities or individuals.

- For administrative fees or governmental funds paid, the legal and effective evidence shall be the issued treasury bills.

- For sums of money paid to overseas entities or individuals, the legal and effective evidence shall be receipts signed by them and the tax authorities may require them to provide confirmation certificates issued by overseas notary organizations if they suspect the signed receipts.
- Legal and effective evidence may be other as specified by the State Administration of Taxation.

Calculation of Tax Payable

Business tax practices proportional tax rate and the method for calculating tax amount is simple. There are three calculation methods according to the different tax bases of business tax.

The formula for calculating tax payable according to total amount of business income is as follows:

Tax payable = Business turnover × Applicable business tax rate

The formula for calculating tax payable according to the difference of business incomes is as follows:

Tax payable = (Business turnover – Business turnover allowed by tax law for deduction) × Applicable business tax rate

The formula for calculating tax payable according to composite assessable price is as follows:

Tax payable = Business cost or project cost × (1 + Cost-profit ratio) / (1 – Applicable business tax rate × Applicable business tax rate)

Tax Preference

Provisions on minimum threshold

The applicable scope of business tax's minimum threshold is limited to individuals.

The range of business tax's minimum threshold is specified as follows:

1) For tax payment on a periodic basis, a monthly business turnover of RMB1,000–5,000.
2) For tax payment on a transaction-by-transaction basis, a business turnover each time (day) of RMB100.

The finance bureaus and tax administrations in all provinces, autonomous regions, and municipalities directly under the central government shall determine the locally applicable threshold within the specified range and report it to the Ministry of Finance and the State Administration of Taxation for filing.

Business tax is exempted if the taxpayer's business turnover is less than the minimum threshold specified by the competent finance and tax authorities under the State Council, and the total business tax shall be calculated and paid if it reaches the minimum threshold.

The *Detailed Rules for the Implementation of the Provisional Regulations on Business Tax of the People's Republic of China* which came into force as of January 1, 2009, expands the preference applicable to the laid-off to all individual business taxpayers.

Statutory tax-exempt items

The following items are exempt from business tax:

1) Nursing services provided by nurseries, kindergartens, homes for the aged, welfare institutions for the handicapped, matchmaking services and funeral services. Services provided on an individual basis by the disabled.

2) Services provided on individual basis by the disabled refer to services provided by the disabled themselves to society.

3) Medical services provided by hospitals, clinics and other medical institutions.

4) Educational services provided by schools and other educational institutions, and services provided by students participating in work-study programs.

   Schools and other educational institutions refer to ordinary schools and various schools that are approved to be set up by departments of education administration of the people's governments at or above the region and city levels or at the same level, with academic diplomas for students recognized by the state.

5) Agricultural mechanical ploughing, irrigation and drainage, prevention and treatment of plant diseases and insect pests, plant protection, insurance for farming and animal husbandry, and related technical training services, breeding and the prevention and treatment of diseases of poultry, livestock and aquatic animals.

   Agricultural mechanical ploughing refers to farming (including ploughing and weeding, planting, reaping, threshing and plant protection etc.) using agricultural machinery for agriculture, forestry and animal husbandry; irrigation and drainage refer to irrigating or draining of farmland; prevention and treatment of plant diseases and insect pests refer to the forecasting, prevention and treatment of diseases and insect pests in agriculture, forestry, animal husbandry and fishery; insurance for farming refers to the businesses of providing insurance for plants and animals of industries covering crop farming, fish breeding, and poultry raising and animal husbandry; related technical training services refer to technical training that is related to agricultural mechanical ploughing, irrigation and drainage, prevention and treatment of plant diseases and insect pests and plant protection and that aims to help farmers obtain knowledge of insurance of agriculture and animal husbandry; the scope of tax exemption for breeding and the prevention and treatment of diseases of poultry, livestock and aquatic animals include the provision of medicines and medical instruments related to this service.

6) Admission fees for cultural activities conducted by memorial halls, museums, cultural centers, cultural protective units, art galleries, exhibition halls, academies of painting and calligraphy, and libraries, and admission fees for cultural and religious activities conducted at places of religious worship.

Cultural activities conducted by memorial halls, museums, cultural centers, cultural protective units, art galleries, exhibition halls, academies of painting and calligraphy and libraries refer to cultural activities that are conducted on their own sites and are within the taxable scope of tax item of culture and sports industry. The admission fees refer to the income obtained from selling tickets of first admission. The admission fees for cultural and religious activities conducted at places of religious worship refer to the income obtained from selling tickets for cultural and religious activities conducted in temples, abbeys, mosques and churches.

Supplementary preference items

1) Business tax is exempted for income obtained from an insurance company's premium of restitutionary life insurance business lasting more than one year. Restitutionary life insurance business refers to ordinary life insurance, pension insurance and health insurance, with a period lasting for at least one year and where the capital and profit will

be returned on the expiry date.

Business tax is exempted for specific kinds of ordinary life insurance, pension insurance and health insurance set up by insurance companies once they are examined and verified by the Ministry of Finance and the State Administration of Taxation and included into the tax-exemption list, while business tax is levied on those not included in the list.

2) Business tax is exempted for the income obtained by entities and individuals (including foreign-funded enterprises, research and development (R&D) centers established by foreign investment, foreign enterprises and individuals) engaged in technical transfer and technical development and related technical consultation and service. Technical transfer refers to the transferer's acts of compensatory transfer of his ownership or right of use of patents and non-patented technologies to others; technical development refers to the developer's acts of R&D conducted for new technologies, new products, new processes or new materials and their systems on a commission basis; technical consultation refers to provision of feasibility studies, technical forecasting, specialized technical investigation, analysis and evaluation reports for special technical projects; technical consultation and services related to technical transfer; and technical development refers to technical consultation and services provided by the transferor (or consigner) in accordance with the provisions of the contract on technical transfer or development to help the transferee (consignee) master the technologies transferred (or developed on a commission basis).

Technical development and technical transfer businesses with exemption of business tax are specified in the *Circular of the Ministry of Finance and the State Administration of Taxation on Relevant Tax Collection Issues Related to Implementing the Decisions of the Central Committee of the Communist Party of China and the State Council on Strengthening Technical Innovation*, Developing high technology and realizing industrialization refer to technological development and technical transfer businesses within the domain of natural science.

3) Business tax is exempted for individual's transfer of copyright.

4) Business tax is exempted for transfer of land use rights to agriculturists for agricultural production.

5) Business tax is exempted for labor union's sanatoria that can be regarded as "other medical institutions."

6) Business tax is exempted for administrative fees and funds approved by the financial department of the central authority or of the provincial

government to be incorporated into budget control or special financial account management, no matter whether they are charged by administrative units or government-sponsored institutions.

7) Business tax is exempted for charges collected by legislative organizations, judicial authorities and administrative organizations if in conformance with the following conditions: firstly, the charges are allowed in formal documents of the State Council, provincial people's government or its subordinate financial and price department and the charging standards conform to provisions of these documents; secondly, the charges are directly collected by legislative organizations, judicial authorities or administrative organizations.

8) Business tax is exempted for membership fees charged by social organizations according to the standards specified by financial departments or civil administration departments. Social organizations refer to non-profit non-governmental mass and social organizations approved by the competent state authorities in charge of mass organizations to be established within the territory of China, such as associations, societies, unions, research institutes, foundations, sodalities, promotion organizations and chambers of commerce. Membership fees of mass organizations refer to the amount of money collected from individual members and corporate members by social organizations in accordance with organizational regulations within the scope allowed by state laws and policies.

Party membership dues and membership fees collected by all parties, the Communist Youth League, labor unions, the Women's Federation, the China Association for Science and Technology, the China Federation of Youth, the China Federation of Taiwan Compatriots and the All-China Federation of Returned Overseas Chinese shall be treated with reference to the stipulations mentioned above.

9) For economic entities of logistics which are separated from the original logistics management department of colleges and universities and are of independent accounting and corporate capacity (hereinafter referred to as entities of logistics of colleges and universities), business tax is exempted for their rent and services income obtained from operating apartments for students and teachers and providing logistics services for teaching; however, business tax shall be levied according to current provisions on rent and various service incomes obtained from providing services to the social community by making use of logistics service facilities such as apartments for students or teachers.

Business tax is exempted for rental income obtained from student apartments that are built by social investment to provide accommodation for students of colleges and universities and are allowed to collect rent according to the uniform charging standards of the higher education system; however, business tax shall be levied according to current provisions for the rental income obtained from providing accommodation to the social community by making use of student apartments.

Business tax is exempted for the income obtained by dining halls that are located on campus, and practice socialized management and independent accounting for their catering services provided to teachers and students; business tax shall be levied according to current provisions for the income obtained from providing catering services to the social community.

10) Business tax is exempted for the income obtained from issuing public accumulation funds for housing construction as individual housing loans at entrusted banks appointed by the administration center for public accumulation funds for housing construction.

11) Business tax is provisionally exempted for public housing and low-rent housing rented at the price specified by the government; business tax is provisionally levied according to the tax rate of 3% for residential housing rented by individuals at the market price.

12) Business tax is exempted for loan transactions issued to financial institutions by the PBOC. Business tax is levied for loans issued to enterprises by the PBOC or issued by its entrusted financial institutions.

13) Business tax is provisionally exempted for transactions between financial institutions. Transactions between financial institutions refer to inter-branch fund transactions, fund transactions between financial enterprises and the PBOC and inter-bank fund transactions from which interest income is obtained, excluding services provided to one another.

14) Business tax is exempted for financial institutions' sum of money whose actual cash value is more than the book value.

15) Business tax is exempted for the income of medical services provided by non-profit medical institutions at the price specified by the state. Medical institutions include hospitals of all levels and kinds, clinics, community health service centers (stations), first-aid centers (stations), urban and rural health centers, nursing homes, sanatoriums and clinical examination centers etc. Medical services refer to the services of examination, diagnosis, treatment, rehabilitation, preventive health

care, child delivery, planned parenthood and relevant medicines, medical materials and appliances, ambulances, ward lodging and meals provided by the medical institutions to the patients.

Various taxes are levied as specified for the income obtained by profit-making medical institutions. However, in order to support the development of profit-making medical institutions, the income obtained from medical services that is directly used for improving medical and health conditions is exempt from business tax from the date of acquisition of registration for practice for three years. Business tax is exempted for the income obtained at the price specified by the state from the medical services provided by sanitary institutions such as disease control agencies and maternity and child care institutions. Sanitary institutions such as disease control agencies and maternity and child care institutions include sanitation and anti-epidemic stations (disease control centers) and dispensaries for various specialized diseases sponsored by governments at all levels and by relevant departments, maternity and child care stations, maternal and infant health care agencies, and child health care institutions sponsored by governments at all levels, as well as blood stations (centers) sponsored by governments at all levels.

16) The following preference policies were put into force as of January 1, 2005, in order to properly implement preference policies on business tax related to re-employment of laid-off workers:

- Business tax is levied on individual business activities carried out by laid-off workers whose individual business acts have employees numbering no more than seven. For laid-off workers' business activities employing at least 8 employees, preference polices on business tax related to newly-established service enterprises shall be implemented no matter whether their business license is marked as individual units of industry and commerce or not.

- Service enterprises refer to those engaged in business activities specified by the item "service industry" of the current business tax. The merger, separation, restructuring, reorganization, extension, relocation, change of business, bring-in of new members, change of relationship of administrative subordination, change in enterprise name and change of legal representative of original enterprises shall not be regarded as new establishment of enterprises.

17) Business tax is exempted for 3 years since the date of receipt of tax registration certificate for demobilized military cadres, urban demobbed soldiers and their dependents engaged in individual operations.

Individual operations refer to individual operations involving at most seven employees. For demobilized military cadres, urban demobbed soldiers and their dependents engaged in individual operations involving at least 8 employees, demobilized military cadres and their dependents shall enjoy relevant business tax preference policies for newly-established enterprises and urban demobbed soldiers shall enjoy those for newly-established service enterprises no matter whether their business licenses are marked as individual units of industry and commerce or not.

18) For credit guaranty and re-guarantee agencies of non-profit medium-sized and small enterprises within the national pilot scope, local governments may decide to grant exemption of business tax for 3 years from that start of their income obtained from guarantee businesses.

19) According to the *Provisional Regulations on Business Tax of the People's Republic of China* and its detailed rules on implementation, the incidence of business tax is the act of compensatorily providing taxable services, transferring intangible assets or selling real estate. Transfer of property rights of enterprises refers to overall transfer of enterprise assets, rights of credit, liabilities and labor force, moreover the transfer price is not determined only by the value of assets and these acts are completely different from enterprises' acts of selling real estate and transferring intangible assets. Therefore the acts of transfer of property rights of enterprises do not fall into the incidence of taxation of business tax and no business tax is levied.

20) Business tax is provisionally exempted for price difference income obtained by boards of management of social security funds and use of social security funds by the investment manager for purchasing securities and investing in funds, stocks and bonds.

21) Provisions on exemption of business tax for special funds for housing maintenance are as follows. The special fund for housing maintenance is an agency fund owned by all proprietors. The special fund is used for repair, renewal and renovation of common areas, facilities and equipment after expiry of the property warranty period. In view of the special characteristics of ownership and use of special funds for housing maintenance, business tax is exempted for special funds for housing maintenance collected by the competent department of real estate or its designated institution, public accumulation fund management center, development enterprise or property management organization.

22) Business tax is exempted for price difference income obtained by enterprises in China entrusted by QFII for dealing in securities.

23) For individual's donation of real estate to others free of charge, business tax is exempted in three scenarios i.e. inheritance, heritage disposition and other donation of real estate free of charge. However taxpayers shall provide relevant evidentiary materials to the tax authorities according to different conditions when transacting the application procedures for exemption of business tax.

- In the case of inheritance of real estate, the inheritor shall submit the "notarial deed for right of inheritance," property ownership certificate and registration form of the individual's donation of real estate free of charge issued by notary organizations.
- In case of testator's disposition of real estate, the heir by testament or the devisee must submit the "notarial deed for testament," "notarial deed for right of inheritance of testament" or "notarial deed for acceptance of bequest" property ownership certificate and registration form of the individual's donation of real estate free of charge issued by notary organizations.
- In case of other donations of real estate free of charge, the recipient shall submit the property owner's "notarial deed for donation" and the recipient's "notarial deed for acceptance of donation," or hold the "notarial deed for donation contract" transacted by them together, and the property ownership certificate and registration form of the individual's donation of real estate free of charge.

The original documents of the above material evidence must be submitted and tax authorities shall check them properly. If these materials are all provided with the correct and standard entries, they will be returned to the presenter after the registration form of the individual's donation of real estate free of charge is signed, and copies of the relevant notarial deeds will be retained and procedures for business tax exemption will be transacted at the same time.

For taxpayers engaged in tax exempt or tax reduction items, the business turnovers for tax exemption or tax reduction items shall be accounted for separately, if they have not been separately accounted, no exemption or reduction is allowed.

Administration of Tax Collection

The occurrence time of tax liability

The time at which a liability to business tax arises shall be the date on which the business proceeds are received or documented evidence of the right to collect business proceeds is obtained by the taxpayer for providing taxable services, transferring intangible assets or selling real estate. Business proceeds received as mentioned refer to the sum of money collected during or after the occurrence of the taxpayer's taxable act. The date on which documented evidence of right to collect business proceeds is obtained is the date of payment determined in the written contract, or the date on which taxable acts are completed if no written contract is signed or the date of payment is not determined in the written contract.

For some items, regulations on implementation of business tax specify as follows:

1) For taxpayers transferring land use rights or selling real estate in the form of advance payment, the time at which a liability to tax arises is the date on which advance payment is received.

2) For taxpayers providing services for the construction industry or leasing industry in the form of advance payment, the time at which a liability to tax arises is the date on which advance payment is received.

3) For taxpayers donating real estate or land use rights to other entities or individuals free of charge, the time at which a liability to tax arises is the date on which real estate ownership or land use rights are transferred.

4) For taxpayers conducting acts of self-construction, the time at which a liability to tax arises is the time at which self-built buildings are sold.

5) The time at which a liability for withheld tax arises is the date on which the withholding agent receives the business income or obtains documented evidence of the right to collect business proceeds.

Assessable period

Assessable periods for business tax payment are 5 days, 10 days, 15 days, 1 month or 1 quarter. The actual assessable period of taxpayers shall be determined by the competent tax authorities according to the magnitude of the tax payable by the taxpayer. Tax that cannot be assessed at regular periods may be assessed on a transaction-by-transaction basis.

Taxpayers who adopt one month or one quarter as an assessable period shall report and pay tax within 15 days following the end of the period. If an assessable period of 5 days, 10 days or 15 days is adopted, the tax shall be prepaid within 5 days following the end of the period and a monthly return shall be filed with any balance of tax due settled within 15 days from the first day of the following month.

The tax payment deadlines for withholding agents shall be determined with reference to the stipulations of the above paragraphs.

1) The assessable period is one quarter for banks, financial companies, trust and investment corporations, credit cooperatives, and foreign enterprises' resident representative offices. Tax declaration and payment shall be within 15 days of the expiry of the assessable period.

2) The assessable period is one month for the insurance industry.

Place of payment

1) Taxpayers providing taxable services shall declare and pay tax to the local competent tax authorities where the taxable services take place. However taxpayers engaged in the transportation business shall declare and pay tax to the local competent tax authorities where the business establishment is located.

2) Taxpayers transferring land use rights shall declare and pay tax to the local competent tax authorities where the land is located. Taxpayers transferring other intangible assets shall declare and pay tax to the local competent tax authorities where the establishment is located.

3) For entities and individuals leasing land use rights and real estate, the place of tax payment is where the land and real estate are located; for entities and individuals leasing movable property such as articles and equipment, the place of business tax payment is where the business establishment of the leasing organization is located or the individual resides.

4) Individuals selling immovable properties shall declare and pay tax to the local competent tax authorities where the immovable properties are located.

5) Taxpayers providing taxable services in a different county (or city) shall declare and pay tax to the local competent tax authorities where the taxable services take place. The local competent tax authorities where the establishment is located or the taxpayer resides shall collect the overdue tax which has not been declared and paid to the local competent tax authorities where the taxable services activities have taken place.

6) For taxpayers whose contracted works involve two or more provinces, autonomous regions or municipalities directly under the central government, tax shall be declared and paid to the local competent tax authorities where the business establishment is located.

7) Tax withheld by withholding agents shall be declared and paid to the

competent tax authorities where the establishment is located or the withholding agents reside.

5
Chapter

Customs Duty

An Overview

Some concepts and effects

Concepts

Customs duty is a kind of commodity tax levied in accordance with laws for goods and commodities inbound and outbound movement through the customs territory. Customs territory is also called the customs territory realm, which is the realm for thorough implementation of the *Customs Law of the People's Republic of China.* Generally, a country's customs territory is consistent with its national boundary limits. However there are some countries that form a customs union and have a unified customs territory, implement uniform customs laws and decrees and outward tax regulations, and only collect duty when goods from or to other countries go into or out of the common customs territory. The customs territory of these countries is bigger than the national boundary limits, for example, the European Union. On the contrary, the national territory is bigger than the customs territory when one country establishes a free trade zone or free port within its national territory, for example, Hong Kong and Macau maintain their status of free port pursuant to the *Basic Law*, so they belong to separate customs territories.

Effects

Raising state financial funds

The tax structure of most developed countries shows that customs duty is a small portion of the overall fiscal revenue and show a descending tendency, but for some developing countries, especially those strongly dependent on import and export, levy of customs duty is still an important way of obtaining fiscal revenue. Since the founding of new China, customs duty as a part of state fiscal revenue has accumulated considerable financial funds for China's economic development. After joining the World Trade Organization (WTO), China began to reduce customs duty by stages pursuant to the undertakings made on joining the WTO and the proportion of customs duty in the fiscal revenue will gradually decrease. However customs duty will still play an important role in raising state financial funds with the increasing expansion of China's foreign trade.

Adjusting industrial structure and import and export trade

Customs duty is an important economic lever for a country to use in adjusting industrial structure and import and export trade and to affect domestic industrial structure and import and export scale by setting high and low tax rates and reduction and exemption of tax. Generally, customs duty is exempted or a low tax rate is practiced to encourage import of advanced technology and key equipment necessary for domestic production, and the products necessary for people's lives but in short supply from domestic production; a high tax rate is practiced for domestically produced oversupplied products and luxury goods in order to restrict import. The policy of export tax rebate is practiced for most exported goods in order to enhance international competitiveness of China's exported commodities; export customs duty is levied for some special exported goods to protect China's scarce resources and meet domestic demand.

Safeguarding the rights and interests of the state and promoting the development of foreign economic relations and trade

Right of taxation is a part of state administrative power and the levy of customs duty for imported and exported goods directly influences the sovereignty and economic benefit among countries. In modern society, customs duty has become an important weapon for governments around the world to safeguard their own political and economic rights and interests. In accordance with the principles of equality, mutual benefit and reciprocity, and with the WTO tariff schedule, China safeguards state economic rights and interests and promotes the further development of foreign economic relations and trade by making use of multiple tariffs.

Classification

In terms of the directions of goods

Import duty. This is a kind of customs duty levied for goods and articles moved from abroad into China.

Export duty. This is a kind of customs duty levied for goods and articles moved from China to abroad.

Transit duty. This is a kind of customs duty levied for goods staying at China's ports for movement to other countries.

In terms of the different taxation objectives

Protective duty. Protective duty refers to the customs duty levied primarily to safeguard the economic development of China. Protective duty is mainly reflected by import duty and usually a higher tax rate is set.

Financial duty. Financial duty refers to the customs duty levied primarily to increase fiscal revenue.

In terms of the differentiated treatment according to importing countries

Heavier duty

Heavier duty refers to a kind of provisional import surtax levied after collection of general import duty for imported goods of some exporting countries and producing countries for a particular reason (such as discrimination, retaliation, protection and economic demand). It includes anti-dumping duty, anti-subsidy duty, retaliatory duty etc.

1) Anti-dumping duty: this is an import surtax levied for dumping products. Dumping refers to the act whereby the products of one country squeeze into the market of another country for competitive sale at a price lower than the normal value and lead to great loss or major damage to a particular industry established in that country.

2) Anti-subsidy duty: this is an import surtax levied by the importing country for foreign goods directly or indirectly accepting export subsidy when they are imported to the country.

3) Retaliatory duty: this is a discriminatory duty practiced for commodities imported from other country by a country which holds that its exported commodities are treated with unfair discrimination.

Preferential duty

Preferential duty refers to preferential treatment granted to some special goods of the beneficiary country by practicing a preferential tax rate lower than the ordinary tax rate. It includes mutually preferential duty, preferential duty, general preferential duty and most favored nation treatment.

1) Mutually preferential duty: this refers to a conventional duty between two countries mutually granting each other a preferential tax rate lower than that granted to other countries, with the purpose of developing bilateral trade relation.

2) Preferential duty: this refers to a duty of very low import tax rate or even exemption adopted by countries with special relations, either unilaterally or bilaterally. The preferential degree is higher than that of mutually preferential duty.

3) General preferential duty: this is a universal, non-discriminatory and non-reciprocal preference of customs duty granted by developed

countries to goods (finished products and semi-finished products) exported by developing countries in the course of international trade. Universality means that preference of customs duty is practiced for products imported from developing countries, including finished products and semi-finished products. Non-discrimination means that all developing countries enjoy general preferential treatment without discrimination or exception. Non-reciprocal preference means that developed countries granting preference of customs duty to developing countries shall not request the same preference of customs duty from developing countries, and other developed countries shall not request the same applicable preferential customs duty by invoking the principle of most favored nation treatment.

4) Most favored nation treatment: this means that one contracting country unconditionally grants the preferential treatment given to any third country currently and in future to other members.

In terms of different taxation standards

Ad valorem duty. This is a customs duty calculated and levied based on the price of goods. China practices ad valorem duty for almost all imported commodities.

Specific duty. This is a customs duty calculated and levied according to measuring units such as weight, length, volume and area.

Compound duty. This is a customs duty practicing both ad valorem duty and specific duty for the same kind of imported goods.

Sliding-scale duty. This is a customs duty where the rate moves from low to high for imported goods as their price moves from high to low, which enables import duty rate to decrease with the increase of the price of imported goods and increase with the decrease of the price of imported goods.

China's policies on customs duty

Policies on customs duty refer to the standards of conducts for a country to achieve specific economic and political objectives by means of customs duty in a certain historical period. Different countries in different periods have different policies on customs duty, which is mainly dependent on factors such as politics, economy and industrial policies. Generally, policies on customs duty can be classified into financial duty and protective duty, but it is difficult to completely separate them and so policies on customs duty of countries worldwide are usually mixed duty policies. China is no exception. China's policies on customs duty are specifically embodied by the following principles: tax exemption or low tax is practiced for import of fine animal and plant breeds, fertilizer, forage, agents, precision instruments, meters, key mechanical equipment and grains which are necessary for building the national economy and for people's livelihood but which cannot be produced or supplied in sufficient quantity domestically; import rate for raw material is generally lower than that for semi-finished products and finished products and the rate shall be much lower especially for raw material that is subject to natural conditions and where domestic production cannot be quickly developed; tax rate on parts and components of mechanical equipment, instruments and meters that cannot be produced domestically shall be lower than that on complete machines; a higher tax rate shall be set for products requiring protection domestically and products with a large price difference at home and abroad; export duty is not levied for the most-exported commodities in order to encourage export. However export duty may be appropriately levied as necessary for commodities of limited capacity in the international market but with strong competitiveness and scarce raw materials, materials and semi-finished products, the export of which shall be restricted.

Object of Taxation and the Taxpayers

Object of taxation

Objects of taxation of customs duty are goods and articles permitted to pass into and out of the territory of China. Goods refer to commodities for trade purpose; articles refers to luggage and personal postal articles carried by incoming passengers, items for personal use and items for gifts carried by service staff onboard various means of transport, and personal effects coming in territory by other means. Unless otherwise specified by the state, import duty or export duty shall be levied by the Customs in accordance with the *Customs Import and Export Tariff of the People's Republic of China* (hereinafter referred to as the *Customs Import and Export Tariff*). The Customs shall levy import duty for purchasing and importing goods originally made in China from overseas in accordance with the *Customs Import and Export Tariff*. Taxation measures for luggage and personal postal articles of incoming passengers shall be separately formulated by the Customs Tariff Commission of the State Council.

Taxpayers

There are two kinds of taxpayers subject to customs duty.

Taxpayers for goods imported and exported for trade purposes

Taxpayers for goods imported and exported for trade purposes are consignees and consigners of goods. Consignees and consigners of goods imported and exported are legal persons or other social organizations obtaining foreign trade rights in accordance with the laws and importing or exporting goods.

Taxpayers for goods imported and exported for non-trade purposes

Taxpayers for goods imported and exported for non-trade purposes are owners of articles passing in and out of the territory, including owners of articles and those presumed to be owners.

1) For articles carried into the territory, the owners are presumed to be their carriers.
2) For separately transported luggage, the owners are presumed to be the corresponding passengers passing in and out of the territory.
3) For articles coming into the territory by postal means, the owners are presumed to be the recipients.
4) For articles going out of the territory by post or other means, the owners are presumed to be the senders or consigners.

Tariff, Tax items and Rates

An overview of import and export tariff

Import and export tariff is the applicable customs tariff schedule that is formulated according to relevant state policies on customs duty, promulgated by a certain legislative procedure and implemented for imported and exported goods and articles. It is the basis for the Customs to collect duties. Import and export tariff is mainly the tax rate schedule, and usually also includes decrees on implementation of tariff, relevant explanations and appendixes on use of tariff. Existing tariffs in China include appendixes such as the *Regulations of the People's Republic of China on Import and Export Duties the Explanations of Applicability of Tax Rates,* the *Import Tariff of the People's Republic of China the Export Tariff of the People's Republic of China,* the *Table of Tariff Items and Rates of Ad Valorem Duty Specific Duty Compound Duty and Sliding Scale Duty of*

Imported Commodities, the *Table of Tariff Quotas Items and Rates of Imported Commodities,* the *Table of Provisional Tariff Rates of Imported Commodities,* the *Table of Provisional Tariff Rates of Exported Commodities and the Table of Ex-Tariff Rates of IT Products.*

The table of tariff rates is the main part of the tariff and includes two parts, namely the catalogue of categories of tariff commodities and the column of tariff rates. The catalogue of categories of commodities include the tariff line and commodity name. The tariff line is the commodity number in tariff classification and the catalogue of commodity classification summarizes the various commodities and simplifies them into categories of a limited number of commodities according to their different characteristics, numbers commodities and arranges them in sequence, forms tariff lines, and lists the names of commodities that shall be listed in each line. Commodity names are generally classified and arranged in sequence according to their natural quality and processing stage. The column of tariff rates is fixed according to the contents of commodity categories one by one. China's current import tariff is of four columns while the export tariff is of one column.

China is a contracting party of the *International Convention for Harmonized Commodity Description and Coding System* (hereinafter referred to as the "Convention"). As required by the Convention, a contracting party's import and export tariff shall be formulated and revised on the basis of the *Harmonized Commodity Description and Coding System* (hereinafter referred to as the "Harmonized System"). China's Customs began to formally implement the import and export tariff and catalogue commodities in accordance with the classification principles and contents of the Harmonized System as of January 1, 1992.

Commodity classification in China's current tariff is fully based on the commodity classification principles, structure and commodity names included in the catalogue of the Harmonized System. The Harmonized System is an integral, systematic, universal and correct international trade commodity classification system mainly consisting of commodity items and sub-items. There are various commodities, names and specifications, more than 7,000 commodity lines of eight-digit numbers, 22 categories, and 99 chapters with items and sub-items. The first two numbers of the commodity code represents the "chapter," the first four numbers represent the "item," and the fifth and the sixth represent the "sub-item." Classification and arrangement of listed commodity names follow a certain rules. Seen from the point of view of classifications, they are classified basically according to production categories i.e. products of a same production category are classified into the same category. Seen from the point of view of chapters, they are classified basically according to commodity attributes or functions and purposes. Within each chapter, commodity items are generally arranged in sequences of animal, plant and mineral, and it is relatively obvious that raw materials are anterior to finished products, products of low processing degree are anterior to those of high processing degree, and specific breeds are anterior to ordinary breeds.

The World Customs Organization (WCO) revises the Harmonized System every 4–6 years in order to adapt to the development of international trade, science and technology. The latest revision was based on the 2000 edition of the Harmonized System and was executed by all contracting parties of the Convention as of July 1, 2007. China, as one contracting party, also made great adjustments to the tariff in 2006 based on the Harmonized System. This adjustment was the largest-scale adjustment of import and export tariff in recent ten years, involving the change of 1,600 eight-digit tax numbers, accounting for over 20% of all eight-digit tax numbers, mainly related to categories of mechanical and electrical products, chemical products, textiles, woodworks, and steel materials and products. Since China had practiced new consumption tax items and rates since April 1, 2006, the 2007 edition adjusted the relevant contents. On the basis of the eight-digit number of the customs tariff, the new tariff added ten-digit numbers, including name of commodity, import rate (most favored nation rate, China-Pakistan rate, general rate), VAT rate, export rebate rate, measuring unit, regulatory conditions, columns of corrective and normative commodity name in English, plus the *Table of Provisional Tariff Rates of Imported Commodities*, the *Table of Tariff Rates of Ad Valorem Duty and Compound Duty of Imported Commodities*, the *Table of Tariff Quotas and Rates of Imported Commodities*, the *Table of Ex-Tariff Rates of IT Products*, the *Table of Relevant Tariff Rates of China-ASEAN Free Trade Area (FTA)*, the *Table of Consumption Tax Rates of Imported Commodities*, the *Table of Preferential Tax Items and Rates*, the *Table of Tariff Items and Rates Arranged for Preferential Duty of Mainland China Hong Kong SAR and Macau SAR*, and the *Table of Export Tariff and Provisional Rates of Exported Commodities*.

For the purpose of further implementing relevant taxation and industrial policies and adapting to the demands of scientific and technological progress and enhancement of export administration, tax items in the 2009 edition of the import and export tariff were appropriately increased and decreased under the principles of items of the Harmonized System of the WCO, and the increased items include products that were exported more year by year and required enhancement of export management, such as xylitol, shortening and footwear, products supporting development of agriculture and rural economy such as bamboo wares, anti-HIV drugs, high-tech products such as soldering tin and silicon single crystal rods, and environmentally-friendly products. Moreover some items of individual products were deleted. After the adjustment, the total number of items in the import and export tariff were increased to 7,868 in 2009 from 7,758 in 2008.

Tariff rates and application

Tariff rates of import duty

Setting and applicability of tariff rates

Before entry to the WTO, China had two columns of tariff rates of import duty i.e. general rate and preferential rate. Tax is levied according to the general rate on imported goods originally produced in countries or regions without a relevant mutually beneficial agreement on customs duty signed with China, and tax is levied according to the preferential rate on imported goods originally produced in countries or regions with a relevant mutually beneficial agreement on customs duty signed with China. After entry to the WTO, China's import duties are categorized as most favored nation tariff rate, contractual tariff rate, preferential tariff rate, normal tariff rate, tariff rate quota rate and others, and a temporary tariff rate may be applied to imported goods within a specified period.

The most favored nation tariff rate is applied to imported goods originating from other WTO members or regions to which most favored nation treatment is applicable in a collective manner, or to imported goods originating from countries or regions with which China has signed bilateral trade agreements containing provisions for granting mutual most favored nation status, and to imported goods originating from within the territory of China.

The contractual tariff rate is applicable to imported goods originating from relevant contracting parties with which the People's Republic of China has signed regional trade agreements containing provisions on preferential tariff rates. Currently the contractual tariff rate (namely the tariff rate under the *Bangkok Agreement*) is applied to imported commodities under 739 items for three members of the *Bangkok Agreement* i.e. South Korea, Sri Lanka and Bengal.

The preferential tariff rate is applicable to imported goods originating from countries or regions with which China has a signed trade agreement containing provisions on special preferential tariff rates. Currently the preferential tariff rate (namely the preferential tariff rate under the *Bangkok Agreement*) is applied to imported commodities under 18 items originating from Bengal.

In cases where imported goods to which most favored nation tariff rate is applicable are subject to temporary tariff rates, the temporary tariff rate shall apply. In cases where imported goods to which the contractual tariff rate or preferential tariff rate is applicable are subject to the temporary rate, the lower tariff rate shall apply. Imported goods subject to the normal tariff rate are not subject to the temporary tariff rate. For imported goods subject to tariff rate quota administration as specified by the state, the tariff rate quota rate will be applied within the tariff rate quota, and the applicable provisions shall come into play in terms of the application of tariff rate on imported goods beyond the tariff rate quota allowed.

The normal tariff rate is applied to imported goods originating from countries or regions other than those mentioned above. The most favored nation tariff rate may be applied to imported goods subject to normal tariff rate if approved by the Tariff Commission of the State Council. The list of countries or regions qualified for most favored nation tariff rate, contractual tariff rate and preferential tariff rate shall be determined by the Tariff Commission of the State Council.

Tariff level and structure

China had a total tariff level of about 42% (arithmetic average level of the preferential tariff rate) and a general tariff rate of 56% in 1992. There were several big adjustments to the total tariff level, which was reduced to 40% in December 1992, to 36% in January 1994, to 23% in April 1996 and to 17% in October 1997. In 2002, China's total tariff level (arithmetic average level of the preferential tariff rate) was reduced from 15.3% to 12%, with average decreasing amplitude of 21.6%. Among 7,316 tax items, rates on 5,332 items were reduced to varying extents, with the decrease being up to 73%. The average tariff rate on industrial products was 11.6% and that on agricultural products (including aquatic products) was 15.6%, respectively reduced by 23% and 17.5% compared with those in 2001. After tariff reduction, the average tariff rate was 15.8% for agricultural products (excluding aquatic products), 14.3% for aquatic products, 6.1% for crude oil and petroleum products, 8.9% for wood, paper and products made out of them, 17.6% for textiles and clothing, 7.9% for chemical products, 17.4% for transportation facilities, 9.6% for mechanical products and 10.7% for electronic products. The total average level of general tariff rate was about 57%. In 2004, China's total tariff level (arithmetic average level of the preferential tariff rate) was further reduced to 10.4%.

China further reduced import tariffs for commodities under 5 items such as fresh strawberries from January 1, 2009. Since the scope of commodities of reduced tariff was small and so was the decreasing amplitude of tariff rate, total tariff level was not affected much in 2009 and remained at 9.8%, which was same as that in 2008. The average tariff rate was 15.2% for agricultural products and 8.9% for industrial products. After this reduction of tariffs, China had basically fulfilled the undertaking on tariff reduction made for entry to the WTO except that 5 commodities including strawberries as mentioned above had one year before expiry of the tariff reduction implementation period, with the total tariff level reduced to 9.8% from 15.3% (on entry to the WTO).

Tariff rate structure of imported commodities are mainly embodied by the fact that tariff rate increases with the increase of product processing degree, in other words, among unrenewable resources, general resource products, raw materials, semi-finished products and finished products, unrenewable resources are of lower tariff rates and finished products are of higher tariff rates.

Tariff rates of export duty

China has one column of tariff rate of export duty i.e. export tariff rate. The state usually encourages export of commodities and practices export tax rebate for most exported commodities. Therefore export tariff is only levied on a small number of resource products and semi-finished products that are easily competed for and require normative export orders. A temporary tariff rate may be applied to exported goods within a specific period. China had 36 items of export tariff in 2002 which included five rates i.e. 20%, 25%, 30%, 40% and 50%. The temporary tariff rate was applied to exported commodities under 23 tax items, including 16 items for zero rate and the other 7 items respectively for rates of 5%, 7%, 10% and 20%. Tariff rates on exported commodities were slightly adjusted and the Customs Tariff Commission made adjustments of the export tariff on textiles on June 1, 2005: export tariff rates were improved for 74 kinds of textiles under 39 eight-digit tax items among 148 textiles on which export tariff was levied from January 1, 2005; export tariff was levied for a single yarn of flax (tariff line 53061000); export tariff rates were reduced for 3 products among 148 textiles on which export tariff was levied from January 1, 2005; and levy of export tariff was stopped for 2 products. From January 1, 2007, a temporary tariff rate was applied to some exported commodities such as steel billet, and a seasonal temporary tariff rate was applied to carbamide exported in general trade and small-scale border trade.

In order to relieve business difficulties faced by industries involving textiles, steel and fertilizers, the import tariff was reduced for some production raw materials with larger domestic demand in the form of a reduction of the temporary tariff rate in 2009, and the policies on canceling export tariff on some steel products and adjusting the seasonal tariff for exported fertilizers such as carbamide came into force on December 1, 2008, which would continue to be applied, and the special export tariff rate on some fertilizers would be reduced at the same time.

Special customs duties

Special customs duties include retaliatory duties, anti-dumping duties, countervailing duties and safeguard duties. Measures governing goods subject to special duties, country or region of application, tariff rate, period, and method of levy shall be determined and published by the State Council Tariffs Commission and implemented by the General Administration of Customs.

1) Retaliatory duties refer to heavier duties levied for commodities imported from another country by a country which holds that its exported commodities are subject to inequitable and unequal treatment. Where any country or region levies discriminating duties or grants other discriminatory treatment to goods originating from China, China will levy retaliatory duties for imported goods originating from this country or region. Today, retaliatory duties are one of the weapons of the "trade war."

2) Anti-dumping duties and countervailing duties are additionally levied for dumped goods of foreign countries while the levy of normal import duty is to counterbalance the subsidy of other countries. Dumping may occur if a country promotes its products to other countries at a price lower than production cost, and the importing country may levy anti-dumping duty of not more than the dumping margin.

3) Safeguard duties mean that general safeguard measures may be taken in accordance with the relevant WTO rules if the import quantity of a certain category of commodity rises sharply and relevant industries in China are thereby endangered or damaged significantly. In other words, measures such as increasing import duty on this commodity or limiting import quantity within a specific period may be taken after negotiation with countries or regions of substantial interest resulting from this commodity, so as to protect the relevant industries in China from damage.

Provisions on Country of Origin

Origin criterion refers to the standard for a country (region) to judge its production or manufacture and it is the basis for issuing certificate of origin. Any product in line with origin criterion is regarded as a product of the country (region). Origin criterion is the core of origin rules. Nowadays, various countries (regions) classify origin criteria of goods into two categories, i.e. wholly obtained product criterion and substantial transformation criterion. Correct determination of the country of origin of imported goods is the basis for correct use of all columns of tariff rates and calculation of customs duty payable since different tariff rates are applied to imported goods originated from different countries or regions. China basically adopts two international origin criteria, namely "criterion for obtaining products totally from one country" and "substantial transformation criterion." For goods produced by two or more countries (regions), the origin shall be the country (region) finishing substantial transformation.

Criteria for obtaining products from one country

This criterion is applicable to goods completely obtained in one country (region). Goods completely obtained in one country (region) refer to:

1) Animals born and raised in that country (region);
2) Animals caught, fished or gathered in the field in that country (region);
3) Unprocessed articles obtained from live animals in that country (region);
4) Plants and plant products harvested in that country (region);
5) Minerals excavated in that country (region);
6) Other articles naturally generated in that country (region) beyond the scope of 1) to 5);
7) Waste and scrap materials produced during production that been discarded or collected as materials in that country (region);
8) Goods collected in that country (region) that cannot be restored or repaired, or parts or materials recycled from the goods;
9) Aquatic animals and other goods obtained by the ships with the flag of the country legally in the sea area outside its territorial waters;
10) Products obtained by processing articles listed in 9) legally on a factory ship bearing the flag of the country legally;
11) Goods obtained from the seabed or subsoil of the seabed outside territorial waters where the country has special rights of excavation; and
12) Products completely produced out of articles listed from 1) to 11) in that country (region).

Criteria for substantial transformation

Substantial transformation criterion is applicable to goods produced by two or more countries (regions). The origin shall be the country (region) finishing the substantial transformation.

The criterion for substantial transformation is based on the change of tariff classification. Where the change of tariff classification fails to embody substantial transformation, the ad valorem percentage and manufacturing procedure will serve as supplementary criteria.

1) Change of tariff classification means that after the materials from other countries (regions) are manufactured and processed in a country (region), tax item classification of the goods obtained changes in the *Import and Export Tariff of the People's Republic of China*.

2) The ad valorem percentage refers to the percentage of the value added part greater than the value of goods obtained after raw materials originating from other countries (regions) are manufactured and processed in a country (region).

3) Manufacturing or processing procedures refer to the major procedures deciding the fundamental characteristics of goods obtained after manufacturing and processing in a country (region).

Calculation of Customs Value and Tax Payable

Customs value is the price based on which the Customs levies duty and is the base of customs duty. The *Customs Law* specifies that the customs value of imported and exported goods shall be identified by the Customs based on the transaction value of the goods. If the transaction value cannot be ascertained, the customs value shall be determined by the Customs according to the law. The Customs of China has put into full execution the *WTO Valuation Agreement* since entry into the WTO, followed the objective, fair and uniform principles and examined and finalized the customs value of imported and exported goods in accordance with the *Provisions of the Customs of the People's Republic of China for Assessment of Duty on Imported and Exported Goods*.

Customs value of imported goods

Customs value based on transaction value

The *Provisions of the Customs of the People's Republic of China for Assessment of Duty on Imported and Exported Goods* promulgated on May 1, 2006, specifies that the customs value of imported goods shall be identified by the Customs on the basis of the transaction value of the goods and shall include the freight, insurance premium and relevant expenses before the goods are transported to the loading spot within the territory of China. Where there are relevant expenses that are not accounted into the customs value or should be deducted, the Customs shall adjust the transaction value.

Calculation of customs value

For transactions based on FOB of overseas ports, freight and insurance premium actually paid before the goods are shipped from the overseas port of dispatch or delivery to the territory of China shall be additionally added. The calculation formula of customs value is as follows:

Customs value = FOB + Freight + Insurance premium

For transactions based on the price of goods transported to the port within the territory of China plus insurance premium, the calculation formula of customs value is as follows:

Customs value = Price of goods + Freight + Insurance premium

Adjustment of customs value

The following fees shall be included in the customs value of imported goods:

1) Commission and brokerage fees except purchase commission to be borne by the buyer;
2) Fees for containers borne by the seller that are considered to be an integral part of the goods sold in the course of examining and identifying the customs value of the goods;
3) Expenses of packaging materials and packaging labor fees borne by the seller;
4) Money for materials, tools, moulds, consumption materials and similar goods provided by the seller free of charge or below cost and capable of being amortized with appropriate percentages, which are related to the production of the goods and to the sales of the goods within the territory of China, as well as expenditure incurred for the related services of overseas development and design;
5) Royalties related to the goods and to be borne by the seller, which serves as a condition for the sale of the goods within the territory of the People's Republic of China; and

6) Benefits obtained by the seller from the buyer directly or indirectly from the resale, disposal or use of goods after importation.

The following tax revenue and fees shall not be included in the customs value of imported goods:

1) Fees with regard to the construction, installation, assembly, servicing and technical services provided to goods, such as workshops, machinery, equipment etc., after importation;

2) Transportation and related fees and insurance incurred after the unloading of imported goods that have arrived at their destination within China; and

3) Import duties and domestic taxes.

Method to evaluate imported goods

Where transaction price of imported goods does not conform to the provisions of the tax law or is unable to be determined, the Customs shall evaluate customs value in accordance with the following sequence:

1) Transaction value of the same goods that are sold into the territory of the People's Republic of China at the same time or at approximately the same time.

2) Transaction value of the similar goods that are sold into the territory of the People's Republic of China at the same time or at approximately the same time.

3) Unit price of the said imported goods, same goods or similar goods that are sold to buyers without a special relationship with the seller in the maximum quantity at the first level of sales links, which occurred at the same time or approximately at the same time as the importation of the goods; however, items such as sales profit, general expense, paid commission, transportation expenses and relevant expense, import duty and inland revenue stipulated in tax law shall be deducted.

4) The price is calculated according to the summation of the following items: cost of materials used to produce the goods, processing fee, normal profits and general expenses and transportation expenses for sales of the same or similar goods within China, related fees and insurance fees of the goods occurred within China

5) Price valuated using reasonable methods.

Customs value of goods imported by special means

In terms of goods imported by means of leasing, the customs value will be the rental of the goods.

For goods imported by means of processing trade, the customs value of the goods will be identified based on the overseas processing fees, cost of materials, transportation cost and related fees and insurance fees incurred during the course of transporting the said goods back into the country.

Customs value of exported goods

Customs value based on transaction value

Customs value of exported goods will be identified by the Customs based on the transaction value of the goods and the transportation, related fees and insurance fees of the goods arriving at the departure point within China but before loading. Transaction value of export goods refers to the total amount of money charged by the seller to the buyer directly or indirectly for the export of the goods at the time of export from China.

Transaction value of export goods refers to the total amount of money charged by the seller to the buyer directly or indirectly for the export of the goods at the time of export from China. Commission paid overseas included in the transaction value of exported goods shall be deducted if it is not listed separately. The following tax revenue and fees shall not be included in the customs value of exported goods:

1) Export duty
2) The transportation fees, related fees and insurance fees not included in the customs value of export goods arriving at the departure point within the People's Republic of China but before loading
3) Commission separately listed to be afforded by the seller in the transaction value of exported goods

The calculation formula for transaction value of exported goods is as follows:

Customs value = FOB / (1 + Export tariff rate)

Method to evaluate exported goods

Where the transaction price of exported goods cannot be determined, the Customs shall evaluate the customs value in accordance with the following sequence:

1) Transaction value of the same goods that are exported to the same country or region at the same time or at approximately the same time.
2) Transaction value of similar goods that are exported to the same country or region at the same time or at approximately the same time.

3) The price calculated according to the cost, profits and general expenses, transportation fees, related fees and insurance fees of the goods incurred within China for producing the same or similar goods within China.
4) Price valuated using reasonable methods.

Calculation of customs duty payable

Calculation of ad valorem duty payable:

Ad valorem duty payable = Customs value × Applicable tariff rate

Calculation of specific duty payable:

Specific duty payable = Quantity of goods taxable × Unit tax

Calculation of compound duty payable:

Customs duty = Quantity of goods taxable × Unit tax + Customs value × Applicable tariff rate

Calculation of sliding scale duty payable:

Customs duty = Customs value × Sliding scale duty rate

Import Duty on Luggage and Postal Items

Import duty on luggage and postal items is levied on luggage carried by incoming passengers, personal postal articles, and includes customs duty, and VAT and consumption tax. The tax is levied by the Customs on a commission basis.

Object of taxation

Objects of taxation of import duty on luggage and postal items include taxable luggage, personal postal articles, gifts and personal articles coming into the territory by other means, termed imported articles for short.

Taxpayers

Taxpayers of import duty on luggage and postal items include incoming passengers carrying the articles into China, service staff onboard various means of transport, receivers of entering postal articles, and consignees of articles imported by other means.

Taxable articles for personal use mentioned above do not include automobiles or motorcycles and their fittings and accessories. For import of taxable automobiles, motorcycles, and their fittings and accessories for personal use, customs duty, VAT and consumption tax shall be paid in accordance with the relevant tax laws and regulations.

Tax rates

China's import duty on luggage and postal items has experienced adjustments more than once and there are three levels of proportional tax rates i.e. 50%, 20% and 10%.

1) The tax rate is 50% for cigarettes and liquor.
2) The tax rate is 20% for textiles and products made from these, cosmetics, video cameras, camcorders, digital cameras and other electrical appliances, cameras, bicycles, watches and clocks (including fittings and accessories).
3) The tax rate is 10% for books, newspapers, publications, education-dedicated films, slides, original audio tapes and video tapes, gold, silver and products made from them, foods, beverages and other commodities.

Adjustment of tariff rates of import duty on luggage and postal items shall be determined by the Tariff Commission of the State Council.

Calculation of tax payable

The ad valorem method is applied to import duty on luggage and postal items. Tax on taxpayers shall be calculated and paid according to tax rate and the customs value of taxable goods effective on the day when the customs issues the payment of duties.

The formula for calculating payable import duty on luggage and postal items is as follows:

Duty payable = Customs value × Applicable tariff rate

Where customs value shall be determined by the Customs with reference to the overseas normal retail price of taxable articles.

The payment of duty on articles for personal use shall be made by the taxpayers prior to their release by the Customs.

Recovery, pursuit and refunding

In cases where after granting access to taxpayer's taxable articles, the customs discovers that duties on imported luggage and postal items have not been levied in entirety, it shall recover the duties from the taxpayer within one year, starting from the day of duty payment being granted.

Upon discovery of a taxpayer's short or non-payment of customs duty on imported luggage and postal items goods due to a breach of the Customs regulations, the Customs is entitled to pursue the unpaid duty within 3 years from the date of the breach.

Where an over-levy of duty on luggage and postal items is discovered or confirmed by the Customs, the Customs shall refund the money without delay; the duty payer is also entitled to ask the Customs for the refund within 1 year from the date of duty payment.

Tax Preference and Administration of Tax Collection

Tax preference

Reduction and exemption of customs duty is a special regulatory measure for encouraging and considering some taxpayers and taxation objects. There are three kinds of duty reduction and exemption: statutory reduction and exemption, special reduction and exemption, and temporary reduction and exemption. According to the *Customs Law*, duty reduction and exemption other than the statutory reduction and exemption shall be determined by the State Council.

Statutory reduction and exemption

For duty reduction or exemption definitively listed in tax law on imported and exported goods with allowable duty reduction or exemption according to the tax law, the Customs may perform direct reduction or exemption and the taxpayer does not have to apply. Generally, the Customs has no follow-up administration of items with statutory duty reduction or exemption. According to the *Customs Law of the People's Republic of China* and the *Regulations of the People's Republic of China on Import and Export Duties,* duty may be exempted for the following goods when investigated by the Customs to be true and accurate:

1) Goods for which the customs duty is less than RMB10.
2) Advertising material and trade samples of no commercial value.
3) Materials donated free of charge by foreign governments or international organizations.
4) Fuels, materials, food and drink necessary in the course of transportation carried by the entry and exit transportation vehicles.

5) Raw materials, auxiliary materials, spare parts, components, fittings and packaging materials imported for overseas manufacturers to process and assemble finished products and to produce export goods shall be exempted from import duty by the Customs in accordance with the number of finished products actually produced and exported; alternatively, import duty may be levied firstly for imported materials, parts, components and fittings, and then the duty refunded in accordance with the number of finished products actually produced and exported.

6) For samples, exhibitions, construction equipment, construction vehicles, engineering vessels, instruments and tools for installing equipment, television or filmmaking instruments, containers of goods, costumes and property of troupes that are imported or exported on a temporary basis upon approval by the Customs and are taken out of or into the territory within 6 months again, customs duty may be temporarily exempted after the goods consignee or consignor pays the Customs guarantee or provides warranty equivalent to the duty payment.

The Customs may grant an appropriate reduction or exemption for imported goods under any of the following circumstances: 1) goods suffering damage or loss in the course of overseas transportation or loading; 2) goods suffering damage or loss due to force majeure after loading but before Customs release; 3) goods suffering damage, leakage or decay before Customs inspection which is proven not to be caused by careless storage or storage.

Special reduction and exemption

Special reduction and exemption is also called special or policy-oriented duty reduction and exemption as specified by the State Council or the departments empowered by the State Council by promulgating laws and regulations beyond the statutory reduction and exemption determined by the *Customs Law of the People's Republic of China* and the *Regulations of the People's Republic of China on Import and Export Duties*. Goods liable for special duty reduction or exemption are generally limited to some regions, enterprises and uses, and the Customs needs to have follow-up administration and statistics of reduction and exemption, for example, duty reduction or exemption for imported products used for science, technology and education, articles dedicated for the disabled, and donated materials for poverty relief.

Donated materials for poverty relief and charity purposes

Upon approval by the State Council, the Ministry of Finance, the State

Administration of Taxation and the General Administration of Customs promulgated the *Provisional Measures on Exempting Import Tax Levied upon Donated Materials for Poverty-Relief and Charity Purposes* (hereinafter referred to as "the *Measures*") to promote the healthy development of public welfare undertakings. Import duty and VAT in the link of import are exempted for materials directly used for poverty relief and charity purposes donated free of charge by donors such as natural persons, legal entities or other organizations outside the territory of China to social organizations aiming at providing humanitarian aid and developing poverty relief and charity undertakings established legally with the approval of the competent authorities of the State Council and relevant departments of the State Council and the people's governments of provinces, autonomous regions or municipalities directly under the central government. Poverty relief and charity undertakings refer to social charity and welfare undertakings related to non-profit poverty relief and charitable aid. The *Measures* specify the categories and names of donated materials enjoying duty exemption.

Special-purpose articles for the disabled

To support the rehabilitation of the disabled, the State Council promulgated the *Interim Measures for Exemption from the Import Duties on Special-Purpose Articles for the Disabled*, exempting import duty and VAT in the link of import for specified special-purpose articles for the disabled. The special-purpose articles for the disabled specified in the *Interim Measures* which cannot be produced by domestic rehabilitation and welfare organizations, artificial limb factories and rehabilitation hospitals for disabled soldiers are exempted from import duty and VAT in the link of import. The *Interim Measures for Exemption from the Import Duties on Special-Purpose Articles for the Disabled* specifies the categories and names of special-purpose articles for the disabled which enjoy duty exemption.

Articles for scientific research and teaching

With a view to promoting the development of scientific research and education, the State Council formulated the *Interim Provisions for Exemption from Import Duties on Articles for Scientific Research and Teaching*. Where scientific research institutes and schools, without the object of profit-making and within reasonable quantities, import articles for scientific research and teaching which cannot be made in China, and use these articles directly for scientific research or teaching, exemption of import duties and VAT or consumption tax shall be granted.

The *Interim Provisions for Exemption from the Import Duties on the Articles for Scientific Research and Teaching* specifies the qualifications and categories of scientific research institutes enjoying this preference and the articles enjoying duty exemption.

Processing and trade products

1) Processing and assembling, and compensation trade. Processing and assembling are processing materials supplied by clients, processing with supplied samples and assembling with supplied parts. This means that overseas merchants provide all or some of the raw materials, parts, spares and packing materials, and provide equipment where necessary. The Chinese party processes and assembles these according to the other party's requirements, delivers the finished products to them for sale, and charges processing fees. Money provided by merchants for purchasing equipment is paid off through processing fees. Compensation trade refers to a trade model under which overseas merchants provide the production technology or equipment, or domestic entities import production technology by foreign export credit, and the Chinese enterprise amortizes the opposite side's money for technology and equipment or for loan and interest by back selling products. Since this helps to rapidly enhance production technology of exported products, improve the quality and variety of products, expand exports and increase foreign exchange income, China grants a certain degree of tariff preference: imported materials are not liable but are allowed for bonded processing to produce finished products and back sell for export; import of non-priced equipment and import of priced equipment of merchants is implemented with respective reference to provisions on duty exemption for foreign investment projects and domestic investment projects; duty may be exempted for residual materials or added products which are approved to be sold in China if their value is within 2% of the total value of the imported materials and is less than RMB3,000.

2) Processing with imported materials. Enterprises with the approved right of import and export import materials by using the designated sum of foreign exchange, process or assemble finished products, and export them. This is called processing with imported materials and tariff preferences are as follows: for exported materials used specially for processing and exporting commodities, the Customs shall exempt

the import duty according to the actual quantity of commodities processed and re-exported; import duty is exempted for exports of processed finished products, while import duty is levied as specified for materials and finished products sold in China; for by-products, seconds and leftover materials, the Customs shall levy, reduce or exempt duty based on the analysis and evaluation of their useful value; duty may be exempted for residual materials or added products which are approved to be sold in China if their value is within 2% of the total value of imported materials and is less than RMB5,000.

Imported and exported goods from export processing zones

The state establishes export processing zones in order to strengthen and improve processing trade administration, strictly control the domestic sales of processed trade products, protect the relevant domestic industries, provide a more relaxed business environment for export processing enterprises, and boost the export of domestically produced raw materials, parts and spares. The main duty preference policies for export processing zones are as follows:

1) Import duty and tax in the import link are exempt for machinery and equipment required by production infrastructure projects entering export processing zones from overseas, capital construction materials required by production factories and storage facilities, machinery, equipment, moulds, spares and parts for repair required by production activities of enterprises in export processing zones, and office supplies of a reasonable quantity used by enterprises and administration agencies themselves in export processing zones;

2) The bonded system is practiced for raw materials, parts and spares, components, wrapping materials and consumable materials required for processing export products by enterprises in export processing zones;

3) For goods transported out of processing zones, the Customs handles customs clearance according to the relevant provisions and levies according to the finished products;

4) Goods entering processing zones from outside are regarded as exported goods and export rebate rate may be handled in compliance with the provisions.

Imported and exported goods of bonded areas

In order to create a more improved investment and operational environment and carry out processing and sorting, packaging, transportation, storage, commodity exhibition and entrepot trade, China has established bonded areas within the territory which are special areas completely isolated from the outside world for storing and processing bonded goods under the Customs' monitoring and administration. The main tariff preference policies of bonded areas are as follows: 1) import duty and tax in the import link are exempted for machinery, equipment, capital construction materials and production vehicles that are imported for use in the bonded area; raw materials, parts and spares, components and wrapping materials imported for processing export products; and transit goods for storage and products processed in the bonded area and transported out of the territory; 2) raw materials, spares and parts, and packaging materials imported by the enterprises in the bonded area to be used for producing and processing export products, and transit goods, shall be held in bond; 3) export tariff is generally exempted for goods transported from bonded areas to overseas.

Materials imported through border trade

In order to encourage border areas to actively develop border trade and economic cooperation with nations adjacent to China, the state has formulated relevant policies and measures for supporting and encouraging border trade and border area's foreign economic cooperation. Border trade is of two forms i.e. trade among border residents and small-scale border trade. Trade among border residents refers to commodity exchange activities of border residents within 20 km of the border line at government-approved open spots or appointed marketplaces. Import duty and tax in the link of import are exempted for articles for daily use imported by border residents by border trade, with a daily value per person less than RMB8,000. Small-scale border trade refers to trade activities between enterprises with approved small-scale border trade operating rights that are within the administrative regions of border counties (or banners) and cities along the land border line and are approved by the state to be opened to the outside world and the enterprises or other trade agencies in border areas of neighboring countries through land border ports. Import duty and tax in the import link are exempted by one half for commodities originating from neighboring countries imported by small-scale border trade enterprises through appointed border ports, except for cigarettes, liquor, cosmetics and other commodities when it must be levied in accordance with the regulations.

Temporary reduction or exemption

Temporary reduction or exemption is temporarily granted to some taxpayers due to special reasons other than statutory and special reduction or exemption. This reduction or exemption is approved on a case-by-case basis and is issued through a special document. Generally there are limitations on unit, variety, quantity and time, so it cannot be used as reference for implementation. China has now basically cancelled temporary reduction or exemption to unify tax law and make the tax burden fair.

Administration of tax collection

Declaration and payment of customs duty

Taxpayers of imported goods shall, within 14 days of the declaration of entry of transportation vehicles, declare the goods to the Customs at the entry-exit location. Taxpayers of exported goods shall declare to the Customs after the arrival of the goods at the area under the Customs' supervision and 24 hours before loading. The Customs shall calculate payable customs duty and tax in the import link on a commission basis in accordance with the tariff classification and customs value, and file and issue the letter of payment of duty. Taxpayers shall pay duties to the designated banks within 15 days of the day when the Customs issues the letter of payment of duty. In cases where the customs duty payer fails to pay the duties within the specified period of time due to force majeure or under the circumstances where the State is adjusting its taxation policies, they may delay their payment of duties subject to the approval of the General Administration of Customs, with the longest delay being no more than 6 months.

Where duties are not paid within the specified period of time, the Customs shall levy a fine for overdue payment. The overdue fine is levied at 0.5‰ per day of the duty owed from the day following the expiry day of the due payment period to the day of payment of all duty. The calculation formula is as follows:

Overdue fine of duty = Unpaid taxable duty × 0.5‰ × Number of overdue days

Compulsory execution of customs duties

In cases where the taxpayers or guarantors fail to pay duties after three months upon the expiration of the duty payment period, the Customs may adopt compulsory measures upon approval from the governor of the Customs directly subordinated to the General Administration of Customs or from the authorized governor of the Customs subordinate to the Customs directly subordinated to the General Administration of Customs as follows:

1) Notification in writing to the banks or other financial institutions with

which the taxpayer, withholding agent or tax payment guarantor has opened an account to withhold and remit the amount of tax from its deposits;

2) Sale of dutiable goods in accordance with the law and use of the proceeds from the sale to make good the amount of tax payable;

3) Withholding and sale of the goods or other property of the taxpayer, withholding agent or tax payment guarantor with a value equivalent to the amount of tax payable, and use of the proceeds from the sale to make good the amount of tax payable.

4) At the same time as implementing the mandatory measures, the Customs shall implement the relevant mandatory measures to collect the overdue fine which has not been paid by the taxpayer, withholding agent or tax payment guarantor

Recovery, pursuit and refund of customs duties

For these three scenarios occurring in the course of levy of customs duties, the *Customs Law* makes specifications respectively in *Article 62* and *Article 63*.

Recovery

In cases where after granting access to imported and exported goods and articles moving in and out of the territory, the customs discovers that duties are not levied or not levied in entirety, it shall levy duties on the taxpayer within one year starting from the day of duty payment or access being granted to goods or articles.

Pursuit

If the short-payment or non-payment of the duty is due to a breach of the Customs regulations by the obligatory duty payer, the Customs is entitled to recover this part of unpaid duty within 3 years.

Refund of over-levy

Refund of over-levy means that the Customs has levied too much duty and shall refund to the over-payment to the original taxpayer immediately after the discovery; if the duty payer knows there has been an excessive levy, it is entitled to ask the Customs to refund the over-levy within one year of the date of duty payment. According to the *Regulations of the People's Republic of China on the Administration of the Import and Export of Goods*, consignees and consigners and their agents may state reasons in writing and submit original duty receipts to the Customs to apply for a duty refund within one year of the date of the duty payment in any of the following circumstances, and no application will be accepted beyond the time limit: 1) duty is over-paid due to the Custom's mistaken levy; 2) shortage of imported goods approved by the Customs for exemption from inspection is discovered after duty payment, and investigated and recognized by the Customs; 3) goods for which export duties have been paid fail to be exported due to certain reasons, and an application has been filed for a customs declaration to move the goods back into the country, which has been investigated and recognized by the Customs. The Customs shall reply in writing and notify the refund applicant within 30 days upon accepting the application for duty refund.

Settlement of disputes over duty payment

Where the obligatory duty payer is involved in a dispute over duty payment with the Customs in the course of duty levy and payment, the *Article 64* of the *Customs Law* specifies that the duty payer shall first make the payment of the duty and then apply to the Customs for an administrative reconsideration of the case. If the reconsideration decision is considered unacceptable, the obligatory duty payer may take legal action at the People's Court. The administrative reconsideration specified in this law is an administrative reconsideration by the customs. The interested party of duty is specified as the duty payer in *Article 64* of the *Customs Law*. The duty payer may request a review of the Customs' administrative acts and ask the administrative organs of reconsideration to review the legality and appropriateness and to make a decision, and the duty payer has the right to institute legal proceedings if he is not satisfied with the reconsideration decision. The legal basis for this are the *Administrative Litigation Law of the People's Republic of China*, the *Administrative Reconsideration Law of the People's Republic of China*, and measures for implementing relevant administrative reconsideration. In the course of administrative reconsideration and administrative lawsuits related to customs duty collection and administration, the principles of levying duties in accordance with the law, stopping and correcting illegal acts and incorrect behavior in the course of collection and administration of duties, safeguarding the legitimate rights and interests of duty payers, and safeguarding the interests of the state shall be upheld.

6
Chapter

Enterprise Income Tax

An Overview

Some concepts

Enterprise income tax is a category of tax levied on the income obtained from the production and business activities of domestic enterprises and other organizations, and is an important means for the state to participate in the profit distribution of enterprises.

Evolution

Current enterprise income tax is originated from the merger of enterprise income tax (hereinafter referred to as original enterprise income tax) and income tax for foreign-invested enterprises and foreign enterprises. Original enterprise income tax was formed by the combination of state-owned enterprise income tax, collectively-owned enterprise income tax and private enterprise income tax in 1994.

The system of enterprise income tax after the founding of new China and before the reform and opening up

The basic scheme for unifying national taxation policies was approved at the national taxation conference in 1994, including measures for levying enterprise income tax and individual income tax. In 1950, the then Government Administration Council promulgated the *Main Points of the Implementation of Tax Policy* and specified 14 categories of tax revenues, including three categories involving tax collection for income i.e. industrial and commercial tax (the part of income tax), income tax on interest earnings, and income tax on salaries and remunerations.

Since the levy of industrial and commercial tax (a part of income tax) began in 1950, its taxation object was mainly the taxable income of private enterprises, collectively-owned enterprises and individual businesses. Since the relevant government departments directly participated in the operation and management of state-owned enterprises, their financial accounting systems were very different from that of general enterprises, so state-owned enterprises handed over profits to superior departments without paying income tax. This system was designed adapted to the requirements of the highly centralized planned economy management system at that time.

China experienced two major taxation reforms in 1958 and 1973, mainly with the purpose of simplifying the taxation, with the industrial and commercial tax (the part of income tax) mainly levied from collectively owned enterprises. State-owned enterprises were only liable for industrial and commercial tax but not for income tax. Private enterprises did not exist after the socialist transformation in 1958. At this stage, various tax revenues accounted for an increasing proportion of financial revenue, up to about 50%; however, the profit handed over by state-owned enterprises was a main source of state financial revenue. Commodity tax and labor service tax levied on the domestic sales link were a main part of tax revenue, up to more than 70% of the total revenue, while the income tax handed over by industrial and commercial enterprises accounted for a minor proportion of the total revenue.

The system of enterprise income tax after the reform and opening up

The end of 1970s saw the beginning of China's attempts to practice its reform and opening-up policy. The construction of the taxation entered a new development period, and tax revenue gradually became the main source of governmental financial revenue; meanwhile, taxation became an important means of state macro-economic control.

First, the system of enterprise income tax during 1978–1982

After the reform and opening up, taxation reform was carried out step by step during the Seventh Five-Year Plan in order to introduce foreign capital, techniques and skills, and facilitate foreign economic and technical cooperation. The *Income Tax Law of the People's Republic of China on Chinese-Foreign Equity Joint Ventures* was approved and promulgated at the 3rd Meeting of the Standing Committee of the 5th NPC in September 1980. Enterprise income tax rate was set at 30%. Moreover, local income tax was levied at a rate of 10% for payable amount of income tax. The *Income Tax Law of the People's Republic of China for Foreign Enterprises* was adopted at the 5th Meeting of the Standing Committee of the 4th NPC in December 1981, and it specified a five-grade progressive tax rate of between 20% and 40% for the amount in excess of a specific amount of income. Local income tax was levied at a rate 10% for payable amount of income tax. The abovementioned reform marked the beginning of the income tax system reform matched to China's socialist planned market economy system.

Second, the system of enterprise income tax during 1983–1990

In 1983, the State Council decided to carry out the trial implementation of "substitution of tax payment for profit delivery" for state-owned enterprises throughout the country as a important measure of enterprise reform and urban reform. In other words, the system of state-owned enterprises' handover of profits to the state implemented for more than 30 years after the founding of new China was changed to the system of enterprises' payment of income tax.

The State Council promulgated the *Regulations of the People's Republic of China on Income Tax of State-owned Enterprises (Draft)* and the *Measures for Levying Regulatory Tax on State-owned Enterprises* in September 1984, which marked the determination of the distribution relationship between the state and state-owned enterprises in legal form. Taxpayers of income tax of state-owned enterprises are state-owned enterprises with independent economic accounting, with large and medium-size enterprises practicing a proportional tax rate of 55% and small-size enterprises practicing an eight-grade progressive tax rate of between 10% and 55% for the amount in excess of a specific amount. Taxpayers of regulatory tax on state-owned enterprises are large and medium-size state-owned enterprises and the rate is decided by the competent fiscal and taxation departments.

The State Council promulgated the *Interim Regulation of the People's Republic of China on Enterprise Income Tax* in April 1985, practicing an eight-grade progressive tax rate of between 10% and 55% for the amount in excess of a specific amount, and concurrently suspending the industrial and commercial tax (the part in income tax) originally levied on collectively-owned enterprises.

The State Council promulgated the *Interim Regulations of the People's Republic of China on Income Tax of the Private Enterprise* in June 1988, specifying a tax rate 35%.

The promulgated systems on "substitution of tax payment for profit delivery" for state-owned enterprises and income tax for collectively owned enterprises and private enterprises redefined the distribution relationship between the State and enterprises and brought China's enterprise income tax system to a new stage.

Third, the system of enterprise income tax during 1991–1994

In order to adapt to the new situation of building a system of socialist market economy, further expanding the reform and opening up and pushing state-owned enterprises to the market, the state successively unified income tax of foreign-invested enterprises and that of domestically funded enterprises.

The 7th NPC in April 1991 incorporated the *Income Tax Law of the People's Republic of China for Chinese-Foreign Equity Joint Ventures* with the *Income Tax Law of the People's Republic of China for Foreign Enterprises* and formulated the *Law of the People's Republic of China on Income Tax for Foreign-invested Enterprises and Foreign Enterprises* which was put into force as of July 1, 1991.

The State Council incorporated the *Regulations of the People's Republic of China on Income Tax of the State-owned Enterprises (Draft)*, the *Measures for Levying Regulatory Tax on State-owned Enterprises,* the *Interim Regulations of the People's Republic of China on Enterprise Income Tax* and the *Interim Regulations of the People's Republic of China on Income Tax of the Private Enterprise* on December 13, 1993, and formulated the *Interim Regulations of the People's Republic of China on Enterprise Income Tax* which came into effect as of January 1, 1994. The abovementioned reform marks an important step towards a legal, scientific and normalized income tax system.

Fourth, the system of enterprise income tax during 1994–2007

There were two systems of enterprise income tax in 1994, for domestically funded enterprises and foreign-invested enterprises (including foreign-invested enterprises and foreign enterprises) respectively, which had differing elements of tax system including taxpayers, deductable items and preference policy.

Enterprise income tax is applicable to domestically-funded enterprises and taxpayers are state-owned enterprises, collectively owned enterprises, private enterprises, jointly-run enterprises, joint-stock enterprises and other organizations within the territory of China. The objects of taxation are taxpayers' income obtained from domestic and overseas production and business operations and other incomes. The amount of income taxable for taxpayers is their gross income in each tax year minus the amount of deductable items. Pre-tax deduction with a limit or of standard amount is practiced for enterprise's expenditure for salaries, public welfare donations, advertising expenses, staff education appropriations, staff welfare funds, and employee labor union funds. The statutory benchmark tax rate is 33% and enterprises with annual tax payable of less than RMB30,000 and those with annual tax payable of between RMB30,000 and RMB100,000 qualify for preferential tax rates of 18% and 27% respectively.

The *Law of the People's Republic of China on Income Tax for Foreign-Invested Enterprises and Foreign Enterprises* is applicable to foreign-invested enterprises and the taxpayers are foreign-invested enterprises and foreign enterprises. The objects of taxation are incomes obtained from production and business operations and other incomes of foreign-invested enterprises and foreign enterprises. The amount of income taxable for taxpayers is their gross income in each tax year after deducting the amount of deductible items. The enterprises basically implement measures of pre-tax deduction of cost and expenses according to the facts. A proportional tax rate of 30% is implemented for enterprise income tax and the local income tax is levied at a rate of 3% according to the amount of income taxable, so the composite tax rate is 33%. In order to increase the policy efforts to attract foreign investment, the state has implemented a series of tax preference policies, mainly including the "two-year exemption and three-year halved payment" preferential policy of enterprise income tax for foreign-invested production enterprises, the "five-year exemption and five-year halved payment" preferential policy of enterprise income tax for foreign-invested enterprises investing in ports, piers and energy, and low tax rates of 15% and 24% for foreign-invested production enterprises in regions such as special economic zones and economic and technological development zones.

The *Enterprise Income Tax Law of the People's Republic of China* was adopted at the 5th Session of the 10th NPC on March 16, 2007, and the *Regulations on Carrying out the Enterprise Income Tax Law of the People's Republic of China* was adopted at the 197th Session of the State Council on November 28, 2007, which came into force as of January 1, 2008.

Characteristics

Enterprise income tax is an important means of normalizing and handling the distribution relationship between the state and enterprises, and it is of different nature of that of commodity and service tax. Its main characteristics include four aspects as follows.

First, enterprises are classified into resident enterprises and non-resident enterprises. Current enterprise income tax classifies enterprises into two categories i.e. resident enterprises and non-resident enterprises. Resident enterprises shoulder unlimited obligation to pay tax; in other words, for incomes obtained domestically and overseas, income tax shall be paid to the Chinese government. Non-resident enterprises shoulder limited obligation to pay tax. For income obtained within China, income tax shall be paid to the Chinese government.

Second, the object of taxation is the amount of income taxable. The object of taxation of enterprise income tax is the amount of income taxable which is the balance of the gross taxable income in one tax year deducting costs, expenditures, taxes and losses according to the provisions of enterprise income tax law but not the total profit calculated according to the provisions of the accounting system.

Third, the tax levy principle is taxation on capacity. The objects of taxation of enterprise income tax are income obtained from production and business operations and other incomes, and the tax levied is proportional to the income, which embodies the principle of a rational incidence of taxation and unlike commodity and service tax which levies tax as long as there is income regardless of gains or losses.

Fourth, the method of tax levy is on an annual basis and payment in advance in installments is practiced. The base of enterprise income tax system is the amount of income taxable in one tax year. Generally, tax is paid in advance in monthly or quarterly installments and tax payments are settled after the end of each tax year, and any payment in excess shall be refunded and any deficiency shall be made up.

Legislative principles

Enterprise income tax is an important means for handling the distribution relation between the state and enterprises. Whether the tax system is reasonably designed not only affects the burden of enterprises and the fiscal revenue of the state but also influences the sustainable development of the overall national economy. Therefore the following principles should be followed in the course of formulation of laws and regulations on enterprise income tax.

The first is the principle of equity. The principle of equity is a perpetual principle of human society, while enterprise income tax is one of the main categories of taxes for handling the distribution relationship between the state and enterprises, so an equitable tax burden is very important for distributing the value created by enterprises. From the macroscopic perspective, it is necessary to guarantee governmental fiscal revenue and adapt to governmental economic regulation by tax collection. In other words, governmental fiscal revenue should be guaranteed without affecting the initiative for production and operation of enterprises. From the microscopic perspective, there should be equity among enterprises and among industries, so all enterprises shall bear an equitable tax burden unless otherwise specified. Therefore the new enterprise income tax law unifies tax rates, pre-tax deduction standards and tax preference policies.

The second is the principle of the outlook of the scientific development. The scientific development concept is of fundamental importance for human survival, so the levy of enterprise income tax should aim for a rational distribution relationship between the government and enterprises. It should also facilitate the long-term sustainable development of the overall national economy. Therefore the formulation of laws and regulations on enterprise income tax should benefit the rational utilization of resources, ecological balance, and environmental protection.

The third is the principle of exertion of the macro-control. Taxation is an important lever for regulating the economy and how to regulate the economy by using the regulations on enterprise income tax is an important issue worthy of study. China needs to regulate the economy by using laws and regulations on enterprise income tax while taking into consideration the facts that it has a vast territory, much unbalanced economic development, large gaps between regions and industries, an irrational economic structure, and lags behind in technical progress.

The fourth is the principle of international comparison. Enterprise income tax is a category of tax universally levied throughout the world. Although there are different names for it in different countries, there is no big essential difference. With the increasing expansion of policies on opening up to the outside world and the rapid development of global economic integration, objects paying income tax to the Chinese government are not only domestic enterprises but also involve many foreign enterprises. Therefore universal international practice as mentioned above must be taken into consideration in the course of formulation of laws and regulations on enterprise income tax.

The fifth is the principle of convenient collection and administration. Enterprise income tax is the most difficult to calculate among all categories of taxes, and it is related to all incomes, costs and expenses of an enterprise in one tax year and the deduction of all taxes other than income tax paid by enterprises and creditable VAT. Errors may occur in the course of collection and administration due to carelessness. Therefore laws and regulations on enterprise income tax should be formulated to try to make them simple, lucid and convenient for operation and implementation.

Effects

As in important lever for regulating the distribution relationship between the state and enterprises, enterprise income tax has two main effects as follows:

First, it helps to extensively gather financial funds.

Enterprise income tax is a tax of very extensive coverage. Any enterprise obtaining income regardless of whether it is a domestically funded enterprise or a foreign-invested enterprise shall pay income tax, so enterprise income tax has a strong power to gather revenue and this effect will become more outstanding with the rapid development of the national economy and the increasing improvement of the enterprise's economic benefit.

Second, it helps to effectively implement tax regulation and control.

As one of the important means of state macro-control, enterprise income tax is helpful for gathering revenue as well as effectively implementing state industrial and social policies. For example, the national industrial restructuring can be promoted by implementing a series of tax preference policies.

Object of Taxation and the Taxpayers

Object of taxation

Objects of taxation of enterprise income tax refer to income obtained from production and business operation, other income and liquidation income.

In terms of resident enterprises

Objects of taxation of resident enterprises are gains obtained domestically and overseas. These gains include gains from selling goods, providing labor services, transferring assets, equity investment gains such as dividends and bonuses, and gains from interest, rent, royalties, donations and other gains.

In terms of non-resident enterprises

If a non-resident enterprise sets up an organization or establishment within the territory of China, it shall pay enterprise income tax on its incomes sourced inside the territory of China and on incomes sourced outside the territory of China but actually connected with the said organization or establishment. If a non-resident enterprise has no organization or establishment within the territory of China, or its income have no actual connection to its organization or establishment inside the territory of China, it shall only pay enterprise income tax on the income sourced inside the territory of China.

The actual connection as mentioned above means that a non-resident enterprise possesses stock rights and creditor's rights for obtaining gains by setting up an organization or establishment within the territory of China and possesses, manages and controls the assets for obtaining gains.

Sources of gains

1) Gains obtained from sales of goods shall be determined according to the place where the transaction activities occur.
2) Gains obtained from provision of labor services shall be determined according to the place where the labor services occur.

3) Gains obtained from transfer of assets.

Gains obtained from transfer of real estate shall be determined according to the place where the real estate is located.

Gains obtained from transfer of movable property shall be determined according to the place where the enterprise or organization transferring the movable property is located.

Gains obtained from transfer of equity investment shall be determined according to the place where the invested enterprise is located.

4) Gains obtained from equity investment such as dividends and bonuses shall be determined according to the place where the enterprise participating in distribution of gains is located.

5) Gains obtained from interest, rents and royalties shall be determined according to the place where the enterprise or organization burdening or paying for the gains is located, or the place where the individual burdening or paying for the gains resides.

6) Other incomes shall be determined by the competent finance and tax authorities under the State Council.

Taxpayers

The enterprises and other organizations which obtain income within the territory of China shall be payers of the enterprise income tax. *Article 1* of the *Enterprise Income Tax Law of the People's Republic of China* specifies that the enterprises and other organizations which obtain income (hereinafter referred to as "the enterprises") within the territory of China shall be the payers of the enterprise income tax and shall pay their enterprise income taxes according to the present law, except for sole individual proprietorship enterprises and partnership enterprises.

Resident enterprises

Resident enterprise means an enterprise which is set up under Chinese law within the territory of China, or set up under the law of a foreign country (region) but the actual management organ of which is within the territory of China. Such enterprises here include state-owned enterprises, collectively owned enterprises, private enterprises, jointly-run enterprises, joint-stock enterprises, foreign-invested enterprises, foreign enterprises and other organizations with income obtained from production and business operations and with other incomes. "Other organizations with income obtained from production and business operations" refers to organizations such as government-sponsored institutions and public organizations registered according to the law with the approval of the relevant department of the state. Public organizations and government-sponsored institutions that carry out many kinds of business operations and compensatory services in the course of accomplishment of national business plans, and obtain operating income other than appropriations of financial departments and various charges approved by the Ministry of Finance and competent price authorities, shall be regarded as enterprises and included in the incidence of taxation if they are of business operation characteristics.

The actual management organs refer to organs practicing essential and overall management and control of enterprise production and operation, staff, finance and assets, and they shall meet three conditions as follows: first, that they practice essential management and control of the enterprise; second, that they practice overall management and control of the enterprise; third, that the objects of management and control are enterprise production and operation, staff, finance and assets.

Non-resident enterprise means an enterprise which is set up under the law of a foreign country (region), the actual management organ of which is not within the territory of China but which has organizations or establishments within the territory of China, or which does not have any organization or establishment within the territory of China but has income sourced in China.

Organizations or places as mentioned above refers to organizations or places for carrying out production and business operations activities within the territory of China, including:

1) Administrative organs, operating organs and administrative offices;
2) Factories, farms and places for exploiting natural resources;
3) Places for providing labor services;
4) Places for engineering works covering construction, installation, assembly, repair and exploration;
5) Other organs or place for carrying out production and business operation activities.

For non-resident enterprises consigning business agents to carry out production and business operation activities within the territory of China, including consigning organizations or individuals to sign contracts or storing or delivering goods on their behalf, the agents shall be regarded as organizations or places set up by non-resident enterprises within the territory of China. For example, a company is registered and set up in the United States according to the laws of the United States and the company has its actual management organ in the United State and sets up executive offices in Shanghai and Guangzhou to facilitate sales. This company falls within the category of a non-resident enterprise in China.

Tax Rates

Proportional tax rate is practiced for enterprise income tax.

1) The basic tax rate is 25%. It is applicable to resident enterprises and non-resident enterprises which set up organizations or places within the territory of China and their gains are related to these organs or places.

2) The low tax rate is 20%. It is applicable to non-resident enterprises that have no organization or establishment within the territory of China, or their income presents no actual connection to its organization or establishment inside the territory of China. However the tax rate of 10% is applicable in the course of actual taxation (refer to relevant contents about tax preference).

3) Preferential tax rate. As well as the basic tax rate and low tax rate, the state also practices preferential taxation measures for some special enterprises, for example, for small low-profit enterprises the enterprise income tax shall be levied at a reduced tax rate of 20% and for important high-tech enterprises which need to be supported by the state, the enterprise income tax shall be levied at the reduced tax rate of 15%.

Tax Base

Income tax is levied on net income. The amount of income does not fully reflect the taxable capacity of taxpayers, so only by levying on net income can taxation on capacity be realized and an equitable tax burden be embodied. The amount of income taxable is the tax base of enterprise income tax and the determination of income taxable is an important content of the income tax law. According to the provisions of the enterprise income tax law, the amount of income taxable is the balance of an enterprise's total income amount of each tax year after deducting tax-free income, tax-exempted income, deductable items as well as the permitted remedies for losses of the previous year(s). The primitive formula is as follows:

The amount of income taxable = Total income – Tax-free income –
Tax-exempt income – Deductable items – Losses of the previous year(s)

The computation of taxable income of an enterprise shall, in principle, be on an accrual basis. This means that income and expenses that belong to the current period shall be regarded as income and expenses of the current period no matter received or paid or not; income and expenses that do not belong to the current period shall not be regarded as income and expenses of the current period even if they have been received or paid (unless otherwise specified by the competent finance and tax authorities under the State Council).The principle of accrual base is the base for specifying accounting recognition from the perspective of time, and its core is to recognize revenues and expenditures and profits of enterprises in accordance with the duration of the actual influence of the rights-obligation relationship. Accounting of income, costs and expenses on an accrual base is able to more accurately embody actual financial conditions and business performance during each accounting period. Enterprise income tax law has precise specifications on the computation of taxable income and the main contents include gross income, deduction scope and standards, tax treatment of assets, make-up of loss etc.

Gross income

An enterprise's gross income refers to the monetary and non-monetary income obtained from various sources and includes income from sale of goods, provision of labor services, transfer of assets, dividends, bonuses and other equity investment gains, interest, rentals and royalties, and income from accepting donations and other incomes.

The enterprise's monetary income includes cash, bank deposits, accounts and notes receivable, and bond investments to be held to maturity and debt exemptions. Taxpayer's non-monetary income includes fixed assets, biological assets, intangible assets, equity investment, goods in stock, bond investments not to be held to maturity, labor services, and relevant rights and interests. The amount of income from these non-monetary assets shall be determined according to fair value which is the value determined according to the market price. Details of income compositions are as follows:

Recognition of general income

1) Income obtained from selling goods. This refers to the income from enterprise's sales of commodities, products, raw materials, wrappers, low-priced and easily-worn articles and other goods in stock.
2) Income obtained from providing labor services. This refers to the income from an enterprise's engaging in construction and installation, repair and replacement, communications and

transportation, warehouse leasing, finance and insurance, post and telecommunications, consultancy brokering, culture and sports, scientific research, technical services, educational training, catering and accommodation, intermediary, health care, community services, tourism, entertainment, processing, and providing other labor service activities.

3) Income obtained from transferring property. This refers to the income obtained from an enterprise's transferring properties such as fixed assets, biological assets, intangible assets, stock rights and creditor's rights.

4) Equity investment gains, such as dividend and bonus. This refers to an enterprise's income obtained from equity investment. For equity investment gains, such as dividends and bonuses, the income shall be recognized according to the date on which the entity invested in makes decisions on profit distribution, unless otherwise specified by competent financial and tax authorities under the State Council.

5) Interest income. This refers to income from an enterprise providing funds to others but which constitutes no equity investment or others' occupation of its funds, including interest on deposit, interest on credit, bond interest and interest on arrears.

6) Rental income. This refers to the income from an enterprise providing right of use of fixed assets, wrappers and other tangible assets.

7) Royalty income. This refers to the income from an enterprise providing right of use of patent rights, non-patent technology, trademark rights, copyrights and other royalties. Income from royalties shall be recognized according to the contract stipulated date of payment of royalties by their users.

8) Income from accepting donations. This refers to the income from an enterprise accepting monetary and non-monetary assets granted free of charge by other enterprises, organizations or individuals. Income from accepting donations shall be recognized according to the date of payment of actual receipt of donated assets.

9) Other incomes. These refer to an enterprise's other incomes except those mentioned above, including income from overage of enterprise assets, income from due to failure of withdrawal of guarantee deposit of wrappers beyond the time limit, payable bills and accounts actually unable to be paid, accounts receivable already itemized as bad debt losses which are recovered later, income for debt restructuring, income from subsidy, and income from penalty and exchange earnings.

Recognition of special income

1) Where goods are sold by the installment payment methods, the income may be recognized according to the date of collection as specified in the contract.

2) Where the enterprise processes and manufactures large-scale mechanical equipment, vessels or aircraft, engages in construction, installation, assembly works or provides other labor services for more than one year, the income may be recognized according to the progress of the project or the amount of work completed.

3) Where the income is obtained based on product-sharing, the income may be recognized according to the date on which the enterprise shares products, and the amount of income is determined according to fair value of products.

4) Where the enterprise has non-monetary assets transactions and uses goods, assets and labor services for donation, debt redemption, fund raising, advertising, samples, staff welfare or profit distribution, these acts shall be regarded as sales of goods, transfer of assets or provision of labor services, except for those otherwise specified by the competent financial and tax authorities of the State Council.

Tax-free income and tax-exempt income

In order to support and encourage some special taxpayers and projects or to avoid influencing the normal running of an enterprise through tax levy, the state implements special policies of no tax or tax exemption for some income of enterprises in order to lighten the enterprise's burden and promote coordinated development of the economy. Taxable income amount is approved to be credited, or funds for special purpose are treated as non-taxable income, to lighten the enterprise's burden and increase the enterprise's expendable funds.

Tax-free income

Financial appropriations

These refer to financial funds appropriated by people's governments at all levels for organizations such as public organizations and government-sponsored institutions incorporated into budget control, except for those otherwise specified by the State Council or the competent financial and tax authorities of the State Council.

Administrative fees

These are expenses charged for specific objects and incorporated into fiscal administration in the course of implementing social public management and providing special public services to citizens, legal persons or other organizations in accordance with the relevant provisions of laws and regulations and with the approval of the State Council according to the specified procedures.

Governmental funds

These are financial funds with special purpose collected by the enterprise on behalf of the government in accordance with the relevant provisions of laws and administrative regulations.

Other tax-free income as prescribed by the State Council

These are financial funds obtained by the enterprise and approved by the State Council and specified for a special purpose by the competent finance and tax authorities under the State Council.

Tax-exempt income

1) Interest income from treasury bonds. In order to encourage enterprises to actively purchase national debt and support national reconstruction, the tax law specifies that enterprise income tax is exempted for interest income obtained from purchase of national debt.
2) Dividends, bonuses and other equity investment gains generated between qualified resident enterprises. These are investment gains of resident enterprises obtained by directly investing in other resident enterprises.
3) Dividends, bonuses and other equity investment gains which are obtained from a resident enterprise by a non-resident enterprise with organs or establishments inside the territory of China and have actual connection with such organs or establishments. These gains do not include the investment gains obtained from continuous holding stocks that are distributed to the public by resident enterprises and are listed for transaction for less than 12 months.
4) Income of qualified non-profit organizations.

Deductable items

Principles of pre-tax deduction

Deductable items and amounts declared by the enterprise shall be true and legitimate. True means that the enterprise is able to prove that the relevant expenditures have truly occurred; legitimate means that it conforms to the provisions of the tax laws of the state, and the provisions of tax laws and regulations shall prevail if there is any discrepancy with other laws and regulations. Generally, pre-tax deduction shall conform to the following principles unless otherwise specified by taxation laws and regulations:

1) The principle of accrual base. This means that the enterprise's expenses shall be deducted within their respective occurrence period but not be recognized for deduction when they are actually paid.

2) The principle of proportionality. This means that the deduction of the enterprise's expenses shall be in proportion with the enterprise's income. The enterprise's expenses shall not be declared for deduction earlier or later than the designated date unless otherwise specified.

3) The principle of relevance. Deductible expenses of the enterprise must be directly related to acquisition of taxable income from the perspective of their natures and sources.

4) The principle of certainty. This means that the amount of deductible expenses of the enterprise must be certain no matter when it is paid.

5) The principle of rationality. This refers to necessary and normal expenditures that conform to the convention of production and business activities and shall be recorded into profits and losses of the current period or relevant asset costs.

Scope of deductable items

The *Enterprise Income Tax Law of the People's Republic of China* specifies that when calculating the taxable income amount, reasonable expenditures which have an actual connection with the business operations of an enterprise, including costs, expenditures, taxes, losses etc. may be deducted.

Costs

These refer to cost of sales, cost of goods sold, business expenses occurred in the course of production and operating activities, and other costs i.e. the enterprise's costs for selling commodities (products, materials, leftovers, waste materials, waste and old materials etc.), providing labor services, and transferring fixed assets and intangible assets (including transfer of technology).

Expenditures

These refer to the enterprise's selling (operating) expenses, management fees and financial expenses incurred in one tax year for producing and operating commodities and providing labor services. Relevant expenses that have been incorporated into costs are excepted.

Selling expenses refer to expenses that occur when selling commodities and shall be paid by the enterprise, including advertising expenses, transportation expenses, loading and unloading expenses, packing charges, exhibition fees, insurance premiums, sales commission (purchasing price of a commodity where the import commission adjustment can be directly determined), service charges for sales on a commission basis, operating lease premiums and marketing department's travel expenses, salaries, welfare expenses etc.

Management fees refer to expenses spent by the enterprise's administrative departments for providing various supporting services for managing and organizing business operations.

Financial expenses refer to the enterprise's expenses incurred for gathering operating funds, including the net interest expense, the aggregate net loss, service charges of financial agencies and other non-capitalized expenditures.

Taxes

These refer to various taxes and their extra charges other than enterprise income tax and creditable VAT. In other words, they are taxes and extra charges for sales of products paid by the enterprise as specified, including consumption tax, business tax, urban maintenance and construction tax, customs duty, resource tax, land value increment tax, house tax, vehicle and vessel usage tax, land use tax, stamp tax and educational surtax.

Losses

These refer to the enterprise's inventory loss, damage, abandonment loss of fixed assets and goods in stock occurred in the course of production and business operating activities, losses due to transferred property and bad debts, losses caused by force majeure such as natural disasters, and other losses.

The balance of the enterprise's losses compensation of the person in charge and insurance indemnities shall be deducted as specified by the competent financial and tax authorities of the State Council.

An enterprise's assets already itemized as losses which are recovered in full or in part in a subsequent tax year shall be included in the income of the year.

Other expenses

These refer to relevant reasonable expenses that are related to production and business operating activities and occur in the course of production and business operating activities other than costs, expenditures, taxes and losses.

Standards of deductable items

Expenditure on wages and salaries

Reasonable expenditure on wages and salaries incurred by enterprises are permitted to be deducted according to the facts. Expenditure on wages and salaries refers to all cash or non-cash labor rewards paid by the enterprise to its staff by virtue of the tenure of an office or employment in each tax year, including basic salaries, bonuses, allowances, subsidies, year-end extras, overtime wages and other expenses related to staff's tenure of an office or employment.

Employee welfare expenses, labor union expenditure and employee education expenses

Employee welfare expenses, labor union expenditure and employee education expenses incurred by an enterprise shall be deducted as per the standards. Those not greater than the standard amount shall be deducted according to the actual amount, and those greater than the standard amount shall be deducted according to the standard.

First, for employee welfare expenses incurred by an enterprise not more than 14% of the gross payroll is permitted to be deducted.

Second, for labor union expenditure appropriated by an enterprise not more than 2% of the gross payroll is permitted to be deducted.

Third, for of employee education expenses not more than 2.5% of the gross payroll is permitted to be deducted and the excess may be carried forward for deduction in later tax year(s) unless otherwise specified by the competent financial and tax authorities of the State Council.

Social insurance

First, "five insurances and one fund" i.e. social insurance, including basic old-age insurance, medical insurance, unemployment insurance, work injury insurance, maternity insurance as well as the housing accumulation fund paid for employees by an enterprise in accordance with the scope and standard specified by the relevant competent departments of the State Council or provincial people's governments are permitted to be deducted.

Second, supplementary endowment insurance and supplementary medical insurance paid for employees by an enterprise within the scope and standard specified by the competent financial and tax authorities of the State Council are permitted to be deducted. Personal safety insurance paid by an enterprise for workers for special jobs in accordance with relevant state provisions and deductible commercial insurance according to provisions of the competent financial and tax authorities of the State Council are permitted to be deducted.

Third, commercial insurance paid by an enterprise for investors or employees is not permitted to be deducted.

Interest expenses

Interest expenses incurred in the course of an enterprise's production and business operations are deducted according to the following provisions:

First, interest expenses of non-financial enterprises for borrowing money from financial enterprises, interest expenses of deposits of financial enterprises, interest expenses for inter-bank borrowings and interest expenses of enterprises for issuing bonds as approved can be deducted according to the facts.

Second, the part of interest expenses of nonfinancial enterprises for borrowing money from financial enterprises not greater than the amount calculated according to the interest rates of similar loans in the same period of financial enterprises can be deducted according to the facts and the excess is not permitted to be deducted.

Borrowing costs

First, reasonable borrowing costs requiring no capitalization occurring in the course of production and business operations are permitted to be deducted.

Second, where the enterprise borrows money for purchasing and building fixed assets, intangible assets and stock requiring more than 12 months to achieve prescribed merchantable status, reasonable borrowing costs incurred in the course of purchasing and building the relevant assets shall be capitalized and recorded into costs of relevant assets in the form of capital expenditure; borrowing costs occurring after delivery of relevant assets may be deducted within the current period of occurrence.

Exchange losses

The enterprise's exchange losses caused by conversion of monetary assets and liabilities into RMB according to the closing spot mid-rate at the end of the tax year in the course of monetary operation are permitted to be deducted except for the part that has been included into relevant asset costs and is related to profit distribution with the owners.

Business reception expenses

60% of the actual amount of an enterprise's business reception expenses related to production and business operations are deducted, but the deduction shall not be more than 5‰ of the sales (operating) income in the same year.

Advertising expenses and business promotion fees

The part of an enterprise's advertising expenses and business promotion fees meeting requirements and not more than 15% sales (business) income in the same year is permitted to be deducted unless otherwise specified by the competent finance and tax authorities under the State Council; the excess is permitted to be carried forward for deduction in later tax year(s).

Advertising expenses and sponsorship expenditures that an enterprise declares for deduction shall be clearly distinguished. Advertising expenses that an enterprise declares for deduction must meet the following conditions: the advertisement shall be produced by specialized agencies authorized by industrial and commercial departments; expenses have been actually paid and relevant invoices have been obtained; and the advertisement has been propagated through certain media.

Special funds for environmental protection

Special funds withdrawn according to relevant provisions of laws and regulations for environmental protection and ecological restoration are permitted to be deducted. No deduction is permitted if use of these special funds is changed after withdrawal.

Insurance premiums

Insurance premiums paid by the enterprise for participating in property insurance are permitted to be deducted.

Leasing expenses

Leasing expenses paid by an enterprise for leasing fixed assets required by production and business operation shall be deducted according to the following methods:

First, leasing expenses incurred for leasing fixed assets in the form of an operating lease shall be uniformly deducted according to the term of lease. Operating lease refers to a lease with no transfer of ownership.

Second, for leasing expenses incurred for leasing fixed assets in the form of a financing lease, the depreciation charge shall be withdrawn and deducted by installments for the part that forms a proportion of the value of fixed assets obtained from the financial lease. Financial lease refers to a kind of lease which essentially transfers all risks and rewards related to the ownership of an asset.

Labor protection expenses

Reasonable labor protection expenses incurring in an enterprise are permitted to be deducted. Generally, labor protection expenses refers to expenditure incurred for providing staff with working clothes, gloves, articles for safety protection, heatstroke prevention and cooling. Pre-tax deduction is not permitted for labor protection materials issued by the enterprise in the form of cash.

Expenditure for public welfare donations

As regards an enterprise's expenditure on public welfare donations, the portion within 12% of the total annual accounting profit calculated in accordance with the provisions of the uniform accounting system of the state is permitted to be deducted.

Public welfare donations refer to an enterprise's donations performed through social organizations of public welfare or the people's governments at or above the county level and their departments for public welfare undertakings specified by the *Law on Donation for Public Welfare Undertakings of the People's Republic of China*.

Expenses related to assets

An enterprise's expenses incurred for transfer of various fixed assets are permitted to be deducted. Depreciation fee of fixed assets and amortization charges for intangible assets and deferred assets are permitted to be deducted.

Allocation of head office's expenses

Expenses that are paid by a non-resident enterprise with an establishment or site in China to the overseas head office in connection with production or business operations of the establishment or site and are reasonably allocated shall be permitted to be deducted after verification of documents of proof issued by the head office in respect of the scope of the expenses, quotas, basis and methods of allocation.

Loss of assets

The enterprise's net loss of inventory shortage and spoilage of fixed assets and current assets occurred in the current period is permitted to be deducted after the enterprise's provision of inventory check data and the competent tax authorities' verification; the enterprise's input tax not creditable from output tax due to reasons such as inventory shortage and spoilage and abandonment is regarded as the enterprise's loss of assets and is permitted for pre-tax deduction as specified together with inventory loss.

Other deferred assets that are permitted to be deducted as per the provisions of relevant laws, regulations and related tax laws of the state, such as membership fees, reasonable convention expenses, travel expenses, penalties and expenses in litigation.

Non-deductible items

When calculating the taxable income amount, the following expenditures may be non-deductable:

1) Such equity investment gains as dividends and bonuses paid to the investors.
2) Payment for enterprise income tax.
3) Surcharge for overdue payment of taxes which is imposed by tax authorities on a taxpayer violating the provisions of tax laws and regulations.
4) Pecuniary penalties, fines, and losses of confiscated properties, referring to punishment imposed by relevant departments and fines and confiscation of properties imposed by judicial authorities on a taxpayer violating the relevant provisions of laws and regulations of the state.
5) Donation expenses in excess of the prescribed standard.
6) Sponsorship expenditures, referring to an enterprise's various non-advertising expenses that are not related to production and business operating activities.
7) Unverified reserve expenditures, referring to reserve expenditures failing to meet the requirements on reserve for impairment of assets and risk reserve put forward by the competent finance and tax authorities under the State Council.
8) Management fees paid among enterprises, rents and royalties paid

among business institutions within enterprises, and interest paid among business institutions within non-bank enterprises are not permitted to be deducted.

9) Other expenditures with no relation to the obtainment of revenues.

Make-up of loss

The losses suffered by an enterprise during a tax year may be made up by the income of the following year, and if the income of the following tax year is not sufficient to make up for the losses, the losses may be made up in the continuing and consecutive tax years. However the maximum term may not exceed five years and this make-up shall be calculated continuously year by year in sequence. Moreover an enterprise may not offset the losses of its overseas business organs against the profits of its domestic business organs in the consolidated calculation of its enterprise income taxes.

The losses as mentioned refer to the negative amount after tax-free and tax-exempted income and each deductable item are deducted from the total income amount of each tax year in accordance with the provisions on enterprise income tax law and the provisional regulations.

Taxation on Assets

Assets are accumulated by capital investment, so capital expenditures and expenses for transfer, establishment and development of intangible assets shall not be regarded as costs and expenses and deducted from total income once and for all, but shall be deducted only by depreciation or amortization in installments. In other words, depreciation charges of fixed assets used in the course of a taxpayer's business operation and amortization charges of intangible assets and long-term deferred expenditures may be deducted. According to the provisions of tax laws, assets included in a taxpayer's taxation are mainly fixed assets, biological assets, intangible assets, long-term deferred expenditures, investment assets and inventory, and their tax base is historical cost. Historical cost refers to the actual expenditure on obtaining assets. For appreciation or depreciation of assets during an enterprise's holding period of assets, the tax base of each asset shall not be adjusted unless the gains and losses can be determined according to the provisions of the competent financial and tax authorities of the State Council.

Taxation on fixed assets

Fixed assets refer to non-monetary assets held and used for more than 12 months by an enterprise for producing products, providing labor services, leasing or operating management, including houses, buildings, machines, machinery, means of transportation and other equipment, and appliances and tools related to production and business operating activities.

Tax base

Tax bases of fixed assets are generally based on the original value. The specific provisions are as follows:

1) For purchased fixed assets, the tax bases are purchase price, relevant taxes paid and other expenses that bring the fixed asset to the expected conditions for use.

2) For self-constructed fixed assets, the tax bases are the expenditure made before completion settlement.

3) For fixed assets financed by leasing, the tax bases are the total payment stipulated in the leasing contract and relevant expenses of the leasee incurred in the course of signing of the leasing contract; if the total payment is not stipulated in the leasing contract, the tax bases are the fair value of the assets and relevant expenses of the leasee incurred in the course of signing the leasing contract.

4) For fixed assets with inventory profit, the tax base is the full replacement value of similar fixed assets.

5) For fixed assets obtained in the forms of donation, investment, exchange of non-monetary assets and debt restructuring, the tax bases are the fair value of the assets and relevant taxes paid.

6) For fixed assets other than fixed assets reconstructed, fixed assets for which the full amount of depreciation has been allocated and fixed assets obtained by leasing, the tax bases are the expenditures for reconstruction incurred in the course of reconstruction.

Scope of depreciation

When calculating the taxable income amount, the enterprise's depreciation of fixed assets calculated as specified is permitted to be deducted. However neither depreciation nor deduction is permitted for the following fixed assets:

1) Fixed assets which have not yet been put into use, among which houses and buildings are not included.

2) Fixed assets which are rented through commercial lease.

3) Fixed assets which are rented out through finance leasing.

4) Fixed assets for which depreciation has been fully allocated but which are still in use.

5) Fixed assets with no relation to the business operations.

6) The land which is separately evaluated and entered into the account as an item of fixed asset.

7) Other fixed assets for which no depreciation may be calculated for deduction.

Methods of calculating depreciation

1) Depreciation of fixed assets of an enterprise shall be calculated commencing with the month following the month in which they are first put into use. The calculation of depreciation shall cease in the month following the month in which the fixed assets cease to be used.

2) An enterprise shall, in accordance with the nature and use of a fixed asset, reasonably ascertain its expected net salvage value. Once an enterprise decides the expected net salvage value of the fixed asset, it shall not be changed randomly.

3) Depreciation of fixed assets calculated according to the straight-line method is permitted to be deducted.

Period of depreciation

Minimum periods of depreciation of fixed assets are as follows unless otherwise specified by the competent finance and tax authorities under the State Council:

1) The period is 20 years for houses and buildings.

2) The period is 10 years for airplanes, railway rolling stock, ships, machinery, mechanical apparatus, and other production equipment.

3) The period is 5 years for appliances, tools and furniture related to production and business activities.

4) The period is 4 years for means of transportation except airplanes, railway rolling stock and ships.

5) The period is 3 years for electronic equipment.

Methods of depreciation for enterprises engaging in mineral resources

For enterprises dealing with mineral resources such as petroleum and natural gas, expenses incurred before the beginning of commercial production, and methods for dealing with depletion and depreciation of relevant fixed assets, shall be otherwise specified by the competent finance and tax authorities under the State Council.

Taxation on biological assets

Biological assets refer to living animals and plants. Biological assets are classified as consumptive biological assets, productive biological assets and public welfare biological assets. Consumptive biological assets refer to the biological assets held for sale, or biological assets to be harvested as agricultural products in the future, consisting of growing field crops, vegetables, commercial forests, livestock on hand etc. Productive biological assets refer to the biological assets held for the purpose of producing agricultural products, rendering labor services, renting etc., consisting of economic forests, fuel forests, productive livestock, draught animals etc. Public welfare biological assets refer to the biological assets with the main purpose of protection or environmental protection, consisting of wind break and sand fixation forests, water and soil conservation forests, water conservation forests etc.

Tax base

Tax bases of biological assets shall be determined according to the following methods:

1) For purchased productive biological assets, the tax bases are purchase price and relevant taxes paid.
2) For productive biological assets obtained in the forms of donation, investment, exchange of non-monetary assets and debt restructuring, the tax bases are the fair value of the assets and relevant taxes paid.

Methods and period of depreciation

Depreciation of productive biological assets calculated according to the straight-line method is permitted to be deducted. Depreciation of productive biological assets of an enterprise shall be calculated commencing with the month following the month in which they are first put into use. The calculation of depreciation shall cease in the month following the month in which the productive biological assets cease to be used.

An enterprise shall, in accordance with the nature and use of a productive biological asset, reasonably ascertain its expected net salvage value. Once an enterprise decides the expected net salvage value of the productive biological asset, it shall not be changed randomly.

Minimum periods of depreciation of productive biological assets are as follows: 10 years for biological assets such as forests and 3 years for biological assets such as livestock.

Taxation on intangible assets

Intangible assets refer to assets that are used by an enterprise for a long term without material state, including patents, trademark, copyrights, right to use land sites non-patented technology and goodwill, etc.

Tax base

Tax bases of intangible assets shall be determined according to the following methods:

1) For purchased intangible assets, the tax bases are purchase price, relevant taxes paid and other expenses that bring the fixed asset to the expected conditions for use.

2) For self-developed intangible assets, the tax bases are expenditures incurred during the period from the time when the asset meets the capitalization conditions to the time when the expected purposes of use are realized.

3) For intangible assets obtained in forms of donation, investment, exchange of non-monetary assets and debt restructuring, the tax base is the fair value of the asset and relevant taxes paid.

Scope of amortization

An enterprise is allowed to deduct the amortized expenditures of intangible assets calculated under the related provisions when calculating the taxable amount of income.

For the following intangible assets, no amortized expense may be calculated:

1) The intangible assets are developed by the enterprise itself and the expenditures have been deducted when calculating the taxable income amount.

2) The self-created business reputation.

3) The intangible assets with no relation to the business operations.

4) Other intangible assets for which no amortized expense may be calculated for deduction.

Methods and period of amortization

The amortization of intangible assets shall be calculated using the straight-line method. The amortization period in respect of intangible assets shall not be less than ten years. Intangible assets transferred or assigned or used as investments, where the useful life is stipulated by laws or regulations or in the contract, may be amortized over the period of their useful life as specified or contracted. Expenditures for purchasing business reputation are permitted to be deducted upon the overall transfer or liquidation of an enterprise.

Taxation on long-term deferred expenditures

Long-term deferred expenditures refer to an enterprise's expenses that shall be amortized for one or more years. The following expenditures incurred by an enterprise shall be deemed as long-term deferred expenditures when calculating the taxable income amount. Those amortized according to following provisions are permitted to be deducted:

1) Expenditures for rebuilding a fixed asset, for which depreciation has been fully allocated.
2) Expenditures for rebuilding a rented fixed asset.
3) Expenditures for major repairs of a fixed asset.
4) Other expenditures which shall be deemed as long-term deferred expenditures.

An enterprise's expenditures for repairing fixed assets may be deducted within the current period of occurrence. For an enterprise's expenditures incurred on major repair and improvement, the value of assets may be added if depreciation of relevant fixed assets has not been fully allocated; if depreciation of relevant fixed assets has been fully allocated and can be used as long-term deferred expenditures, they may be averagely amortized within a specified period.

The expenditures for rebuilding a fixed asset refer to the expenditures incurred for altering a house or building structure and prolonging its service life. Expenditures for rebuilding a fixed asset for which depreciation has been fully allocated may be amortizated in installments according to the predicted remaining useful life; expenditures for rebuilding a rented fixed asset may be amortized in installments according to the residual leasing period as contracted; for a rebuilt fixed asset with extended useful life, the depreciation period shall be moderately extended for other expenditures for rebuilding except for rebuilding expenditures of a fixed assets and a rented fixed asset whose depreciation has been fully allocated.

The expenditures for major repairs of a fixed asset shall be amortizated in installments according to the remaining useful life.

The expenditures for major repairs of a fixed asset as mentioned in the enterprise income tax law refer to expenditures meeting all the following conditions:

First, expenditures for repair account for more than 50% of the tax base when the fixed asset was obtained.

Second, the useful life of the fixed asset is extended for more than 2 years after repair.

Other expenditures that shall be regarded as long-term deferred expenses shall be amortized beginning with the month following the month in which expenditure occurs and the period of amortization shall not be less than three years.

Taxation on inventories

Inventories refer to products or commodities held by an enterprise for selling, products in process, materials consumed in the course of production, or provision of labor services.

Tax base

Costs of an inventory are determined according to the following methods:

1) For an inventory obtained by paying in cash, the costs are purchase price and relevant taxes paid.
2) For an inventory obtained by means other than paying in cash, the costs are fair value of an inventory and relevant taxes paid.
3) The costs of agricultural products harvested by a productive biological asset are necessary expenses for the materials, labor, and indirect apportionment etc. during the course of output or gathering.

Methods of calculating costs

An enterprise may select one of three methods for calculating the costs of inventories used or sold i.e. first-in and first-out, weighted average, and specific identification. Once a method has been adopted for use, no change shall be made thereto.

If an enterprise transfers an asset, it is permitted to deduct the net value of the asset when calculating the taxable income amount. Net value of the asset refers to the balance of tax base of relevant assets and properties once depreciation, depletion, amortization and reserve have been deducted as specified.

Unless otherwise specified by the competent finance and tax authorities under the State Council, gains or losses due to transfer of relevant assets shall be ascertained at the time of transaction in the course of enterprise restructuring, and the tax base of relevant assets shall be determined again according to the transaction price.

Taxation on investment assets

Investment assets refer to assets formed by an enterprise's external equity investments and credit investments.

Costs

For investment assets, the investment costs shall be determined according to the following methods:
1) For investment assets obtained by paying in cash, the costs are purchase price.
2) For investment assets obtained by means other than paying in cash, the costs are fair value of assets and relevant taxes paid.

Methods of deducting costs

When calculating the taxable income amount, an enterprise may not deduct the costs of the investment assets during the period of external investment; costs of investment assets are permitted to be deducted when an enterprise transfers or disposes of investment assets.

Taxation on Business Transactions of Affiliated Enterprises

What are affiliated parties?

Affiliated parties refer to enterprises, other organizations or individuals which have one of the following relationships with the enterprise:
1) Direct or indirect control in relation to such areas as capital, business operations, and purchases and sales.
2) Direct or indirect control by a third party.
3) Other mutually beneficial associations.

Taxation on business transactions between affiliated enterprises

1) As regards the costs of an enterprise and its affiliated parties for jointly developing or accepting intangible assets, or jointly providing or accepting labor services, they shall, when calculating the taxable income

amount, apportion them according to the arms length principle.

2) When an enterprise and its affiliated parties apportion costs, they shall apportion costs according to the principle of matching costs with expected reward and submit relevant data within the period specified by the tax authorities according to their requirements.

3) If an enterprise and its affiliated parties apportion costs in violation of the two provisions mentioned above, their respectively apportioned costs shall not be deducted when calculating the taxable income amount.

4) An enterprise may propose the pricing principles and calculation methods for the transactions between it and its affiliated parties to the tax organization, and the tax organization and the enterprise shall, upon negotiations and confirmation, achieve an advance pricing arrangement. Advance pricing arrangement means that an enterprise proposes pricing principles and calculation methods for affiliated transactions in future years to the tax authority, and the tax authority and the enterprise, upon negotiations and confirmation, achieve an agreement.

5) When an enterprise submits its annual enterprise income tax returns to the tax authority, an annual report on the affiliated transactions between it and its affiliated parties shall be attached.

When the tax authority investigates the affiliated transactions, the enterprise and its affiliated parties, as well as other enterprises in relation to the affiliated transactions under investigation shall, according to the relevant provisions, provide the related materials.

Related materials refer to:

- Materials such as formulation standards, calculation methods and instructions in relation to affiliated transactions in corresponding period.
- Materials in relation to resale (transfer) price or final sale (transfer) price of property, property use rights and labor services involved in affiliated transactions.
- Materials such as product price, pricing method and profit level comparable with those of the investigated enterprise that are provided by other enterprises in relation to the investigation of affiliated transactions.
- Other materials in relation to affiliated transactions.

6) If an enterprise which is set up in a country (region) where the actual tax burden is apparently lower than the tax rate of 25% on a resident enterprise or is controlled by a resident enterprise or by a Chinese resident fails to distribute the profits or decreases the distribution not

by virtue of reasonable business operations, the portion of the aforesaid profits attributable to this resident enterprise shall be included in its income for the current period.

The abovementioned "controlled" means:

- A resident enterprise or a Chinese resident directly or indirectly holds more than 50% of the voting shares of a foreign enterprise or they together hold more than 50% of shares of this foreign enterprise.
- The shareholding ratio of a resident enterprise or a resident enterprise and a Chinese resident does not reach the standard specified above but there is substantial control of the foreign enterprise's shares, capital, business operation, purchases and sales.
- The actual tax burden is apparently lower means that the actual tax burden is apparently lower than 50% of the income tax rate of 25% specified by the enterprise income tax law.

7) As regards an enterprise's interest expenditures for any credit investments and equity investments accepted from its affiliated parties in excess of the prescribed criterion, the enterprise may not deduct them when calculating the taxable income amount. An enterprise's credit investments obtained from affiliated parties include the following:

- Credit investments provide by affiliated parties through non-affiliated third parties.
- Credit investments provided by non-affiliated third parties and guaranteed by affiliated parties with joint and several liability.
- Credit investments with credit nature that are obtained indirectly from other affiliated parties.

Equity investments refer to the investments accepted by an enterprise with no need to pay the principal and interest, with the investor having ownership of the enterprise's net assets.

Adjustment of transactions between affiliated enterprises

Methods of adjustment

The tax law designs the following adjustment methods specific for affiliated enterprises making false income declarations:

1) Comparable uncontrolled price method, referring to the pricing method according to the price of the same or similar transactions performed by parities without affiliation relationships.
2) Resale price method, referring to the pricing method according to the

price of resale of commodities purchased from affiliated parities to transaction parities without affiliation relationships deducting the gross profit on sales of same or similar transactions.

3) Cost-plus method, referring to the pricing method according to cost plus reasonable expenses and profits.

4) Transactional net margin method, referring to the method for determining profits according to the net profit level obtained from same or similar transactions among parities without affiliation relationships.

5) Profit split method, referring to the method for distributing consolidated profits or losses of an enterprise and its affiliated parties among all parties according to reasonable standards.

6) Other methods conforming to the arms length principle.

Verification

When the tax authority investigates the affiliated transactions, the enterprise and its affiliated parties, as well as other enterprises in relation to the affiliated transactions under investigation, shall provide the related materials according to the relevant provisions. Where an enterprise does not provide materials about transactions with its affiliated parties or provides false or incomplete materials and fails to truly reflect information on transactions, tax authorities may adopt the following methods when verifying taxable income amount according to the provisions of enterprise income tax law:

1) Verification by referring to the profit levels of same or similar enterprises.

2) Verification according to an enterprise's costs plus reasonable expenses and profits.

3) Verification according to a reasonable proportion of the overall profit of affiliated enterprise groups.

4) Verification through other reasonable methods.

If an enterprise has different opinions on the taxable income amount verified by tax authorities according to the abovementioned methods, relevant evidence shall be provided and the verified taxable income amount shall be adjusted after verification by the tax authorities.

If an enterprise makes any arrangement not for any reasonable commercial purpose which causes the decrease, exemption or delay of its tax payment, the tax authority may make special adjustments on the tax payment of the enterprise according to the provisions of tax laws and regulations, collect the overdue tax and additionally charge for interest from June 1 of the year following the tax year to the date of payment of overdue tax. The additionally charged interest shall not be deducted when calculating taxable income amount.

The interest shall be calculated according to the benchmark loan interest rate of RMB in the same period as the overdue tax payment period published by the People's Bank of China in the tax year, plus 5 percentage points.

If an annual report on the affiliated transactions is attached when an enterprise submits its annual enterprise income tax returns to the tax organ according to the provisions of enterprise income tax law, the interest may be calculated only according to the specified benchmark loan interest rate of RMB.

If a transaction between an enterprise and its affiliated parties does not conform to the arms length principle, or the enterprise makes any other arrangement not for any reasonable commercial purpose, the tax authorities shall have the right to adjust tax payment within 10 years from the tax year when this transaction occurs.

Calculation of Tax Payable

For resident enterprises

Tax payable by resident enterprises equals taxable income amount multiplied by the applicable tax rate and the basic calculation formula is as follows:

*Tax payable by resident enterprise = Taxable income amount ×
Applicable tax rate – Tax deducted and exempted – Creditable tax*

The above formula shows that the amount of tax payable by a resident enterprise is dependent on two factors, namely taxable income amount and applicable tax rate. There are two methods for calculating taxable income amount in the actual process.

Direct calculation method

Under the direct calculation method, the balance after tax-free and tax-exempt income and each deductable item as well as the permitted remedies for losses of the previous year(s) being deducted from an enterprise's total income amount of each tax year shall be the taxable income amount. The calculation formula is the same as that mentioned above i.e.:

*Taxable income amount = Total income – Tax-free income –
Tax-exempt income – Deductable items – Remedies for losses*

Indirect calculation method

Under the indirect calculation method, the taxable income amount is the total accounting profit plus or minus the amount of items adjusted according to the provisions of the tax law. The calculation formula is as follows:

Taxable income amount = Total accounting profit ± Amount of items adjusted

The amount of tax adjustment items includes two aspects: the first is the amount that shall be adjusted due to inconsistency between an enterprise's financial accounting and tax regulations; the second is the amount of tax of an enterprise that is permitted to be deducted according to the provisions of the tax law.

For overseas income

If an enterprise has already paid overseas the enterprise tax for the following income, it may deduct it from the payable tax amount of the current period. The limit of tax credit shall be the payable tax amount on such income calculated under the present law. The part exceeding the limit of tax credit may, during the five subsequent years, be offset from the balance of the limit of tax credit of each year minus the tax amount which ought to be offset in the current year:

1) A resident enterprise's taxable income is sourced from outside the territory of China.

2) Taxable income is obtained outside the territory of China by a non-resident enterprise having organizations or establishments inside the territory of China, and that income has effective connection with those organizations or establishments.

As regards dividends, bonuses and other equity investment gains earned outside the territory of China by a resident enterprise from a foreign enterprise which it controls directly or indirectly, the portion of income tax on this income paid outside the territory of China by the foreign enterprise may be treated as the allowable tax credit of the resident enterprise's overseas income tax amount and be deducted within the limit of tax credit as provided for in the enterprise income tax law.

Direct control as mentioned above means that a resident enterprise directly holds more than 20% of the shares of a foreign enterprise.

Indirect control as mentioned above means that a resident enterprise indirectly holds more than 20% of the shares of a foreign enterprise, and the specific measures for determining this are otherwise formulated by the competent finance and tax authorities under the State Council.

Income tax paid outside the territory of China refers to the tax of the nature of enterprise income tax that should be paid and has been actually paid for an enterprise's income sourced from outside the territory of China according to China's tax laws and regulations on overseas incomes. When an enterprise credits enterprise income tax according to the provisions of the enterprise income tax law, it shall provide relevant tax payment receipts for the tax year issued by tax authorities outside China.

The limit of tax credit refers to the tax payable for an enterprise's gains sourced from outside the territory of China calculated according to the enterprise income tax law and the implementation rules. Unless otherwise specified by the competent finance and tax authorities under the State Council, this credit limit should be calculated respectively for countries (regions) but not for items according to the following formula:

Credit limit = (Total tax payable for gains sourced from both inside and outside the territory of China × The amount of tax payable for the source country) / Total income payable for both inside and outside of the territory of China

The five subsequent years refer to five successive tax years from the following year when an enterprise's income tax amount paid outside the territory of China for incomes sourced from outside the territory of China exceeds the credit limit.

For non-resident enterprises

For income of a non-resident enterprise that has no organization or establishment within the territory of China, or if its income has no actual connection to its organization or establishment inside the territory of China, the taxable income amount shall be calculated according to the following methods:

1) As regards dividends, bonuses and other equity investment gains, interest, rentals and royalties, the taxable income amount shall be the total income amount.

2) As regards income from assigning property, the taxable income amount shall be the balance of the total income amount lessening the net value of the property.

3) As regards other incomes, the taxable income amount shall be calculated according to the methods as mentioned in the preceding two items by analogy.

Net value of the asset refers to the balance of tax base of the asset after depreciation, depletion, amortization and reserve have been deducted as specified.

Tax Preference

Tax preference refers to encouragement through and consideration on taxation given to some special taxpayers and taxation objects and it is an important means of implementing financial policies. With the help of tax preference, the government is able to guide enterprises to engage in industries that are encouraged by the state, encourage and guide social investment, accordingly increase employment, optimize economic structure and resource allocation, regulate revenue allocation, promote economic development, and ultimately realize the macroscopic economic objectives of the state and overall coordinated development of the economy and society.

Tax reduction and exemption

Enterprise income tax may be exempted or reduced for the following income. However the enterprise engaged in items whose development is restricted or prohibited by the state shall not enjoy preference of enterprise income tax.

Income obtained from engagement in the agriculture, forestry, husbandry and fishery industries

Enterprise income tax may be exempted or reduced for an enterprise's income generated from engagement in agriculture, forestry, animal husbandry or fishery.

Income obtained from investments in and business operations of the state-sponsored public infrastructure projects

Important public infrastructure projects supported by the state mentioned in the *Enterprise Income Tax Law* refer to projects involving ports, docks, airports, railways, highways, power stations, water conservancy etc. as specified in the *List of Public Infrastructure Projects Enjoying Enterprise Income Tax Preference*.

For income generated from investment in and business operations of the important public infrastructure projects supported by the state, enterprise income tax shall be exempted for the first three years as of the tax year to which the first revenue coming from production or operation contributes, and shall be levied at half for the fourth to the sixth years.

An enterprise operating and constructing items specified in this provision in contract form and by insourcing, and using them internally, shall not enjoy preferences on enterprise income tax as specified in this provision.

Income obtained from projects on environmental protection, energy and water conservation

For income generated from projects of environmental protection, energy and water saving, enterprise income tax shall be exempted for the first three years as of the tax year to which the first revenue coming from production or operation contributes, and shall be levied at half for the fourth to the sixth years.

Projects of environmental protection, energy and water saving which satisfy the related requirements include projects related to public sewage treatment, public waste treatment, comprehensive development and utilization of biogas, technical innovation for energy saving and emission reduction, and sea water desalinization. Specific conditions for and scope of projects are formulated by the competent finance and tax authorities under the State Council jointly with other relevant departments of the State Council and promulgated after approval by the State Council.

If a project mentioned above enjoying preferences of tax exemption or reduction as specified is assigned within the period of tax exemption or reduction, the assignee may enjoy the specified preferences within the residual period since the date of consignment; if a project is consigned after expiry of the period of tax exemption or reduction, the assignee shall not repeatedly enjoy preferences of this project.

Income obtained from technological transfer

Exemption or reduction of enterprise income tax for the income generated from transfer of technologies which satisfy the related requirements as specified by the enterprise income tax means that enterprise income tax is exempted on not more than RMB5 million of the income obtained from an enterprise's transfer of technology ownership within one tax year, and enterprise income tax is levied by half for the portion over RMB5 million.

Tax preference for hi-tech enterprises

As regards important hi-tech enterprises which need to be supported by the state, enterprise income tax shall be levied at the reduced tax rate of 15%. Important hi-tech enterprises which need to be supported by the state refer to enterprises which have their own core independent intellectual property rights and also meet the conditions as follows:

1)   Their products (services) are within the specified scope of hi-tech sectors mainly under the state support.

2) Expenses for research and development are not less than the specified proportion of sales income.

3) The income from hi-tech products (services) is not less than the specified proportion of total income of the enterprise.

4) The number of scientific and technical personnel is not less than the specified proportion of total workforce.

5) Other conditions specified by the *Measures for the Determination of Hi-Tech Enterprises*.

The *Hi-tech Sectors Mainly under the State Support and the Measures for the Determination of Hi-tech Enterprises* are formulated by the competent science and technology, finance, and tax authorities under the State Council jointly with other relevant departments of the State Council, and promulgated after approval by the State Council.

Tax preference for small and low-profit enterprises

For a small low-profit enterprise, enterprise income tax shall be levied at a reduced tax rate of 20%. Conditions of small low-profit enterprises are as follows:

1) For industrial enterprises, the annual taxable income amount shall not be more than RMB0.3 million, if the number of employees is not more than 100, the total assets shall not be more than RMB30 million.

2) For other enterprises, the annual taxable income amount shall not be more than RMB0.3 million, if the number of employees is not more than 80, the total assets shall not be more than RMB10 million.

Tax preference for additional deductions

Preference for additional deductions mainly includes two aspects as follows.

1) Expenses for research and development refer to an enterprise's expenses for researching and developing new technologies, products and processes. If there is no intangible asset formed and included into the profits and losses of the current period, 50% of the expenses for research and development may be additionally deducted on the basis of deduction according to the facts as specified; if there is an intangible asset formed, the amortization shall be carried out according to 150% of the cost of the intangible asset.

2) For wages paid by an enterprise to disabled employees, an additional deduction of 100% of the wages is implemented based on deduction according to the facts of wages aid to disabled employees. The scope of

disabled persons is as specified in the relevant provisions of the *Law of the People's Republic of China on the Protection of Disabled Persons*. Methods for additional deduction of wages paid to other employees whose employment is encouraged by the state are otherwise specified by the State Council.

Tax preference for startup investment enterprises

If a startup investment enterprise engages in important startup investments which need to be supported and encouraged by the state, it may deduct a certain proportion of the investment amount from the taxable income amount. Deduction from the taxable income amount means that for a startup investment enterprise that has invested in small and medium–sized unlisted hi-tech enterprises in the form of equity investment for more than 2 years, the taxable income amount of this startup investment enterprise may be credited with 70% of its investment amount in the year when the share holding time has been 2 years; if it is insufficient for credit in the same year, it is permitted to be carried forward for deduction in later tax year(s).

Tax preference for accelerated depreciation

In case an enterprise needs to accelerate the depreciation of any fixed asset by virtue of technological progress or for any other reason, it may curtail the term of depreciation or adopt a method for accelerated depreciation. Fixed assets for which curtailing the term of depreciation or adopting a method for accelerated depreciation are allowed include the following:

1) Fixed assets with rapid upgrade and replacement of products by virtue of technological progress.
2) Fixed assets which experience strong vibration and high corrosion throughout the year.

In case of the method of curtailing the term of depreciation, the minimum period of depreciation shall not be less than 60% of the specified period of depreciation; in case of the method of accelerated depreciation, the double declining balance method or sum of the years digits method may be adopted.

Tax preference for downsized income

Preference for downsized income means that as regards the income earned by an enterprise from producing products complying with the industrial policies of the state by comprehensively utilizing resources, the income may be downsized in the calculation of the amount of taxable income.

Comprehensive utilization of resources means that an enterprise uses resources specified in the *List of Comprehensive Utilization of Resources Enjoying Enterprise Income Tax Preference* as main raw materials, and the incomes earned from producing products that are not restricted or forbidden by the state and comply with the industrial policies of the state, shall be downsized to 90% of the total income.

The proportion of raw materials as mentioned above shall not be less than the criterion specified by the *List of Comprehensive Utilization of Resources Enjoying Enterprise Income Tax Preference*.

Tax preference for tax credit

Credit of tax amount means that 10% of the amount of an enterprise's investment in purchasing and using special equipment for protecting the environment, saving energy and water, work safety etc. as specified in the *List of Special Equipment for Protecting the Environment Enjoying Enterprise Income Tax Preference,* the *List of Special Equipment for Saving Energy and Water Enjoying Enterprise Income Tax Preference* and the *List of Special Equipment for Work Safety Enjoying Enterprise Income Tax Preference* may be credited from the amount of tax payable in the same year; if it is insufficient for credit in the same year, it is permitted to be carried forward for credit in the 5 subsequent tax years.

Enterprises enjoying this enterprise income tax preference must actually purchase special equipment as mentioned above and put it into use; enterprises transferring or renting out the purchased special equipment within 5 years shall stop enjoying enterprise income tax preferences and repay the amount of enterprise income tax that has been credited.

The list of enterprise income tax preferences is formulated by the competent finance and tax authorities under the State Council jointly with the other relevant departments of the State Council, and promulgated after approval by the State Council.

For an enterprise engaging in items applicable to different enterprise income tax treatments, the income of preference items shall be separately calculated and the period expenses of the enterprise shall be reasonably amortized; in the case of no separate calculation, no enterprise income tax preference shall be granted.

Tax preference for autonomous regions

The autonomous authorities of an autonomous region of ethnic minorities may determine to reduce or exempt the enterprise income tax for enterprises within the said autonomous region. If the decision on deduction or exemption is made by an autonomous prefecture or county, it shall be reported to the people's governments at all levels.

Autonomous regions refer to autonomous regions, autonomous prefectures and autonomous counties that practice regional national autonomy in accordance with the provisions of the *Law of the People's Republic of China on Regional Autonomy.* However enterprise income tax shall not be reduced or exempted for enterprises engaged in industries restricted or forbidden by the state in autonomous regions.

Tax preference for non-resident enterprises

Non-resident enterprises shall be subject to the enterprise income tax at the reduced rate of 10%. However enterprise income tax may be exempted for the following income:

1) Income from interest of loans provided by a foreign government to the Chinese government.
2) Income from interest of concessional loans provided by international financial institutions to the Chinese government and resident enterprises.
3) Other incomes approved by the State Council.

Tax preference for the development of western regions

Domestically-funded enterprises and foreign-invested enterprises which are set up in the western regions and engage in industries encouraged by the state may enjoy enterprise income tax at the reduced rate of 15% during the period from 2001 to 2010.

Newly established enterprises that are engaged in transport, power, water conservancy, post, and broadcast television in the western regions and the proportion of income from these businesses is more than 70% of the total income of the enterprise may enjoy the following preferential policies on enterprise income tax: enterprise income tax shall be exempted for domestically-funded enterprises from the date of start of production and business operation (equivalent to from the tax year to which the first revenue coming from production or operation contributes) for the first two years as of the tax year to which the first revenue coming from production or operation contributes, and shall be levied at half for the third to the fifth years; enterprise income tax shall be exempted for foreign-invested enterprises with a business period more than 10 years from the profit-making year for the first 2 years and shall be levied at half for the third to the fifth years.

Enterprises set up in the western regions with income obtained from the following business operating activities in tourist attractions and spots determined by competent tourism authorities of people's governments at county level and above in the western development region which accounts for more than 70% of the total operating income may be subject to enterprise income tax at the reduced rate of 15% during 2007–2010: 1) Selling tickets (including admission tickets, through tickets, monthly tickets and annual tickets within tourist attractions and spots and admission tickets for literature and art, sports and other comprehensive performance within an enclosed area with an entrance guard); 2) Providing guide services within tourist attractions with entrance guards; and 3) Providing tourist transport services (including providing services to tourists by various vehicles, pleasure boats, cableways, slideways and other means of transportation) within tourist attractions with entrance guards. For enterprises meeting all the conditions mentioned above, enterprise income tax shall be levied at half for the third to the fifth years and the taxable income amount shall be calculated according to an income tax rate of 15% for implementation by half.

Withholding at Source

Withholding agents

If a non-resident enterprise has no organization or establishment within the territory of China, or its income has no actual connection to its organization or establishment inside the territory of China, the enterprise income tax on the income shall be withheld at source and the withholding agent is the payer. The tax amount shall be withheld by the withholding agent for each payment or payment due when each payment occurs or each payment is due.

The payer refers to the entity or individual directly bearing the obligation of paying relevant sums of money to a non-resident enterprise in accordance with relevant legal provisions or contract stipulations.

Payment includes currency payments and non-currency payments such as cash payment, payment by remittance, payment by bank transfer and payment by equity exchange.

The amount due for payment refers to payables that the payer shall include in relevant costs and expenses according to the principle of accrual basis.

As regards the payable income taxes on the incomes obtained by a non-resident enterprise within the territory of China from undertaking engineering projects or providing labor services, the payer of the project price or remuneration may be designated as the obligatory withholder by the tax authority.

Withholding methods

When the withholding agent withholds tax, the tax amount shall be calculated according to the calculation method aforementioned for the non-resident enterprise.

If the withholding agent fails to withhold tax that should be withheld in accordance with law or to fulfill the withholding obligation, it shall be paid by the enterprise at the place where the income occurs. If the enterprise fails to do so, the tax authority may recover the payable tax of the enterprise from its other income items within the territory of China which ought to be paid by the enterprise.

The place where the income occurs refers to the place of income generation determined according to the principle specified in *Article 1* of the *Regulation on Carrying out the Enterprise Income Tax Law*. If there are more than one places of income generation within the territory of China, the enterprise may choose one for declaring and paying enterprise income tax.

Other incomes of the enterprise obtained within the territory of China refer to incomes obtained from various sources obtained within the territory of China.

When recovering the payable tax of the enterprise, the tax authority shall inform the enterprise of the recovery reason, amount, time limit for payment and payment mode.

A withholding agent shall, within 7 days after the date of withholding, turn over to the state treasury the tax payments which it withholds each time and submit a report form on the enterprise income taxes withheld to the local tax authority.

Administration of Tax Collection

Place of payment

The tax payment place of a resident enterprise shall be its place of registration unless it is otherwise provided for in any tax law or administrative regulation. However, if its place of registration is outside the territory of China, the tax payment place shall be the place at which its actual management organization is located. The place of registration of an enterprise refers to the enterprise's place of domicile registered in accordance with the relevant provisions of the state.

A resident enterprise which has set up operational organizations without legal person status inside the territory of China shall, on a consolidated basis, calculate and pay its enterprise income taxes. When an enterprise calculates and pays its enterprise income taxes, the taxable income amount shall be uniformly accounted; the specific measures shall be otherwise formulated by the competent finance and tax authorities under the State Council.

If a non-resident enterprise sets up an organization or establishment within the territory of China, it shall pay enterprise income tax on its income sourced inside the territory of China and on incomes sourced outside the territory of China but actually connected with the said organization or establishment. If a non-resident enterprise has set up two or more organizations or establishments within the territory of China, it may choose to have its main organization or establishment make a consolidated payment of enterprise income tax upon the examination and approval of the tax authority. If a non-resident enterprise needs to add, merge, move or close an organization or establishment, or stop the business of an organization or establishment after paying enterprise income tax on a consolidated basis upon approval, its main organization or establishment making a consolidated payment of the enterprise shall income tax report to the local authority in advance; the main organization or establishment requiring change of payment of enterprise income tax on a consolidated basis shall be handled in accordance with the provisions of the preceding paragraph.

If a non-resident enterprise has no organization or establishment within the territory of China, or its income has no actual connection to its organization or establishment within the territory of China, the tax payment place shall be the place where the withholding agent is located.

Enterprises may not pay their enterprise income taxes on a consolidated basis unless approved by the State Council.

Assessable period

Enterprise income tax is calculated on an annual basis and paid in advance in monthly or quarterly installments. Tax payments are settled after the end of each tax year, and any payment in excess shall be refunded and any deficiency shall be made up. The tax year for enterprise income tax begins on the first day of January and ends on the thirty-first day of December of the Gregorian calendar. Enterprises commencing business operations in the middle of a tax year or actually operating for a period of less than 12 months in any tax year due to such factors as merger or shutdown shall use the actual period of operations as the tax year. Enterprises that undergo liquidation shall use the period of liquidation as the tax year.

An enterprise shall submit an annual enterprise income tax return for the settlement of tax payments to the tax authority and settle the payable or refundable amount of taxes within 5 months after the end of each year.

If an enterprise terminates its business operations in the middle of a year, it shall apply to the tax authority for calculating and paying the enterprise income taxes of the current period within 60 days after the actual date of termination of its business operations.

Tax declaration

An enterprise shall submit an enterprise income tax return for advance payment to the tax authority and pay the tax in advance within 15 days after the end of the month or quarter in case of advance payment on monthly or quarterly basis.

When an enterprise submits an enterprise income tax return, the financial statements and other related materials shall be attached in accordance with the related provisions.

Before deregistration formalities are handled, an enterprise shall make a declaration to the tax authority and pay the enterprise income taxes based on the income of the liquidation.

Enterprise income taxes to be paid according to the enterprise income tax law shall be calculated based on RMB. If any income is calculated based on a currency other than the RMB, the taxes shall be calculated and paid after such income is converted into RMB.

Regardless of profits or losses of an enterprise within a tax year, it shall submit to the tax authority an enterprise income tax return for advance payment and an annual enterprise income tax return, and financial statements and other related materials shall be attached in accordance with the relevant provisions.

7

Chapter

Individual Income Tax

An Overview

Some concepts

Individual income tax is a kind of tax levied for various taxable incomes obtained by an individual (natural person) and it embodies the allocation relationship between the state and the individual.

In the early years of the new China, the then Government Administration Council promulgated the *Main Points of the Nationwide Implementation of Tax Policy* at the beginning of the 1950s, which specified that individual income was liable for two taxes, namely income tax on interest earnings and income tax on salaries and remunerations. Since China practiced a low wage system then and residents had a low income from wages and salaries, and few of them had bank savings, the income tax on salaries and remunerations was not levied continuously and the income tax on interest earnings was cancelled in 1959 although it has been levied from 1950.

After the 11th Central Committee of the CPC, China began to implement its policy of opening up. Due to more and more foreign investment thereafter, China promulgated the *Individual Income Tax Law of the People's Republic of China* at the 3rd Meeting of the Standing Committee of the 5th NPC on September 10, 1980, which aimed to safeguard China's tax rights and interests In order to better regulate the income level of self-employed individuals and to protect their lawful rights and interests, the State Council promulgated and implemented the *Law of the People's Republic of China on Income Tax of Urban and Rural Self-employed Individuals* on January 7, 1986, and changed the practice of levying industrial and commercial income tax for self-employed individuals which had started after the founding of new China. In view of the increasing improvement in the living standards of ordinary people and the fact that the individual income tax law formulated in 1980 was basically inapplicable to the actual income level of China's residents, the State Council promulgated on September 25, 1986, and implemented on January 1, 1987, the *Individual Income Regulation Tax of the People's Republic of China*. From then on, there were three co-existing taxes for individual income. With the development of the economic situation, the co-existence of three taxes for individual income gradually demonstrated problems such as lack of standardization of the taxation and an unfair tax burden in the course of implementation, which affected the full functions of taxation. The current taxation on individual income tax consists of five amendments. The first amendment is in accordance with the *Decisions Regarding the Amendment (of the Individual Income Tax Law of the People's*

Republic of China) passed at the 4th Session of the Standing Committee of the 8th NPC on October 10, 1993; the second amendment is in accordance with the *Decisions Regarding the Amendment (of the Individual Income Tax Law of the People's Republic of China)* passed at the 11th Session of the Standing Committee of the 9th NPC on August 30, 1999; the third amendment is in accordance with the *Decisions Regarding the Amendment (of the Individual Income Tax Law of the People's Republic of China)* passed at the 18th Session of the Standing Committee of the 10th NPC on October 27, 2005; the fourth amendment is in accordance with the *Decisions Regarding the Amendment (of the Individual Income Tax Law of the People's Republic of China)* passed at the 28th Session of the Standing Committee of the 10th NPC on June 29, 2007; and the fifth amendment is in accordance with the *Decisions Regarding the Amendment (of the Individual Income Tax Law of the People's Republic of China)* passed at the 31st Session of the Standing Committee of the 10th NPC on December 29, 2007.

Characteristics

China's current individual income tax has mainly the following characteristics:

Classification-based levy

Worldwide taxation of individual income tax is usually classified into three kinds, namely taxation of classified income, taxation of comprehensive income and taxation of classified and comprehensive income (taxation of mixed incomes). China currently practices the taxation of classified incomes; in other words, individual incomes taxable are classified into 11 categories to which are applied different deductions of expenses and tax rates. This practice helps to simplify tax payment formalities, strengthen tax collection administration, and control the tax from sources.

Multiple tax rates

Current individual income tax consists of many forms of tax rates. Progressive tax rate and proportional tax rate are implemented respectively according to different taxable incomes. Progressive tax rate is practiced for income obtained from wages and salaries, income obtained from productions of self-employed individuals, and income obtained from contracted or leased operation of enterprises or institutions. Proportional tax rate is practiced for other taxable incomes. The individual income gap is reasonably regulated by many forms of tax rates.

Multiple expense deduction methods

According to the requirements of a tax system with classified incomes, different expense deduction methods are currently adopted for the levy of individual income tax. At present there are many methods of deduction of individual income tax such as deduction of a constant amount, deduction at a constant rate, restricted deduction according to facts, and deduction according to facts. Moreover the expense is not deducted for passive incomes.

Self-declaration and withholding declaration

There are two methods of declaration of individual income tax at present i.e. the taxpayer's self-declaration and the paying unit's withholding declaration. That can be withheld in the payment link of taxable income is withheld by the withholding agent. If there are incomes from wages and salaries obtained from two or more places within the territory of China, incomes obtained from outside the territory of China, and taxable incomes under no withholding agent, the method of self-declaration began to be practiced as of January 1, 2006 for taxpayers with an annual income of more than RMB120,000. This provision not only facilitates collection administration, it also helps to control loss of tax.

Effects

Current individual income tax in China features three effects:

To regulate income distribution gap

Since the implementation of the reform and opening up policies, and especially since the establishment of the socialist market economy system, the gap in individual income China has been expanding continuously and the income distribution gap between regions, between industries, between rural and urban areas, and among residents has increasingly widened. To a large extent his gap resulted from an imperfect system during the period of economic transition. Levy of individual income tax in conformance with the principle of equitable tax burden is able to transfer a part of income of high earners to the state, which is objectively helpful for relieving the contradiction of unfair distribution of social wealth. At the same time, relevant provisions on aspects such as expense deduction criteria and tax rates of individual income tax will not discourage the initiative of high earners for production and business operation and working, and can maintain the fundamental living needs of low earners.

To gather funds for national reconstruction

Today, the tax structure in some Western countries is mainly based on income tax and the scale and proportion of individual income tax are both very large. Individual income tax has a strong regulating power. China's individual income tax is of a relatively low proportion in financial revenue, far lower than the level in developed countries. However with the continuous improvement of the socialist market economy system and development of the economy, the income level of Chinese residents will further improve, the individual income tax system will increasingly improve, and the income from individual income tax will gradually increase and its fund gathering and regulatory functions will certainly assume an important position.

To develop the foreign trade

Taxation is an important tool for safeguarding the rights and interests of the state. The right of taxation is an important part of state sovereignty and any sovereign country shall exercise this power. Levy of individual income tax on foreigners obtaining income in China and Chinese workers overseas embodies China's exercise of tax jurisdiction on the basis of the principle of reciprocity, which safeguards the rights and interests of the state and promotes foreign economic and technical cooperation and exchanges.

Taxpayers

Taxpayers of individual income tax refers to individuals who are domiciled in the People's Republic of China, or who are not domiciled but have resided in the People's Republic of China for at least one year, or who are not domiciled or are domiciled for less than one year but obtain income within the territory of China, including Chinese citizens, individual industrial and commercial businesses, foreign individuals, and compatriots from Hong Kong, Macau and Taiwan.

In accordance with the decisions of the State Council, enterprise income tax is no longer levied for individual proprietorship enterprises and only the individual income tax is levied for income obtained by the investor himself from production and business operations as of January 1, 2000. If the partner of a partnership enterprise is a natural person, individual income tax shall be paid; if the partner is a legal person or other organization, enterprise income tax shall be paid.

Since taxpayers of individual income tax are natural persons and they are usually of complex circumstances in real life, the criteria to use for determining their identities and tax obligations is inevitably an issue for the individual income tax laws of all countries.

Resident taxpayers and non-resident taxpayers

In order to effectively exercise tax jurisdiction, China adopts two international criteria, namely domicile and residence time, to classify resident taxpayers and non-resident taxpayers.

Criteria for determination

The domicile criterion and resident time criterion specified by the tax law are two parallel criteria for determining resident identity, and an individual may be determined as a resident taxpayer once he meets either criterion.

According to domicile

Individuals who have domicile in China means individuals with their permanent registered address, family or economic interests, habitually reside in the People's Republic of China. This criterion adopted in China is based on the "habitual domicile," which refers to the place an individual shall return to with reasons such as study, work and visiting relatives are eliminated and there is no reason to remain in other places, but it does not refer to the place that an individual resides in actually or resides in within a specific period of time. It is an important basis for determining if a taxpayer is a resident or non-resident. The concept of "domicile" mentioned in tax law is different from the normal use of the word "domicile."

According to time span

Resident time refers to the number of days during which an individual actually resides in the territory of one country. In real life, a considerable number of individuals have no domiciles or habitual residences in a country, but stay in this country for a relatively long time and obtain income, so the country should regard them as residents and exercise tax jurisdiction. During the practice of taxation of individual income tax in all countries, the length of residence time of individuals has become a criterion for judging the residence time of residents and non-residents, and China's individual income tax law also adopts this criterion.

Residence for one year within the territory of China means that an individual resides within the territory of China for 365 days within one tax year (from the first day of January to the thirty-first day of December,) and an individual who meets this criterion is a resident taxpayer. When days of residence are calculated, temporary trips out of the territory of China shall be regarded as residence in China and the number of days of residence in China shall not be deducted. "Temporary trips outside the territory of China" as mentioned here shall mean absence from the People's Republic of China for not more than 30 days during a single trip or not more than a cumulative total of 90 days over a number of trips within the same tax year.

Definitions

According to above two criteria, China's resident taxpayers and non-resident taxpayers are defined as follows:

Resident taxpayers

Resident taxpayers refer to individuals who are domiciled in the People's Republic of China or who are not domiciled but have resided in the People's Republic of China for at least one year. They include categories listed as follows:

1) Chinese citizens and foreign nationals who have settled within the territory of China. However this does not include overseas Chinese who have Chinese nationality and have not settled on China's mainland but live abroad, or compatriots living in Hong Kong, Macau and Taiwan.

2) Foreigners, overseas Chinese and compatriots from Hong Kong, Macau and Taiwan who reside in the territory of China from the first day of January to the thirty-first day of December.

3) Investors of sole proprietorship enterprises and partnership enterprises. From January 1, 2000, investors of sole proprietorship enterprises and partnership enterprises also became individual income taxpayers.

Non-resident taxpayers

Non-resident taxpayers refer to individuals who are not domiciled in the People's Republic of China or who are not domiciled but have resided in the People's Republic of China for less than one year. In other words, non-resident taxpayers refers to individuals whose habitual residence is not within the territory of China, or who do not reside in China or reside for less than one year within the territory of China within one tax year.

Moreover, it should be noted that for individuals with no domicile within the territory of China should conform to the following provisions on the number of days of residence in China and days of actual work in China as of July 1, 2004:

The first is for judging tax obligations and calculating the number of days of residence in China. For individuals who have no domicile in China, the number of days of their residence in China shall be calculated, in order to judge their tax obligations according to tax law and agreed or arranged provisions based on their days of actual stay. The day when these individuals mentioned above enter, leave or go back and forth to China shall be regarded as one day and calculated into the number of days of actual stay in China.

The second is as for the day when an individual enters or leave China and the calculation of the period of actual working in China. For individuals who take positions at organizations both within the territory of China and overseas, or only at overseas organizations but have no domicile within the territory of China, the day when they enter, leave or go back and forth to China shall be regarded as half a day and calculated into the number of days of actual stay within the territory of China.

Tax obligations of resident and non-resident taxpayers

Taxpayers shoulder unlimited obligations to pay tax and they shall pay individual income tax for any income taxable whether it originates from inside or outside of the territory of China.

Non-resident taxpayers shoulder limited obligations to pay tax and they shall pay individual income tax only for the taxable income that originates from inside the territory of China.

The concept of "within the territory of China" in current tax law refers only to China's mainland and does not include Hong Kong, Macau and Taiwan for the time being.

Source of income

Determination

Determination of source of income is an important basis for determining whether individual income tax should be levied for this income. The issue of determination of source of income is relatively unimportant for resident taxpayers since they shoulder unlimited obligations to pay tax. However the determination of source of income is very important for non-resident taxpayers since they shall pay tax only for income originating within the territory of China. For China's individual income tax, the determination of source of income shall be based on embodying the essence of the economic activities and meanwhile the principle of facilitating collection and administration by tax authorities shall be followed, as specified in details as follows:

1) For income obtained from wages and salaries, the source is the location of the companies, enterprises, government-sponsored institutions, organizations, groups, and schools at which the taxpayers work or are employed.

2) For income obtained from production and business operations, the source is the location where production and business activities are realized.

3) For income obtained from remuneration of labor services, the source is the location where taxpayers actually provide labor services.

4) For income obtained from transfer of real estates, the source is the location of the real estate; for incomes from transfer of movable property, the place of source is the location where the transfer is realized.

5) For income obtained from lease of property, the sources are the locations where the leased property is used.

6) For income obtained from interest, dividends and bonuses, the source is the location of the enterprises, bodies and organizations paying interest, dividends and bonuses.

7) For income obtained from royalties, the source is the location where the royalties are used.

Income obtained within the territory of China

1) Income obtained from wages and salaries obtained from working at entities or economic organizations such as companies, enterprises, government-sponsored institutions, organizations, groups, and schools.

2) Income obtained from remuneration of labor services provided within the territory of China.

3) Income obtained from production and business activities within the territory of China.

4) Income obtained from a lessee's use of property leased by an individual within the territory of China.

5) Income obtained from transfer of assets such as houses, buildings and land use rights, and other assets within the territory of China.

6) Income obtained from royalties for using patent rights, proprietary technology, trademark rights, copyright and other concessionary rights within the territory of China.

7)   Income obtained from interest, dividends and bonuses obtained from companies, enterprises or economic organizations within the territory of China due to holding various bonds, stocks and stock rights of China.

It shall be noted that the place of source of income is a concept different from the place of payment of income and that they are sometimes consistent with each other and sometimes inconsistent.

Provisions on relief of tax obligations of residents and non-residents

These provisions on relief of tax obligations are mainly designed for individuals who possess no domicile within the territory of China but continuously or accumulatively reside within the territory of China within one tax year.

For individuals who have no domicile within the territory of China but continuously or accumulatively reside within the territory of China for not more than 90 or 183 days, individual income tax is levied if their income obtained from wages and salaries obtained within the territory of China are paid by employers outside of the territory of China but not by organizations set up within the territory of China by the employers. They only pay tax for income obtained from wages and salaries paid by enterprises or individual employers or organizations within the territory of China during the period of their actual working within the territory of China.

For individuals who have no domicile within the territory of China but continuously or accumulatively reside within the territory of China for more than 90 or 183 days but less than one year, they shall pay individual income tax whether their incomes obtained within the territory of China are paid by enterprises or individual employers within the territory of China or by those outside of the territory of China. For incomes from wages and salaries obtained by individuals from outside the territory of China, individual income tax is not paid except for individuals who act as a director or senior manager at enterprises within the territory of China and fulfill duties overseas, and are paid by enterprises within the territory of China for their director's fees or wages and salaries. For income obtained from wages and salaries paid by enterprises within the territory of China for acting as a director or senior manager at enterprises within the territory of China, the individuals shall declare to pay individual income tax whether they fulfill duties outside the territory of China or not.

For individuals whose income obtained from wages and salaries are paid by overseas employers but not by organizations with the territory of China, their monthly tax payable shall be declared and paid as scheduled if it is specified in advance that they continuously or accumulatively reside within the territory of China for more than 90 or 183 days within one tax year. In case it is unable to specify this in advance, their monthly tax payable may be declared and paid together with that of the preceding month(s) within 7 days of the month following the date when 90 days or 183 days are reached.

Individuals who have no domicile within the territory of China but reside within the territory of China for more than one year but less than five years shall pay individual income tax completely for all incomes from within the territory of China. For income from outside the territory of China, individual income tax maybe paid only for the portion paid by companies, enterprises, other economic organizations or individuals within the territory of China upon the approval of the competent tax authorities. If individuals as mentioned above temporarily leave the territory of China during their residence period, tax is only paid for the portion of income obtained from wages and salaries during this period paid by enterprises or individual employers within the territory of China.

Individuals who have no domicile within the territory of China but reside within the territory of China for more than five years shall pay individual income tax completely for all incomes from within and outside the territory of China from the sixth year.

Items of Taxable Income

The classification-based taxation is applicable to China's individual income tax, and all incomes of taxpayers are classified, according to their income sources, into 11 categories with different provisions on levy of individual income tax.

Wages and salaries

This refers to wages, salaries, bonuses, year-end extras, profit shares, subsidies, allowances and other incomes related to the tenure of an office or employment that is derived by individuals by virtue of the tenure of an office or employment.

Generally, income obtained from wages and salaries belong to income obtained from dependent individual labors. Dependent individual labors mean that the labor of individuals is appointed and arranged by others and that they accept management, and persons (excluding owners of private enterprises) working at or serving in companies, factories, administrative units and government-sponsored institutions. Their labor remunerations obtained from the organizations mentioned above are embodied in the form of wages and salaries. Among this category of remunerations, subjects of income of wages and salaries are slightly different. Generally, income of laborers (workers) directly engaged in production, business operations or services are called wages i.e. the incomes of the so-called "blue collar" workers; incomes of laborers (public servants) directly engaged in social public service or management are called salaries i.e. the incomes of the so-called "white collar" workers. However, in the course of actual legislation, all countries merge wages and salaries into one item for levying individual income tax for the purpose of simple and easy implementation.

Besides wages and salaries, bonuses, year-end extras, profit shares, subsidies and allowances are also within the scope of wages and salaries. For year-end extras and profit shares regardless of categories and obtainment status, tax is levied by treating them as income obtained from wages and salaries. However, subsidies and allowances have some exceptions.

Tax law specifies that tax is not levied for some subsidies and allowances that do not belong to wages and salaries. These items include:

1) Subsidies for the only child of one couple.

2) Subsidies, margin of allowances and subsidies for non-staple foods that are not included in the gross payroll under the pay system of public servants,

3) Allowance for child nurseries.

4) Subsidies for travel expenses and allowances for meals. Allowances for meals refer to overtime meal allowances that are received by individuals who work in urban or suburban areas on business and are not able to eat at the work unit or return for meals according to provisions of the Ministry of Finance, the actual number of overdue meals and the specified criterion. Subsidies and allowances paid by the enterprise to employees in the name of allowances for overall meals shall not be included.

Bonuses refer to those with a nature of wages or salaries and the scope of tax-free bonuses is otherwise specified in tax law. For the issue of levy on income obtained by those retiring early in the course of an enterprise's downsizing for efficiency and the institutional reform of administrative units, government-sponsored institutions and social groups, current provisions are as follows:

1) Wages and salaries obtained from the original work unit by an early retired individual within the period from handling early retirement formalities to the statutory retirement age do not belong to retirement wages and shall be liable for individual income tax according to the

item of "income of wages and salaries."

2) An individual's lump-sum income obtained from the original work unit after finishing early retiring formalities shall be averaged for the months from finishing the early retirement formalities to retirement age, merged with the income from "wages and salaries" received in current month, and the applicable tax rate is determined based on the balance of this income after deducting the expenses criterion of the current month, and individual income tax will be levied according to the applicable tax rate and the sum of wages and salaries in the current month and the lump-sum income after deducting the expenses criterion.

3) If an individual is reemployed during the period from finishing early retirement formalities to retirement age, the income from "wages and salaries" obtained after reemployment shall be merged with the income from "wages and salaries" obtained from the original work unit in the same month and the individual shall declare and pay individual income tax to the competent tax authorities.

For a taxi business unit practicing contracting or leasing of a single taxi for taxi drivers, the income of taxi drivers from business operation for passengers and cargoes shall be levied according to income from wages and salaries.

Production and business operations of self-employed individuals

This can be further categorized into:

1) Income derived by self-employed individuals who engage in industry, handicrafts, construction, transportation, commerce, the food and beverage industry, the service industry, the repair industry, and production and business in other industries.

2) Income derived by individuals who engage in the provision of educational, medical, advisory and other services activities for considerations, with approval from the relevant government authorities and after having obtained licenses,.

3) All taxable income related to the production and business operations of the above self-employed individuals.

4) Income of an individual from lottery sales on a commission basis shall be liable for individual income tax according to the item "income obtained from production and business operations of self-employed individuals."

5) Other incomes derived by individuals from engagement in self-employed activities.

Other taxable incomes irrelevant to production and business activities obtained by self-employed individuals and individuals engaged in production and business shall be liable for individual income tax according to relevant provisions on other taxable items.

Income obtained by taxi drivers of individual operation shall be liable for individual income tax according to the item of income from production and business operations of self-employed individuals.

If the taxi belongs to an individual but is subordinate to a taxi operating unit or an enterprise or institution to which the driver pays management fees, or the taxi operating unit transfers taxi ownership to the driver, the income obtained by the driver from operation and business related to passengers and cargoes shall be liable for tax according to the item of income from production and business operations of self-employed individuals.

Other taxable incomes irrelevant to production and business activities obtained by self-employed individuals and individuals engaged in production and business shall be liable for individual income tax according to the relevant provisions on other taxable items. For example, income of interest on bank deposits and stock dividends from overseas investment shall be separately liable for individual income tax according to the provisions on the tax item "dividend, interest and bonuses."

If the individual investor of a sole proprietorship enterprise or a partnership enterprise pays with business capital for himself, his family members and relevant persons non-productive expenditures irrelevant to enterprise production and business and financial expenditures such as purchase of cars and houses, this shall be regarded as the enterprise's allocation of profit for an individual investor and shall be merged into the individual investor's income from production and business. Individual income tax shall be levied according to the item of "income from production and business operations of self-employed individuals."

Insourcing and leasing activities

This refers to income obtained from an individual's insourcing or leasing activities. Insourcing can be classified into many categories such as for production and business operations, procurement, sales, and construction and installation.

Remuneration of labor services

This refers to income obtained from an individual's independent labor services.

These labor services include the following:

1) *Design*. Various construction and process designs etc. provided to the client according to his requirements.

2) *Decoration*. Consigned works of decoration and ornamentation of objects to improve their appearance or make them suitable for special applications.

3) *Installation*. Engineering businesses such as assembly and emplacement of machines and devices, installation of auxiliary facilities connected with machines and devices, insulation, corrosion prevention, heat preservation and painting according to the client's requirements.

4) *Drawing*. Drawing plans, stereograms and perspectives on a certain scale based on the image, volume, area and distance, etc. of a material object or a concept on a commission basis.

5) *Assay*. Businesses of examining components and properties of an object by physical or chemical methods on a commission basis.

6) *Testing*. Businesses of testing properties and quality of articles by instruments or meters or other means for the client.

7) *Medical treatment*. Businesses of medicares such as diagnoses and treatments.

8) *Law*. Acting as a defense counsel and legal adviser, writing statements of defense and bills of complaint on a commission basis.

9) *Accounting*. Businesses of accounting on a commission basis.

10) *Consultancy*. Businesses of providing answers and explanations to the client's questions on politics, economy, science and technology, law, accounting and culture.

11) *Lectures*. Businesses of giving lectures, reports and introductions as invited (employed).

12) *News*. Businesses of providing news information and writing news.

13) *Broadcast*. Labor services engaged in broadcast.

14) *Translation*. Businesses of translation (including interpretation) of Chinese and foreign languages or words on a commission basis.

15) *Examination and approval of manuscripts*. Businesses of examining and checking written or graphic works.

16) *Calligraphy and painting*. Businesses of calligraphy, painting and inscription according to the client's requirements or of one's own accord.

17) *Sculpture*. Businesses of sculpting seals, stamps, plaques, stone tablets, jade articles and sculptures for the clients.

18) *Movies and television*. Businesses related to shooting movies and television programs by acting as actors, directors, sound engineers,

dressers, props personnel, producers and photographers in the movies and television programs as invited or employed.

19) *Sound recording*. Services recording audio tapes for the client by recording devices or services for being recorded as invited for speech, singing or interview.

20) *Video recording*. Services recording images and programs for the client by video recording devices or services for being recorded as invited for performance and interview.

21) *Play*. Businesses related to participating in artistic plays such as drama, music, dance and Chinese folk arts.

22) *Performance*. Businesses related to performances of acrobatics, sports, martial arts, bodybuilding, fashionable dress, breathing exercises and other skillful performance activities.

23) *Advertisement*. Businesses related to propaganda and relevant services for issues such as introduction of commodities, business service items, culture and sports programs or announcement and declaration by using books, newspapers, magazines, broadcasting, television, cinema, posters, guideposts, display windows, neon lamps, light boxes, walls and other media.

24) *Exhibition*. Businesses of holding exhibition activities such as painting and calligraphy exhibitions, photographic exhibitions, miniature gardening exhibitions, stamp exhibitions, personal collection exhibitions and exhibitions of flowers, birds, insects and fish.

25) *Technical services*. Businesses of providing technical guidance and aid based on professional skills.

26) *Introduction services*. Businesses of introducing the supply party and the demand party for negotiations or introducing products and business servicing items.

27) *Brokering services*. Brokering businesses to help to realize various transactions by introducing both parties and providing labor services.

28) *Agency services*.

29) *Other services*. Labor services other than the 28 items of labor services as mentioned above.

Remuneration of authors

This refers to income derived by individuals by virtue of the publication of their work in books, newspapers and periodicals.

Income obtained from this remuneration is distinguished from income obtained from remuneration of personal services such as translation, manuscripts examination and approval, painting and calligraphy, and is regarded as a separate item of taxable income and liable for a light tax burden, this is mainly based on the following considerations: income from author's remuneration is a kind of intellectual and artistic product requiring high intelligence for its creation; income from author's remuneration is lower than remuneration of personal services.

Royalties

This refers to the individual's income obtained from providing right of use of patent rights, trademark rights, copyrights, non-patented technology and other chartered rights. Incomes from providing right of use of copyright do not include income from author's remuneration.

Patent right refers to the exclusive right of the patent applicant or his successor in title for implementing invention and creation within a specific period of time which is granted by the patent administration department under the State Council in accordance with the laws. For patent rights, many countries only list the income obtained from provision to others for use into the royalties, but list the income obtained from transfer of patent rights as a taxation object of capital gains tax. Since there is no capital gains tax in China, the income of individuals from providing and transferring patent rights are listed into royalties for levying individual income tax.

Trademark refers to the exclusive right to use a trademark enjoyed by trademark registrants. Copyright refers to an author's exclusive right to literary, artistic and scientific works. For an individual's income obtained from providing or transferring trademark rights, copyrights, proprietary technology and technical know-how, individual income tax shall be paid in accordance with the laws.

Interest, dividends and bonuses

This refers to income obtained from interest, dividends and bonuses that are derived by individuals by virtue of their possession of creditor's rights and share rights. Interest refers to interest that is derived by individuals by virtue of their possession of creditor's rights, including the interest on deposits, the interest on loans and the interest on bonds. Individual income tax shall be levied on the income obtained from an individual's interest except the interest from government debts and financial bonds issued by the state. Dividends and bonuses refer to an individual's dividends and bonuses obtained from possession of stock rights. Income obtained from dividends and bonuses shall be liable for individual income tax unless otherwise specified.

If the individual investor of enterprises other than a sole proprietorship enterprise or a partnership enterprise pays with business capital for himself, his family members or relevant persons nonproductive expenditures irrelevant to enterprise production and business and financial expenditures such as purchase of cars and houses, this shall be regarded as the enterprise's allocation of profit for the individual investor and shall be liable for individual income tax according to the item of "income obtained from interest, dividends and bonuses." The aforementioned expenditures of an enterprise are not permitted to be deducted before individual income tax.

Property leasing

This refers to income derived by individuals from the lease of buildings, land use rights, machinery, equipment, means of transportation and other property.

Income obtained by individuals from subleasing property belongs to the incidence of taxation of "income obtained from lease of property" and the individual income tax shall be paid by the sub-lessor. Taxpayers shall be determined based on equity security; in case there is no equity security, the competent tax authorities shall make a determination according to actual conditions. If the owner of the title dies and there is rental income from lease of the property during the period of handling the formalities of succession of title, the taxpayers shall be the individuals receiving the rent.

Transfer of assets

This refers to income obtained derived by individuals from the assignment of negotiable securities, share rights, structures, land use rights, machinery, equipment, means of transportation and other property.

Individual sales of self-owned houses

According to the provisions of the *Individual Income Tax Law of the People's Republic of China*, individual income tax shall be levied for income obtained from an individual's sales of self-owned houses according to the item of "income obtained from transfer of property."

1) The amount of taxable income from an individual's sales of self-owned houses shall be determined according to the following principles:
   - If an individual sells self-owned houses other than purchased public

houses, the amount of taxable income shall be determined according to the relevant provisions of the individual income tax law.

- If an individual sells a purchased public house, the amount of taxable income shall be the balance of the sale price of the purchased public house less the price of economically affordable housing of the same area standard, the price originally paid for areas more than the housing area standard, income return paid to the financial unit or original property unit, and reasonable expenses as specified by the tax law.

  Purchased public house refers to public housing purchased at cost price (or standard price) by an urban employee in accordance with the policies and provisions on reform of the urban housing system specified by the state and people's governments at county level and above.

  The price of economically affordable housing shall be determined according to the criterion specified by people's governments at county level and above.

- For housing built cooperatively by employees by collecting funds at cost price (or standard price), housing projects for low-income urban residents, economically affordable housing, and relocation housing, the taxable amount of income shall be determined with reference to that of the purchased public house.

2) In order to encourage individuals to change and purchase housing, the payable individual income tax for selling existing housing may be totally or partially exempted according to the value of newly purchased housing for taxpayers who sell self-owned housing and plan to purchase new housing at market price within one year after the sale. Specific provisions are as follows:

   - Individual income tax payable for an individual's sale of existing housing shall be paid to the local competent tax authorities in the form of security of tax payment before handling the formalities of transfer of title. When tax authorities collect security of tax payment, they shall officially issue "Receipts for Security of Tax Payment" to taxpayers and put the receipts into a special account for reserve.

   - In case an individual purchases housing again within one year after the sale of the current housing, the security of tax payment shall be refunded according to the amount of money for purchase. If the amount of money for purchase is more than or equals to the amount for sale of the original housing (if the original housing is purchased public housing, the amount of sale of the original housing shall be less the income return paid to the financial unit or original property unit according to provisions, similar hereinafter), the security of tax payment shall be refunded completely; if the amount of money for purchase is less than the amount for sale of the original housing, the security of tax payment shall be refunded according to the ratio of the amount of money for purchase to the amount for sale of the original housing and the balance shall be turned over to the treasury as individual income tax.

- If case an individual does not purchase housing again within one year after the sale of the current housing, all the security of tax payment shall be turned over to the treasury as individual income tax.
- If an individual applies for refund of the security of tax payment, he shall provide the competent tax authorities with legal and effective contracts of housing sale and purchase and other relevant evidence required, and shall not handle formalities on refunding the security of tax payment before the competent tax authorities check and confirm them.
- An individual selling and purchasing housing involving two or more administrative regions and meeting conditions of refund of the security of tax payment shall apply to the local competent tax authorities where the security was paid for refund.

3) If enterprise institutions sell self-built housing to staff at a price lower than the cost of purchase or construction, individual income tax shall conform to the following provisions.

- In accordance with the relevant provisions of policies on reform of the housing system, if state organs, enterprise institutions and other organizations (hereinafter referred to as units) sell public housing to staff at a cost price of the housing reform specified by the local people's government at or above the county level during the period of housing system reform, staff income obtained from the price difference because the housing reform cost price they paid is lower than housing construction cost price or market price shall be liable for individual income tax.
- Besides the scenarios mentioned above, if units sell housing to staff at a price lower than the cost price of purchase or construction, the part of price difference paid less by staff belongs to taxable income for individual income tax, which shall be paid according to the item of "income obtained from wages and salaries" in accordance with

relevant provisions of the *Individual Income Tax Law of the People's Republic of China* and its implementing rules. The "part of price difference" refers to the difference between the price actually paid by staff for purchasing housing and the cost price of housing purchase or construction.

- For the aforementioned taxable income obtained by staff, individual income tax shall be calculated and levied by referring to the taxation method of annual lump-sum award specified by the *Circular of the State Administration on Issues of Calculation and Levy of Individual Income Tax for Individual's Annual Lump-sum Award*; in other words, the amount of all incomes is divided by 12 and then the applicable tax rate and quick calculation deduction are determined according to the quotient and the table of tax rates specified by the individual income tax law. The tax to be paid is then calculated according to the amount of all incomes, applicable tax rate and quick calculation deduction and provisions of the tax law. Tax not previously levied is no longer pursued and the tax is not refunded.

4) Exemption of individual income tax is continued for the income obtained by an individual for assignment of the sole living house used for more than 5 years.

5) In order to guarantee full and correct implementation of policies on individual income tax related to transfer of housing, administrative departments for real estate transactions at all levels shall enhance cooperation and collaboration with the tax authorities, and the administrative departments for real estate transactions shall provide timely information on local real estate transactions to the competent tax authorities.

6) If an individual whose certificate of title to a house property bears the name of one owner for his current self-owned house purchases a house at a market price in the name of the property owner's spouse, or both husband and wife, within one year after sale of the house, full or partial exemption of individual income tax may be granted for the income of the property owner from sale of the house in accordance with *Article 3* of the *Circular of the Ministry of Finance the State Administration of Taxation and the Ministry of Construction on Issues Concerning the Levy of Individual Income Tax on the Income from an Individual's Sales of Houses*; if a house is purchased again at the market price in the name of others, no exemption of individual income tax shall be granted for the income from the property owner's sale of house.

Transfer of equities

According to the provisions of the *Regulations for the Implementation of the Individual Income Tax Law of the People's Republic of China*, measures for the levy and collection of individual income tax on income from the transfer of shares shall be separately formulated by the Ministry of Finance and implemented upon approval by the State Council. The State Council has decided that individual income tax is temporarily not levied on income from the transfer of shares.

Transfer of shares of quantitative assets

Individual income tax is temporarily suspended for quantitative assets obtained by staff in the form of shares when a collective ownership enterprise is restructured into a joint-stock cooperative enterprise; when an individual transfers shares, the balance of the amount of income from transfer deducting the expenditures actually paid by an individual for obtaining the shares and reasonable transfer expense shall be liable for individual income tax according to the item of "income obtained from transfer of assets."

Contingent income

This refers to income derived by individuals from winning awards, prizes and lotteries, and other incomes of an occasional nature. Winning awards refers to awards won by participating in various contests and winning a place in the finals; winning prizes and lotteries refers to awards obtained after specified procedures of drawing lots for participating in various rewarding activities related to sales, savings and purchase of lotteries. Individual income tax payable for contingent incomes shall be withheld by the award issuing units or organizations.

Other incomes

Except aforementioned Individual incomes taxable, other individual incomes necessary for taxation shall be determined by the financial departments of the State Council. Incomes derived by individuals for whom the taxable items are difficult to be determined shall be decided by the competent tax authorities.

Tax Rates

Tax rates of individual income are specified for different taxable income events.

Wages and salaries

Nine grades of progressive tax rates are applied to income obtained from wages and salaries, and tax rates range from 5% to 45% (see Table 7.1).

Table 7.1. **Tax rates of individual income obtained from wages and salaries**

Grade	Monthly taxable income	Tax rate (%)	Quick calculation deduction
1	For not more than RMB500	5	0
2	For more than RMB500 but not more than RMB2,000	10	25
3	For more than RMB2,000 but not more than RMB5,000	15	125
4	For more than RMB5,000 but not more than RMB20,000	20	375
5	For more than RMB20,000 but not more than RMB40,000	25	1,375
6	For more than RMB40,000 but not more than RMB60,000	30	3,375
7	For more than RMB60,000 but not more than RMB80,000	35	6,375
8	For more than RMB80,000 but not more than RMB100,000	40	10,375
9	For more than RMB100,000	45	15,375

Self-employed individuals and insourcing and leasing activities

Five grades of progressive tax rates ranging from 5% to 35% are applicable to income obtained from production and business operations of self-employed individuals and to income obtained from insourcing and leasing operations of enterprises or institutions (see Table 7.2).

Table 7.2. Tax rates of income obtained from production and business operations of self-employed individuals and income obtained from insourcing and leasing activities

Grade	Yearly taxable income	Tax rate (%)	Quick calculation deduction
1	For not more than RMB5,000	5	0
2	For more than RMB5,000 but not more than RMB10,000	10	250
3	For more than RMB10,000 but not more than RMB30,000	20	1,250
4	The portion more than RMB30,000 but not more than RMB50,000	30	4,250
5	For more than RMB50,000	35	6,750

Remuneration of labor services

A proportional tax rate of 20% is applied to incomes from remuneration of labor services. Excessively high incomes from remuneration of labor services shall be subject to an additional levy according to specific measures formulated by the State Council.

According to the provisions of the *Regulations for the Implementation of the Individual Income Tax Law of the People's Republic of China*, "a specific payment of income from remuneration of personal service is excessively high" shall mean a payment received as remuneration of personal services with an amount of taxable income exceeding RMB20,000. That part of taxable income which exceeds RMB20,000 but does not exceed RMB50,000 shall, after the amount of tax payable is calculated in accordance with the tax law, be subject to an additional levy at the rate of 50% of the amount of tax payable. That part which exceeds RMB50,000 shall be subject to an additional levy at the rate of 100% of tax payable. Therefore three graded progressive tax rates of 20%, 30% and 40% are applicable to income obtained from remuneration of labor services (see Table 7.3).

Table 7.3.   Tax rates of income obtained from remuneration of labor services

Grade	Taxable income	Tax rate (%)	Quick calculation deduction
1	For more than RMB20,000	20	0
2	For more than RMB20,000 but not more than RMB50,000	30	2,000
3	For more than RMB50,000	40	7,000

Remuneration of authors

A proportional tax rate of 20% is applied to income obtained from author's remuneration and 30% tax is reduced from the taxable amount. Therefore the actual tax rate is 14%.

Royalties, interest, dividends and bonuses, lease of property, contingent income, and other incomes

A proportional tax rate of 20% is applied to income obtained from royalties, income obtained from interest, dividends and bonuses, incomes from lease of property, contingent income, and other incomes.

According to the approval of the State Council and the decisions of the Ministry of Finance and the State Administration of Taxation, individual income tax was exempted for income obtained from interest on savings deposits as of October 9, 2008. However, it should be noted that exemption is not granted for all interest obtained after October 9, 2008, but that tax shall be calculated according to different time slots of interest on savings deposits, and income obtained from interest generated before October 9, 2008, shall still be liable for tax according to the relevant provisions.

It should be noted that there are different distribution modes since there are many forms of insourcing (leasing) business operations, therefore different tax rates are applied to income obtained by contractors and lessees according to the provisions of the insourcing or leasing contract (agreement) as shown in the following two scenarios:

1) The contractor and the lessee have no proprietary right to the enterprise operation achievements; however, if they obtain some incomes as specified according to the contract (agreement), a nine grade progressive tax rate ranging from 5% to 45% is applicable to the incomes according to the item of income obtained from "wages and salaries."

2) If the contractor and the lessee possess the enterprise operation achievements after paying some expenses to the party issuing the contract or the leasor as specified by the contract (agreement), a five grade progressive tax rate ranging from 5% to 35% is applicable to their incomes according to the item of incomes from insourcing or leasing operations of enterprises or institutions.

Tax Base

Determination

The tax law specifies that seven sources of income i.e. remuneration of labor services, author's remuneration, royalties, interest, dividends and bonuses, lease of property, contingent income and other incomes shall be taxed on the amount received in each time period. Correct division of "time" is of great significance for correctly calculating individual income tax and guaranteeing state tax revenue. Specific provisions are as follows:

Remuneration of labor services

Income obtained from remuneration of labor services are specified as follows according to the characteristics of different items of labor services:
1) If there is only a lump-sum income, the time is determined according to the time of obtainment of this income.
2) If there is income continuously obtained from one task, the time is determined according to the obtainment within one month.

Remuneration of authors

In the case of income obtained from author's remuneration, the time is determined according to the income derived on each instance of publication. The specific subdivisions are as follows:
1) Income obtained from republication of the same works shall be regarded as another remuneration of the purposes of levy of individual income tax.
2) If one work is serialized in installments in newspapers or periodicals before publication, or it is published before it is serialized in installments in newspapers or periodicals, it shall be regarded as twice the remuneration of the purposes of levy of income tax. In other words, serialization in installments is regarded as one time, and publication as another.
3) For income obtained from serialization in installments in newspapers or

periodicals, all incomes obtained after accomplishment of serialization in installments are merged for a one time levy of individual income tax.

4) Income obtained from author's remuneration paid in advance or in several installments for publication of a work shall be merged into one time for calculation.

5) The remuneration added due to increase of page(s) after publication of a works shall be merged with that obtained previously into one time for the calculation and levy of individual income tax.

Royalties

In the case of income obtained from royalties, one time is the incomes derived from each transfer of a certain use right. A taxpayer may have more than one concessionary right and the right of use of each concessionary right may be provided to others more than once. Therefore it is specified that the "time" of income from royalties is determined by the obtainment of income from each transfer of each right of use. If the income for this time of transfer is paid in installments, the income of all times shall be added into one for the levy of individual income tax.

Lease of property

In the case of income obtained from the lease of property, the time is determined according to the obtainment of income during one month.

Interest, dividends and bonuses

In the case of income obtained from interest, dividends and bonuses, the time is determined according to the obtainment of income when interest, dividends or bonuses are paid.

Contingent income

In the case of contingent income, the time is determined according to the obtainment of each income.

Other incomes

In the case of other incomes, the time is determined according to the obtainment of each income.

Criteria of expense deduction

Since individual income tax is levied on classified incomes, the criteria of expense deduction are specified according to different classifications. There are three deduction methods for different incomes i.e. the fixed-amount method, the fixed-rate method and the accounting method, as detailed as follows:

Wages and salaries

For income obtained from wages and salaries, the amount of taxable income shall be the balance of the monthly income after deducting an expense of RMB2,000 (RMB1,600 each month before March 1, 2008).

Scope of additional expense deduction

The *Regulations for the Implementation of the Individual Income Tax Law of the People's Republic of China* have special provisions on the applicable scope and criteria of additional expense deductions:

Applicable scope of additional expense deductions is as follows.

1) Foreigners working in foreign investment enterprises and foreign enterprises in the People's Republic of China.

2) Foreign experts hired to work in enterprises, institutions, social organizations and government agencies in the People's Republic of China and receiving income obtained from wages and salaries.

3) Individuals who are domiciled in the People's Republic of China and derive income from wages and salaries by virtue of their tenure of an office or employment outside the People's Republic of China.

4) Others determined by the Ministry of Finance and obtaining income obtained from wages and salaries.

Criteria of additional expense deduction

Monthly income obtained from wages and salaries of persons as mentioned above is subject to an additional deduction of RMB2,800 after the initial deduction of RMB2,000.

For overseas Chinese and compatriots from Hong Kong, Macau and Taiwan, the above criteria for additional expense deductions shall be referred to for implementation.

Production and business operations of self-employed individuals

For the income obtained from production and business operations of self-employed individuals, the amount of taxable income shall be the balance of total income in each tax year after deducting costs, expenses and losses. Costs and expenses mean all direct expenditures, indirect expenses allocated as costs, as well as marketing expenses, administrative expenses and financial expenses incurred by taxpayers while engaging in production and business; losses mean all non-operating expenditures incurred by taxpayers in the course of production and business.

If a taxpayer engaging in production or business fails to provide complete and accurate tax information and is unable to correctly calculate the amount of taxable income, his amount of taxable income shall be determined by the competent tax authorities.

For the investor of a sole proprietorship enterprise, the amount of taxable income shall be all the income from production and business; for investors of a partnership enterprise, the amount of taxable income of each investor shall be determined according to all the income from production and business and the allocation proportion stipulated in the partnership agreement. If the partnership agreement does not stipulate the allocation proportion, the amount of taxable income of each investor shall be determined by averagely according all the income from production and business and the number of partners.

Income obtained from production and business as mentioned include the incomes allocated by the enterprise to the investors and the income (profit) retained by the enterprise in that year.

Insourcing and leasing

For income obtained from insourcing and leasing operations of enterprises or institutions, the amount of taxable income shall be the balance of total income in each tax year after deducting necessary expenses. "Total income in each tax year" refers to the operating profit shared according to the provisions of the contract of insourcing and leasing operations and the income of wages and salaries; "deducting necessary expenses" refers to monthly deduction of RMB2,000.

Remuneration of labor services, remuneration of authors, royalties and lease of property

For incomes from remuneration of labor services, income obtained from author's remuneration, incomes from royalties and incomes for lease of property, the expense deduction is RMB800 if the income of each time is not more than RMB4,000 and 20% of expense is deducted if the income of each time is more than RMB4,000. The balance is the amount of taxable income.

Transfer of property

For income obtained from transfer of property, the amount of taxable income shall be the balance of income obtained from transfer of property after deducting the original value of the property and reasonable expenses.

The original value refers to:

1) In the case of negotiable securities, the price for which they were purchased and related expenses paid according to regulations at the time of purchase;

2) In the case of buildings, the construction expenses or purchase price, and other related expenses;

3) In the case of land use rights, the amount paid to acquire the land use rights, land development expenses and other related expenses;

4) In the case of machinery, equipment, vehicles and vessels, the purchase, freight, installation expenses and other related expenses; and

5) In the case of other property, the original value shall be determined by reference to the above methods.

If a taxpayer fails to provide complete and accurate vouchers concerning the original value of the property and is unable to correctly calculate the original value of the property, the original value of the property shall be determined by the tax authorities in charge. Reasonable expenses refer to relevant expenses paid in accordance with regulations at the time of sale.

Interest, dividends and bonuses, contingent income, and other incomes

For income obtained from interest, dividends and bonuses, contingent income and other incomes, the amount of taxable incomes is the amount of incomes each time.

Special provisions on the tax base

1) In the case of donations by individuals of their incomes to educational and other public welfare undertakings, and to areas suffering from serious natural disasters or poverty, through social organizations or government agencies in the People's Republic of China, that part of the amount of donations which does not exceed 30% of the amount of taxable income declared by the taxpayer may be deducted from the amount of taxable income.

2) Welfare and relief donations by taxpayers through the China Population Welfare Foundation and the China Guanghua Science and Technology

Foundation may be deducted within 30% of the amount of taxable income.

3) In the case of donations by individuals to rural compulsory education through non-profit social organizations and state organs, full deduction is permitted from the amount of income before payment of individual income tax. The scope of rural compulsory education refers to primary schools and junior high schools and special schools belonging to this age group that are established in rural townships (excluding townships where the municipal government of a county or a county-level city is located) and in villages by governments and social organizations. The taxpayer's donations to schools which combine rural compulsory education with high school education also enjoy this pre-tax deduction.

4) In the case of donations by individuals to the Red Cross through non-profit social organizations and state organizations, full deduction is permitted from the amount of income before payment of individual income tax.

5) If an individual's income is used as expenditures for supporting non-affiliated scientific research institutions, colleges and universities to research and develop new products, technologies and processes, full deduction is permitted from the amount of income during the levy of individual income tax in the next month (for incomes from wages and salaries) or next time (for incomes levied in each time) or the current year (for incomes levied yearly), and the insufficient part, if any, shall not be carried forward.

Tax Deduction on Overseas Income

For resident taxpayers, the central government levies tax on their incomes from both inside and outside the territory of China according to the tax jurisdiction on the principle of nationality. However, for a resident's income from a foreign country, income tax of the relevant country has generally been paid or imposed. The tax law makes provisions on the deduction of the amount of tax that has been paid for overseas income in order to avoid the problem of duplicate taxation in two countries for one transnational income of a taxpayer, and to safeguard the rights and interests of China.

The tax law specifies that for a taxpayer's income obtained overseas, individual income tax paid overseas is permitted to be deducted from the amount of tax payable. However, the deduction amount shall not be more than the amount of tax payable for the taxpayer's overseas income which is calculated according to the provisions of China's tax law.

The amount of individual income tax paid overseas means the amount of income tax payable, and actually paid, on income derived by a taxpayer from sources outside the People's Republic of China, according to the laws of the country or regions from which that income was derived.

The amount of tax payable calculated according to the provisions of China's tax law means the amount of tax payable on income derived by a taxpayer from sources outside the People's Republic of China. It shall be computed separately for each different country or region and for each different taxable item, in accordance with the standards for the deduction of expenses and the applicable tax rates stipulated in the tax law. The sum of the amounts of tax payable in the different taxable items within the same country or region shall be the limit for deductions for that country or region, or in other words, the limit for deductions shall be calculated separately for each country and item.

If the actual amount of individual income tax paid by a taxpayer in a country or region outside the People's Republic of China is less than the limit for deductions for that country or region computed in accordance with the provisions of the preceding paragraph, the balance shall be paid in the People's Republic of China. If the amount exceeds the limit for deductions for that country or area, the excess portion may not be deducted from the amount of tax payable for that tax year. However, the excess portion may be deducted from any unused portion of the limit for deductions for that country or region during subsequent tax years, for a maximum period of five years.

When taxpayers apply for approval to deduct the amounts of individual income tax paid outside the People's Republic of China in accordance with the tax law, they shall provide the original tax payment receipts issued by the tax authorities outside the People's Republic of China.

In order to ensure correct calculation of the limit for deductions and reasonable deduction of tax paid outside the People's Republic of China, the tax law specifies that individuals who are domiciled in the People's Republic of China, or who are not domiciled but have resided in the People's Republic of China for at least one year, shall calculate the amounts of tax payable for income derived from sources within and outside the People's Republic of China separately.

Calculation of Tax Payable

For wages and salaries

Formula for calculation of tax payable for income obtained from wages and salaries is as follows:

Tax payable = Payable income × Applicable tax rate – Quick calculation deduction
= (Monthly income amount – RMB2,000 or RMB4,000) × Applicable tax rate – Quick calculation deduction

For Production and business operations of self-employed individuals

Formula for calculation of tax payable for income of self-employed individuals is follows:

Tax payable = Payable income × Applicable tax rate – Quick calculation deduction
= (Total annual income – costs, expenses and losses) × Applicable tax rate – Quick calculation deduction

Calculation on self-employed individuals

1) In the case of levy of individual income tax in accordance with laws for income obtained from production and business of self-employed individuals, the expense deduction criterion is unified at RMB24,000 each year (RMB2,000 each month).

2) Reasonable expenditures of wages and salaries actually paid by self-employed individuals to their employees are permitted for pre-tax deduction of cost and expenses.

3) Expenditures on labor union funds, employee welfare expenses and employee education expenses appropriated and paid by self-employed individuals shall be respectively deducted according to the facts from the total amount of wages and salaries within the criteria of rates of 2%, 14% and 2.5%.

4) The part of a self-employed industrial and commercial household's advertising expenses and business promotion fees not more than 15% of sales (business) income in the same year is permitted to be deducted according to the facts; the excess is permitted to be carried forward for deduction in the later tax year(s).

5) The self-employed industrial and commercial household's business reception expenses within each tax year related to production and business operation are deducted at 60% of the actual amount, but the deduction shall not be more than 5% of the sales (business) income in the same year.

6) Individual income tax shall be levied on incomes of self-employed individuals for their dedicated engagement in industries of planting, fish

breeding and poultry raising, stockbreeding and fishery. In the case of engagement in the aforementioned four industries where incomes are of separate accounting, the incomes shall be merged with the income obtained from production and business of other industries according to the principles of preceding paragraphs; if their incomes cannot be separately accounted, individual income tax shall be levied for all the incomes.

7) Other taxable incomes irrelevant to production and business activities obtained by individual self-employed individuals and individuals engaged in production and business shall be liable for individual income tax according to the relevant provisions on other taxable items.

Calculation on sole proprietorship enterprises and partnership enterprises

For income of sole proprietorship enterprises and partnership enterprises obtained from production and business operations, there are two methods as follows for calculating the individual payable income tax.

Audit collection

1) When individual income tax is levied in accordance with the laws on the income of self-employed individuals, sole proprietorship enterprises, and partnership enterprises obtained from production and business, their expense deduction criterion is unified at RMB24,000 each year (RMB2,000 each month).

2) Reasonable expenditures on wages and salaries actually paid by self-employed individuals, sole proprietorship enterprises and partnership enterprises to their employees are permitted for pre-tax deduction of cost and expenses according to the facts.

3) Expenditures of labor union funds, employee welfare expenses and employee education expenses appropriated and paid by self-employed individuals, sole proprietorship enterprises and partnership enterprises shall be deducted according to the facts from the total amount of wages and salaries within the criteria of rates 2%, 14% and 2.5%.

4) Advertising expenses and business promotion fees of a self-employed industrial and commercial household, sole proprietorship enterprise and partnership enterprise of not more than 15% of the sales (business) income in the same year is permitted to be deducted according to the facts; the excess may be carried forward for deduction in later tax year(s).

5) The business reception expenses of a self-employed industrial and commercial household, sole proprietorship enterprise and partnership

enterprise within each tax year related to production and business operations may be deducted for 60% of the actual amount, but the deduction shall not be more than 5% of the sales (business) income in the same year.

6) The amount of income taxable of a partnership enterprise is determined as follows.

A partnership enterprise refers to a partnership enterprise set up in accordance with the laws and administrative regulations of China. The taxpayer of a partnership enterprise is all partners. If the partner of a partnership enterprise is a natural person, individual income tax shall be paid; if the partner is a legal person or other organization, enterprise income tax shall be paid.

The principle of "allocation before taxation" is practiced for a partnership enterprise's income obtained from production and business and for other incomes. Income obtained from production and business and other incomes include the incomes that are allocated by a partnership enterprise to all partners and the incomes (profits) retained by the enterprise in the same year. The amount of taxable income of a partner in a partnership enterprise shall be determined according to some principles. First, the amount of income taxable of a partner in a partnership enterprise shall be determined according to incomes from production and business of the partnership enterprise and other incomes, and the allocation proportion as stipulated in the partnership agreement. Second, if the proportion is not stipulated or the stipulation is undefined, the amount of income taxable shall be determined according to incomes from production and business of the partnership enterprise and other incomes and the allocation proportion negotiated by the partners. Third, if no settlement can be reached through negotiation, the amount of income taxable shall be determined according to income obtained from production and business of the partnership enterprise and other incomes, and the proportion of subscribed capital. Fourth, if it is impossible to determine the proportion of subscribed capital, the amount of income taxable shall be averagely determined according to income obtained from production and business of the partnership enterprise and other incomes, and the number of partners. The partnership agreement shall not stipulate allocation of all profits to an only some of the partners.

Verification collection

Verification collection models include collection of fixed amount, collection according to verified taxable income rate, and other reasonable collection modes.

In the case of collection according to verified taxable income rate, the calculation formula for of tax payable is as follows:

Tax payable= Taxable income amount × Applicable tax rate

Taxable income = Total income × Taxable income rate
= Expenditure of costs and expenses / (1-Taxable income rate) × Taxable income rate

Taxable income rates for individual income tax are shown in Table 7.4.

Table 7.4.   Taxable income rates of individual income tax

Industry	Rate of taxable income (%)
Industry, transportation and commerce	5–20
Construction and real estate development	7–20
Catering services	7–25
Entertainment	20–40
Other industries	10–30

For insourcing and leasing operations

The calculation for individual income tax payable for income from insourcing and leasing operations of enterprises or institutions is as follows:

Tax payable = Payable income × Applicable tax rate – Quick calculation deduction
= (Yearly income – Necessary expenses) × Applicable tax rate – Quick calculation deduction

For income from insourcing and leasing operations of enterprises or institutions, the amount of taxable income shall be the balance of total incomes in each tax year after deducting necessary expenses.

If the period of insourcing and leasing operations is less than one year within one tax year, the tax year shall be the actual period of operations.

Quick calculation deduction applicable to the income obtained from insourcing and leasing operations of enterprises or institutions is the same as that applicable to the income obtained from production and business operations of self-employed individuals.

For remuneration of labor services

For income obtained from remuneration of labor services, the calculation method of individual income tax payable is as follows:

In case of income each time less than RMB4,000:

Tax payable = Taxable income × Applicable tax rate
        = (Income each time – 800) ×20%

In case of income each time more than RMB4,000:

Tax payable = Taxable income × Applicable tax rate
        = Income each time × (1 – 20%) × 20%

In case of the amount of income taxable each time more than RMB20,000:

Tax payable = Payable income × Applicable tax rate – Quick calculation deduction
        = Income amount each time × (1 – 20%) × Applicable tax rate –
        Quick calculation deduction

For remuneration of authors

The calculation of tax payable for income obtained from remuneration of authors is as follows:

In case of income each time less than RMB4,000:

Tax payable = Taxable income × Applicable tax rate × (1 – 30%)
        = (Per time income – 800) × 20% × (1 – 30%)

In case of income each time more than RMB4,000:

Tax payable = Taxable income × Applicable tax rate × (1 – 30%)
        = Income each time × (1 – 20%) × 20% × (1 – 30%)

For royalties

For income obtained from royalties, the calculation for individual income tax payable is as follows:

In case of income each time less than RMB4,000:

Tax payable = Taxable income × Applicable tax rate
        = (Income each time – RMB800) × 20%

In case of income each time more than RMB4,000:

Tax payable = Taxable income × Applicable tax rate
        = Income each time × (1 – 20%) × 20%

For interest, dividends and bonuses

For income from interest, dividends and bonuses, the calculation formula of individual income tax payable is as follows:

Tax payable = Taxable income × Applicable tax rate
          = Income each time ×120%× Interest 5%

For lease of property

For income obtained from lease of property, the amount of income taxable is generally the balance of the income obtained by an individual each time after a fixed-amount or fixed-rate deduction of specified expenses. If the income each time is not more than RMB4,000, the expense is deducted by a fixed amount of RMB800; if the income each time is more than RMB4,000, the expense is deducted at a fixed rate of 20%.The income from the lease of property each time is the income obtained within one month.

When the amount of taxable income from lease of property is determined, tax and extra charges of education funds paid in the course of a taxpayer's lease of property may be deducted from the income from lease of property by providing tax payment receipts. As well as specified expenses and relevant taxes and charges, items permitted to be deducted also include repair costs actually assumed by the taxpayer for leasing the property if effective and correct credence can be provided. The repair cost permitted to be deducted is limited to RMB800 each time and that not deducted in one time is permitted to be deducted continually next time until it is completely deducted.

For the income from an individual's lease of property, the following expenses may be deducted in sequence when individual income tax is calculated and paid:

1) Taxes paid in the course of lease of property.
2) Repair costs actually assumed by the taxpayer for leasing the property.
3) Expense deduction criterion specified by the tax law.

The calculation of tax payable is as follows:

In case of income each time (month) less than RMB4,000:

Taxable income = Income each time (month) – Item permitted to be deducted – Repair cost (not more than RMB800) – RMB800

In case of income each time (month) more than RMB4,000:

Taxable income = [Income each time (month) – Item permitted to be deducted – Repair cost (not more than RMB800)] × (1 – 20%)

The calculation of tax payable is as follows:

Tax payable = Taxable income × Applicable tax rate
= Income each time ×20%

For transfer of property

The calculation of tax payable for income obtained from transfer of property is as follows:

Tax payable = Taxable income × Applicable tax rate
= (Total income – Original value of the property – Reasonable taxes)
×20%

For contingent income

The formula for calculation of tax payable for contingent income is as follows:

Tax payable = Taxable income × Applicable tax rate
= Income each time × 20%

For other incomes

The formula for calculation of tax payable for other incomes is as follows:

Tax payable = Taxable income × Applicable tax rate
= Income each time × 20%

Special provisions

Provisions on the levy for an individual's annual lump-sum award

A lump-sum award refers to the lump-sum award granted to employees by withholding agents such as administrative organs, enterprises or institutions in accordance with the economic benefit of the whole year and the comprehensive appraisal of the employee's achievements in the whole year. A lump-sum award also includes the year-end extras and the annual pay and performance pay cleared by organizations practicing an annual salary system and performance pay measures in accordance with the appraisal results.

A taxpayer's annual lump-sum award is separately regarded as the wages and salaries of one month for calculating and paying tax and the tax is withheld by withholding agents as of January 1, 2005, according to the following tax calculation measures:

1) The annual lump-sum award obtained by an employee in one month is divided by 12, and then the applicable tax rate and quick calculation deduction are determined according to the quotient.

   If an employee's income from wages and salaries is less than the expense deduction amount specified by the tax law in the month when the annual lump-sum award is granted, the applicable tax rate and quick calculation deduction shall be determined according to the methods mentioned above on the basis of the balance of the annual lump-sum award less "the difference between an employee's income from wages and salaries in the month and the amount of expense deduction.

2) Tax is calculated and levied for an employee's lump-sum award obtained in the month according to the specified applicable tax rate and quick calculation deduction according to the following formulas:

   • If an employee's income from wages and salaries in the month is more than (or equals to) the expense deduction amount specified by tax law, the applicable formula is as follows:

   Tax payable = An employee's annual lump-sum award obtained in the month × Applicable tax rate – Quick calculation deduction

   • If an employee's income from wages and salaries in the month is less than the expense deduction amount specified by tax law, the applicable formula is as follows:

   Tax payable = (An employee's annual lump-sum award obtained in the month – The difference between an employee's income from wages and salaries in the month and the amount of expense deduction) × Applicable tax rate – Quick calculation deduction

3) Within one tax year, this tax calculation method is permitted to be used only once for each taxpayer.

4) For organizations practicing an annual salary system and performance pay, the annual salary and performance pay granted to an individual at the year's end shall conform to the provisions on annual lump-sum award.

5) Various awards other than the annual lump-sum award obtained by an employee, such as half-year award, quarterly award, overtime award, advanced individual award and attendance award shall be uniformly merged with the income from wages and salaries in the month and the individual income tax shall be paid in accordance with the provisions of the tax law.

Exemption of individual income tax on the individual's income obtained from severance payment

The "severance payment" that can be exempted for individual income tax as mentioned in *Clause 7* of *Article 4* of the *Individual Income Tax law of the People's Republic of China* refers to the severance payment received by an individual which meets the retirement and resignation conditions specified by the *Provisional Regulations of the State Council on Retirement and Resignation of Workers* and accords with the criterion for severance payment specified by these provisional regulations.

An individual's income from severance payment not meeting the retirement and resignation conditions and severance payment criterion specified by the above regulations shall belong to the income from wages and salaries related to their tenure of an office or employment, and the individual income tax shall be calculated and paid according to the income from wages and salaries in the month of obtainment. However in view of the fact that the severance payment, as the employer's economic compensation to the retired and resigned, is usually granted once and for all in a larger amount and that the retired and resigned may have no regular income within a period, the higher income from severance payment obtained by the retired and resigned once and for all may be regarded as obtainment of lump-sum income of wages and salaries of several months in accordance with the relevant provisions on calculation and levy of tax on income from wages and salaries as specified by the *Individual Income Tax Law of People's Republic of China* and be divided into wages of several months based on the criterion of original total income from monthly wages and salaries. The amount of payable individual income tax and the tax amount shall be calculated after the income of salaries is obtained. However, if the income is divided according to the abovementioned method into wages and salaries of more than 6 months, it shall be calculated according to the average division for 6 months. Tax payable for all the income of an individual from severance payment shall be withheld by the original employer when paying severance payment and turned over to the treasury within 7 days of the next month. In case of tenure of an office and employment again within 6 months after an individual's resignation, the income of an individual from severance payment for which individual income tax has been paid is no longer merged with the income from wages or salaries obtained from tenure of an office and employment again for calculation and repayment of individual income tax.

Taxation methods for an individual's economic compensation obtained from discharging the labor contract

On the basis of the spirit of the *Circular of the Ministry of Finance and the State Administration of Taxation on the Issue of Exemption of Individual Income Tax on the Income from Lump-sum Compensation of an Individual from Discharging the Labor Contract with the Employer*, and the *Circular of the State Administration of Taxation on the Issue of Exemption of Individual Income Tax on the Income from Lump-sum Compensation of an Worker of a State-owned Enterprise from Discharging the Labor Contract*, the provisions below shall be followed as of October 1, 2001:

1) If an enterprise declares bankruptcy in accordance with the law, individual income tax is exempted for the income from the lump-sum settlement allowance obtained by the enterprise employee.

2) For an individual's lump-sum compensation obtained from discharging the labor contract with the employer (including economic compensation, living allowance and other subsidies granted by the employer), individual income tax is exempted for the part of income which is within 3 times the local workers' average wages of the last year; the part more than 3 times the local average wages may be regarded as lump-sum income of wages and salaries of many months and may be averagely calculated within a specific period. The method is as follows: the part of lump-sum compensation income more than 3 times the local average wages is divided by the number of years an individual has worked in the enterprise (it is 12 if the number is more than 12) and the quotient is used as an individual's income from monthly wages and salaries for calculating and paying individual income tax according to the provisions of the tax law. In case of an individual taking tenure of an office and employment again after the discharge of the labor contract, the lump-sum compensation income for which tax has been paid is no longer merged with the income from wages or salaries obtained from tenure of an office and employment again for calculation and repayment of individual income tax.

3) Public accumulation funds for housing construction, medical insurance, endowment insurance and unemployment insurance paid by an individual according to the actual proportions specified by state and local governments while receiving the income of lump-sum compensation may be deducted when individual income tax is calculated and levied for the income of lump-sum compensation.

Taxation on an individual's income obtained from subsidies for official business transport and communications

For an individual's income from subsidies for business transport and communications obtained from the reform of official business transport and communications, individual income tax is calculated and levied according to the item of income from "wages and salaries" after deduction of a certain criterion of official business expense. If monthly distributed, they are merged into the income from "wages and salaries" of the same month for calculating and levying individual income tax; if not monthly distributed, they are divided into the corresponding month and merged with income from "wages and salaries" of that month for calculating and levying individual income tax.

The deduction criterion of official business expenses shall be calculated by the local provincial tax administrations according to the investigation into the actual expenses of official business transport and communications of taxpayers, determined after submittal to the provincial people's governments for approval, and submitted to the State Administration of Taxation for filing.

Taxation on unemployment insurance premium

Unemployment insurance premium actually paid by urban enterprises and institutions and their employees according to the proportion specified in the *Regulations on Unemployment Insurance* shall not be included into the employee's income from wages and salaries in the current period and is exempted for individual income tax; in the case of unemployment insurance premium paid by a larger proportion, the excess part shall be included into the employee's income from wages and salaries in the current period and the individual income tax shall be calculated and levied in accordance with the laws.

Individual income tax is exempted for the unemployment insurance premium received by the unemployed meeting conditions specified in the *Regulations on Unemployment Insurance*.

Taxation on income obtained from wages and salaries of Chinese workers in foreign-invested enterprises, foreign enterprises and foreign institutions in China

If incomes obtained from wages and salaries of Chinese workers in foreign-invested enterprises, foreign enterprises and foreign institutions in China are respectively paid by the employment unit and dispatch unit, the paying units shall withhold individual income tax in accordance with the provisions of the tax law. Meanwhile, the amount of taxable income of taxpayers shall be the balance of all monthly income from wages and salaries after deducting specified expenses according to the provisions of the tax law. In order to facilitate tax collection administration, the method of deducting expenses by one party is used in the case where wages and salaries are respectively paid by the employment unit and dispatch unit. In other words, expenses shall be deducted from wages and salaries paid only by the employment unit according to the provisions of the tax law, and individual income tax shall be calculated and withheld, while expenses shall not be deducted from wages and salaries paid by the dispatch unit and the payment amount shall be directly used for determining the applicable tax rate and for calculating and withholding individual income tax.

The taxpayers abovementioned shall hold original salary description certificates, salary sheets and original tax payment receipts provided by both paying units, choose one local tax authority to which to permanently declare monthly income obtained from wages and salaries, settle the individual income tax on the income from wages and salaries, and any payment in excess shall be refunded and any deficiency shall be made up. The specific time limit for declaration shall be determined by the tax authorities of the province, autonomous region or municipality directly under the central government.

Measures for levy of individual income tax on an individual's income obtain from purchase and disposal of creditor's rights

In accordance with the relevant provisions of the *Individual Income Tax Law of the People's Republic of China*, an individual shall pay individual income tax in accordance with the item of "income obtained from transfer of property or the income obtained from claiming creditor's rights through the relevant judicial or administrative procedures after purchase of creditor's rights by tender offering, auction, or other means.

If an individual obtains "packaged" right of credit in the way abovementioned and only disposes a part of the creditor's rights, the amount of taxable income shall be determined according to the following measures:

1) The income from disposal of a part of creditor's rights each time is regarded as the income from transfer of property each time for the purpose of levying tax.

2) The taxable income shall be determined according to the sum of estimated value or market value of monetary assets and non-monetary

assets obtained by an individual.

3) The cost of disposal of creditor's rights (i.e. the original value of the asset) shall be calculated according to the following formula:

Cost of disposal of creditor's rights at current time = Actual expenditure of an individual for purchasing "packaged" creditor's rights × [Book value of creditor's rights disposed currently (or value announced by auction agencies) / Book value of "packaged" creditor's right (or value announced by auction agencies)]

4) Auction bidding charges, litigation fees, audit assessment fees and reasonably paid taxes in the course of an individual's purchase and disposal of creditor's rights are permitted to be deducted when calculating individual income tax.

Measures for levying individual income tax for taxpayer's repossession of transferred stock equity

If the stock equity transfer contract has been fulfilled, and the change of stock equity has been registered, and the income has been obtained, the transferor's income from stock equity transfer shall be levied for individual income tax according to the laws. After the act of transfer, both parties sign and enforce an agreement on terminating the original stock equity transfer contract and returning stock equities, and this is another act of transfer of stock equity and the individual income tax levied for the preceding transfer acts are not refunded.

If the stock equity transfer contract is not fully fulfilled and the original stock equity transfer contract is terminated, and the transferred stock equity is recovered at the origin due to execution of decisions of the commission of arbitration on termination of stock equity transfer contract and supplementary agreements, the return on equity does not exist within the termination of stock equity transfer relationship since the stock equity transfer act has not been fully realized, and the taxpayer shall not pay individual income tax in accordance with the relevant provisions of the individual income tax law and the tax administration law.

Tax Preference

Preference on exemption of individual income tax

1) Awards for science, education, technology, culture, health, sports and environmental protection granted by provincial people's governments,

departments of the State Council, the Chinese People's Liberation Army (PLA) organizations above corps level, and foreign organizations and international organizations.

2) Interest on national debts and state-issued financial bonds.

3) Subsidies and allowances issued under state uniform provisions.

4) Welfare benefits, survivors pensions and relief payments.

5) Insurance indemnities.

6) Soldier's military severance payment and demobilization payment.

7) Settlement payment, severance payment, retirement payment and retirement living allowances received by public servants and workers under state uniform provisions.

8) Public accumulation funds for housing construction, medical insurance, endowment insurance and unemployment insurance paid by an enterprise or an individual according to the provisions of provincial people's governments shall not be included into the individual's income from wages and salaries in the current period, and the individual income tax shall be exempted, while the excess paid outside of the specified proportion shall be liable for individual income tax.

Individual income tax is levied when an individual receives originally collected and saved public accumulation funds for housing construction, medical insurance, or endowment insurance.

9) Individual income tax is exempted for an individual's income from interest on education savings and other special savings or special funds of a nature defined by the financial department of the State Council.

10) Issues on awards granted to those who act heroically. Individual income tax is exempted, upon approval of the competent tax authorities, for awards or prizes granted to those who act heroically by foundations or organizations of a similar nature which are approved by people's governments at or above county level or the competent authorities of people's governments at or above county level which have their own organizational constitutions.

11) Individual income tax is exempted for the income from service charges for withholding interest tax of tax officers engaged in withholding work at depository institutions.

12) Individual income tax is exempted for awards of students obtained from participating in the activities of the "Little Changjiang Scientists."

13) The income derived by the diplomatic agents, consular officers and other personnel who are exempt from tax under the provisions of the relevant laws of China.

The income mentioned above shall mean income that is tax-exempt under the *Regulations of the People's Republic of China Concerning Diplomatic Privileges and Immunities* and the *Regulations of the People's Republic of China Concerning Consular Privileges and Immunities.*

14) The income exempted from tax as stipulated in the international conventions to which the Chinese government is a party and in agreements it has signed.

Preference on reduction of individual income tax

In case of any of the following circumstances, individual income tax may be reduced as approved:

1) Income of the disabled, the aged without families, and the families of revolutionary martyrs.
2) Great loss caused by serious natural disasters.
3) Other circumstances of tax reduction approved by the financial department of the State Council.

The ranges and periods of the reductions of above-mentioned tax reduction items shall be stipulated by the people's governments at all levels.

Preference on temporary exemption of individual income tax

1) Housing subsidies, food allowances, moving fees and laundry fees obtained by individual foreigners in the non-cash form or in the form of being reimbursed for what they spend.
2) Subsidies for both domestic and overseas business trips obtained by individual foreigners according to reasonable criteria.
3) The part of relative visiting fees, language training fees, children's education fees obtained by individual foreigners which is examined and approved to be reasonable by the local tax authorities. Relative visiting fees enjoying exemption of individual income tax are limited to expenses for taking transport vehicles of an individual foreigner incurred between his employment location and home place (including the place where his spouse or parents live) no more than twice a year.
4) Income from dividends and bonuses of individual foreigners gained from foreign-invested enterprises.
5) Bonuses of individuals gained from reporting and assisting to uncover illegal and criminal acts.
6) Service charges for withholding gained as specified by individuals for

providing withholding formalities.

7) Income obtained by an individual for assignment of the sole living house used for more than 5 years.

8) For senior experts (experts and scholars enjoying special government allowances) who reach retirement age but genuinely need to postpone retirement in accordance with the *Provisional Regulations of the State Council on Issues Concerning Retirement of Senior Experts* and the *Circular of the General Office of the State Council on Issues Concerning Examination and Approval of Suspension of Retirement of Outstanding Senior Experts*, their income from wages and salaries during the extended period for retirement shall be regarded as retirement salary and be exempted from individual income tax.

9) Individual income tax is exempted for the income gained by foreign experts from wages and salaries who meet any of the following circumstances:
   - Foreign experts directly sent to work in China by the World Bank according to its special loan agreement.
   - Experts directly sent to work in China by the organizations under the United Nations.
   - Experts working in China for projects aided by the United Nations.
   - Experts sent by a donor country to China for work for that country's projects of non-reimbursable assistance.
   - Cultural and educational experts coming to China for the signed cultural exchange projects by two governments for not more than 2 years and whose incomes obtained from wages and salaries are paid by their countries.
   - Cultural and educational experts coming to China for international exchange projects for not more than 2 years and whose incomes obtained from wages and salaries are paid by their countries.
   - Experts coming to China for scientific research according to agreements of non-governmental organizations whose incomes obtained from wages and salaries are paid by their countries.

10) Individual income tax on incomes obtained from shares and cash paid to holders of tradable shares in the form of consideration by holders of non-tradable shares in the course of equity division reform shall be temporarily exempted.

11) Individual income tax is exempted for removal compensation obtained by relocation households according to the criteria specified by the state on measures for administration of demolition and relocation of urban houses.

12) Individual income tax is temporarily exempted for an individual's

income from a single scratch-and-win receipt of not more than RMB800; if the income is more than RMB800, individual income tax shall be levied based on the total amount according to the item of "contingent income" as specified by the individual income tax law.

Administration of Tax Collection

Tax withholding and remittal

Withholding agents and scope of withholding and remittal

Withholding agents

Entities or individuals paying individual income tax such as enterprises (companies), government-sponsored institutions, governmental agencies, mass organizations, army troops and the self-employed are withholding agents of individual income tax.

Institutions stationed in China do not include embassies and consulates, the United Nations and other international institutions enjoying diplomatic privileges and immunities in accordance with laws.

Scope of withholding and remittal

Individual income tax shall be withheld if a withholding agent pays an individual with the following incomes:
1) Income obtained from wages and salaries;
2) Income obtained from insourcing and leasing operations of enterprises or institutions;
3) Income obtained from remuneration of labor services;
4) Income obtained from author's remuneration;
5) Income obtained from royalties;
6) Income obtained from interest, dividends and bonuses;
7) Income obtained from lease of property;
8) Income obtained from transfer of property;
9) Contingent income;
10) Other incomes liable for tax determined by the financial departments under the State Council.

Obligations and responsibilities of withholding agents

1) Withholding agents shall appoint personnel of financial and accounting

departments paying taxable income or other departments as the taxation personnel who handle specific processes of withholding individual income tax.

Relevant leaders of withholding agents shall provide conveniences for withholding activities and support taxation personnel to fulfill their obligations; if a change of taxation personal is confirmed, this shall be reported in a timely way to the competent tax authorities.

2) Legal representatives (or the main responsible persons of an organization) of withholding agents, responsible persons of financial and accounting departments and relevant personnel actually handling withholding activities jointly bear legal liabilities for fulfilling withholding obligations in accordance with the laws.

3) If different departments of the same withholding agent pay taxable incomes, they shall report these to taxation personnel for summarizing.

4) When withholding agents withhold tax, they must issue withholding certificates uniformly printed by tax authorities to taxpayers and indicate in detail the taxpayer's personal information such as name, work unit, home address, resident identification card number or passport number (in case of neither of these certificates, another certificate of effective evidence is acceptable). If it is inconvenient to issuing withholding certificates for income obtained from wages and salaries and income obtained from interest, dividends and bonuses due to the number of taxpayers, withholding certificates may not be issued upon approval of the competent tax authorities but taxpayers must be informed in a certain form that tax has been withheld. If a taxpayer demands a withholding certificate from a withholding agent in order to hold a tax clearance certificate, the withholding agent shall not refuse.

Withholding agents shall actively apply to tax authorities to receive withholding certificates to withhold tax based on these. Taxpayers may refuse informal withholding certificates.

5) For tax that should be withheld but is not withheld by a withholding agent, the tax payable shall still be paid by the taxpayer and a fine imposed on the withholding agent of more than 50% of the tax amount that should have been withheld but has not been withheld and up to 3 times that amount.

6) The withholding agent shall keep a withholding account book, correctly reflect withholding of individual income tax, and fill in the report form of withheld individual income tax and other relevant materials accurately.

Time limit of withholding

A withholding agent shall, within 7 days after the date of withholding, turn over to the state treasury the tax payments which it withholds every month and submit the report form of withheld individual income tax, withholding certificate, table of details of the taxpayer containing such details as the payer's name, work unit, position, income and tax amount, and other relevant materials requested by tax authorities.

Once it has been investigated and verified that a withholding agent has not submitted tax payment information, or has submitted false tax payment information, in violation of the above provisions, the sum of money paid to individuals that was not reflected in the table of details of individual income shall not be deducted as cost when the amount of taxable income of a withholding agent is calculated.

If a withholding agent is unable to submit the report form of withheld individual income tax and other relevant materials as scheduled due to special difficulties, they may be declared later with the approval of the tax authorities at a county level.

Self-declaration

Taxpayers

1) Taxpayers with an annual income of more than RMB120,000 as of January 1, 2006.
2) Taxpayers obtaining income of wages and salaries obtained from two or more places within the territory of China.
3) Taxpayers obtaining income from outside the territory of China.
4) There is no withholding agent although taxable income is obtained.
5) Other circumstances as regulated by the State Council.

Taxpayers with an annual income of more than RMB120,000 shall report and pay tax to the local competent tax authorities after the end of a tax year in accordance with these regulations no matter whether they have paid the full amount of individual income tax for all their incomes; other taxpayers shall report and pay tax to the local competent tax authorities after the obtainment of income in accordance with the provisions on self-declaration administration measures. Moreover, it should be noted that taxpayers with an annual income of more than RMB120,000 do not include individuals have no domicile within the territory of China and reside within the territory of China for less than one year. Taxpayers obtaining income from outside the territory of China refer to individuals who are domiciled in the People's Republic of China, or who are not domiciled but have resided in the People's Republic of China for at least one year.

Details

After the end of a tax year, taxpayers with an annual income of more than RMB120,000 shall fill in the individual income tax return (applicable to declaration by taxpayers with an annual income of more than RMB120,000) and submit this to the competent tax authorities together with copies of an effective personal identification certificate and other materials required by the competent tax authorities.

Income obtained from wages and salaries, production and business operations of self-employed individuals, insourcing and leasing operations of enterprises or institutions, remuneration of labor services, income obtained from author's remuneration, royalties, interest, dividends and bonuses, lease of property, transfer of property, contingent income, and other incomes determined to be liable by the financial departments of the State Council.

Income sourced from tax exemption. In other words, awards for science, education, technology, culture, heath, sports and environmental protection granted by provincial people's governments, departments of the State Council, the PLA, organizations above the corps level and foreign organizations and international organizations; interest on national debts and state-issued financial bonds; subsidies and allowances granted according to uniform state regulations i.e. special government subsidies and allowances, and allowances for academicians and senior academicians, granted according to *Article 13* of the *Regulations for the Implementation of the Individual Income Tax Law of the People's Republic of China* as specified by the State Council, and other allowances and subsidies exempted from individual income tax as specified by the State Council; welfare benefits, survivors' pensions and relief payments; insurance indemnities; soldiers' military severance payment and demobilization pay; settlement payment, severance payment, retirement payment and retirement living allowances received by public servants and workers under state uniform provisions. "Paid in accordance with uniform regulations of the state" shall mean special government subsidies issued in accordance with the State Council regulations and allowances and subsidies that are exempt from individual income tax by the State Council regulations

Income sourced from temporary exemption of tax. In other words, income derived by the diplomatic agents, consular officers and other personnel who are exempt from tax under the provisions of the relevant laws of China; income exempted from tax as stipulated in the international conventions to which the

Chinese government is a party and in agreements it has signed.

Income sourced from outside the territory of China which can be exempted for tax, such as endowment insurance, medical insurance, unemployment insurance and public accumulation funds for housing construction paid for individuals by their organizations as specified.

Methods for calculating the annual amount of various incomes

1) For income obtained from wages and salaries, the calculation shall be based on the amount of income of RMB2,000 per month without deduction and the additional deduction expense (RMB2,800 per month).

2) For income obtained from remuneration of labor services and incomes from royalties, the relevant taxes paid by taxpayers in the course of providing labor services or transferring royalties shall not be deducted.

3) For income obtained from lease of property, the relevant taxes paid by taxpayers in the course of lease of property shall not be deducted; income of taxpayers from lease of property obtained over years are regarded as income of the year when the income is actually obtained.

4) For an individual's income obtained from transfer of houses, taxable income rates (5%, 10%, 15%) shall be respectively converted according to actual levy rates (1%, 2%, 3%) for calculating annual income if individual income tax is levied by verification collection.

5) Income obtained from interest on an individual's savings deposit and income obtained from interest on an enterprise's bonds is regarded as annual income actually obtained by taxpayers.

6) For self-employed individuals and investors of sole proprietorship enterprises, the levy rate shall be converted into taxable income rate for calculating the amount of taxable income if individual income tax is levied by verification according to the levy rate. After investors of partnership enterprises determine the amount of taxable income according to the methods mentioned above, the partners shall determine the amount of taxable income according to the distribution ratios specified in the partnership agreement. If there is no specified distribution ratio, the amount of taxable income shall be determined according to the average based on the number of partners. If a partner invests into two or more enterprises, the annual income of the partner shall be the sum of taxable income amounts from all enterprises invested.

7) For income obtained from transfer of shares, the amount of taxable income shall be the positive number after incomes from transfer of shares

offsetting losses within a tax year, and the amount of taxable income shall be zero if there is a negative number after offset of gains and losses.

Time limit for self-declaration

1) Taxpayers with an annual income of more than RMB120,000 shall report and pay tax to the local competent tax authorities within three months after the end of a tax year.

2) If the tax payable obtained from production and business operations of self-employed individuals and investors of sole proprietorship enterprises and partnership enterprises is paid in advance in monthly installments, the taxpayers shall report and pay tax within seven days after the end of a month; the taxpayers shall report and pay tax within seven days after the end of a quarter in the case of advance payment in quarterly installments. After the end of a tax year, the taxpayers shall settle within three months.

3) For lump-sum incomes of taxpayers from insourcing and leasing operations of enterprises or institutions, the taxpayers shall report and pay tax within 30 days from the day when the incomes are obtained; if the incomes of taxpayers from insourcing and leasing operations are obtained several times within one tax year, the taxpayer shall report and pay in advance within 7 days in the following month after the obtainment and settle within 3 months after the end of a tax year.

4) Taxpayers obtaining income outside the territory of China shall report and pay tax to the competent tax authorities within the territory of China within 30 days after the end of a tax year.

5) Except in the above circumstances, taxpayers shall report and pay tax to competent tax authorities within 7 days in the following month after the obtainment of other incomes.

6) If a taxpayer fails to report and pay tax within the prescribed time limit and needs to postpone, they shall act according to the provisions of *Article 27* of the *Tax Administration Law of the People's Republic of China* and *Article 37* of the *Detailed Rules for Implementation of the Tax Administration Law of the People's Republic of China*.

Methods and Place of self-declaration

Methods of declaration

Taxpayers may declare by telegram or post, and may also directly declare to the competent tax authorities or by other modes specified by the competent tax authorities. In the case of the use of post, the declaration evidence shall be the receipt of the registered letter and the actual declaration date shall be the date of the postmark.

Taxpayers may also entrust qualified tax agencies or others to handle the declaration.

Place of declaration

1) If the taxpayer holds a post or is employed in an organization within the territory of China, they shall declare to the competent tax authorities at the place where they hold a post or are employed.

2) If the taxpayer holds a post or is employed at two locations, they shall choose one location and always declare to the competent tax authorities there.

3) If the taxpayer holds no post or is not employed within the territory of China and their annual incomes include incomes from production and business operations of self-employed individuals or incomes from insourcing and leasing operations of enterprises or institutions (hereinafter referred to as incomes from production and business), they shall declare to the competent tax authorities at one place of actual business.

4) If the taxpayer holds no post or is not employed within the territory of China and their annual incomes do not include incomes from production and business, they shall declare to the competent tax authorities at the place of registered permanent residence. If they have registered permanent residence within the territory of China is different to their habitual residence, they shall choose one location to always declare to the competent tax authorities there. If they have no registered permanent residence within the territory of China, they shall declare to the competent tax authorities at the place of habitual residence.

5) For taxpayers of other incomes, declaration locations are as follows:
   - In case of income obtained from wages and salaries derived from two more locations, they shall choose one location to always declare to the competent tax authorities there.
   - For income obtained from outside the territory of China, they shall declare to the competent tax authorities at the place of registered permanent residence within the territory of China. If they have registered permanent residence which is different to their habitual

residence, they shall choose one location to always declare to the competent tax authorities there. If they have no registered permanent residence within the territory of China, they shall declare to the competent tax authorities at the place of habitual residence.

- Self-employed individuals shall declare to the competent tax authorities at the place of actual business operation.
- If the investors of sole proprietorship enterprises and partnership enterprises establish two or more enterprises, tax declaration locations shall be determined according to different circumstances.

If the established enterprises are all of a nature of sole proprietorship, they shall declare to the competent tax authorities at the place of actual business operation; if an enterprise is of the nature of a partnership, they shall declare to the competent tax authorities at the place of habitual residences; if there is discrepancy between the habitual residences of individual investors of an enterprise of the nature of a partnership and the place of business operation, they shall choose one location of business operation to always declare to the competent tax authorities there; taxpayers shall declare to the competent tax authorities at the place where incomes are obtained for other circumstances other than those mentioned above.

Taxpayers shall not change the tax declaration location without approval and they must report to the original competent tax authorities for filing in case of change due to special circumstances.

Withholding service charge

Tax authorities shall pay service charge at a rate of 2% to withholding agents for them to use as withholding expenditures and to reward those tax withholding personnel with better performance.

8 Chapter

Resource Taxes

An Overview

Some concepts

Resources are all the material wealth that exists in nature and that can increase mankind's benefits through processing, modification and utilization. There are diversified resource expression methods: minerals, water, solar energy, wind power, forests, wild animals and plants, the sea, land, manpower, funds and information. Minerals and land are the two resources most closely associated with our daily production and life: the former can be divided into metal minerals and non-metal minerals, energy minerals and non-energy minerals, rare minerals and non-rare minerals; the latter can be divided into agricultural land and non-agricultural construction land. With the constant enhancement of mankind's natural development and utilization power and the constant deepening of dependence on resources, resources extension is showing a constantly expanding tendency in general. For instance, when water for production and domestic use was rich in reserves, and development and utilization did not cost too much, we did not regulate and limit its utilization through charges and taxation. With the constant reduction in amount of usable water, the development and utilization cost of water becomes higher and higher, and therefore usable water has become a rare resource and regulation and limitation of development and utilization through tax and charges have become normal. Similar examples include human resources. We can conclude that transfer from infinite resources, free resources and resources waste to finite resources, priced resources and resources saving is a demonstration of mankind's civilization and progress; at the same time, it is an inevitable requirement of the sustainable development concept.

Resource taxes is a general term for a tax category covering the exploitation (or development) of natural resources and the levying of differential benefits. According to the tax setup pattern, it is divided into general resource taxes and special resource taxes. The former is levied on the work unit and individual obtaining natural resources exploitation or utilization rights for the purpose of demonstrating national natural ownership or monopoly rights of natural resources. The funds obtained are exclusively used for compensation of natural resource consumption—it is generally based on the absolute rent theory. The latter is levied on the work unit and individual occupying and utilizing superior resources for the purpose of collecting differential benefits of superior resources to the country and creating competition conditions with equal opportunities for the exploitation or development taxpayer of superior and inferior resources.

It is generally based on the differential rent theory. The taxpayer is mainly the work unit or individual obtaining the exploitation rights of mineral resources or development and utilization rights of land resources; and the tax base form is divided into physical volume and value volume. The former adopts the exploitation volume, sales volume and self-consumption volume of mineral resources as well as occupying volume of land resources as the tax base; the latter adopts the sales income from mineral resources and the transfer income and value-added income of land resources as the tax basis. The resource taxes with physical volume as the tax base generally uses the quantitative and quota levying method; the resource taxes with value volume as the tax basis generally uses the price and fixed rate levying method. According to the tax rate form it is divided into differential proportional tax rate by classification and grade, differential quota tax rate by classification, grade and region, progressive tax rate upon excessive rate, and margin tax rate. The quota tax rate and proportional tax rate are the most frequently adopted.

Characteristics

Finiteness of levying scope

The tax levying object in China's contemporary resource taxes is limited to two categories listed in the tax law: mineral resources (including salt) and land. Other resources are temporarily not integrated into the levying scope—they are regulated through charges or other methods. The selectivity of the tax levying object and finiteness of tax levying scope are determined by China's actual conditions of short history of resource taxes and less experience.

Universality of regulation of differential benefits

Natural resources vary in the respect of sufficiency and rarity, high/low quality, abundance and scarcity. Under market economic conditions, the same resources have different economic benefits given differences in the reserves, exploitation or development difficulty and utilization efficiency. China's contemporary resource taxes is mainly levied on the differential benefits arising from relative superiority of natural conditions; at the same time, it considers the universality of regulation of resources benefits.

Simplicity of levying methods

The tax rate design of resource taxes is in accordance with the differential tax with a certain margin (except for the land VAT). According to the exploitation volume, sales volume, occupying volume or utilization volume of taxable resources, the tax is calculated according to the quantitative and quota method—the levying method is rather simple and convenient compared with the priced and fixed rate turnover tax, income tax and property tax based on commodity turnover volume, income and property assessment value.

Income imbalance

Resources are natural material wealth; the geological distribution is uneven, exploitation or development difficulty varies, and resource quality and differential benefits change with the constant deepening of exploitation or development activities. Therefore the resource tax source and tax standard cannot remain unchanged. This determines a certain imbalance in the income space and time.

Transfer of tax burden

The resource tax levied on natural resources has to transfer to the lower reaches with constant extension of commodity circulation procedure regardless of the constitution as a part of resource product price or addition to the price; ultimately, the commodity buyer or consumer has to bear the resource taxes—it is the transfer feature of resource taxes.

Effects

The resource taxes have a long development history and has a very important status in the tax system of various countries. China's contemporary resource taxes are composed of four major taxes including resource tax, urban land utilization tax, land VAT and farming land use tax. In spite of the small total annual income in various taxes (above RMB100 billion) and low ratio of total tax volume (about 2%), it is acquiring a very important status in China's taxation. It is one of the hot spots in the tax system reform.

To secure national financial income

China has confirmed the paid development principle for state-owned resources. In the socialist market economic conditions, the state has to share resources development interests among all the resources developers including state-owned enterprises (SOEs) through tax—it is a necessary measure to assure the realization of resource ownership in the economy and regulate the distribution relationship between the state and enterprise. Therefore the universal levying principle is confirmed for the resource tax; any enterprise and individual is a resource taxpayer so long as they exploit the national taxable resources. The different quality and geological location of exploited mineral resources often lead to rather large difference in the production and business status of mineral resources exploitation enterprises. Since a part of the benefits made by enterprises with excellent resources exploitation conditions cannot reflect the enterprise efforts, the state has to make a proper regulation of the benefits beyond the normal level in order to create fair competitive conditions between the enterprises. At present, China's elementary products have a rather low price and most of the resource benefits are reflected in the processing industry; resource tax is helpful for changing the low price of resource products, making a reasonable adjustment to the industrial structure and increasing the financial income of the place of origin of the resource.

To protect resources and to improve the efficiency of resource utilization

The resource tax is useful in protecting state-owned resources and upgrading the efficiency of resources utilization. The urban land utilization tax enhances land management through economic measures, changing free-of-charge utilization to paid utilization, promoting rational and economical land utilization and upgrading the land utilization benefits, making a proper regulation of the land differential income between different areas and sections, encouraging enterprises to enhance economic verification, and smoothing the distribution relationship between the state and the land user. For instance, land VAT is good for enhancing the national macro-regulation and control of real estate development and transactions; blocking land purchasing and sales and assuring the national land equity.

To rationally utilize special land resources

The resource taxes can protect special land resources. For instance, the state can enhance land management through farming land use tax and tax methods, reduce occupation of farming land, and thus protect agricultural land resources.

The Resource Tax

An overview of mineral resource tax

Some concepts

The resource tax is a quantitative and quota tax levied on work units and individuals engaged in mineral product exploitation and salt production within the boundary of China. It is also known as the mineral resource tax, and is an important tax in China's resource taxes.

China's resource tax system for mineral resources started in 1984 (the second step of substitution of tax payment for profit delivery) in the initial period of reform and opening-up. The legal basis is "In the paid exploitation of mineral resources, related enterprises must pay the resource tax and resource compensation according to related national stipulations" stipulated in the *Law of the People's Republic of China on Mineral Resources*. It confirmed the concept of priced resources, finite resources and state-owned resources, and made clear the obligations of paying resource tax and (or) resource compensation to the state in the development and utilization of state-owned mineral resources.

Given its short tax history and lack of experience, the resource tax is only aimed at crude oil, natural gas, coal, metal mineral products and non-metal mineral products. In implementation it is only levied on a minority of enterprises such as coal and petroleum, adopting product sales income as the tax calculation base and implementing progressive tax levying upon excessive rate according to the sales profitability rate. With the reduction of sales profitability rate of resource products, the State Council decided to change the price and fixed rate levying method into the quantitative and quota levying method as of January 1, 1986, on the basis of basically maintaining the original tax burden for the purpose of stabilizing the resource tax income. In December 1993, the State Council promulgated the revised *Interim Regulations of the People's Republic of China on Resource Tax*, expanded the levying scope of resource tax and unified the levying and management measures. The new regulations were implemented as of January 1, 1994.

With the gradual taking root of the concept of sustainable development and a scientific development outlook in recent years, people's consciousness of resource and environmental protection has been enhanced. In order to change the long-term pattern of poorly-organized exploitation of mineral resources, cheap utilization, losses, waste, serious environmental pollution and inadequate cost compensation, the state has upgraded the sales price of mineral products several times. On this basis it has implemented numerous structural regulations on the quota standard of resource tax to give a better play to its positive role in increasing financial income and protecting the resources environment.

Characteristics

Compared with other taxes, the resource tax has the following characteristics:

Narrow levy scope

China's contemporary resource tax is only aimed at mineral resources and salt; other resources are not involved. Therefore the levying scope is rather narrow and this is related to China's rather short levying period and lack of experience. With the gradual deepening of reform and constant upgrading of productive forces, other resources not listed into the object of resource tax are expected to be gradually integrated into the scope of the tax.

Levy on in-quota and quantitative basis

Generally, the resource tax calculation basis includes resource exploitation volume, sales volume, sales income and sales profitability rate; the tax rate is divided into the quantitative and quota method and the priced and fixed rate method. Since 1986, China has changed the levying and management method of resource tax as follows. It adopts the sales volume of taxable mineral products and salt as the tax calculation basis and implements quantitative and quota levying. Practice has proven that this method is simple and convenient, and easy for the paying and levying parties to operate. Therefore the *Interim Regulations of Resource Tax* implemented as of January 1, 1994, have continued this method.

Tariff with differential margins

The contemporary resource tax regulations are based on China's actual conditions of a vast territory and a great difference in the resources storage structure and development conditions in various areas, and have designed the differential margin tax according to products based on the price and profitability rate of different mineral products, distinguished various tax standards for different mineral resources and mining areas, made regular regulation, and demonstrated the spirit of equal burden.

A tax shared by central and local governments

According to the related stipulations on tax category and tax source distribution in the tax system implemented as of 1994, the resource tax is a tax shared by central government and local government. This means that the special institution affiliated to the State Administration of Taxation is responsible for levy on and management of the ocean petroleum resource tax and collecting all the income in the central treasury; and the local tax bureau at various levels is responsible for levying and managing the mineral resources tax (including the salt tax) and collecting all the income in the local government's treasury. In view of the rather small ratio of ocean petroleum resource tax, the contemporary resource tax can be taken as local tax to a certain degree.

Effects

The resource tax on mineral products and salt has the following objectives and significance:

To promote a rational exploitation and utilization of mineral resources

According to the related stipulations of the constitution and the *Law of the People's Republic of China on Mineral Resources,* all the mineral resources within the territory of China belong to the state; no work unit or individual may exploit state-owned mineral resources without approval as this is illegal and will be penalized by the authoritative institution. Work units and individuals approved to exploit and develop state-owned mineral resources have to pay certain resource exploitation expenses or tax to the state. The resource tax is not only a concrete demonstration of the state's ownership of resources in terms of economic benefits, but also an effective method of protecting state-owned resources, maintaining storage and the exploitation balance, realizing effective utilization and preventing casual exploitation and excavation, losses or waste, and benefit loss.

To regulate of the differential income of resources

Mineral resources are a natural material wealth not processed by mankind. Therefore the geological distribution, volume of reserves, grade and exploitation difficulty are not determined at our discretion. The same resource may have different reserve volumes, grades and exploitation conditions, and it is inevitable that different profitability rates are caused by the different costs of exploitation by enterprises and individuals of the same resources. Enterprises and individuals exploiting high-quality resources can produce more benefits with less input; while enterprises and individuals exploiting poor-quality resources suffer from a low benefit, high input situation. These different economic benefits are caused by the difference in natural conditions; they are not necessarily associated with the subjective efforts and business management level. Therefore it is necessary to formulate a proper regulation of the differential resource incomes arising from the disparity in natural conditions by using charges or tax-levying methods, thus cracking down on over-exploitation of rich resources, abandonment of poor resources and waste of rare resources, and creating fair competition conditions for the various resources exploitation enterprises and individuals. The resource tax is an important economic lever to give play to such a function.

To secure a stable financial revenue for local governments

The state has to intervene in the economic benefits distribution of exploitation and development enterprises and individuals of state-owned mineral resources, and generally this is divided into charges and tax-levying methods. In practical economic life there are numerous charges levied on resources exploitation and development enterprises (mining permit expenses, mining area contracting expenses, mining area rent, mining area environmental governance expenses, surface collapse repair expenses of the mining area and mining area security expenses are only some of the frequently seen items and forms of these charges). The multiplicity of charges, diversity of charging items, variability of charging scope and standards, and lack of transparency of utilization of charges are not well coordinated. This has not only aggravated the economic burden of legal resources exploitation and development enterprises and individuals, and seriously interrupted normal business activities, but has also hindered the formation of a normal price comparison relationship between resource products and lower reaches processing products and basic function of market mechanism in the guidance of effective resources collocation. Therefore elimination of expenses and establishment of tax, or transformation of administrative fees into taxes, is adopted to establish the interest distribution pattern with resource tax as the object—it is of great theoretical and realistic significance in regulating the economic interests distribution relationship between the state and resources exploitation and development enterprises and individuals, promoting the formation of a reasonable price mechanism between resource products and processed products, and forming a stable and reliable source of financial funds for the local government.

The system of resource tax

Scope of levying

Given the short history of resource tax in China and the limited experience but widespread and complex distribution of resources, it is difficult to levy tax on all the resources exploited. Therefore China's contemporary resource tax only includes mineral products and salt. Specifically, the scope of resource tax includes:

Mineral products

1) Crude oil as exploited natural crude oil
2) Natural gas as natural gas exploited for special purposes and as exploited in synchronization with crude oil
3) Coal as in raw coal, excluding coal washing and coal dressing based on raw coal processing
4) Raw non-metallic minerals
5) Raw black metal minerals
6) Raw metallic minerals

Salt

1) Solid salt
2) Liquid salt

Taxpayers

The taxpayers of resource tax are the work units and individuals exploiting taxable mineral products or production salt within the boundary of China.

Taxable mineral products or production salt are the mineral products or production salt listed according to the contemporary tax law.

The work unit is a state-owned enterprise, collective enterprise, private enterprise, stock enterprise, other enterprise, administrative unit, business unit, military unit, social organization, foreign-funded enterprise or foreign enterprise.

The individual is an individual business operator or foreign personnel.

In the cooperative exploitation of petroleum and natural gas between China and foreign countries, the authorities levy only levy the mine area utilization expense according to the contemporary stipulations; they do not temporarily levy the resource tax.

Therefore a cooperative exploitation enterprise of petroleum and natural gas between China and foreign countries is not the taxpayer of resource tax.

The *Interim Regulations of Resource Tax* stipulate the deduction and payment personnel: the work unit purchasing mineral products without tax is the deduction and payment person of resource tax. The work unit purchasing mineral products without tax is defined as an independent mine, combined enterprise, or other work unit. The independent mine is a work unit which only conducts mining or mining and dressing and is in accordance with independent accounting and profits and losses; the produced raw ores and concentrates are mainly sold to other units. The combined enterprise is an enterprise of continuous production in mining, dressing and smelting (or processing), or an enterprise of continuous production in the mining and smelting (or processing). The mining unit is Level II or below in the accounting unit of the enterprise. Other work units include individual business operators purchasing mineral products without tax.

In the purchasing of mineral products without tax—raw ore—the deduction and payment personnel are obliged to deduct and pay the resource tax according to the deduction tax standard verified by the provincial (autonomous region, municipality) people's governments and based on purchased quantity.

Tax rates

According to the idea of "universal levying, differential regulation," the resource tax is levied according to the quantitative and quota method. "Universal levying" applies to the resource tax on all taxable mineral products and salt exploited within the boundary of China; "differential regulation" applies to the regulation of differential resource income arising from differing of natural conditions in accordance with a rather high tax standard.

The Ministry of Finance and related departments of the State Council have to confirm the taxpayer's concrete applicable tax standard according to the resource status of taxable products exploited or produced by the taxpayer and within the tax margin stipulated in the regulations; it also has to make a regular regulation according to the changes of resources exploitation conditions (see Table 8.1 for the *Table of Tax Items and Amount of Resource Tax*).

For non-ferrous metal and non-metal raw ore for which taxes have not been listed in the tax laws, it is up to the provincial-level people's governments (or those of autonomous regions or municipalities directly under the central government) to decided whether to levy tax on these and the decisions must be reported to the Ministry of Finance and the State Administration of Taxation for filing.

If taxpayers exploit or produce taxable products which belong to different tax items, the tax amount of taxable products which belong to different tax items should be calculated respectively. If the tax amount of taxable products under different tax items cannot be calculated or provided correctly, they will be levied using the higher tax standards.

Table 8.1.   Tax item and amount of resource tax

Tax item	Tax margin
Crude oil	RMB14–30/ton
Natural gas	RMB7–15/thousand m^3
Coal	RMB0.3–5/ton
Raw non-metallic ore	RMB0.5–20/ton or m^3
Raw black metal ore	RMB2–30/ton
Raw non-ferrous ore	RMB0.4–30/ton
Salt	
Liquid salt	RMB10–60/ton
Solid salt	RMB2–10/ton

Note: The Ministry of Finance and the State Administration of Taxation adjusted the tax rates on crude oil and natural gas on July 1, 2005. The amount of taxes given in this table is the standard after the adjustment which is comparatively higher than the lower limit of standard of amount of taxes given when the provisional regulation was issued in 1994.

Tax base

The tax calculation base of resource tax is levy duty. The determination method of levy duty is as follows:

General provisions on levy quantity

1)   Sales quantity is levy quantity for sales of dutiable products which are exploited or produced by the taxpayer.
2)   Quantity of owned (or unproduced) goods is levy quantity for own dutiable products which are exploited or produced by the taxpayer.

Special provisions on levy quantity

There are some special conditions regarding actual production business activities.

1)   It shall be converted to levy quantity according to the output of tax-paid products or directing tax organization if the taxpayer fails to provide sales quantity or tax-paid products or transfer and usage quantity correctly.
2)   Tax shall be levied according to the quantity of crude oil used for

thickened oil, high condensation oil or thin oil which cannot be classified or is difficult to divide.

3) Actual sales and owned quantity of processing products shall be converted to quantity of coal as levy quantity according to comprehensive recovery rate if transfer and usage volume of crude oil cannot be calculated correctly before continuous processing.

4) Raw coal shall be converted into quantity of crude ore according to selected ore ratio for crude ore of metallic and non-metallic ore products if failing to master transfer and usage quantity of the taxpayers for crude ore. The calculation formula is as follows:

Selected ore ratio = Quantity of fine ore / Consumable crude ore

The different kinds of tax-paid products exploited or produced by the taxpayer must be checked. The tax shall be increased in the case of failure to provide information on the quantity of different kinds of tax-liable products correctly.

Calculation of tax payable

The calculation formula is shown as follows for when payable tax can be calculated according to the levy quantity of taxable products and regulated unit tax.

Payable tax = Levy quantity × Unit tax

Withheld tax payable = Quantity of untaxed ore products purchased × Applicable unit tax

From the formula we can see that payable tax shall be calculated by levy duty quantity and suitable unit tax.

Tax preference

Tax reduction and exemption items

These have to abide by the principle ideas of ordinary levy and differential regulation for resource tax. Therefore, there are few tax-exempt items. The main tax exemption items include:

1) Tax-free crude oil for heating and well repair during exploitation.

2) People's governments at all levels shall determine tax reduction or exemption properly during exploitation by the taxpayer or production of tax-payable products if major losses are caused due to sudden

accidents or natural disasters.

3) The North China Sea Salt Resource Tax shall be temporarily levied at RMB15 per ton after February 1, 2007. Resource taxes on South China Sea Salt, Lake Salt and Well Mine Salt shall be temporarily levied at RMB10 per ton. That of liquid salt shall be temporarily levied at RMB2 per ton.

4) Resource tax cannot be levied temporarily for coal seam gas exploited on the ground since January 1, 2007. Coal seam gas refers to irregular natural gas which is associated with coal resources in coal seams and the surrounding rock. It is also called coal gas from coal mines.

5) Other tax reduction and exemption items regulated by the State Council shall include:

That levy quantity shall be checked individually for tax reduction and exemption items of the taxpayer. Non-individual failing to provide the correct levy quantity is not entitled for tax reduction or exemption.

Provisions on exported tax-paid products without return (or exemption) of resource tax

Resource tax regulations are only levied for unit and person of tax-payable products which shall be exploited or produced in China. Resource tax is not be levied for imported ore products or salt. It will not be levied for imported taxable products, and paid resource tax also cannot be levied or returned for exported taxable products.

Administration of tax collection

Taxpayers of resource tax shall declare payment tax according to regulations if there are tax payment obligations on the current day to receive sales amount, gain or claim for sales credit and transfer and usage of self-produced and owned tax-payable products.

Occurrence time of tax liability

Occurrence time of tax liability is shown as follows if the taxpayer sells tax-paid products:

1) Occurrence time of tax payment obligation is the date of receipt of the amount regulated by the sales contract if the taxpayer adopts the amount receipt settlement model in phases.

2) Occurrence time of tax payment obligation is the current day to issue

tax-payable products if adopting the settlement mode of pre-received goods amount.

3) Occurrence time of tax payment obligation is the current day of payment received of the sales amount, or claim for sales amount credit if the taxpayer adopts other settlement modes.

Occurrence time of tax payment obligation for self-produced and owned taxable products of the taxpayer is the current day to transfer and use taxable products.

Occurrence time of tax payment obligation to withhold obligor's deduction tax is the current date of the first loan or issue of payable goods amount credit.

Assessable period

Tax payment period is the term of tax payment after tax payment obligations. The tax payment term for resource tax is 1, 3, 5, 10 or 15 days, or 1 month. The tax payment term of the taxpayer shall be checked by the relevant tax organization according to actual conditions. Tax need not be calculated or paid according to a fixed term. It can also be calculated or paid according to the situation.

The taxpayer shall declare tax within 10 days of the expiration date if paying tax by regarding 1 month as a period. It should pre-pay tax within 5 days of the expiration date if paying for tax by regarding 1, 3, 5, 10 or 15 days as a period. It should also declare and pay tax and settles the tax of the previous month within 10 days of the first day of the next month.

Place of payment

A taxpayer paying resource tax shall pay the tax to the competent tax organization in the location of exploitation or production taxable products.

The tax authorities of provinces, autonomous regions and municipalities directly under the central government shall determine the taxable products of taxpayers which are exploited or produced within the scope of provinces, autonomous regions and municipality directly under the central government.

Tax shall be levied for exploited ore products at the exploitation location if resource tax which should be paid by the taxpayer comes from multi-provincial exploitation and the subordinate production unit(s) and checking unit(s) are not in the same province, municipality or municipality directly under the central government. Payable tax shall be calculated and allocated by unit with individual checking responsibility for own profit and loss according to actual sales (or owned volume) in the exploitation location plus the appropriate unit tax.

Urban Land Use Tax

An overview

Some concepts

Urban land use tax is levied according to actual urban land area used by a unit or person in China. It is the second most important tax for the national land tax system.

Land tax originated in China early as an ordinary levy duty. In general, the national levy for village land is called the rural holding or agricultural tax. Tax levy on urban land is called real estate tax or land use tax. The Government Administration Council regulates levy of real estate tax in accordance with the *National Tax Administration Implementation Rules* issued in 1950 after establishment of new China. It issued the *Provisional Regulations on Urban Real Estate Tax* in August 1951 to consolidate real estate tax and estate tax into urban real estate tax. Urban real estate tax levied on enterprises was added into the industrial commercial tax when this was introduced in 1973. The State Council determined to restore land use tax when changing tax laws in 1984. However, it also determined to retain tax without a temporary levy duty due to deficient levy conditions. The State Council issued the *Provisional Regulations of Urban Land Use Tax of the People's Republic of China* on September 27, 1988, to come into effect on November 1, 1988. It issued the *Decisions to Modify Provisional Regulations of Urban Land Use Tax of the People's Republic of China* on December 31, 2006. It modified some clauses of urban land use tax with a great adjustment of tax standard. It unified the tax burden of internal and external capital enterprises and authorized governments at all levels directly under the central government to formulate detailed implementation methods. Such decisions have been executed since January 1, 2007.

Characteristics

Urban land use tax has the following characteristics compared with other taxes:
1) There are triple attributes for property tax, resource tax and behavior tax for duty levy on use of urban land;
2) The regional quota amplitude tax rate is designed using actual land area as the tax base for quota levy;
3) The tax is paid by year using a multiple levy system; and
4) Local tax organizations shall be responsible for levy, and all incomes

belong to the local government.

Effects

Levy of urban land use tax has following objectives and significance:

To secure a rational arrangement of land resources and economical use of land

According to the regulations in the constitution, ownership of urban lands belongs to the state. Units and individuals have to pay certain taxes to government if they are allowed to use urban land. However, urban land use tax is different from the urban land use fee. Levy of urban land use tax not only reflects the principles that "those who use the land will pay the fee (tax)," "the more the use, the more the fee (tax)," and "those who do not use the land will not pay the fee (tax)," but also reflects the government's policy to handle the benefit distribution relationships among land users, urge land users to save the use of lands, increase land use efficiency, and stimulate formation of a land circulation market and rationalization of arrangement of town and county construction by means of a standard, unified, ordinary, fair and transparent form of taxation.

To adjust differential revenues of land

Land is a kind of very precious natural resource. Because the environments of land use in different urban areas are different, their potential economic values differ. Tax amounts in different ranges are designed for urban land use tax according to scarcity and frequency of utilization of urban lands all over the China. This is beneficial to adjusting different revenues resulting from different grades, and promoting fair competition among users of urban lands.

To fine-tune the local tax system

Although urban lands belong to the state in China, they are still managed according to different grades based on territorial jurisdiction. Urban land use tax is a kind of local tax and levied by various grades of local tax authorities. Tax revenues belong to various grades of local governments. Therefore strengthening of management of urban land use tax is beneficial not only to increasing local financial revenues but also to promoting levels of urbanization and stimulating the comprehensive progress of the local society and economy.

The system of urban land use tax

Object of taxation

All lands within cities, counties, towns, and industrial and mining districts, no matter whether belonging to the state or to collective groups, are objects of urban land use tax.

Cities refer to cities established with the approval of the State Council. The taxation range of cities covers the inner city and the suburbs.

Counties refer to locations of people's governments at county level. The taxation range of counties covers the cities and towns where people's governments at county level are located.

Towns refer to the towns established with the approval of the people's governments at all levels. The taxation range of towns covers the area under the particular people's governments of the town.

Industrial and mining districts refer to locations of large-scale industrial and mining enterprises where towns may be established in line with the requirements of the State Council but have not been designated as towns, and where industrial and commercial enterprises are abundant and populations are dense. Industrial and mining districts must be approved by the people's governments at all levels.

Taxpayers

The taxpayers of urban land use tax are units and individuals who use state-owned land in cities, counties, towns, and industrial and mining districts.

Unit(s) hereinafter refers to state-owned enterprises, collective enterprises, privately-owned enterprises, joint-equity enterprises, foreign-invested enterprises, foreign enterprises and other enterprises, and public institutions, social organizations, governmental offices, armed forces and other units. Individual(s) hereinafter refers to privately or individually-owned businesses and other individuals.

Taxpayers of urban land use tax specifically include:

1) The unit or individual which owns the land-use right;
2) If the unit or the individual which owns the land-use right is not at the location of the land, person who actually uses the land or uses it on behalf of the owner shall be the taxpayer;
3) If the land-use right has not been decided or there are unresolved disputes , the taxpayer shall be the actual user of the land; and
4) If land-use rights belong to more than one party and all parties are taxpayers, tax shall be paid by each party respectively.

Tax rates

Land use tax adopts fixed tax rates as per district differential range. The tax amount payable per year for land per square meter is specified respectively for large cities, medium cities, small cities and counties, towns, and industrial and mining districts. The specific standards are as follows:

1) Large cities RMB1.5–30
2) Medium cities RMB1.2–24
3) Small cities RMB0.9–18
4) Counties, towns, and industrial and mining districts RMB0.6–12

The designation as large city, medium city and small city is based on the standards stated in the *Ordinance of City Planning* issued by the State Council and the officially-registered non-agricultural population at the public security department. Cities with a population of over 500 thousand will be deemed as large cities, between 200 thousand and 500 thousand will be medium cities, and less than 200 thousand will be small cities. Urban land use tax rates are listed in Table 8.2.

Table 8.2. Tax rates of urban land use

Grade	Population	Tax amount per square meter (RMB)
Large cities	More than 500 thousand	0.5–10
Medium-sized cities	200 thousand to 500 thousand	0.4–8
Small-sized cities	Less than 200 thousand	0.3–6
Counties, towns and industrial and mining districts	—	0.2–4

Tax base

The tax basis on urban land is the area of land actually occupied by the taxpayer.

The area of land actually occupied by the taxpayer shall be decided as follows:

1) An area of land which is measured and determined by units assured by the people's governments at all levels will be the final decision.
2) An area of land which has not been measured yet but for which a land use certificate issued by governmental authorities is owned by the taxpayer will take the area of land given on the final certificate.

3) An area of land for which a land use certificate has not been issued should be reported accurately by the taxpayer and the relevant tax should be paid accordingly. Adjustment can be made after verification and issue of the land use certificate.

Calculation of tax payable

Tax amount payable for urban land use tax is the product of the area of actually occupied taxable lands and the applicable to-be-paid tax amount. Its computational formula is as follows:

Tax payable per year = Area of actually occupied taxable lands (square meter) × Applicable to-be-paid tax

Tax preference

Tax items under the law

1) Lands used by government offices, mass organizations and armed forces themselves.
2) Lands used by units themselves which enjoy appropriations from national financial departments.
3) Lands used by religious temples, parks and places of interests themselves.
   - Lands used by religious temples themselves refer to lands used for holding religious services and for the livelihood of religious people in the temples.
   - Lands used for parks and places of interests refer to lands used for public tourism and lands for the office works of their management units.
   - Productive or operative lands and other lands of the abovementioned units are not covered by the tax exemption.
4) Public lands for urban streets, squares and green belts.
5) Productive land directly used for agriculture, forestry, animal husbandry and fishery.
   This refers to special land directly used for planting, and breeding and raising animals, not does not include processing sites for agricultural and sideline products, living quarters or office activities.
6) Land which have been approved for mountain dredging and ocean filling and reformed waste land can be exempted from land use tax for 5 to 10 years after the month of coming into use.
   The specific period of tax exemption will be decided independently by

each province, autonomous region and municipality directly under the central government in accordance with the regulations in the *Tentative Regulations on Urban Land Use Tax of the People's Republic of China*.

7) Lands used by medical care institutions themselves, such as not-for-profit medical institutions, disease control institutions and maternity and child care institutions, can be exempted from urban land use tax. Lands used by for-profit medical care institutions themselves can be exempted from urban land use tax for three years. This policy was implemented in 2000.

8) Lands used by enterprises to build schools, hospitals, nurseries and kindergartens of which the function can be clearly differentiated from other of the enterprise functions can be exempted from urban land use tax.

9) Lands of tax units used by tax-exempt entities without charges (such as lands of railway and civil aviation units used by public security and customs units) shall not be subject to urban land use tax. Land of tax-exempt entities used by taxable units should be levied with urban land use tax on the tax units. For multistoried buildings on lands mutually used and of which ownership is shared by tax-exempt entities and taxable units, urban land use tax will be levied on tax units as per the proportion of area of the structure occupied by them.

10) Lands self-used by branches subordinate to the head office of the People's Bank of China (including the State Administration of Foreign Exchange) which exercises national administrative functions will be exempted from land use tax.

11) In order to reflect the country's industrial policies and support the development of key industries, policy limits of tax exemption and tax relief have been made for lands of resources such as petroleum, electricity and coal, lands for traffic and water conservancy facilities such as civil ports and railways, and special lands for the three-line adjustment enterprises, the salt industry, quarry and posts and telecommunication industry.

Deductible tax items allowed by local tax authorities

1) Land used by privately-owned residential houses and courtyards
2) Land for residential housing rental by real estate management departments before adjustment and reform of house rent.
3) Land used by civil administration departments for setting up welfare factories in which the handicapped occupy a certain proportion.

4) Land used by groups or individuals to build various kinds of schools, hospitals, nurseries and kindergartens.

5) Land on which capital projects are under construction should in principal be taxed according to the urban land use tax. But for some capital projects, especially for large-scale capital projects supported by national industrial policies which cover large areas, and have a long construction period and no operating income, if taxpayers have genuine difficulties in paying the tax, the local tax authorities of each province, autonomous region and municipality directly under the central government can decide according to actual conditions whether to reduce or cancel the land use tax.

6) Land used by real estate development enterprises to build commodity houses should in principal be liable for urban land use tax according to the regulations. But in cases where tax payment before sale of commodity houses is genuinely hard to realize, the local tax authorities of each province, autonomous region and municipality directly under the central government can decide according to the actual conditions but based on strict principles whether to postpone or reduce or cancel the tax.

7) For privately-owned houses primarily managed by real estate management departments, after policies have been made clear, the property rights of those houses will be returned to their owners. But if houses are still lived in by the original residents who still pay rent to the house owners on the basis of standards of rent decided before the adjustment and reform of house rents by real estate management departments, and the house owners have genuine difficulties in paying land use tax, the local tax authorities of each province, autonomous region and municipality directly under the central government can periodically reduce the tax amount or exempt them from urban land use tax according to actual conditions.

Administration of tax collection

Occurrence time of tax liability

1) For purchased newly-built commodity houses, taxpayers should pay urban land use tax from one month after the house has been handed over for use.

2) For purchased inventory houses, with private transfer of ownership registration, taxpayers should pay urban land use tax from the month after the month when the real estate ownership registration authorities

issue certificates of real estate ownership.

3) For leased and borrowed real estate, taxpayers should pay urban land use tax from the month after the month of delivery of the to-be-leased or to-be-borrowed real estate.

4) Real estate development enterprises should pay urban land use tax for using; leasing and borrowing commodity houses constructed themselves from the month after the month of use or hand-over.

5) Cultivated lands newly requisitioned by taxpayers should be liable for urban land use tax one year after the date of approval of requisition.

6) Uncultivated lands newly requisitioned by taxpayers should be liable for urban land use tax from the month after the month of approval of requisition.

Place of payment

Urban land use tax shall be paid at the location of the land and levied by the local tax authorities. Tax revenue will be brought into the management of the local financial budget. Specifically, there are two conditions: one is that if land used by taxpayers belongs to different provinces, autonomous regions or municipalities directly under the central government, the taxpayer should pay urban land use tax to the respective tax authorities where the land is located; the other is that if land used by taxpayers are within one province, autonomous region or municipality directly under the central government, places of tax payment will be decided by each province, autonomous region and municipality directly under the central government.

Assessable period

Urban land use tax will be calculated by the year and paid in installments. The specific assessable period for tax payment will be decided by the people's governments at all levels.

Land Value Increment Tax

An overview

Some concepts

Land value increment tax is a kind of tax levied on the value added obtained by units or individuals who transfer use rights of state-owned land, above-ground buildings and other attached objects thereon, and obtain income from transfer of real estate. It is the third most important tax category in China's land tax system.

Land value increment tax is a new tax implemented since the tax reform in 1993 in China. The State Council promulgated the *Provisional Regulations on Value-added Tax of the People's Republic of China* in December 1993, which came into force as of January 1, 1994.

Characteristics

Compared with other taxes, land value increment tax has the following characteristics:

1) It is levied for the acts of compensatory transfer of the use rights of state-owned land, above-ground buildings and other attached objects thereon, and it has the multiple attributes of property tax, resource tax, turnover tax and tax for special purposes.

2) Value added of real estate transfer is the basis for tax calculation. Tax is levied according to the rate on value.

3) In accordance with the land value increment rates, four grades of progressive tax rates are used and the marginal tax rates are higher.

4) Tax is levied only in the link of real estate transfer and the one-link tax system is practiced.

5) Local tax authorities are in charge of tax levy, and all tax revenue belongs to the local government.

Effects

To regulate land value-added gains and to increase the fiscal revenue of local governments

The tertiary industry is a key industry of China, and the real estate industry is the pillar industry of the tertiary industry. During the boom years in some countries, real estate industry has been one of the industries with the largest investment, the fastest increment speed, the highest added value and the strongest driving force for industrial structure adjustment and regional structure adjustment. Among an ordinary family's tangible assets, real estate usually accounts for a large proportion. Urban land in China belongs to the state, and units or individuals only have the right of use. With the development of the urban economy, constant improvement of integrated supporting facilities, improvement of efficiency of land use and enlargement of development degree, real estate in urban regions has seen a larger appreciation. Levy of land value increment tax on acts of transfer of real estate is advantageous to regulating land value-added gains, safeguarding the rights and interests of the state, increasing the fiscal income of local government, and alleviating severe unfair social allocation caused by the flow of enormous profits into the pockets of some units and individuals.

To restrict real estate speculation and to standardize trading orders in the real estate market

Since the implementation of land system reform and housing commercialization in the late 1990s, real estate in China has experienced unprecedented development and played a key role in increasing domestic demand, further improving people's livelihood and promoting fast and steady economic growth. However there has been over-investment in the real estate industry, serious imbalance between total amount and supply-demand structure, excessive rise of real estate prices, and prevalence of speculation in real estate, which brought great risks to the industry's healthy development and the smooth operation of the national economy. Land value increment tax is levied on the value added of transferred use rights of real estate. Progressive tax rates are practiced, or in other words the levy is proportional to the value added, which is advantageous to restricting excessive speculation and investment in real estate. When computing the value added, it is allowed to deduct the land transfer fees and development cost and expenses for land improvement, which is advantageous in restricting deliberate evasion of land transfer fees, encouraging development and utilization of state-owned land, and standardizing trading order on the real estate market.

To improve local taxation

Land value increment tax is a kind of local tax which is levied by local tax authorities, and all the tax revenue belongs to the local government. Levy of land value increment tax and enhancement of the administration of land value increment tax will not only help to increase the local fiscal income, encouraging the local government to improve the overall urban environment, but also help to improve the local tax system, enlarging the scale of local tax revenue and creating favorable conditions for the perfection of division of the tax system and the financial system.

The system of land value increment tax

Object of taxation

General provisions on the scope of collection

The scope of collection of land value increment tax is the use rights of state-owned land, above-ground buildings and other attached objects thereon. The above-ground buildings and other attached objects mentioned here mean all the buildings, structures and all sorts of attached objects constructed on the land and all the plants or other objects which are attached to the land and cannot be moved if damage may happen to them from the removal.

Criteria for collection scope

1) The use right of the transferred land belongs to the state. Land value increment tax is levied on the act of transfer of use right of state-owned land, above-ground buildings and other attached objects thereon. According to the constitution and the *Land Administration Law of the People's Republic of China*, land in cities is owned by the state. Land in rural areas and sub-urban areas are owned by collectives except some that is owned by the state as prescribed by laws. Only use right of state-owned land can be compensatorily transferred. Land owned by collectives cannot be directly transferred; it can only be transferred after it is expropriated by the state.

2) Use right of land and ownership of above-ground buildings and other attached objects thereon must be transferred. Land value increment tax is levied on acts of transfer of right over state-owned land, above-ground buildings and other attached objects thereon. It contains two tiers of meaning. The first is that the collection scope of land value increment tax does not include the revenue from transfer of use right of state-owned land. The transfer of use right of state-owned land means that the state, as a land user, transfers use right of the land to the land users for a certain period of years and land users pay the state transfer fees. It belongs to the primary market of land. Transfer of usufruct of state-owned land means acts of re-transfer after the land user obtains the use right of the land in form of transfer, including sale, exchange and gift, and it belongs to the secondary market of land buying and selling. The second is that the collection scope of land value increment tax does not include the acts of transfer of use right of land or housing property, such as the letting of housing property.

3) Transfer income shall be obtained. Compensatory transfer of real estate is liable to land value increment tax, while real estate transferred without compensation in form of inheritance or gift is not.
   Only in the case that the three conditions above are simultaneously satisfied does the transfer income fall into the collection scope of land value increment tax. It must be emphasized that land value increment

tax shall be paid according to the stipulations regardless of sole transfer of use right of state-owned land or transfer of usufruct of land together with above-ground buildings and other attached objects.

Special provisions on above-ground buildings

1) Real estate rent. In the case of rent of real estate, although the leasor obtains the income, the use right of the land and the housing property has not been transferred. Thus this does not fall into the collection scope of land value increment tax.

2) Mortgage of real estate. The ownership of real estate property and the use right of land does not change during the mortgage period. The owner of the property and user of the land have rights of possession, use and benefits etc. Although the housing property owner and land user have obtained certain mortgage loans during the mortgage period, in fact these loans shall be returned to the loaner with interest after the mortgage period. So for the mortgage of the property, land value increment tax shall not be levied during the mortgage period. After the expiry of mortgage period, land value increment tax is levied according to whether there is transfer of possession of the real estate. The transfer of real estate ownership due to debt payment by real estate shall be included in the scope of collection of land value increment tax.

3) Exchange of real estate. This act leads to the transfer of housing property and use right of land, and both parties in the exchange obtain material income. According to the *Provisional Regulations on Land Value Increment Tax*, it falls into the scope of collection of land value increment tax. But for the exchange of self-occupied housing property between two individuals, land value increment tax can be exempted upon verification by the local tax authorities.

4) Pool and investment on real estate property. For pool and investment on real estate property, the party of pool and investment uses land (real estate) to invest or as the pool condition, transfers the real estate to the enterprises of investment and pool and enjoys exemption of land value increment tax temporarily. In the case of re-transfer of the real estate by enterprises of investment and pools, land value increment tax shall be levied. It should be noted that only non-real estate enterprises having foreign investment and pool of real estate are temporarily exempted from land value increment tax in the case of transfer, while land value increment tax shall be paid in the case of re-

transfer by enterprises of investments and pools. However, real estate enterprises' foreign investments and pool shall be regarded as sale, and land value increment tax shall be levied in the initial investment link and land value increment tax shall not be levied upon the re-transfer of enterprises of investments and pool.

5) Cooperative housing. For cooperative housing with one party providing land and the other party providing funds, land value increment tax for self-occupied housing which is distributed proportionately shall be exempted upon completion. Transfer after completion shall be levied for land value increment tax.

6) The real estate is transferred in the form of inheritance or donation. This is transfer of real estate without compensation since there is no income, so it cannot be included into the scope of land value increment tax. It should be noted that the inheritance of real estate here includes two kinds i.e. inheritance of legitimate heirs and inheritance of non-legitimate heirs, and none needs to pay the land value increment tax. The donation of real estate here only includes two circumstances: the first is that the property owner and owner of the land use right donates the housing property and use right of land to his directive relative or his direct heir. The second is that the property owner and the owner of the land use right donates housing property and use right of land to education, civil administration or other social welfare and charitable undertakings.

7) Agent-construction of real estate. For real estate development companies, although income is obtained, there is no transfer of real estate ownership and the income is in essence income obtained from labor services, so it does not fall into the collection scope of land value increment tax.

8) Re-assessment of real estate. This mainly means a reassessment of real estate by state-owned enterprises while checking the assets and a subsequent increase in value. Although in this case the real estate has value added, its ownership has not been transferred and there is no income for the owner of the housing property and land use right, so it does not fall into the collection scope of land value increment tax.

9) Enterprise mergers and transfer of real estate. In the merger of enterprises, land value increment tax is exempted if the merged enterprise transfers real estate to the merging enterprise.

Taxpayers

Taxpayers of land value increment tax are units or individuals transferring use right of land, above-ground buildings and other attached objects thereon, and thereby obtaining incomes.

Units means various enterprises (including state-owned enterprises, collectively-owned enterprises, privately-run enterprises, foreign-invested enterprises, foreign enterprises, joint-stock enterprises and other enterprises), administrative units, institutions, social organizations, and other organizations. Individuals include individual operators and other individuals.

Tax rates

Land value increment tax practices a four-grade progressive tax rate, which encourages normal real estate developers and operators with lower tax rates and restricts speculators in real estate and property, and gives play to the state's macro-control function.

The four grades progressive tax rates are shown in Table 8.3.

Table 8.3.   Four-grade progressive tax rates for land value increment tax

Grade	Ratio of value added to the sum of deductable items	Tax rates (%)	Quick calculation deduction (%)
1	The portion not more than 50%	30	0
2	The portion more than 50% and less than 100%	40	5
3	The portion more than 100% and less than 200%	50	15
4	The portion more than 200%	60	35

Tax base

The tax base of land value increment tax is the value added from sale of real estate. Provisional regulations provide that value added is the balance of the incomes from transferring the real estate of the taxpayer minus the amount of statutory deductable items.

Determination of incomes

The incomes from transferring real estate include monetary income, income in kind, and other income.

1) Monetary income. Monetary income refers to credit instruments including cash, cash in bank, check, cashier's order, postal order and etc. and securities of treasury bill, financial bond, corporate bond, stock and etc. from transferring real estate by the taxpayer. The essence of this type of income is the collection from transferring land-use rights and building property rights by the assignor.

2) Physical income. Physical income refers that to income in a variety of physical forms from transferring real estate by the taxpayer, such as real estate including steel, cement and other building materials, buildings, and land.

3) Other incomes. Other income refers to income from intangible assets or the rights of property value obtained from transferring real estate by the taxpayer, such as patent rights, trademark rights, copyrights, right of using proprietary technology, land-use rights, goodwill rights etc.

If any of the following situations occurs we should conduct the income verification based on the evaluated price of the real estate and collect the land value increment tax:

1) Concealment or false declaration of the transaction price of real estate. This means that the taxpayer does not declare or declares at a low price the land use right, constructions, and attachments.

2) Fraudulence over deductable items. This means that the taxpayer does not disclose the deductable items in the tax declaration.

3) The transaction price of transferring real estate is obviously and unwarrantably lower than the evaluated price. This means that the actual transaction price of real estate which is declared by taxpayer is lower than the price as evaluated by a real estate appraisal organization, and the taxpayer cannot provide the proper evidence for this.

If the taxpayer conceals or falsely declares the price of real estate, the price should be evaluated according to the transaction price of similar real estate. The tax office will determine the income from transferring real estate according to the evaluated price.

If the taxpayer provides a fraudulent amount for deductable items, the price should be evaluated according to the cost price which is the replacement cost price multiplied by depreciation rate, and standard land value when the land-use right was obtained. The tax office will determine the amount of deductable items according to the evaluated price.

If the transaction price of transferring real estate is unwarrantably lower than the evaluated price, the tax office will determine the incomes from transferring real estate according to the evaluated price of the real estate.

The evaluated price of real estate means the evaluation by a real estate appraisal organization which is approved by the government, according to the same district or similar real estate, and affirmed by the local tax office.

Determination of deductable items

The calculation of the amount of land value increment tax refers to tax collection on the balance of revenue minus each deductable items approved by the government, which is not tax collection on the incomes of transferring real estate, and the balance is the value added from transferring real estate. The deductable items approved by tax law are as follows:

1) Payment of land use rights
   - The payment amount of land use right acquirement includes the following two items:
   - The land cost for acquirement of land use rights. If the land use right is acquired by transfer agreement, bid invitation, auction etc., the land cost is the land transfer fees paid by the taxpayers; if the land use right is acquired by administrative transfer, the land cost is the land transfer fees according to the relevant provisions; if the land use rights are acquired by transfer, the land cost is the amount paid to the primary land use right holders.
   The relevant costs paid in accordance with national provisions. This refers to the registration and transfer formalities fee paid in accordance with national provisions when acquiring the land use right.

2) Cost of real estate development
   The cost of real estate development refers to the cost of real estate development, including compensation for expropriation and demolition, prophase engineering cost, installation engineering cost, infrastructure cost, public supporting facility cost, indirect cost in development etc.
   - Compensation for expropriation and demolition. This consists of compensation for expropriation, farmland conversion tax, labor force settlement allowance, compensation for above-ground and underground demolition, and the cost for arranging buildings for relocation.
   - Prophase engineering cost. This consists of expenses for planning, designing, project feasibility study, hydrology, geology, surveying, mapping, leveling, and connecting to water and electricity supply and transport facilities.

- Installation engineering cost. This is paid to the contractor who undertakes the installation engineering.
- Infrastructure cost. This consists of expenses for paths, water supply, power supply, gas supply, waste water discharge, flood discharge, communications, lighting, environmental sanitation, afforestation and etc.
- Public supporting facility cost. This includes the expenses of public supporting facilities which cannot be transferred.
- Indirect cost in development. This refers to the expenses of organizing and managing the development project, including wages, employee services and benefits, depreciation costs, repair costs, administrative expenses, utility bills, labor protection fees, revolving house amortization etc.

3) Expense of real estate development

Real estate development expenses are selling expenses, managing expenses and financial expenses relevant to real estate development. According to the modern financial and accounting rules this expense, which is a period expense, should be included in the current profits and losses and not be split according to cost accounting object. As a deductable item of land value increment tax, the real estate development cost should not be deducted according to expenses of real estate development but in accordance with the *Detailed Rules for the Implementation of the Provisional Regulations of the People's Republic of China on Land Value Increment Tax*.

The *Detailed Rules for the Implementation of the Provisional Regulations of the People's Republic of China on Land Value Increment Tax* provide that the interest expenses of financial expense, which can be split according to real estate transfer and have the certification of a financial institution, may be deducted but may not exceed the amount calculated according to the loan interest rate of the same kind and period from a commercial bank. Other real estate development costs should be deducted at 5% of the balance of the payment amount of acquiring the land use right plus real estate development cost. If the interest expenses of financial expense cannot be split according to real estate transfer or the certification of a financial institution cannot be provided, the real estate development cost should be deducted from at 10% of the amount of balance of the payment for acquiring the land use right plus real estate development cost. The detailed proportion of deduction is provided by the people's governments of each province and municipality.

In addition, the treasury department and State Administration of Taxation provide two special rules on interest expense of amount of deductable items: one is that the floating range should be in accordance with the relevant provisions and the parts which exceed the come-up amplitude may not be deducted; another is that the interest and penalty interest of exceeding the length of maturity may not be deducted.

4) Relevant tax on transferring real estate

Relevant tax on transferring real estate refers to the business tax, city maintenance and construction tax, and stamp tax during transfer of real estate. The educational surtax on transferring real estate should be deducted as tax.

Specifically, according to the *Financial Regulations of Construction and Real Estate Development Enterprises*, the stamp tax is included in management expenses and thus it will not be deducted. The stamp tax paid by the other taxpayer (0.5‰ of the amount of the transfer certificate of property) is allowed to be deducted.

5) Other deductable items

20% of the balance of amount of acquiring land- use right plus real estate development cost should be deducted for the taxpayer who is engaged in real estate development. It should be pointed out in particular that this provision only applies to the taxpayer who is engaged in real estate development and not to other taxpayer. The aim of this provision is to restrain illegal trading and, protect the enthusiasm of the normal development investor.

6) Price evaluation of old buildings and constructions

Evaluated price of old buildings and constructions refers to the balance of replacement cost price evaluated by real estate appraisal organizations approved by the government multiplied by the rate of depreciation, during transfer of used buildings and constructions. The evaluated price should be confirmed by the local tax office.

Replacement cost price refers to the cost price of building new buildings and constructions with the same area, level, structure and construction standard, according to the price of building materials and expenses of labor when transferring the old buildings and constructions. The rate of depreciation is a discount according to the usage.

In addition, land value increment tax should be collected based on the amount of deductable items which consist of the relevant cost which is paid when transferring old buildings according to the evaluated price of buildings and constructions, the land cost of acquiring the land use right, and national provisions, and the tax which is paid in the transfer. If the land cost has not been paid when acquiring the land use right or the taxpayer cannot provide evidence of the land cost which has been paid, is may not be deducted in the collection of land value increment tax.

In addition, if the taxpayer transferring the land use right is developing and transferring in stages or groups, the determination of amount of deductable items should be quantified according to the proportion of the transferred land use right area in the gross area, or building area, or in other ways approved by the tax office.

Calculation of tax payable

Land value increment tax is collected according to the value added from transferring real estate and the approved tax rate. There are three detailed calculation methods.

Multi-step calculation method

Land value increment tax is collected according to four levels of progressive rate, thus determination of the tax payable by the original method should be in accordance with the following steps:

First, calculate the amount of land value added:

Amount of land value added = Gross incomes of transferring real estate – Amount of deductable items

Then, calculate the land value added rate:

Land value added rate = Amount of land value added / Amount of deductable items × 100%

Then, calculate the amount of land value added of each grade and class interval: This means to divide the land value added rate from the second step calculation into several parts according to the grades and class intervals determined by the land value increment tax, and then calculate the land value added of each part.

Land value added of each part = Amount of land value added × Land value added of each part

Finally, calculate the tax payable:

Tax payable = ∑(Land value added of each part × Proper tax rate of each part)

Although this multi-step calculation method is in accordance with the principle of the land value increment tax, the computational process is complicated and thus it is less used in practical work.

Quick deduction method

The tax payable of land value increment tax can be also easy calculated by multiplying the value added with the proper tax rate subtracting the amount of deductable items multiplied by the quick calculation deduction rate. This kind of method is called the quick calculation deduction rate method or quick calculation deduction coefficient method, the principle of tax setting is similar to the quick calculation deduction count method, and it is the one most prevalently used in practical work. The formula is:

Tax payable = Land value added × Applicable tax rate –
Amount of deductable items × Quick calculation deduction coefficient

The formula for tax payable of land value increment tax according to the group of sub-value added is as follows:

The value added does not exceed 50% of amount of deductable items:

Tax payable = Value added × 30%

The value added exceeds 50% but not 100% of amount of deductable items:

Tax payable = Value added × 40% – Amount of deductable items × 5%

The value added exceeds 100% but not 200% of amount of deductable items:

Tax payable = Value added × 50% – Amount of deductable items × 15%

The value added exceeds 200% of amount of deductable items:

Tax payable = Value added × 60% – Amount of deductable items × 35%

5%, 15% and 35% in the formulas are quick calculation deduction rates (coefficients).

Tax preference

According to the current situation in China, land value increment tax will be reduced or exempted in the following three circumstances.

For standard residence domiciles

When selling a normal standard residence built by the taxpayer, if the value added does not exceed 20% of the amount of deductible items, the land value increment tax should be exempted. If the value added exceeds 20% of amount of the deductable items, land value increment tax should be paid according to gross value added.

Normal standard residence refers to the building which accords with the standard of a local civil residence. Service flats, villas, western style buildings with two stories or more, holiday villages, and residences which exceed the area, standard and degree of luxury, are not normal standard residences. The provincial government will provide the detailed limits between normal standard residences and others.

If the taxpayer builds a normal standard residence and develops other real estate as well, the value added should be accounted separately; if the value added is not accounted separately or accurately, the normal standard residence will not be liable for the rules of tax exemption.

For real estate being expropriated and repossessed by state

The taxpayer shall be exempt from land value increment tax if real estate is expropriated and repossessed by state construction. The real estate that is being expropriated and repossessed by state construction in accordance with the law refers to the fact that real estate is expropriated or land use right is repossessed by approval of the government due to the requirements of planning implementation of city and state construction.

Where taxpayers transfer original real estate voluntarily when relocation is required because of planning implementation of city and state construction, it shall be exempt from tax in accordance with this regulation.

The units and individuals who conform to the tax exemption regulations above must put forward a tax exemption application to the local tax authority and may be exempted from land value increment tax after being examined and verified by the local tax authority.

For individuals who transfer real estate

Individuals who transfer an original self-use house where the individual has lived for 5 years or above due to job change or improvement of housing conditions may be exempted from land value increment tax after being examined and approved by the local tax authority. If the individual has lived there for over 3 years but less than 5 years, 50% of the land value increment tax shall be levied. If the individual has lived there less than 3 years, the land value increment tax shall be levied in accordance with the regulations.

Individuals selling houses after January 1, 2008, shall be temporarily exempt from land value increment tax.

Administration of tax collection

Tax declaration

In accordance with the *Provisional Regulations on Land Value Increment Tax*, taxpayers shall submit a tax declaration to the local tax authority within 7 days of the day of signing of the real estate transfer contract, and submit the building property rights certificate, land use right certificate, contracts of land transfer and real estate business contract, assessment report of real estate, and other documents related to the real estate transfer, and then pay the land value increment tax within the time limit approved by the tax authority. Taxpayers may execute a regular tax declaration after being checked and approved by the tax authority it is difficult to declare tax for every transfer due to constant real estate transactions. The specific declaration time limit shall be determined by the tax authorities. After dealing with tax procedures, taxpayers shall transact ownership transfer procedures at the real estate and land administrative department with the tax payment receipt.

Taxpayers of land value increment tax are divided into two categories in reality. One is the taxpayers who are engaged in real estate development (this includes as exclusive business and as concurrent business), namely the ordinary real estate development company; the other is other taxpayers. Different contents and methods of transaction of tax declaration apply.

1) Companies engaging in real estate development. Taxpayers shall transact the tax declaration at the tax authority within 7 days of the occurrence of tax liability resulting from signing of a real estate transfer contract or within the time limit regulated by the tax authority in accordance with the tax law, and provide the following certificates and documentation:
   - House property rights certificate, land use right certificate.
   - Contracts of land transfer and real estate business contract.
   - Documents related to real estate transfer, which include: payment for obtaining land use right; financial accounting information on cost of real estate development; documents on expenses of real estate development; tax payment receipt of taxation expenses on real estate transfer; other information related to the real estate.
   - A real estate appraisal report shall be submitted to the tax authority.

This refers to a real estate appraisal report in accordance with the tax law executed by an assessment institution approved by government if tax authorities believe the incomes or deductable items provided by the taxpayer due to real estate transfer are accurate and cannot act as the basis for tax calculation, and a real estate appraisal is necessary.

The tax authority shall examine and check the tax documents above including contracts or texts. The contents concerning tax relief and tax by installments include:

First, the specific date of signing the real estate transfer contract, real estate development contract or setting of project, signing of the land transfer contract, and implementation of development capital in accordance with the regulations of the contract. It shall provide relevant documentation signed before January 1, 1994 for the contracts above, which shall act as the reference basis for tax of this item determined by the tax authority.

Second, types of real estate development. This shall record whether the development item is a common standard house, which shall act as the reference basis of tax determined by the tax authority.

Third, forms of real estate transfer. This shall record whether an item is a one-time sale or sale by stages and adoption of selling method or presale, which shall act as the reference basis for tax declaration and tax payment time determined by the tax authority.

2) Taxpayers other than real estate development companies. This kind of taxpayer shall transact the tax declaration at the local tax authority where the house is located within 7 days of the day of signing the real estate transfer contract, and provide the following documentation:

- House and building property rights certificate, land use right certificate.
- Contracts of land transfer and real estate business contract.
- Real estate appraisal report. There must be an appraisal report made by an assessment institution designated by the government if an old house is transferred.
- Tax payment receipt of taxation expenses on the real estate transfer.
- Other documents related to the real estate transfer, such as original cost of construction or buying price of the real estate.

Assessable period and methods of payment

Land value increment tax shall be levied in accordance with calculation of actual benefits obtained through real estate transfer, so the tax payment time of land value increment tax cannot be regulated uniformly as with other tax categories but is determined specifically by the local tax authority in accordance with different transfers of real estate due the need for consideration of cost and expenses of real estate development and implementation of real estate appraisal. The specific conditions are as follows:

1) Transfer of real estate in a one-time delivery and payment. The local tax authorities shall regulate the taxpayer to pay all the land value increment tax within a number of days before procedures of transfer of names and registration in accordance with the amount of tax amount payable and the time limit of transaction of procedures of transfer of names and registration when taxpayer completes the tax declaration.

2) Transfer of real estate through payment by stages. The tax authority shall determine the specific assessment period for tax payment in accordance with the date of receipt regulated in the contract, namely it shall calculate the total land value increment tax payable, and then the total income from the real estate is divided by the total tax amount, which is the ratio of tax payable to total income. After that, when cost is received, the amount of received cost multiplied by the ratio is the tax amount payable every time, and the tax authority shall regulate that land value increment tax be paid within a number of days after receiving the cost.

3) Transfer of real estate before completion of settlement of project. Land value increment tax may be levied in advance when the taxpayer cannot calculate land value increment tax for income obtained through real estate transfer before completion of settlement of project due to cost accounting or other reasons, and then clear accounts when settlement is carried out after completion of project. There are two conditions as follows:

First, where the taxpayer implements development and construction of a neighborhood and part of the real estate projects have been transferred due to development in advance, but some supporting facilities will be built after transfer. In this situation, tax authorities may levy land value increment tax in advance when income is obtained for items being transferred in advance.

Second, where the taxpayer transfers real estate by pre-sale, the tax authority may levy land value increment tax for income obtained before settlement and delivery procedures. The specific methods shall be formulated by the provincial local tax authority on the basis of local conditions.

In accordance with the regulations of the tax law, where land value increment tax is levied in advance, the land value increment tax shall be cleared if it meets the conditions for clearing.

Place of payment

The tax authority where the real estate is located is responsible for the collection of the land value increment tax. "Location of the real estate" refers to its physical location. Regardless of the location of the organization, business or residence of the taxpayer is, tax shall be declared at the location of the real estate. There are two specific conditions as follows:

1) Where the taxpayer is a legal person. Tax may be declared at the original administrative tax authority where tax registration is transacted when location of the real estate transferred by the taxpayer is in the same location as the organization or business; when location of the real estate transferred by the taxpayer is not in the same location as the organization or business, tax shall be declared at the administrative tax authority where the real estate is located. Where locations of real estate transferred by the taxpayer are in two or more areas, tax shall be declared at the respective locations of the real estate.

2) Where the taxpayer is natural person. When location of the real estate transferred by the taxpayer is in the location as location of residence, tax shall be declared at the tax authority where the residence is located; when location of the real estate transferred by taxpayer is not in the same location as residence, tax shall be declared at the tax authority where the transfer procedures are transacted.

Taxpayers of land value increment tax shall transact the tax declaration at the local administrative tax authority where the real estate is located within 7 days of the day of signing the real estate transfer contract, and submit the building property rights certificate, land use right certificate, contracts of land transfer and real estate business contract, assessment report on the real estate, and other documents related to the real estate transfer to the tax authority. Taxpayers may execute tax declaration at regular intervals after being checked and approved by the tax authority it is difficult to declare tax for every transfer due to constant real estate transfers. The specific declaration time limit shall be determined by the tax authority in accordance with actual conditions.

Land Use Tax

An overview

Some concepts

Land use tax is a kind of lump-sum quota tax levied on entities and individuals occupying land for building or engaging in other non-agricultural construction according to the area of land occupied. It is the first important tax in China's land tax system.

China is a country with a large population and a severe shortage of cultivated land. The agricultural acreage is only about 1.8 billion *mu* (a unit of area, about 666.67 m^2) which is less than 7% of the world total but which supports a population about 22% of the world total. Cultivated land area per capita is about 1.3 *mu*, ranked behind No.110 in the world. Since the reform and opening up to the outside world, the speed of agricultural land's transformation into urban land (usually non-agricultural land) has clearly accelerated with the increasing urbanization, and there are severe problems of abuse of cultivated land, occupation of cultivated land but without utilization, and less utilization but more occupation. Reclamation and improvement of cultivated land lags far behind and the contradiction between supply and demand of cultivated land becomes increasingly prominent, which seriously endangers the leading position of agriculture and damages the sustainable development of the economy and society.

For the purpose of proper use of land resources, enhancement of land administration and protection of cultivated land, the State Council promulgated the *Provisional Regulations of the People's Republic of China on Land Use Tax* on April 1, 1987, and decided to levy land use tax for the occupation of land due to non-agricultural construction. On December 1, 2007, the State Council promulgated the revised *Provisional Regulations of the People's Republic of China on Land Use Tax* which made large adjustments to contents such as taxpayers, tax amount criteria and tax relief, and became effective as of January 1, 2008.

Characteristics

Compared with other land taxes, land use tax has the following characteristics:

1) It is levied for the act of occupation of cultivated land for non-agricultural construction and is of three natures, namely property tax, resource tax and tax for special purposes.
2) It is levied based on the area of cultivated land actually occupied according to the method of amount on volume.
3) Regionally differential quota tax rates are designed in counties according to the quantity of cultivated land per capita.
4) It is only levied in the link of occupation of cultivated land and the one-link tax system is practiced.

5) Local tax authorities are responsible for collection administration, and all revenues belong to local government.

Effects

Levy of land use tax has objectives and significance as follows:

To enhance land administration and to protect agricultural land

One important objective of the levy of land use tax is to increase the cost of land occupation, promote the implementation of state land policies, enhance land administration, restrict land abuse and protect limited land resources.

To increase agricultural income and to stabilize the development of agricultural production

The State Council specifies that the tax levied from land occupation must be totally used as special funds for agricultural development and investment in agricultural development. Therefore levy of land use tax is beneficial to stabilizing agricultural production and strengthening potential for agricultural development.

The system of land use tax

Object of taxation

Land use tax is levied for building or non-agricultural construction by occupation of land within territory of China. It must conform to both of the following two conditions simultaneously; the first is occupation of cultivated land, and the second is building or performing non-agricultural construction.

Cultivated land refers to land for planting farm crops.

Tax is levied for occupation of cultivated land for building or non-agricultural construction by occupying forestland, grassland, land for irrigation and water conservancy, and water surfaces in aquaculture and fisheries areas.

Tax is not levied for occupation of land for irrigation and water conservancy. Occupation of garden land for building or non-agricultural construction shall be regarded as occupation of cultivated land and tax shall be levied.

Taxpayers

Entities or individuals occupying cultivated land for building or non-agricultural construction are the taxpayers of land use tax and shall pay tax according to the regulations.

Entities here include state-owned enterprises, collectively-owned enterprises, private enterprises, joint-stock enterprises, foreign-invested enterprises, foreign enterprises and other enterprises and institutions, social organizations, state organs, troops and other entities; individuals include individual businesses or others.

Upon approval for land occupation, taxpayers shall be the users of land for construction as indicated in the approval documents for conversion of agricultural land; taxpayers shall be the applicants for land use in the case of no indication in approval documents. In the case of land occupation without approval, taxpayers are the actual land users.

Tax rates

Regionally differential quota tax rates are applied. There are four grades of tax amounts according to the area of cultivated land per capita and the economic development situation in each unit of county-level administrative region (see Table 8.4).

Table 8.4.   Criteria of tax for land occupation

Area of cultivated land per capita	Range of tax amount
Regions where the area is not more than one *mu*	RMB10–50 /m^2
Regions where the area is more than one mu but not more than two *mu*	RMB8–40 /m^2
Regions where the area is more than two mu but not more than three *mu*	RMB6–30 /m^2
Regions where the area is not more than three *mu*	RMB5–25 /m^2

People's governments at all levels may check and verify tax amounts applicable to their regions according to the ranges specified in the above table.

The applicable tax amount may be moderately increased for special economic zones, economic and technological development zones, and regions with a developed economy but scant per capita land possession. However the increased portion shall not be more than 50% of the applicable tax amount verified by the people's governments at all levels.

In order to prevent too low criteria of applicable tax amounts verified in different regions, the financial departments and competent tax authorities of the State

Council specify the average tax amounts for all provinces, autonomous regions and municipalities directly under the central government according to the area of cultivated land per capita and the economic development situation (see Table 8.5).

Table 8.5.   Average tax amount for land occupation

Regions	Average tax amount per square meter (RMB)
Shanghai	45
Beijing	40
Tianjin	35
Jiangsu, Zhejiang, Fujian, Guangdong	30
Liaoning, Hubei, Hunan	25
Hebei, Anhui, Jiangxi, Shandong, Henan, Chongqing, Sichuan	22.5
Guangxi, Hainan, Guizhou, Yunan, Shaanxi	20
Shanxi, Jilin, Heilongjiang	17.5
Inner Mongolia, Tibet, Gansu, Qinghai, Ningxia, Xinjiang	12.5

Average applicable tax amounts verified by the people's governments at all levels shall not be lower than the average tax amounts determined by the financial departments and competent tax authorities of the State Council. Tax amounts applicable to county-level administrative regions of provinces, autonomous regions and municipalities directly under the central government shall conform to the *Provisional Regulations of the People's Republic of China on Land Use Tax* and its detailed rules for implementation, and the regulations of the people's governments.

In case of occupation of basic farmland, the applicable tax amounts shall be improved by 50% on the basis of the applicable tax amounts verified by the people's governments at all levels. Basic farmland refers to cultivated land within the scope of a basic farmland protection zone as defined in accordance with the *Regulations on the Protection of Basic Farmland*.

Calculation of tax payable

Land use tax is calculated based on the area of land actually occupied by taxpayers and lump-sum levy is practiced according to the specified applicable tax amounts. The formula for calculating land use tax payable is as follows:

Tax payable = Taxable land area × Applicable unit tax rate

Tax reduction, exemption and refund

1) Exemption of tax on land occupation
   - Land occupied by military facilities.
   - Land occupied by schools, kindergartens, geracomiums and hospitals.
2) Reduction of tax on land occupation
   - A reduced tax amount of RMB2/m^2 is granted for land occupied by railways, highways, airstrips, parking aprons, harbors and shipping channels.
   - For land occupied by rural residents for building houses, land use tax is reduced by half of the local applicable tax amount.
   - Land use tax may be exempted or reduced by half after examination by local township people's governments and approval by county-level people's governments for the families of martyrs, disabled solders and those who have no relatives and cannot support themselves in rural areas, and residents in old revolutionary bases, localities of minority nationalities, and those in remote and poor mountainous areas who face livelihood difficulties.

   Taxpayers' change of use of originally occupied land after exemption or reduction of land use tax in accordance with the regulations shall be liable for land use tax additionally as per the local applicable tax amount the circumstances no longer warrant exemption or reduction.

9
Chapter

Property Taxes

An Overview

Some concepts

Property taxes (the property tax system) are the general term for taxes levied on the possession, use, profits, donation and transfer of real property. The categories of taxes that belong to property taxes are house tax, contract tax, and vehicle and vessel usage tax in the current tax system in China.

Compared with income tax, the differences are as follows: from the point of view of object of taxation, both property taxes and income tax show income. However the object of taxation for property tax is the stock of income, while the object of taxation for income tax is the flow of income. The taxpayer of property taxes is the owner, user, and successor of property income while the taxpayer of income tax is the owner of kinds of incomes. In terms of the tax calculation, property taxes are levied on the value and the property itself while income tax is levied on the incomes derived from property.

As one of the oldest tax categories, property taxes as direct tax used to be the main tax category and one of the main sources of state revenue in pre-capitalist society. With the further development of the commodity economy, property income as the main category of tax has gradually made way for turnover tax and income tax. The status of property taxes has been weakened in the recent several decades.

There are many kinds of classification for property tax categories in accordance with its levy characteristic, including:

Property value tax and capital gains tax

Property taxes are divided into property value tax and capital gains tax in accordance with different bases for tax calculation. The property value tax is a tax levied on the value of property owned by the taxpayer, and the tax standards are total value of property, net value of property, actual value of property. Capital gains tax takes earnings or value added of property as the basis for tax calculation, which is generally allocated into the income tax category.

Static property tax and dynamic property tax

Property tax may be divided into static property tax and dynamic property tax in accordance with different objects of taxation. The static property tax is levied on the property occupied, owned or dominated by the taxpayer at a certain time point. The dynamic property tax is levied on the transfer value or value added of property or property rights when ownership of taxable property or other rights and interests such as right of use is transferred.

General property tax and special property tax

Property tax is divided into general property tax and special property tax in accordance with the different scope of the levy property. General property tax, also called comprehensive property tax, is levied on the value of the whole or total of many kinds of properties owned by the taxpayer. Special property tax, also called individual property tax, is levied on some specific property (such as land and housing) owned by the taxpayer.

Characteristics

Abundant sources

The sources of property taxes include all working achievements (means of production and means of consumption) accumulated in society and natural resources (including land, mountain forest, mineral resources, rivers, shoals etc.) and all kinds of proprietary rights (such as patent rights, copyrights, trademark rights) which present the achievements of mental labor. Property taxes is levied on some specific properties as selected in accordance with financial requirements and the social and economic conditions of society.

Fairness

As a kind of direct tax, property taxes levy on the occupation or domination of property in the consumption sector, so the burden cannot be shifted. Thus property taxes are beneficial to fairness of tax incidence because it can overcome the regressive nature of tax transfer and conforms to the principle of capacity for tax.

Comprehensive revenue collection and administration

Property taxes are levied on property stock accumulated over years in non-tradable fields. However it lacks normal transaction value in non-tradable fields and the cost of stock property does not reflect the current market value as time moves on. Thus evaluation of the current market price must be used as the base for tax calculation. Due to the difficulty of finding a sensible basis for price, it is hard to determine the basis for tax calculation of property tax which is thus complicated for revenue collection and administration.

Small elasticity of tax revenue

The specific characteristics of the object of taxation of property taxes limit the universality of scope of levy. Meanwhile, the property price fluctuation is not as large as that of common commodities. For the sake of revenue collection and management, many countries have fixed the price for value of property for several years, which makes the revenue elasticity of property tax small.

Sources of government revenue

With the development of social economy and expansion of the functions and powers of the state, it is hard for the property taxes, with poor elasticity and difficulty of levy, to meet the demand of raising revenue and economy regulation for government, so the leading role of property taxes in the tax system has been replaced by turnover tax and income tax and has then become a source of revenue of local government.

Effects

To improve macro-control and regulation of tax revenue

Generally, commodity tax and income tax adjust commodity flow or income volume, but the adjustment for property stock transformed from income is limited, so property taxes make up the deficiencies of commodity tax and income tax and then realizes the macro-control and regulation of the social economy through taxation by the state.

To maintain a steady flow of fiscal revenue

There are two objects of taxation for property taxes: one is revenue of property, the other is value of property. The levy on revenue of property can increase fiscal revenue and become a supplementary source of fiscal revenue because of its sufficient source of taxation. The levy on value of property is stable and reliable in revenue because the object of taxation is not affected by constantly varying factors. The stability of object of taxation for property taxes determines the steady growth of property tax with the increase of taxable property and is not affected by economic fluctuation. Therefore property taxes are generally allocated into local tax in those countries where a tax-sharing system is implemented, and thus property tax becomes the main source of fiscal revenue for local government.

To secure a fair wealth distribution

The degree of wealth and taxable capacity of a person is defined by the property owned by the person. Property taxes are beneficial to the rectification of uneven distribution of wealth through income adjustment of the property owner and control of property concentration and implementation of a reasonable distribution of burden. It conforms to the principle of fairness. Meanwhile, the levy on transfer of property promotes the successor standing on their own feet and creates the conditions for fair competition.

House Tax

An overview

Some concepts

House tax is a tax to levied on the house owner or operator in accordance with the residual value of the house or rental income from the house.

After the New China was founded in 1949, the Government Administration Council promulgated the *Regulations for the Implementation of Tax Administration*, which regulated the levy of house tax and real estate tax in China. On August 1951, the then Government Administration Council promulgated the *Interim Regulations on Urban Real Estate Tax* which merged house tax and real estate tax. In 1973, the reform of the industrial and commercial tax system merged the urban real estate tax into the industrial and commercial tax, and continued to levy the urban real estate tax on individuals with houses, wholly foreign-owned enterprises and house property management departments. On October 1984, the State Council recovered the levy of house tax when it implemented the second step of changing profits into tax and reformed the industrial and commercial tax system. However the land in cities belongs to the state in China, and the users of the land have no land ownership, so it divides urban real estate tax into house tax and land use tax. On September 15, 1986, the State Council promulgated the *Provisional Regulations on the Housing Property Tax* which was put into implementation in October 1, 1986. In accordance with the decree of the State Council of the People's Republic of China promulgated on December 31, 2008, it declared the abolition from January 1, 2009 of the *Interim Regulations on Urban Real Estate Tax* promulgated by the then Government Administration Council on August 8, 1951. As of January 1, 2009, foreign-funded enterprises, foreign enterprises and organizations, and foreign individuals pay house tax in accordance with the

Provisional Regulations on the Housing Property Tax of the People's Republic of China.

Effects

The significances of house tax are as follows:

1) It can provide reliable fiscal revenue for local government through collection of house tax;
2) House tax can adjust the income gained by the taxpayer due to inappropriate shifting of taxation;
3) It may enhance the management of housing and improve the service efficiency of housing.

The system of house tax

Object of taxation

The object of taxation of house tax is the house. House refers to a place with roof and building enclosure, and shelter from wind and rain, where people produce, work, study, entertain, live or store goods and materials.

The incidence of taxation of house tax includes city, county town, organic towns and industrial and mining areas, among which:

1) Cities are those which are established after being approved by the State Council.
2) County towns are those areas where the county people's governments are located.
3) Organic towns are those which are established after being approved by the people's governments at all levels.
4) Industrial and mining areas are those where large and medium industrial and mining enterprises are located with developed industry and commerce and concentrated population; an organic town is not established in here although it conforms to organic town standards regulated by the State Council. The levy on house tax in industrial and mining areas must be approved by the people's governments at all levels.

Rural areas are free from incidence of taxation of house tax.

House tax shall not be levied for commodity houses before sale which are built by real estate development enterprises, except for those commodity houses which have been used, rented or lent before sale by real estate development enterprises.

Taxpayers

Objects of taxation of house tax are owners of property rights in the real estate within scope of collection, among which:

1) Operating administrative units pay tax for those houses whose property rights belong to the state. Collective units and individuals pay tax for houses whose property rights belong to collective units and individuals respectively. Units include state-owned enterprises, collectively-owned enterprises, private enterprises, stock enterprises, foreign-funded enterprises, foreign enterprises, other enterprises and public institutions, public organizations, state organs, military and other units. Individuals include privately or individually-owned businesses or any other individual person.

2) The person taking out a mortgage ay for house tax when the property right of a house is pawned. Mortgage of property right is a financing business to obtaining capital when the owner of the property right pawns the property right of a house and means of production to others for a certain period. The person taking out a mortgage may obtain right of domain of the pledged goods within the mortgage period and transfer the mortgage when the person taking out a mortgage pays the mortgagee regulated in tax law that the person taking out a mortgage is the taxpayer because the owner of the property right of the house has no right to dominate the house within the mortgage period of the house.

3) The managing agent or user of the house pays housing tax when the owner of the property right of the house or the person taking out a mortgage is not in the location of the house.

4) The managing agent or user of the house pays housing tax when the property right is not determined or dispute on rent or mortgage is not resolved.

5) The user of the house pays house tax for those tax units and individuals who use the houses of house administrative department, tax-exempt entities, and tax units without lease.

Since January 1, 2009, foreign-funded enterprises, foreign enterprises and organizations, and foreign individuals pay house tax.

Tax rates

Proportional tax rate is adopted in the current house tax in China. There are two forms of tax rate for house tax due to the fact that the basis for tax calculation of house tax is divided into levy ad valorem and levy on rent.

1) Ad valorem: the tax rate is 12% when levied on the residual value, which is equal to house original value minus 10%–30% of the value.

2) Rent-based tax levy: the tax rate is 12%.

Since March 1, 2008, house tax at a 4% tax rate has been levied for individual renting of a house. For houses owned by enterprises and public institutions, public organizations and other organizations, rented by individual to live in, house tax is deducted to a 4% tax rate.

Tax base

The tax base of house tax is the dutiable value or rental income of the house. The levy on dutiable value of the house is called levy ad valorem, while levy on rent is on the basis of rental income of the house.

Ad valorem tax levy

This is payment of house tax in accordance with the residual value which is equal to the original value of the house minus 10%–30% of its value as regulated in the *Provisional Regulations on the Housing Property Tax*. The proportion deducted in various regions shall be determined by the people's governments at all levels.

1) Original value of a house is the original cost of the house recorded under "fixed assets" in the account book in accordance with the regulations of the accounting system. Therefore house tax shall be levied on the basis of house residual value, which is equal to the original cost of the house minus a certain deduction if the original cost of the house is recorded under "fixed assets" in the account book in accordance with the regulations of the accounting system. Otherwise the original value of the house shall be determined and then the house tax levy regulated in accordance with above principle and with reference to similar houses.

2) Original value of house shall include all kinds of accessory equipment which is inseparable from the house or supporting facilities, of which the value is generally calculated independently. These are as follows: heating installation, sanitary installation, ventilation installation, lighting equipment and gas installation; all kinds of pipelines such as steam, compressed air, oil, water supply and drainage; and electricity telecommunications and cable conductor, elevator, lifter, passageway and flat roof. The calculation of original value shall be started from the nearest visiting well or three-way pipe for water pipe, sewer, heating

pipe and gas pipe which belong to house accessory equipment. The electric light net and illuminating line is calculated from the original value from the connecting pipe of the inlet line box.

3) The original value of the house shall be added to when the taxpayer rebuilds or expands the original house.

In addition, the following problems should be noted: first, levy of house tax for houses of joint operation by investment shall be different. For those persons who operate house investment and investors who participate in profits and risk share of investment, house tax is levied on the original value of the house as the basis for tax calculation. For those who obtain fixed income from house rent through house investment and do not share the risk of joint operation, it shall be levied on house tax on the leasor through rental income in accordance with the relevant regulations in the *Provisional Regulations on the Housing Property Tax.* Second, with respect to houses on finance lease, the lease fee including costs, procedure fee and loan interest on purchasing the house is different from "rent" as a result of leasing of a common house, and when the tenancy is terminated the property right of the house shall be transferred to the lessee when the lessee pays back the last lease fee. This is in fact a form of subtle purchasing of fixed assets through installment payment, so it house tax shall be levied in accordance with the calculation of the residual value of the house. With respect to the taxpayer of house tax within the lease term, this shall be determined by local tax authorities in accordance with the specific conditions.

4) Tax regulations for accessory equipment and supporting facilities for the house

Since January 1, 2006, the levy on accessory equipment and supporting facilities of the house as house tax shall be implemented in accordance with the following regulations:

- Any immovable at will accessory equipment and supporting facilities which take the house as carrier, such as water supply and drainage, heating installation, fire-fighting, central air-conditioning, electric and intelligent building equipment, shall be levied for house tax in accordance with the proportion of they represent in the original value of the house, whether they are accounted and checked independently within financial accounting or not.
- For those houses where accessory equipment and supporting facilities change, the value of original relevant equipment and facilities shall be deducted when their value is put in original value of the house.

For those houses where spare and accessory parts is easily damaged and need to be changed constantly, they shall not be included in the original value of the house when changed.

Rent-based tax levy

In accordance with the *Provisional Regulations on the Housing Property Tax*, house rental income is taken as the basis for tax calculation of house tax if the house is leased. The house rental income is remuneration obtained by the owner of the house property rights due to lease of the house. It includes monetary income and income in kind.

A standard rental value shall be determined for levy on rent in accordance with the rental level of local similar housing, rent income may be defrayed in the form of labor or other remuneration.

If the taxpayer fails to declare rent income obtained from individual leased houses accurately or the amount in the declaration is obvious unreasonable compared with the rent income of similar houses in the same district, the tax authorities may check and ratify tax payable by using scientific and reasonable methods in accordance with the *Law of Administration of Tax Collection*. The detailed rules shall be formulated by the local tax authorities of provinces, autonomous regions and municipalities directly under the central government according to the actual local conditions.

Calculation of tax payable

Calculation of ad valorem tax levy

Ad valorem tax levy is on the basis of residual value which is equal to original value of the house minus a certain proportion. The calculation formula is as follows:

Tax payable = Tax payable of original value of house ×
(1 – Deduction proportion) × 1.2%

Calculation of rent-based tax levy

Levy on rent is on the basis of rental income of the house. The calculation formula is shown as follows:

Tax payable = Rental income × 12%

Tax relief

The tax relief on house tax is formulated in accordance with the requirements of national policy and the burden capacity of taxpayers. Offering a certain authority to local governments to grant relief will be beneficial to the handling of local problems, since house tax belongs to local tax.

The specific preferential policies are as the follows:

1) The houses used by state organs, people's organizations and the military are exempt from house tax. However rented houses and houses used in non-self production and business by the tax-exempt entities listed above are not exempted from taxation.

   "People's organizations" are social organizations and groups which are approved for establishment or registration through government departments authorized by the State Council and given funding appropriation by the state.

   The "self-used houses" refer to official houses in these units.

2) The following houses used within the scope of business are exempt from house tax: units whose undertaking expenditures are allocated by departments of finance, such as schools, medical treatment and public health units, child-care centers, kindergartens, gerocomiums, and units of culture, sports and art.

   If the units above are self-supporting in source of payment, they are exempt from house tax for three years from the year of implementing self-support so as to encourage economic self-support. The houses used by the units themselves refer to business houses.

   The houses of affiliated factories, shops, and guesthouses subordinated to the above and which do not act as houses of official business shall pay the house tax.

3) The houses used in religious temples, parks and places of interest are exempt from house tax.

   The houses used in religious temples refer to those houses where religious rites are held and religious personnel live.

   The houses used in parks and places of interest refer to those houses where public go on sightseeing tours and those where administrative unit personnel live.

   The houses used by theaters, food and beverage departments, tea houses and photo studios and tenanted houses, which act as attached business units to religious temples, parks and places of interest, are not exempt from house tax.

4) A non-operating house owned by an individual is exempt from house tax. Non-operating house, which mainly refers to residential housing, is exempt from house tax irrespective of the size of the house.

   An operating house or tenanted house owned by an individual is not exempt from house tax.

5) The houses used by branches of the head office of the People's Bank of China (and including the State Administration of Foreign Exchange) which exercise national public administration functions are exempt from house tax.

6) Other houses which are exempt from house tax after being approved by Ministry of Finance.

   This kind of house is duty-free in accordance with actual conditions due to special circumstances and small scope.

   • Houses that cannot be used due to damage and dangerous buildings may be exempt from house tax when they are terminated for use after being identified by the relevant departments.

   • Houses which are out of service for more than half a year as a result of repairs may be exempt from house tax during the overhaul period. The exemption tax amount shall be deducted by the taxpayer when the taxpayer declares house tax and gives a corresponding description in the attached list or remark column in the declaration form.

   • For those houses which are out of service for more than half a year because of repairs, which may be exempt from house tax, the taxpayers of the houses shall submit the relevant certification documents to the tax authority for checking before the houses are repaired. These include the name and location of the houses, number of title certificate, original value of house, purpose and reasons of house repair, overhaul contract, and start-stop time of repairs. The specific information to be submitted shall be determined by the local tax authority of provinces, autonomous regions and municipalities directly under the central government, and municipalities with independent planning status.

   • Since January 1, 1988, for those resident houses rented by real estate administrative departments where rent is lower than before reform of house rent, levy of house tax may be postponed. For other non-operating houses rented by real estate administrative departments, the amount of house tax shall be determined by provinces, autonomous regions and municipalities directly under the central government in accordance with the tax management system and on the basis of local conditions.

- College logistic entities are exempt from house tax.
- The houses used by non-profit medical institutions, disease control organizations and maternity and child care institutions are exempt from house tax.
- The houses used by elderly service organizations are exempt from house tax. Elderly service organizations are those of welfare and non-profit organizations which provide multi-aspect services such as life care, culture, nursing, and fitness for the elderly, which include elderly social welfare institutes, gerocomiums, elderly service centers, and housing for the elderly (including nursing homes and rehabilitation centers).
- Since January 1, 2000, the following houses are exempt from house tax temporarily: public houses and low-rent houses leased in accordance with price regulated by government, including unit-owned houses rented to workers by enterprises and self-supporting public institutions; public houses rented to residents by real estate administrative department, and private houses rented to residents in accordance with the standard rent regulated by the government in the implementation of the private house policy.
- From January 1, 2006, to December 31, 2008, student hostels which provide accommodation services for college student and collect rent in accordance with charging standard of the higher education system are exempt from house tax.
- Heat supply enterprises which provide heat to and collect heating charges from residents are exempt from house tax. They include professional heat supply enterprises and concurrent heat supply enterprises, and property management companies that provide heat for units and residents in the neighborhood, but do not include those enterprises which engage in heating power production and do not provide heat for residents. The "production houses" that are exempt from house tax refer to workshops used in heat supply for residents. For those enterprises which provide heat for residents and non-residents, tax exemption shall be divided on the basis of the proportion of total income occupied by heat supply; for concurrent heat supply enterprises, tax exemption shall be divided on the basis of proportion of total income from production and management occupied by heat supply.

Administration of tax collection

Occurrence time of tax liability

1) Taxpayers shall pay house tax from the month of start of production and management if the taxpayer uses the original house for production and management.

2) Taxpayers shall pay house tax from the second month of completion of construction if the taxpayer builds a new house for production and management.

3) Taxpayers shall pay house tax from the second month of transaction of acceptance procedure if taxpayer entrusts construction enterprises to build a house.

4) Taxpayers shall pay house tax from the second month of putting into service of the house if the taxpayer purchases a new commodity house.

5) Taxpayers shall pay house tax from the second month of the signing and issuing of the housing management authority certificate by the real estate ownership registration authority after transfer and change of registration of house property is completed.

6) Taxpayers shall pay house tax from the second month of renting out a house if the taxpayer rents or lends a house.

7) Real estate development enterprises shall pay house tax from the second month of use or delivery of a house if they use, rent or lend commodity houses built by themselves.

Assessable period

House tax shall be levied by stages and calculated annually. The specific assessable period for tax payment shall be determined by the people's governments at all levels.

Place of payment

House tax shall be paid in the location of the house. Taxpayers whose houses are located in different places shall pay house tax to the tax authority where each house is located.

Contract Tax

An overview

Some concepts

Contract tax is a kind of tax levy on units and individuals who obtain land use right and house ownership in the process of ownership transfer for land use right and house ownership.

Since China was founded, it abolished the contract tax that existed in the old China. In April, 1950, the then Government Administration Council issued the Provisional Regulations on Contract Tax which lasted for more than 40 years, but cannot meet the requirements of economic development. So the government formulated the *Provisional Regulations of the People's Republic of China on Contract Tax* in 1997 (hereinafter referred to as the *Provisional Regulations on Contract Tax*). Contract tax is a one-time tax and applies to Chinese and foreign-funded enterprises and to Chinese citizens and foreigners.

Characteristics

1) The taxpayer of contract tax is the property transferee.
2) It adopts flat rate within a set range
3) It is levied on both Chinese and foreign taxpayers in China.
4) It is a one-time tax.
5) It belongs to local taxes.

Effects

1) It can increase local financial revenue and accumulate funds for local economic construction.
2) It can regulate and control the real estate market and standardize market transactions, so it guarantees the lawful rights and interests of property owners and reduces disputes over property rights.

The system of contract tax

Object of taxation

The object of taxation of contract tax is the land which transfers right of use and house, which transfers ownership in China.

Transfer of the use right of state-owned land

This refers to the land user authorized to have use right of state-owned land for a limited years when the land user pays charges for transfer of land use right to the state.

Transfer of land use right

Transfer of land use right refers to the action whereby land users transfer a land use right to other units and individuals through sale, gift, exchange or other methods, but excludes the transfer of contract for the management right of collective land in rural areas. The sale of land use right refers to the action of obtaining of money, material object(s), intangible assets or other economic interests if land users use the land use right as trade terms; gift of land-use right is an action whereby the land users transfer the land-use right to the donee voluntarily; exchange of land means that land users exchange land use rights each other.

House purchase and sale

This refers to the action when the house owner sells his/her house to the buyer who pays in cash, material objects, intangible assets or other economic interests.

Gift of house

This refers to the action when the owners of a house transfer their houses to a donee voluntarily.

House exchange

This refers to the action whereby owners of houses exchange houses with each other.

The following actions of transfer ownership of land and houses are treated as transfer of land use right, house sale or house gift, and shall be levied for tax.

1) Taking ownership of land and house as investment and share and pay debt;
2) Bearing ownership of land and house in the form of intangible assets;
3) Bearing ownership of land and house in the form of winning awards;
4) Bearing ownership of land and house in form of purchase in advance or payment of house construction in advance; and
5) Other methods of transfer of ownership of land and houses as determined by the Ministry of Finance in accordance with the provisions

on contract tax.

Taxpayers

Taxpayers of contract tax refer to units and individuals who bear the transfer of ownership of land and houses in China. Ownership of land and house refers to land use right and house property; units refer to enterprise units, public institutions, state organs, military units and social organizations and other organizations; individuals refer to the self-employed and other individuals, including both Chinese citizens and foreigners in China.

Tax rates

This adopts a flat rate within a range of 3%–5% on the basis of taking the unbalanced economic development conditions in China into account.

The specific tax rate shall be determined by provinces, autonomous regions and municipalities directly under the central government in accordance with the tax management system within a range of 3%–5% on the basis of local conditions.

Tax base

The tax base of contract tax is the price of real estate. The tax base of contract tax is different according to different transfer methods of ownership of land and house. There are four conditions as follows:

For transfer of state-owned land use right, sale of land use right, house transaction

With respect to transfer of state-owned land use right, sale of land use right and house transaction is the basis for tax calculation of transaction price. The transaction price is the price determined in ownership transfer contract of land and house, which includes payable money, material objects, intangible assets, or other economic interests.

For gift of house and land use right

The basis for tax calculation shall be checked and ratified by the tax authority in accordance with the market price when the land use right and house are sold.

For exchange of house and land use right

The base for tax calculation is the price margin of exchanged land-use right and house. It is exempt from contract tax when the exchange price is equal, but the party which pays more pays the contract tax when the exchange price is not equal.

The assignor of real estate shall pay contract tax when land use right is obtained through transfer, and the transfer basis for tax calculation is the transfer cost of land use right or land revenue

The tax authority may determine the basis for tax calculation in accordance with market price so as to prevent tax evasion if the transaction price is obviously lower than the market price without reasonable reasons, or the price margin of exchanged land use right and house is obviously unreasonable.

Calculation of tax liability

This adopts a flat rate, and the basic calculation formula is shown as follows:

Tax liability = Base for tax calculation × Tax rate

Tax relief

1)   Where state organs, public institutions, public organizations or military units have land and houses for use in official business, teaching, medical treatment, scientific research and military installations, they shall be exempt from tax.

2)   Staff and workers in cities and towns purchasing public-owned houses for the first time shall be exempt from tax, but limited to within standard areas in accordance with national regulations and approved by the people's governments at or above the county level. Otherwise, tax shall be paid.

3)   From November 1, 2008, for individuals who purchase common house of 90 square meters or below, the tax rate for contract tax shall be dropped to 1% temporarily.

4)   Those who buy a new house due to loss of house resulting from force majeure, they shall enjoy a tax cut or tax exemption.

5)   For those people who bear ownership of land or house again when land or house occupied by the people's governments at all levels, the decision on tax cut or tax exemption shall be determined by the province, autonomous region or municipality directly under the central government.

6)   Taxpayers who hold the land use rights to barren mountains and/or sandy areas, and use these for agricultural production, forestry, animal

husbandry or fishery, shall be exempt from tax.

7) In accordance with the relevant laws and regulations, and the regulations of bilateral and multilateral treaties or agreements established or acceded to by China, foreign embassies, consulates, the United Nations representative offices in China and their diplomatic representatives, consular officials and other diplomatic personnel who bear ownership of land and houses may be exempt from tax after being confirmed by the Ministry of Foreign Affairs.

8) Relevant contract tax policies in enterprise reform

The contract tax policies in enterprise reform are as follows in accordance with the regulations of the Ministry of Finance and the State Administration of Taxation so as to improve the continuous and healthy development of the national economy and promote the deepening of enterprise reform:

- Corporate system reform. This refers to non-corporate enterprises' transformation into a limited liability company (it includes a state-owned exclusive company) or a company limited by shares in accordance with corporation law, or into a company limited by shares from limited liability company.

- In corporate system reform, those corporate system enterprises which without change of investment subject and ratio of investments bear the ownership of the original enterprises' lands and houses can be exempt from contract tax; a company limited by shares through public share offer and launched exclusively to bear ownership of lands and houses of initiators shall be exempt from contract tax; limited liability companies or companies limited by shares in which all workers holding shares transformed from state-owned or collective-owned enterprises, which bear the ownership of the original enterprise lands and houses, can be exempt from contract tax; for others concerning transfer of ownership of lands and houses, they shall not be exempt from contract tax.

- Enterprise combination. This refers to two or more enterprises transforming into one enterprise in accordance with legal provisions and contract. Companies may be merged in two forms i.e. merger by absorption and merger by consolidation. If one company continues and the others are dissolved, this is called merger by absorption; if a new company establishes and all the original enterprises are dissolved, this is called merger by consolidation.

- In the process of enterprise combination if the new party, or existing party which is the same investment subject as before merger, bears ownership of the lands and houses of the dissolved parties, it shall be exempt from contract tax; othewise contract tax shall be levied.

- Division of enterprise. This refers to when an enterprise is divided into two or more investment subjects in accordance with legal provisions and contract. There is division by continued existence and new division. The former refers to when an original enterprise continues to exist and one or several new enterprises derive from part that original enterprise; the latter refers to when the original enterprise is dissolved, and the divided parties establish new enterprises.

- In division of enterprise, where the derived party and the new party bear ownership of the original enterprise's lands and houses, contract tax shall be exempted.

- Share rights restructuring. This refers to the action whereby shares or contribution of capital held by enterprise shareholders changes. It involves share transfer, or investment increase in share rights restructuring. The former refers to shareholders transfer of part or all of the shares or contribution of capital held by them to others; the latter refers to the company raising capital from the public or from specific units and individuals, or issuing shares.

- In share rights restructuring, the unit or individuals who hold the stock rights of the enterprise when land and house ownership of the enterprise fails to transfer shall be exempt from contract tax; in investment increase, those which take ownership of land and houses as shares or investment in the enterprise shall not be exempt from contract tax.

- Bankruptcy of an enterprise. This refers to a legal act whereby an enterprise declares bankruptcy according to the law due to failure of payment of due debt resulting from heavy losses caused by poor management and operation.

- In the period of bankruptcy liquidation of an enterprise, where creditors (staff and workers of the bankrupted enterprise are included) bear ownership of the land and houses of the bankrupted enterprise to compensate for debt, they shall be exempt from contract tax; where non-creditors bear ownership of the land and houses of bankrupted enterprise, they shall not be exempt from contract tax.

Administration of tax collection

Occurrence time of tax liability

The occurrence time of tax liability for contract tax is the day when the taxpayer signs the ownership transfer contract of land and house or the day when the taxpayer obtains the property certificate of ownership transfer contract of land and house.

When taxpayers shall make supplementary payment for contract tax which has been cut or exempted due to the change of purpose of land and house, the occurrence time of tax liability is the day when the purpose of land and house changes.

Assessable period

Taxpayers shall transact a tax declaration at the contract tax collection authority where the land and house are located within 10 days of the occurrence of tax liability, and pay the tax payment within the time limit regulated by the contract tax collection authority.

Where taxpayers conform qualify for contract tax cut or exemption, they shall transact procedures of contract cut or exemption at the contract tax collection authorities where land and house are located within 10 days of the date the ownership transfer contract of land and house is signed.

Place of payment

Contract tax shall be paid to the tax authorities at the place where the land and house are located.

Administration of tax collection

The contract tax collection authority is the financial organization or local tax authority where the land and house are located.

The land management department and house administration department shall provide the relevant data to the contract tax collection authority and assist it to collect contract tax in accordance with the law.

The contract tax collection authority shall provide a tax payment receipt of contract tax when taxpayers pay the tax.

With a tax payment receipt of contract tax and other regulated documentation, taxpayers shall transact ownership change of registration procedures for land and houses at the land management department and house administrative department in accordance with the law. Without a tax payment receipt for contract tax, the land management department and house administrative department will not transact ownership change of registration procedures for land and house.

Vehicle and Vessel Usage Tax

An overview

Some concepts

This is a tax in accordance with the fixed quota system which is levied on vehicles and vessels registered with the vehicle and vessel administrative departments in China.

Collection of vehicle and vessel usage tax has a long history. In 1951, the Government Administration Council promulgated the *Provisional Regulations on Vehicle and Vessel License Tax* and levied vehicle and vessel license tax on units and individuals who used vehicle and vessel; in 1952, the then Government Administration Council promulgated the *Interim Procedures of Tonnage Tax* and levied a tonnage tax on foreign vessels passing in and out of Chinese ports, Chinese vessels rented by foreign merchants, and Chinese and foreign vessels used by Chinese and foreign joint ventures. In 1973, when industrial and commercial tax reform took place, it merged vehicle and vessel license tax levied on domestic enterprises into the industrial and commercial tax and continued to levy vehicle and vessel license tax on vehicles and vessels used by individuals, foreigners, foreign-owned enterprises, Sino-foreign joint ventures and cooperative enterprises. On September 15, 1986, the State Council promulgated the *Provisional Regulations of the People's Republic of China on Vehicle and Vessel Usage Tax*, which was put into practice on October 1, 1986, and applied to units and individuals who owned and used vehicles and vessels. However for foreign-funded enterprises and foreign enterprises, it still levied the vehicle and vessel license tax in accordance with the *Provisional Regulations on Vehicle and Vessel License Tax*.

The levy of vehicle and vessel license tax and vehicle and vessel use tax for vehicles and vessels owned and used by Sino-foreign units and individuals played a positive role in increasing local finance, supervising and encouraging utilization and benefits of vehicles and vessels, and adjusting and promoting development of the social economy. With the establishment and perfection of the socialist market economy, and especially with accession to the WTO, many problems have appeared in the implementation process of the two taxation regulations: one is that two coexistent tax categories cannot conform to the requirements for a unified tax administration and simplified tax system; the second is that the interim period of tax regulations is too long and that tax amount is too low and not unified for Chinese and foreigners; the third is that the supervision method for source of taxation is out of date, which is not beneficial to tax collection and management of tax.

Because of this situation, the State Council promulgated the new *Provisional Regulations of the People's Republic of China on Vehicle and Vessel Usage Tax* on December 29, 2006, and put it into practice on January 1, 2007. These regulations are applicable to foreign and Chinese taxpayers who own taxable vehicles and vessels, and the original *Provisional Regulations on Vehicle and Vessel License Tax and Provisional Regulations on Vehicle and Vessel Usage Tax* were abolished.

Characteristics

1) It is levied on vehicles and vessels only. This is the basic characteristics of vehicle and vessel usage tax, and also the difference between this tax and other tax categories.

2) It is levied in accordance with amount on volume on the base of category, amount and size of vessels and vehicles. Vehicle and vessel usage tax divides the object of taxation into vehicle and vessel, and designates a different tax amount in accordance with amount or size of vessel and vehicle. Compared to the original vehicle and vessel license tax and vehicle and vessel usage tax, the top and bottom limitation difference of tax amount within a range of vehicle and vessel usage tax is larger, but increase at the bottom range is small. For most taxpayers, the total tax burden will not affect the ownership and use of the vehicle or vessel.

3) It is paid by stages annually.

4) The local tax authority is responsible for collection and management of vehicle and vessel tax according to the principle of territorial jurisdiction.

Effects

Vehicles and vessels are important in daily life and in production and operating activities. With the development of the social economy, people's demand for means of transport and for better category, quality and grade of vehicle and vessel is stronger. This promotes investment, consumption and import and export trade, accelerates updating and upgrading of industrial structure and pattern of consumption, promotes development of the transportation industry and benefits the national economy as a whole and people's quality of life. Meanwhile it also makes higher demands on construction and maintenance of infrastructure such as highways, waterways, bridges and tunnels, and brings about great pressure on consumption of resources and energy sources and the ecological environment. Therefore it is necessary to adjust the development scale, speed and structure of vehicles and vessels to make them adapt to the integral development of the national economy, the overall increase in living standards and quality, to what the population, resources, energy sources and ecological environment can bear. Vehicle and vessel usage tax is an important economic lever to regulate and control occupancy and use of vehicles and vessels. It has specific significance in the following aspects from point of its characteristics and tax law regulations: one is that it embodies the tax burden fairness principle of "those who use, pay; those who use more, pay more; no use, no pay"; the second is that it is beneficial to adjusting the structure of vehicle-and-vessel owning, encouraging energy conservation and protecting the environment; the third is that it is beneficial to increasing the holding cost of vehicles and vessels, encouraging effective utilization of vehicles and vessels; and the fourth is that it helps to raise stable and reliable financial funds for the construction and maintenance of transportation.

Collection system for vehicle and vessel usage tax

Object of taxation

The object of taxation for vehicle and vessel usage tax is vehicles and vessels (except for those which are exempt from tax) registered by vehicle and vessel administrative departments in China

Vehicle

Vehicle includes motor vehicle and non-power driven vehicles.

The former refers to those which are driven by fuel oil and electric power, such as cars, tractors and trolleybuses; the latter refers to those which are driven by manpower or animal power, such as tricycles, bicycles and animal powered vehicles.

Vessel

Vessel includes engine driven vessels and non-power driven vessels.

Engine driven vessel refers to those which are driven by fuel, such as passenger ships, cargo ships and hovercraft.

Non-power driven vessels refers to those which are driven by manpower or other power, such as wooden boats, sailing boats, and sampans.

Taxpayers

The taxpayer of vehicle and vessel usage tax is the owner or administrator of the vehicle or vessel which is registered with the vehicle and vessel administrative department in China.

The taxpayer of vehicle and vessel usage tax is the unit or individual who owns the property or administrative and use rights. Unit refers to administrative organs, public institutions, social organizations and enterprises; individual refers to Chinese citizens and foreign individuals in China.

The users of taxable vehicles and vessels shall pay vehicle and vessel usage tax if the owners or administrators fail to pay.

The insurance institution which engages in compulsory motor vehicle liability insurance business is the withholding agent, and it shall collect and pay vehicle and vessel usage tax for the owners or administrators of the vehicle or vessel in accordance with the law.

Tax rates

A quota tax rate is implemented within a range in accordance with the *Provisional Regulations on Vehicle and Vessel Usage Tax*, which regulates an annual tax amount from minimum to maximum for different kinds of vehicles and authorizes finance departments and tax administration departments of the State Council to divide tax items into sub-items of tax within the tax item scope and tax amount range as regulated in tax items and tax amount table on vehicle and vessel usage tax on the basis of actual conditions, and defines the tax amount range of sub-items of tax for vehicles and the specific tax amount for vessels. The specific tax amount for vehicles shall be determined within the regulated tax amount range for the sub-item of tax by the people's governments at all levels. The reason for this is that it is difficult to apply a unified tax to all kinds of vehicles in China. The specific regulations are beneficial to implementation of the tax law. The table of tax items and tax amounts for vehicle and vessel usage tax are shown in Table 9.1.

Table 9.1.   Table of tax items and tax amount of vehicle and vessel usage tax

Tax item	Tax unit	Annual tax amount	Remarks
Passenger service vehicle	Per unit	RMB60–660	It contains electric car
Truck	Weight per ton	RMB60–120	It contains semi-trailer towing vehicle, trailer
Three-wheeled automobile, low speed truck.	Weight per ton	RMB24–120	—
Motorbike	Per unit	RMB36–180	—
Shipping	Net tonnage per ton	RMB3–6	Tugboat and non-power barge shall be calculated in accordance with 50% of vessel tax amount payable

1) In the table of tax items and tax amount of vehicle and vessel usage tax, the passenger service vehicle is divided into large bus, medium bus, small bus and mini-type bus. A large bus is a bus approved for more than 20 passengers, a medium bus is one approved for between 9 and 20 passengers, a small bus one approved for 9 or less passengers, a mini-type bus refers to a bus with total cylinder displacement of engine equal to or less than 1 liter. The annual tax amount within a range for every sub-item of tax is as follows: Coach: RMB480–660; Medium-sized bus: RMB420–660; Small-sized bus: RMB360–660; Mini bus: RMB60–480.
Station wagon levies on vehicles, and vessel usage tax, is in accordance with the tax setting and tax amount for motor trucks.

2) A three-wheeled automobile refers to those motor vehicles registered as tri-car or three wheel farm-oriented carrier vehicle with the vehicle administrative department.

3) Low speed wagon refers to low speed wagon or four-wheel farm-oriented carrier vehicles registered as such by vehicle administrative departments.

4) Professional assignment vehicle refers to a motor vehicle equipped with special equipment or appliances and used in professional assignments; a wheel type special mechanic car is equipped with equipment for loading and unloading, excavation and leveling. The tax tax-setting unit for the professional assignment vehicle and wheel type special mechanic

car is the weight per ton, and the annual tax amount is RMB16–120. The specific tax amount shall be determined within the regulated range by the people's governments at all levels on the base of tax amount standard of truck.

5) The specific tax amount for vessels in tax items and tax amount for vehicle and vessel usage tax is as follows:
   - RMB3 per ton when net tonnage is equal to or less than 200 tons;
   - RMB4 per ton when net tonnage is between 201–2000 tons;
   - RMB5 per ton when net tonnage is between 2,001–10,000 tons;
   - RMB6 per ton when net tonnage is 10,001 tons or above;

Tax base

The base for tax calculation for vehicle and vessel usage tax is divided into unit, net tonnage and load tonnage in accordance with category and property of vehicle.

1) "Unit" is the base for tax calculation for passenger buses, electric cars, motorbikes, bicycles, manpower vehicles and animal power vehicles.
2) Self weight per ton is the base for tax calculation for trucks, professional assignment vehicles, three-wheeled automobiles, and low speed trucks.
3) Net tonnage per ton is the base for tax calculation for vessels.

The tax setting such as approved passenger number, self-weight, net tonnage and horsepower shall be subject to that registered in the vehicle or vessel registration certificate or driving certificate. The tax setting shall be subject that registered in the vehicle or vessel production certificate or import certificate if the taxpayer fails to register with the vehicle and vessel administrative department. In the case of no vehicle or vessel production certificate or import certificate, the local tax authority shall make checks and ratification in accordance with the conditions of the vehicle or vessel on the basis of similar vehicles or vessels.

The tugboat in the Table refers to a professional assignment ship used in towing a transportation ship. Vehicle and vessel usage tax is levied in accordance with net tonnage of 1 ton equal to 2 horsepower of engine power.

If the weight of a vehicle is lower than or equal to 0.5 ton, it shall be calculated by 0.5 ton; if it is more than 0.5 ton, it shall calculate by 1 ton. The weight refers to the curb weight of motor vehicle. When the net tonnage mantissa of ship is lower than or equal to 0.5 ton it is unnecessary to calculate it; if it is more than 0.5 ton, it shall be calculated by the 1 ton. Smaller vehicles and vessels below 1 ton shall be calculated by 1 ton.

Calculation of tax payable

The calculation formula for tax liability for vehicle and vessel usage tax is:

Tax payable of passenger service vehicle or motorbike = Unit amount × Applicable unit tax

Tax amount payable of truck, professional assignment vehicle, three-wheeled automobile, low speed truck = Self-weight tonnage × Applicable unit tax

Tax payable of motor-vessel = Net tonnage × Applicable unit tax

Tax payable of tugboat, non-power barge = Net tonnage × (Applicable unit tax × 50%)

Levy on tugboats for vehicle and vessel usage tax is in accordance with net tonnage of 1 ton equal to 2 horsepower of engine power.

Tax payable of beach wagon = Self-weight tonnage × Applicable unit tax

For newly purchased new vehicles and vessels, tax shall be levied monthly from the month of occurrence of tax liability. The calculation formula is:

Tax payable = (Annual tax payable / 12) × Number of taxable months

Tax relief

Preferential policy on vehicle and vessel usage tax is defined in the *Provisional Regulations on Vehicle and Vessel Usage Tax*, which also authorizes the people's governments at all levels to implement tax relief regularly for taxpayers in difficulties; for bicycles, it may determine the tax amount of vehicle and vessel usage tax or implement tax relief.

1) Statutory tax exemption vehicles and vessels
   - Non-powered vehicles and vessels (non-powered barges are not included);
   - Tractors;
   - Fishing vessels used in fishing and fish breeding;
   - Vehicles and vessels used by the military and armed police;
   - Vehicles and vessels used by the police;
   - Vehicles and vessels that have paid tonnage tax;
   - In accordance with relevant laws and regulations, and regulations of international agreements established or acceded to by China, foreign embassies, consulates, international organization representative

offices in China and relevant personnel whose vehicles and vessels shall be exempt from tax.

2) Relief for special purposes

The people's governments at all levels may implement regular tax relief for public traffic vehicles and vessels in cities and rural areas.

Administration of tax collection

1) Occurrence time of tax liability

The occurrence time of tax liability for vehicle and vessel usage tax is the month registered in vehicle and vessel registration certificate or the driving certificate issued by the vehicle and vessel administrative department. The month marked in the purchasing invoice of a vehicle or vessel is used as occurrence time of tax liability of vehicle and vessel usage tax when the taxpayer fails to register a taxable vehicle or vessel with the vehicle and vessel administrative department. The local tax authority shall check and determine the occurrence time of tax liability if the taxpayer fails to register a taxable vehicle or vessel and provide the purchasing invoice for the vehicle or vessel.

Vehicles and vessels shall not be liable for vehicle and vessel usage tax when they are declared as scrap to the traffic and shipping administrative department. Within a tax year, due to theft, scrapping or loss of the duty-paid vehicle or vessel, the taxpayer may apply for the return of tax payment from the month of theft, scrapping or loss to the end of the tax year at the local tax authority with certificates issued by the relevant administrative department and proof of duty paid. If the taxpayer recovers the stolen vehicle or vessel which has been subject to tax rebate, the taxpayer shall pay vehicle and vessel usage tax since the month the relevant certificate is issued by the public security authorities.

2) Assessable period

Vehicle and vessel usage tax shall be paid in installment annually. The tax year is from calendar January 1 to December 31. The specific assessable period for tax payment shall be determined by the people's governments at all levels.

The reason why the assessable period for tax payment of vehicle and vessel usage tax shall be determined by local governments is based on two points:

- The tax amount payable is different due to various categories and number of vehicles and vessels. Taxpayers who have a large number of taxable vehicles and vessels and who find it difficult to pay the whole tax amount at one time may pay quarterly or half a yearly; for non-powered vehicle and vessels the number of taxpayers is huge and the tax amount payable is small, so taxpayers should pay the whole year's tax at one time.

- It is beneficial to the administration of tax collection when the local authorities are empowered to determine the tax amount payable.

3) Place of payment
- The tax payment place shall be determined by local governments in accordance with local actual conditions, and it is generally the location of the taxpayer. For vehicles and vessels which are used across provinces, autonomous regions and municipalities directly under the central government, the tax payment place is the registration place of the vehicle or vessel.
- The location of taxpayer is the operating place or organization site for each unit, and the place of residence for each individual.
- Source control is implemented for vehicle and vessel usage tax. The tax is collected and managed by the local taxation bureau where taxpayer is located. The local bureau shall not check and levy tax on vehicles from other provinces and cities.
- The users of vehicles and vessels shall pay vehicle and vessel usage tax if the owners or administrators fail to pay.
- The insurance institution which engages in compulsory motor vehicle liability insurance business is the withholding agent of vehicle and vessel usage tax on motor vehicles. It shall collect and pay vehicle and vessel usage tax in accordance with the law.

Taxpayers shall not pay when the withholding agent of motor vehicle and vessel usage tax has collected tax in accordance with the law.

10
Chapter

Taxes for Special Purposes

An Overview

Some concepts

Taxes for special purposes are the general term for a class of taxes levied on certain behaviors of taxpayers (or particular behaviors). Among China's current tax system, the taxes belonging to the category of taxes for special purposes mainly include stamp tax, city maintenance and construction tax, and vehicle purchase tax etc.

In tax distribution activities, economic behaviors as the targets of taxation or the objects of taxation are varied, such as producing, selling and importing and exporting a commodity, providing labor services, developing and utilizing resources, possessing, transferring, leasing and bequeathing property, investing, saving and consuming, buying and selling securities, distributing income etc. Among these, the occurrence, development and continuation of some actions have the characteristics of universality, continuity, permanence and regularity, and thus tax levied on them means abundant tax resources. The scale and growth rate of the tax revenue is positively correlated with the scale and growth rate of economic activities, the purpose of the tax dues is not clearly specified, and the regulation field of the tax is extensive. It is a kind of tax generally levied in all countries in the world and thus there is some comparability between countries worldwide. This kind of tax is typically called the general tax or ordinary tax. But there are some economic behaviors of which the occurrence, development and continuation are occasional, geographic, non-continuous, short-term and irregular, and thus the taxes levied on these special purposes have poor resources, scale and growth rate of tax revenue is often negatively correlated with the scale and growth rate of economic activities, the taxes has no specified purpose or takes seeking revenue as the primary purpose or even is defined as a "sumptuary" tax, and the regulation field of the tax is narrow. This kind of tax has sharp distinctions between different countries and regions.

The relationship between the system of taxes for special purposes and the general taxation

As mentioned above, any tax is closely related with the taxpayers' particular economic behavior and the reason why they are divided into taxes for special purposes and general tax is largely due to the clear distinctions of the purpose of taxation, form of taxation, effect of taxation, length of applicability, legal status and other aspects of the two taxes. In fact the rise and fall and the development of the two taxes have close immanent connections and the dividing standard is relative. Specifically, some taxes may be classified as taxes for special purposes at the beginning and then gradually be transformed into general tax; some taxes may be classified as general tax at the beginning and then be transformed into taxes for special purposes or minor tax with the gradual shrinkage of the tax resource and the obvious decline of its status in the system of taxation during a long period of time. In some countries such taxes are classified as tax for special purposes or minor tax, while in some countries they are the main source of tax revenue and have very prominent position in the tax. Some taxes of a sophisticated nature can be classified as an act of tax or general tax and even defined as general tax, but not all of them are a major tax with abundant tax resources or extensive regulation range.

Overall, as well as collecting general tax universally and accordingly, moderately levying taxes for special purposes on certain specific economic activities or behaviors in accordance with the country's needs, local conditions, the time and the events can to some extent give full play to the advantages of the indirect management and regulation of the taxation leverage so as to make up the deficiency of the general tax and the insufficiency of other economic, administrative and legal instruments in directly managing and regulating these special economic behaviors or activities. In this sense, the taxes for special purposes is a special application of the taxation leverage and a significant expansion in the extension and the function of taxation on the basis of the general tax.

Characteristics and effects

As the taxes for special purposes chooses particular behaviors as the objects of taxation and is highly goal-directed, so its role in regulating the economy is very obvious. The introduction of the taxes for special purposes is to reflect the policy intent of the country in a particular period and to regulate certain particular social and economic acts. The specific categories of taxes for special purposes are constantly changing with the alterations of the policy intent and the specific economic behaviors of the object of taxation, which enables the tax for special purposes to be both temporary and occasional. It is precisely the flexibility of the tax that makes it an important instrument of national macroeconomic control and an indispensable part of the tax system.

Since it has the above characteristics, taxes for special purposes cannot be as stable and reliable as turnover tax and income tax in organizing financial revenue, and the tax revenue from taxes for special purposes usually has a clear purpose or does not take revenue as the primary purpose and even has the characteristics of a "sumptuary" tax. But as a supplementary tax, it plays the role of filling a vacancy.

Stamp Duty

An overview

Some concepts

Stamp duty is a kind of tax levied on organizations and individuals who execute, use and receive taxable documents, and it gets its name as its duty-paid method is to purchase and affix a certain number of stamp tax tickets on the taxable documents.

Stamp duty is a popular tax with a long history in the world. Stamp duty was first introduced in the Netherlands in 1624 the system was then followed by many countries. Currently more than 90 countries and regions have introduced this tax, spanning both developed and developing countries, and in some countries stamp duty revenue makes up a large proportion of overall tax revenue.

Stamp duty was first introduced to China by the Northern Warlords government in 1912 and the Kuo Min Tang (KMT) government announced the *Ordinance of Stamp Duty* in 1927. After the founding of the new China, the Government Administration Council announced the *Ordinance of Stamp Duty* in 1950, and since after that stamp tax was collected nationwide. The *Ordinance of Stamp Duty* was amended in 1953 and 1956, which narrowed the scope and reduced the tax item. After the tax reform of 1958, stamp duty was incorporated into the industrial and commercial consolidated tax and was no longer collected separately. After the reform and opening up, China restored the stamp duty. On August 6, 1988, the State Council issued the *Provisional Regulations of the People's Republic of China on Stamp Duty*, which came into force on October 1, 1988.

Characteristics

First, the objects of taxation of stamp duty are various taxable documents listed in the provisions, which include five categories and thirteen tax items such as contracts, documents for transfer of property rights, business account books and certificates evidencing rights or licenses, and others, which covers all aspects of economic activities. This has obvious differences with other categories of taxes which take the goods, property or value amounts as the objects of taxation.

Second, the stamp duty payable is not directly paid to the tax authorities. Instead the taxpayers shall purchase stamp duty tickets from the tax authorities in advance according to the taxable documents executed, used and received and then affix the stamp duty tickets on the various taxable documents according to the tax payable at one time and cancel each stamp along its border with a seal or a drawn line. This way of self-calculating, self-purchasing and canceling, and self-duty payment is different from the way used for other categories of taxes of declaring and paying taxes directly to the tax authorities by the taxpayers (although in some special cases, the tax can also be paid by way of remittance payment, remittance affix or commissioned collection).

Third, the stamp duty provides for different tax rates according to the nature and characteristics of the taxable documents, of which for the stamp duty paid according to the flat rate, the highest tax rate is 0.4% and the lowest tax rate is 0.005%; and the stamp duty paid according to a fixed amount is RMB5 per document. The tax burden is very light compared with other categories of taxes and is easy for taxpayers to accept. However if the taxpayer violates the regulations, does not affix, affixes less amount than the regulated amount, does not cancel the stamp duty tickets or reuses the used stamp duty tickets, the tax authorities shall impose a fine equal to several times the amount of the regulated tax stamps, reflecting the characteristics of light duty but heavy penalties.

Effects

First, the taxable documents cover a wide range of economic life and is heavily used in tax items listed in the tax laws which must be paid, which provides broad resources for the stamp duty. The stamp duty shall be calculated on the basis of the amount of the economic activities recorded on the taxable documents or the amount in the account books, and the corresponding tax payable will synchronously grow with the continuous expansion of the scale of the economic activities. Meanwhile the calculation of the tax payable for the stamp duty is not directly linked with the operational costs and profitability of the taxpayers, the tax calculation is easy, the cost of collecting tax is low and the revenue is stable without major fluctuations.

Second, contract documents are the true record and legal instruments of economic activities. With the continuous increase in the scale and level of economic activity, various types of contracts, documents, certificates evidencing rights or licenses will increase considerably. Affixing stamps and checking the certificates evidencing rights or licenses can supervise the taxpayers' proper use of various economic contracts and document, enhance awareness of the need to abide by the law, and improve the compliance rate, and thus helps to promote the standardization of economic behaviors and the establishment of market economic order.

Third, the taxpayers shall self-calculate, self-purchase and self-affix the stamp duty tickets, which is conducive to enhancing the taxpayers' self-compliance

The system of stamp duty collection

Object of taxation

Stamp duty is levied on all taxable documents cited in the regulations, specifically including 5 major categories and 13 taxable items.

In terms of contracts

Contracts refer to the contracts concluded in accordance with the *Economic Contract Law of the People's Republic of China*, the *Law of the People's Republic of China on Economic Contracts Involving Foreign Interest* and other relevant contract laws, rules and documents in the nature of a contract, of which documents in the nature of a contract refer to agreements, indentures, invoices, confirmations and other documents of various titles which have the same effect as contracts.

The taxable contracts citied in the regulations include:

1) Purchases and sales contracts, including supply, pre-order, procurement, purchases and sales combination and collaboration, regulation, compensation, trade and other contracts. In addition, it also includes the taxable documents on books, newspapers, periodicals and audio-visual products concluded between the publication and distribution units, such as purchase orders, purchasing quantity order etc.

2) Processing contracts, including processing, customizing, repairing, printing, advertising, surveying and mapping, testing and other contracts.

3) Construction project contracts, including the construction project survey and design contracts and installation project contracts.
   Construction project contracts include turnkey contracts and subcontracts and subcontracting agreements.

4) Property leasing contracts, including housing, ships, aircraft, motor vehicles, machinery, appliances, equipment and other leasing contracts,

as well as the store, counters and other rental contracts of the corporate and individuals.

5) Cargo transport contracts, including civil aviation, railway transport, sea transport, road transport and combined transport contracts, as well as the invoices used as contracts.

6) Warehousing contracts, including warehousing contracts and storage contracts as well as warehouse receipts and other receipts used as contracts.

7) Loan contracts, including the contracts signed between banks/other financial institutions and the borrowers (excluding interbank lending) contracts, the IOUs used as contracts where a loan has been obtained from the bank but no contract has been signed, and finance leasing contracts where finance leasing business operated by banks and other financial institutions is a kind of business achieving financing purpose by the way of financing materials and is an installment fixed assets loan, so therefore finance leasing contracts also belong to the category of loan contracts.

8) Property insurance contracts, including property, liability, warranty and credit insurance contracts, as well as the invoices used as contract. It is divided into five categories: corporate property insurance, motor vehicle insurance, cargo transport insurance, family property insurance and husbandry insurance. Family property co-existing insurance also belongs to family property insurance and shall pay taxes as required.

9) Technology contracts, including technology development, transfer, consulting, service and other contracts, as well as the invoices used as contracts.

10) Other documents in the nature of a contract.

In terms of documents for transfer of property rights

Documents for transfer of property rights are the documents concluded by organizations and individuals for property rights purchases and sales, inheritance, gifting, exchange, division etc., including the documents for the transfer of property rights and copyright, trademark rights, patent rights, proprietary technology etc. The scope of taxation of property transfer refers to documents concluded for property rights transfer of movable and immovable property and the documents concluded for corporate stock transfer registered by the government administrative authorities.

In terms of business account books

Business account books refers to the financial accounting books used to record the production and operating activities of organizations or individuals which can be divided into account books recording the funds and other account books according to the difference in content. Account books recording the funds refers to the account books reflecting the increase or decrease of the amount of funds of the operating units, and other account books refers to the account books recording other production and operating activities not included in the above account books, including the daily books and all kinds of subsidiary ledgers.

In terms of rights or licensing certificates

Certificates evidencing rights or licenses include housing ownership certificates, industry and commerce business licenses, trademark registration certificates, patent licenses and land use permits issued by government departments.

Other documents

Other documents not included in the above four types that are taxable as determined by the Ministry of Finance.

Taxpayers

All organizations and individuals who execute, use or receive taxable documents within the territory of China shall be taxpayers subject to stamp duty, including various types of domestic enterprises, institutions, agencies, organizations, troops, joint ventures, cooperative enterprises, foreign-funded enterprises, foreign enterprises, other economic organizations, institutions in China and other organizations and individuals.

According to the differences of the taxable documents executed, used or received, the taxpayers can be divided into the following six types:

1) Executors to the contract, which refer to the parties of the contract, that is, the organizations and individuals with direct rights and obligations to the documents, not including the guarantors, witnesses and surveyors of the contract. The parties' agents have proxy tax liability.

   A contract is signed by two or more parties and all the parties are the taxpayers.

2) Executors to the documents, which refer to the organizations and individuals executing the documents for transfer of property rights. Tax stamps shall be affixed on the documents for transfer of property rights by the executors to the documents, and if not affixed or the affixed

amount is less than the required amount, then the stamps shall be affixed by the holders of the documents. If the executed documents are signed in the form of a contract, then the parties holding the documents shall affix the full amount of tax stamps due.

3) Executors to the account books, which refer to the organizations and individuals opening and using the business account books.

4) Beneficiaries, which refer to the organizations and individuals receiving and holding the certificates evidencing rights or licenses.

5) Users, which refer to the organizations and individuals executing or receiving the taxable documents in a foreign country but using the taxable documents within the territory China.

For contracts or documents executed by two or more parties, each party is the taxpayer. For certificates evidencing rights or licenses issued by the government, the receivers are the taxpayers.

6) The undersigned of electronic taxable documents.

Tax rates

According to the nature of the taxable documents, the tax rate of the stamp duty has two forms: flat tax rate and fixed amount per document.

Flat tax rate

This applies to all types of economic contracts and documents, account books recording the funds, and documents for transfer of property rights etc. These documents generally contain the amount involved, and the tax payable can be calculated and the stamps can be affixed according to proportions.

The flat rate stamp duty is divided into five grades, respectively, 0.05‰, 0.3‰, 0.5‰, 1‰ and 2‰.

1) Loan contracts are liable to the tax rate of 0.05‰.

2) Purchases and sales contracts, construction and installation project contracts and technology contracts are liable to the tax rate of 0.3‰.

3) Processing contracts, construction survey and design contracts, cargo transport contracts, documents for transfer of property rights and business account books recording the funds are liable to the tax rate of 0.5‰.

4) Property leasing contracts, warehousing contracts and insurance contracts are liable to the tax rate of 1‰.

5) Equity transfer documents (this tax rate was added later and is not cited in *Table of Tax Items and the Tax Rate of Stamp Duty*) are liable to the tax rate of 2‰.

In addition, according to the special provisions of the State Council, stocks publicly issued by joint-stock enterprises, and stock transfer documents executed due to purchases and sales, inheritance and gifts, shall calculate the tax payable according to the actual transaction price on the stock market when the documents were executed and each party to the documents shall respectively pay the stamp duty according to the regulated tax rate.

Norm quota tax rate

This applies to certificates evidencing rights or licenses and other business account books, and the amount of tax to be paid is RMB5 per document as these documents do not belong to funds accounts or have no funds records. This tax payment method is easy for the taxpayers and can also facilitate tax collection and administration by the tax authorities. Tax items and tax rate for stamp duty are shown in Table 10.1.

Table 10.1. Tax items and tax rates of stamp duty

Tax item	Applicable scope	Tax rate	Taxpayer	Remarks
Purchases or sales contracts	Including contracts on supplies, order on purchase, procurement, purchase and marketing, coordination, regulatory supplies, compensation trade, barter trade	Affixing stamps according to 0.3‰ of the amount of the transaction	Executors to the contract	—
Processing contracts	Including processing, customizing, restoration, repairing, printing, advertising, surveying, testing and other contracts	Affixing stamps according to 0.5‰ of the value of the deal	Executors to the contract	—
Construction project survey and design contracts	Including survey and design contracts	Affixing stamps according to 0.5‰ of the deal	Executors to the contract	—

(Cont'd)

Tax item	Applicable scope	Tax rate	Taxpayer	Remarks
Construction and installation project contract	Including construction and installation project contract	Affixing stamps according to 0.3‰ of the contracting amount	Executors to the contract	—
Property leasing contract	Including houses, ships, aircraft, motor vehicles, machinery, appliances, equipment and other leasing contracts	Affixing stamps according to 1‰ of the leasing amount and if less than RMB1, affix stamps according to RMB1	Executors to the contract	—
Cargo transport contracts	Including civil aviation transport, rail transport, sea transport, river transport, road transport and combined transport contracts	Stamps to the equivalent 0.5‰ of the transportation fee	Executors to the contract	For the documents used as a contract, affix stamps according to contract
Warehousing contracts	Including warehousing or storage contracts	Stamps to the equivalent of 1‰ of the storage cost	Executors to the contract	For warehouse receipts used as a contract, affix stamps according to contract
Loan contracts	The loan contracts signed by the banks and other financial institutions or borrowers (excluding interbank lending).	Affixing stamps according to 0.05‰ of the loan amount	Executors to the contract	For the documents used as a contract, affix stamps according to contract
Property insurance contract	Including property, liability, warranty, credit and other insurance contracts	Affixing stamps according to 1‰ of the premium income	Executors to the contract	For the documents used as a contract, affix stamps according to contract

(Cont'd)

Tax item	Applicable scope	Tax rate	Taxpayer	Remarks
Technology contracts	Including technology development, transfer, consulting, service and other technology contracts	Affixing stamps according to 0.3‰ of the amount recorded	Executors to the contract	—
Documents for transfer of property rights	Including documents for transfer of financial ownership and copyright, trademark rights, patent rights, proprietary technology and so on, land use right grant contracts, the land use right transfer contract and real estate sales contract	Affixing stamps according to 0.5‰ of the amount recorded	Executors to the contract	—
Business account books	Account books for the production, operation and funds recording	Affixing stamps according to 0.5‰ of the total amount of paid-in capital and capital reserve and for other account books, affix stamps according to RMB5 per document	Executors to the account books	—
Certificates evidencing rights or licenses	Including the housing ownership certificates, industry and commerce business license, trademark registration certificate, patent license and land use permits issued by the government departments.	Affixing stamps according to RMB5 per document	Beneficiaries	—

Tax base

General provisions

The base for tax calculation of stamp duty is the amount recorded in the various documents. Specific provisions are:

1) The base for tax calculation for purchase and sale contracts is the purchase and sale amount recorded in the contract. In commodity trading activities, contracts signed for commodity trading adopting the approach of exchanging goods with goods are contracts reflecting the economic behavior of purchases and sales. For this kind of contract, the stamp duty shall be calculated according to the total amount of the purchase amount and the sale amount. For the contracts not listing the amount, the tax payable shall be calculated according to the purchases and sales quantity and the price set by the state or the market price.

2) The base for tax calculation of processing contracts is the amount of the processing revenue or hired work revenue. Specific provisions are as follows:

   • For processing and customizing contracts in which the entrusted party provides the raw materials, if the processing fees and raw materials cost are respectively listed in the contract, the tax shall be respectively calculated according to the processing contract and purchase and sale contract and the stamp duty payable is the total amount of the two kinds of tax payable; if the two amounts are not respectively recorded in the contract, the stamp duty shall be calculated based on the total amount in accordance with the processing contracts.

   • For processing contracts in which the entrusting party provides the main materials or raw materials and the entrusted party provides the auxiliary materials, regardless of whether the amount of the processing fees and auxiliary materials costs were recorded, the stamp duty payable shall be calculated on the basis of the total amount of the processing fees and the auxiliary materials costs in accordance with the processing contracts. The amount of the main materials or raw materials provided by the entrusting party shall not be included.

3) The base for tax calculation of construction survey and design contracts is the actual charge.

4) The base for tax calculation of construction and installation project contracts is the contracted amount.

5) The base for tax calculation for property leasing contract is the leasing amount and if the tax calculated is less than RMB1, then affix stamps

according to RMB1.

6) The base for tax calculation of cargo transport contracts is the amount of the actual transport costs, excluding the amount of cargo, handling fees, insurance etc.

7) The base for tax calculation of warehousing contracts is the warehousing costs.

8) The base for tax calculation of loan contracts is the loan amount. The tax law provides different methods of tax calculation according to the different form of the actual loan:

- For loans where a contract is signed and the receipt for the loan (or IOU) is issued once or more than once, the basis for stamp duty calculation is the amount recorded in the loan contract; for loans where only the IOU is issued and is used as a contract, the basis for stamp duty calculation is the amount recorded in the IOU.

- The liquidity revolving loan contract signed between the lender and borrower is usually signed annually (periodically) for which a ceiling is provided and the borrower is required to repay as the money is lent within the prescribed period and ceiling. To avoid increasing the burden on both lenders and borrowers, for this type of contract, the basis for tax calculation is the prescribed ceiling in the contract and the stamps shall be affixed when the contract is signed. If no new contract is signed when the borrower repays as the money is lent within the ceiling, no other stamps shall be affixed.

- For those contracts where the borrower mortgages the property to obtain a certain amount of mortgage loan, the stamps shall be affixed according to the loans. If the borrower is unable to repay the loans and therefore the mortgaged property is transferred to the lender, then stamps shall be affixed based on the documents for transfer of property rights executed by both parties in accordance with the provisions on documents for transfer of property rights.

- For the financing contracts signed by the banks and other financial organizations, the tax payable shall be calculated on the basis of the leasing amount recorded in the contract according to the provisions in the loan contract.

- For lending business, if the lender is a bank syndicate comprised of a number of banks and each member of the bank syndicate bears a certain loan amount, the loan contract is jointly executed by the borrower and the bank syndicate and each party keeps an original. For these contracts, the borrower and the bank syndicate shall affix stamps according to its own loan amount on its own contract original.

- For capital construction loans, if the loan contract is signed annually according to the annual fund use plan and finally the total loan contract is signed according to the total calculation of the loan amount of which the corresponding loan amount of each sub-contract is included, stamps shall be affixed according to the amount of each sub-contract respectively and for the total contract, affixed according to the balance equivalent to the total loan amount deducting the amount of each sub-contract.

9) The base for tax calculation of property insurance contracts is the premiums paid (charged), excluding the amount of property insured.

10) The base for tax calculation of technology contracts is the price, remuneration or royalty recorded in the contract. In order to encourage technology research and development, for the technology development contracts tax is calculated according to the amount recorded in the contract and the research and development budget shall not be included in the basis for tax calculation. If the contract provides for taking a certain proportion of the research and development budget as the remuneration, stamps shall be affixed according to the proportion of the remuneration amount.

11) The base for tax calculation of documents for transfer of property rights is the amount recorded, including documents for the transfer of property rights, trademark rights, patents, proprietary technology and so on. For land use right grant contracts, land use right transfer contracts and real estate sales contracts, stamps shall be affixed according to the provisions on documents for transfer of property rights.

12) The base for tax calculation of business account books recording capital is the total amount of the "paid-in capital" and the "capital reserve." The paid-in capital includes cash, material objects, intangible assets and material assets. The cash shall be determined according to the amount actually received or deposited in the deposit bank of the taxpayer. Material objects refer to housing, machinery etc. and shall be determined according to the value verified by evaluation or the prescribed price in the contract or agreement. Intangible assets and material assets shall be determined by the value verified by the evaluation.

Capital reserve includes accepting donations, legal property revaluation value, capital conversion difference, capital premium etc. In-kind donations shall be determined according to the market price of similar assets or the relevant credentials.

The base for tax calculation of other account books shall be the number of taxable documents.

13) The base for tax calculation of certificates evidencing rights or licenses shall be the number of taxable documents.

Special provisions

1) For the above documents taking "rates," "revenue" and "costs" as the basis for tax calculation, tax is calculated on the basis of the full amount and no amount shall be deducted.

2) If one document involves two or more economic events and the same tax rate does not apply, if the amounts are respectively recorded in the document, then tax payable is calculated respectively according to the corresponding tax rate and stamps shall be affixed according to the total amount of the tax payable. If the amount is not respectively recorded in the document, stamps shall be affixed according to the highest tax rate.

3) For taxable documents where it is applicable to affix stamps to a proportion of the amount, if the amount is not recorded in the document it shall be calculated according to the quantity recorded in the document and the price set by state. If no price is set by the state, then the amount shall be calculated according to the market price and the tax due then calculated according to the tax rate required.

4) The collection of stamp duty on stock exchanges dates back to the continuous development of the stock exchanges in Shenzhen and Shanghai. The existing stamp duty law provides that for stock transfer documents executed due to purchases and sales, inheritance and gifts of stocks publicly issued by the joint-stock pilot enterprise, the tax due shall be calculated according to the actual transaction price on the stock market when the documents were executed, and each party to the documents shall respectively pay the stamp duty by the tax rate of 3 %. [Since September 19, 2008, the collection method of stamp duty on the securities (stock) exchange was adjusted to unilateral collection of stamp duty with the tax rate of 1% and only the transfers are required to pay stamp duty and the transferee no longer needs to pay the tax].

5) For some contracts for which the tax calculation amount is not determined when the contract is signed, such as the transfer revenue in technology transfer contracts, tax is collected according to a certain proportion of the sales revenue or the actual profits; and for property leasing contracts in which the rental standards per month (day) is

provided but the leasing period is not determined, stamps shall be affixed by the quota of RMB5 at first when the contract is signed and additional stamps affixed according to the actual amount when the contract is settled.

6) The tax liability is formed when the taxable contract is signed and the taxpayer shall calculate the tax payable and affix stamps. The stamps shall be affixed regardless of whether the contract is fulfilled or fulfilled on schedule.

   For contracts fulfilled on which the stamps have been affixed, if the amount recorded in the contract is inconsistent with the actual settlement amount after the contract is fulfilled, the taxpayer does not need to handle the tax payment procedure unless the contract amount is adjusted by both parties to the contract.

7) In commodity trading activities, the contracts signed for commodity trading adopting the approach of exchanging goods with goods are contracts reflecting the economic behavior of purchase and sale. For this kind of contact, the stamp duty shall be calculated according to the total purchase amount and the sale amount. For contracts not listing the amount, the tax payable shall be calculated according to the purchases and sales quantity and the price set by the state or the market price.

8) For public institutions with operating revenues, if the undertakings funds are allocated by state revenue and expenditure and the institution implements balanced budget management, stamps shall be affixed according to the provisions on other account books for the account books recording the operating business and no stamps affixed for the account books not recording the operating business. If the undertakings funds are allocated by state revenue and expenditure but the institution implements management of self-controlled revenue and expenditure, its business account books shall respectively calculate the tax payable to the account books recording the capital and other account books according to the corresponding provisions. The business account books used by the branches of cross-regional operations shall calculate and affix stamps by the location where the branches are located. For branches enjoying funds verified and allocated by the higher-level units, the account books recording the funds shall calculate and affix stamps according to the amount of the verified and allocated funds recorded in the book and other account books shall affix stamps on the basis of a fixed amount; and for branches not enjoying funds verified and allocated by the higher-level units, stamps shall be affixed on the

basis of a fixed amount to the other account books per document. To avoid repeatedly calculating and affixing stamps on the same funds, the account books used by the higher-level units to record funds shall calculate and affix stamps on the basis of the total amounts minus the funds allocated to the affiliates.

9) For sub-contracts or subcontracted agreement signed when construction projects are subcontracted to other construction units, the tax payable shall be calculated on the basis of the amount recorded in the new sub-contract or subcontracted agreement.

10) For taxable documents in which the recorded amount is in foreign currency, this shall first be converted into RMB at the foreign exchange rate announced by the State Administration of Foreign Exchange on the day when the documents were executed, and then the tax payable calculated.

11) For various forms of domestic combined transport of cargo, if the whole journey freight was uniformly settled at the departure location, then the tax due shall be calculated on the basis of the whole journey freight. If the freight is settled on different stopovers, then the tax due shall be calculated on the basis of the freight at different stopovers and respectively paid by the parties settling the freight.

For international cargo transport, where the cargo is transported by transport enterprises in China, whether departing from within or outside of China or transferring transport in different stopovers, for tax due on the freight settlement documents held by the transport enterprises in China shall be calculated on the basis of the freight for that journey; and for the freight settlement documents held by the consignor, the tax due shall be calculated on the basis of the whole journey freight. Where import and export cargo is transported by foreign transport enterprises, the freight settlement documents held by the foreign freight transport enterprises shall be exempted from the stamp duty and the freight settlement documents held by the transport enterprises in China shall pay the stamp duty. For the freight settlement documents of international cargo issued in a foreign country, the stamp duty shall be paid when the documents are transferred to China.

Calculation of tax payable

According to the nature of the taxable documents, stamp duty due shall be respectively calculated on the basis of the tax rate or a fixed amount. The calculation method is divided into three categories:

Contracts and documents in the nature of a contract, and documents for transfer of property rights

Tax due = Taxable amount × Applicable tax rate

Financial account books

Tax due = (Paid-in capital + capital reserve) × Applicable tax rate

Certificates evidencing rights or licenses, and other account books

Tax payable = Number of the taxable documents × Fixed amount

Tax relief and exemption

Under the provisions, the following documents are exempted from stamp duty:

1) Copies or transcripts of documents on which the stamp duty has been paid. This refers to the formal signing of the document on which the stamp duty has been paid, the copies or transcripts of which bear no external rights or obligations and are used for the purpose of keeping and checking. But if the original is lost and the copies or transcripts are used as originals, the stamps shall be affixed.

2) Documents executed when the property owner donates the property to the government, social welfare units or schools, of which social welfare units refer to the social welfare units tending the old and childless, and disabled persons.

3) Agricultural products acquisition contracts signed between the acquisition departments designated by the state and village committees or individual farmers.

4) Interest-free, subsidized interest loan contracts.

5) The contracts executed when the foreign governments or international financial organizations provide preferential loans to our government and financial institutions.

6) The leasing contracts signed between the real estate management and individuals for residences.

7) Husbandry insurance contracts.

8) Special freight documents, including military material transport documents, rescue and relief supplies transport documents and transport documents of the engineering temporary supervising line of the newly built railway.

9) From January 1, 2006, to December 31, 2008, stamp duty was exempted from the student hostel leasing contracts signed between the college and

the students.

10) Provisions on exempting stamp duty in the process of enterprise restructuring.

- Stamp duty on financial account books

  First, new enterprises established in the restructuring process of enterprises implementing enterprise restructuring (with a fresh registration of legal entities) where new fund account books are opened to record the funds, or the funds are increased for establishing funds ties, the part with the stamps affixed does not need to affix new stamps and the part which has not paid stamp duty and the newly increased funds shall affix stamps according to the provisions. Corporate restructuring includes: state-owned enterprises establishing wholly state-owned limited liability companies in accordance with the *Company Law of the People's Republic of China*; enterprises transforming into a limited liability company or company limited by shares through increasing the investment or transferring part of the property rights to enable equity participation by others; enterprises forming a new company with part of their property and corresponding debt; and enterprises retaining the debt in the original enterprise and forming a new company with others with its high-quality property.

  Second, if the new company is established by merger or division, for the newly opened capital account books recording the funds, the part with stamps affixed do not need to pay stamp duty and the part having not paid the stamp duty and the newly increased funds shall affix stamps according to the provisions. Merger includes merger by consolidation and merger by re-establishment. Division includes division by continued existence and division by re-establishment.

  Third, the newly increased funds for corporate debt-for-equity shall affix stamps according to provisions.

  Fourth, the increased funds by evaluation in enterprise restructuring shall affix stamps according to the provisions.

  Fifth, the funds transformed from other accounting subjects recorded in the account books of the company to paid-in capital or capital reserve shall affix stamps according to the provisions.

- Stamp duty on all kinds of taxable contracts. For various taxable contracts signed prior to the corporate restructuring yet unfulfilled afterwards, no additional stamp tax will be imposed on those enterprises only subject to changes of their executive bodies.

- Stamp duty on documents for transfer of property rights. Documents for transfer of property rights signed due to enterprise restructuring are exempt from stamp duty.
- Stamp duty on entity transfer in the process of entity division pilot reform. The entity transfer which occurs due to the non-tradable shareholders paying consideration to the tradable shareholders in the process of equity division reform is temporarily exempted from stamp duty.

11) Since November 1, 2008, stamp duty is exempt from the sales or purchases of housing by individuals.

12) Other documents exempt from tax as approved by the Ministry of Finance.

Administration on tax collection

Payment methods

According to the magnitude of tax payable, the times of affixing stamps and the need for tax collection and administration, the stamp duty is collected in the following three ways:

1) Self-affixing of stamps

This means that the taxpayer self-calculates the amount of tax payable, self-purchases and self-affixes the full amount of the stamp duty tickets (hereinafter referred to as "stamping") in accordance with the provisions. This approach applies to the taxpayer holding few taxable documents or holding one kind of document which does not need to pay tax frequently.

2) Remittance affix or remittance payment

Taxpayers who have to pay a large amount of tax and it is inconvenient to affix stamp tickets, or hold the same kind of taxable document for which stamps need to be affixed frequently, in order to simplify the stamping procedures may apply to the tax authorities to replace stamping with a tax payment book or regular payment method.

When the tax payable of a document is over RMB500, the taxpayer shall apply to the local tax authorities to fill in the tax payment book or duty-paid document and affix one sheet to the document, or apply to the tax authorities to add the duty-paid mark on the document instead of stamping.

For units checked and approved to implement the regular payment method, the tax authorities shall issue a remittance payment license. The time limit and the amount limit for regular payment shall be determined by the local tax authorities, but the maximum time limit shall not exceed one month.

3) Commissioned collection method

This refers to the collection method whereby the tax authorities entrust the issuing units of certificates evidencing rights or licenses and the units handling the authentication, notarization and other related issues of taxable documents to collect the stamp duty. These units will take the responsibility of supervising the taxpayers' fulfillment of tax liability according to the laws after accepting the commissioned collection task from the tax authorities and signing the relevant cooperation agreement.

Place of payment

Stamp duty shall be affixed to the taxable documents at the time of execution or upon receipt. This means that the stamp duty shall be affixed to the taxable documents at the time of signing the contract, opening the account books, or receiving the certificates evidencing rights or licenses.

City Maintenance and Construction Tax

An overview

Some concepts

The city maintenance and construction tax is a tax that takes any organization or individual liable to product tax, value-added tax and business tax as the taxpayer, collects tax on the basis of a certain proportion of the actual payment amount of the "three taxes," and shall be used exclusively and completely on urban maintenance and construction.

The city maintenance and construction tax grew out of the urban maintenance and construction additional tax. On February 8, 1985, the State Council promulgated the *Interim Regulations on City Maintenance and Construction Tax of the People's Republic of China* which adjusted the urban maintenance and construction additional tax into city maintenance and construction tax, and came into effect the same year.

Characteristics

First, the city maintenance and construction tax is usually based on the "three taxes" actually paid by the taxpayer and is attached to the tax payment of the "three taxes." It is a kind of tax levied on the object of taxation of other tax and has no specific and independent object of taxation.

Second, the city maintenance and construction tax revenue has a clear taxation purpose and the funds raised shall be used exclusively on the maintenance and construction of urban public utilities and services.

Effects

First, the collection of city maintenance and construction tax is conductive to expanding and stabilizing the resource of necessary funds for urban construction, and accelerating national urban maintenance and construction,

Second, it promotes the development of the emerging cities and the expansion and transformation of the old cities, rapidly changing the archaic conditions of China's urban municipal facilities, improving the living environment of urban residents, driving continuous development of urban maintenance and construction with economic development, and providing a better environment for production development and economy prosperity.

The system of tax collection

Object of taxation

City maintenance and construction tax (referred to as urban construction tax) is levied on the "three taxes" actually paid by the taxpayer, but it is not levied on consumption tax and VAT collected by the customs on import commodities.

Taxpayers

Any organization or individual liable to "three taxes" shall be a taxpayer of city maintenance and construction tax, but currently the city maintenance and construction tax is not levied on foreign-invested enterprises and foreign enterprises.

Tax rates

City maintenance and construction tax implements regionally different flat rates. The tax rate differs based on the different locations of the taxpayer. Specific provisions are:

1) 7% for a taxpayer in a city;
2) 5% for a taxpayer in a county town or township; and
3) 1% for a taxpayer living in a place other than a city, county town or township.

Calculation of tax payable

The urban construction tax the taxpayer should pay is determined by the amount of the "three taxes" actually paid by the taxpayer, which is calculated as:

Tax payable = Amount of the "three taxes" actually paid by the taxpayer × Tax rate

Tax relief and exemption

The amount of city maintenance and construction tax to be paid is based on the "three taxes" actually paid by the taxpayer and is paid simultaneously when the latter are paid, thus no additional relief and exemption shall be provided. However if individual taxpayers have genuine difficulties then provinces, autonomous regions and municipalities can relieve and exempt the tax at their discretion.

1) For export products with consumption tax and VAT reimbursement, the city maintenance and construction tax will not be reimbursed.
2) For tax reimbursement incurred due to the relief and exemption of VAT, consumption tax and business tax, the city maintenance and construction tax collected should be reimbursed at the same time.

Administration of tax collection

Links of taxation

The links of taxation of city maintenance and construction tax are the links of taxation of the "three taxes." As long as taxpayers have "three taxes" liability, the city maintenance and construction tax payable shall be calculated in this link of taxation.

Assessable period

As the city construction tax is paid simultaneously when the "three taxes" are paid by the taxpayer, so its assessable period is respectively consistent with the assessable period of the "three taxes." According to the *Law on VAT of the People's Republic of China* and the *Consumption Tax Law of the People's Republic of China*, VAT and consumption tax both adopt the assessable period of—1 day, 3 days, 5 days, 10 days, 15 days or 1 month. According to the *Business Tax Law of the People's Republic of China*, the assessable period for business tax shall be 5 days, 10 days, 15 days or one month. The specific assessable period for taxpayers of VAT, consumption tax and business tax shall respectively be checked and approved according to the tax payable by the tax authorities in charge and shall not be collected on the basis of a fixed period if the tax can be collected on each transaction.

Place of payment

The collection location of city maintenance and construction tax is the location of taxation of the "three taxes" except in the following circumstances:

1) If organizations or individuals withholding and remitting or collecting and remitting the "three taxes" also assume the obligations of withholding and remitting or collecting and remitting the related city maintenance and construction tax, then the location of taxation is the location of withholding and collecting.

2) For inter-provincial mining oil fields when the subordinate production unit and the accounting unit are not in the same province, the location of the oil well producing crude oil is the location of taxation and the accounting unit shall calculate the tax payable and tax rate on the basis of the productivity of each oil well, and remit and allocate the funds for each oil well to pay the tax due. Therefore the city maintenance and construction tax payable for each oil well shall be calculated by the accounting unit and be remitted and allocated to the location of the oil well with the VAT for the oil well to pay the city maintenance and construction tax simultaneously when the VAT is paid.

3) For revenue from oil transportation of the Pipeline Bureau, the Pipeline Bureau acquiring the revenue shall pay the urban construction tax simultaneously when the Pipeline Bureau pays the business tax.

4) For mobile operators and other organizations and individuals with no fixed location of taxation, the urban construction tax shall be paid according to the applicable tax rate in the operating location of the "three taxes."

Relevant provisions on educational surcharge

Educational surcharge is a surcharge levied on organizations and individuals who are the taxpayers of VAT, consumption tax and business tax, and is calculated on the basis of the actual tax the taxpayers pay.

Educational surcharge is levied on organizations and individuals paying the "three taxes" and its basis for calculation and collection is the "three taxes" actually paid by the taxpayers.

The taxable rate of educational surcharge is 3%. And the educational surcharge is calculated as:

Tax payable = VAT, consumption tax and business tax paid × Applicable tax rate

Still, there are some specific provisions on the relief and exemption of educational surcharge:

1) For import products liable to VAT and consumption tax by the customs, no educational surcharge shall be collected;

2) For tax reimbursement incurred due to the relief and exemption of VAT, consumption tax and business tax, the educational surcharge collected should be reimbursed at the same time. For export products with the VAT and consumption tax reimbursement, the collected educational surcharge shall not be reimbursed.

Vehicle Purchase Tax

An overview

Some concepts

Vehicle purchase tax is a kind of tax levied on organizations and individuals that purchase a taxable vehicle in China.

Vehicle purchase tax, formerly known as vehicle purchase surcharge, is a newly added tax in China's tax system. On October 22, 2000, the State Council promulgated the *Interim Regulations on Vehicle Purchase Tax of the People's Republic of China*, which changed the original vehicle purchase surcharge to vehicle purchase tax and came into force nationwide on January 1, 2001.

Characteristics

1) Levied on taxable vehicles and has a broad scope of taxation.
2) Takes the vehicle purchase price for the tax base, introduces a single proportional tax rate, is easy to calculate and has a transparent tax burden.
3) Levied on both domestic and foreign taxpayers.
4) Implements the one-link tax system at the link of vehicle purchase.
5) Administered by the State Administration of Taxation.

Effects

Since the reform of removing fees and establishing taxes started in the 1990s, China has brought certain budget charges into the overall budget management and has cancelled some charges that increased the burden on taxpayers. It has also brought some charges which really needed to be retained into the standardization of taxation through "transforming administrative fees into taxes" and has implemented administrative measures of "separation of revenue and expenditure." The transformation of vehicle purchase surcharge to vehicle purchase tax was thus introduced, which is an important tax reform initiative.

The transformation of fees into taxation will strengthen the rule of law; and ensure that the tax is paid promptly and in full amount. With the increasing number of taxable vehicles, vehicle purchase tax revenue will grow steadily. Against this background, the government implements the method of including the tax due into the financial budget and of separation between revenue and expenditure, which will essentially eliminate the misappropriation, diversion and embezzlement of funds among the regions and departments so as to ensure the safety of the funds for urban development and road maintenance and to improve its utilization.

Vehicles have become a popular tool in daily life and production rather than being luxury goods. Meanwhile, issues such as traffic congestion, excessive consumption of energy and environmental pollution etc. become increasingly prominent, which requires the adoption of a variety of economic, administrative and legal measures to regulate and guide the production and consumption of vehicles. Vehicle purchase tax is one important measure. The collection of vehicle purchase tax increases the vehicle's purchase cost, increases the financial burden on vehicle buyers, and is conducive to restraining excessive expansion of the desire to purchase vehicles. Meanwhile the implementation of a differential tax policy towards vehicles of different nature and types will help guide the vehicle consumption structure and therefore plays its part in conserving energy, reducing carbon emissions, protecting the environment, improving road traffic, promoting the concept of healthy consumption, guiding the rational allocation of resources, and promoting sustainable economic and social development.

The system of vehicle purchase tax

Object of taxation

The object of taxation of vehicle purchase tax is various taxable vehicle acts as listed in the *Interim Regulations on Vehicle Purchase Tax of the People's Republic of China*. Here the purchase acts refer to the acts of purchasing, importing, self-producing, and endowing, awarding or other ways acquiring taxable vehicles. The specific scope of taxation includes:

Vehicles

This includes various types of vehicles.

Motorcycles

1) Mopeds, which refers to two or three wheel motor vehicles with the

maximum design speed of not more than 50 kilometers per hour and total engine cylinder displacement of less than 50 cubic centimeters.

2) Motor bicycles, which refers to two wheel motor vehicles with the maximum design speed of greater than 50 kilometers per hour and total engine cylinder displacement of greater than 50 cubic centimeters.

3) Motor tricycles, which refers to three wheel motor vehicles with the maximum design speed of greater than 50 kilometers per hour and total engine cylinder displacement of greater than 50 cubic centimeters and empty weight of less than 400 kg.

Trolley buses

1) Trolley buses refer to wheeled public vehicles which are electric-powered and powered by a dedicated transmission cable.

2) Trams, which refers to public vehicles which are electric-powered and drive on a track.

Trailers

1) Full trailers refer to vehicles which have no power equipment, bear weight independently, and are towed by towing vehicles.

2) Semi-trailers refer to vehicles which have no power equipment, bear weight together with the towing vehicles, and are towed by towing vehicles.

Farm vehicles

1) Three-wheel farm vehicles, which refers to three-wheel motor vehicles with diesel engine power of not greater than 7.4 kilowatts, a load not greater than 500 kg, and a maximum speed of not more than 40 kilometers per hour.

2) Four-wheel farm vehicles, which refers to four-wheel motor vehicles with diesel engine power of not greater than 28 kilowatts, a load of not greater than 1,500 kg, and a maximum speed of not more than 50 kilometers per hour.

Taxpayers

The organizations and individuals purchasing taxable vehicles in the People's Republic of China are all taxpayers of vehicle purchase tax. Organizations include state-owned enterprises, collective enterprises, private enterprises, joint-stock enterprises, foreign-invested enterprises, foreign enterprises and other enterprises and institutions, social organizations, state agencies, troops and other units, and individuals includes individual businesses and other individuals.

Tax rate

Tax rate of vehicle purchase tax is 10%. The adjustment of the tax rate of vehicle purchase tax is determined and issued by the State Council.

Tax base

Depending on the circumstances, the base of vehicle purchase tax (also known as taxable value) shall be determined in accordance with the following provisions:

1) The tax base for taxable vehicles purchased by taxpayers for self-use is the vehicle purchasing price and other charges that the taxpayer paid to the seller (including the handling charge, funds, breach of contract payment, packaging costs, transportation costs, storage costs, collecting payments, advance payments and other charges charged by the seller outside the vehicle price), but not including VAT.

2) The tax base for taxable imported vehicles purchased by the taxpayer for self-use is the total amount of customs dutiable value and the tax due for customs duty and consumption tax. The formula is as follows:

   Tax base = Customs dutiable value + Customs duty + Consumption tax

3) The tax base for taxable vehicles produced by the taxpayer, or endowed or awarded by others for self-use, shall be checked and approved with reference to the minimum taxable value of taxable vehicles provided in the provisional regulations of the tax authorities in charge.

The minimum taxable value for different types of taxable vehicles shall be provided with reference to the average trading price of the taxable vehicles in the market by the State Administration of Taxation.

For taxable vehicles produced by the taxpayer for self-use or imported for self-use, if the declared taxable value is lower than the minimum taxable value of the same type of taxable vehicles and the taxpayer has no just cause for this, then the vehicle purchase tax shall be calculated according to the minimum taxable value.

Calculation of tax payable

The vehicle purchase tax calculates tax payable with the method of rate on value. Tax payable is calculated as:

Tax payable = Base for tax calculation × Tax rate

Tax relief and exemption

Taxable vehicles enjoying vehicle purchase tax relief and exemption provided in the provisional regulations include the following:

1) Vehicles used by foreign embassies, consulates and international organizations in China and their diplomatic personnel enjoy tax exemption.

2) Vehicles included in the military weapons equipment order plan of the Chinese People's Liberation Army and the Chinese People's Armed Police Force enjoy tax exemption.

3) Non-transport vehicles with fixtures (such as excavators, graders, forklifts, loaders, bulldozers, etc.) enjoy tax exemption.

4) Flood control special vehicles and forest fire control special vehicles enjoy tax exemption.

5) Domestic sedan cars purchased for self-use by students studying abroad and providing service in China with spot exchange (1 car per person only) enjoy tax exemption.

6) The export sedan cars purchased for self-use by foreign experts who are permanent residents in China (1 car per person only) enjoy tax exemption.

7) From January 20, 2009 to December 31, 2007, vehicle purchase tax at a tax rate of 5% was collected for passenger vehicles with the displacement of 1.6 liters or below purchased by the residents.

8) Other circumstances enjoying tax relief and exemption by the regulations of the State Council according to the provisions.

The vehicles enjoying tax relief or exemption which is no longer within the scope of tax relief or exemption due to transfer, change of use or other reasons shall pay the vehicle purchase tax prior to handling the procedures of transfer of vehicle ownership or changing the vehicle registration procedures.

Administration of Tax Collection

Links of taxation

The vehicle purchase tax shall be paid when the taxpayer is using the vehicle and prior to handling the vehicle registration procedures with the public security organs and other regulatory agencies.

Assessable period

Taxpayer shall declare the tax within 60 days of acquiring the taxable vehicles for self-use through way of purchase, import, self-production, endowment, awarding, or other ways.

Payment of taxation

The taxpayers purchasing taxable vehicles shall report the tax to the tax authorities in charge where the vehicle is registered and the taxpayers purchasing taxable vehicles that do not need to handle vehicle registration shall report the tax to the tax authorities in charge where the taxpayer is.

Tax declaration

The vehicle purchase tax implements the one-link tax system. The taxpayers purchasing the vehicles with vehicle purchase tax paid do not need to pay the vehicle purchase tax.

The taxpayers shall handle the vehicle registration procedures with the duty-paid document or tax-free document issued by the tax authorities in charge. The vehicle management institutions of the public security organs will not handle vehicle registration procedures for the vehicles without a duty-paid document or tax-free document.

References

Documentary Sources

Hu Yijian 胡怡建. 2004. *Shuishou xue* 稅收學 (The Discipline of Taxation). Shanghai: Shanghai University of Finance and Economics Press.

Ma Haitao 馬海濤. 2009. *Zhongguo shuizhi* 中國稅制 (China's Taxation). 3rd ed. Beijing: China Renmin University Press.

Sun Gongliang 孫貢亮. 2009. *Shuifa* 稅法 (China's Tax Law). Beijing: Economic Science Press.

Sun Ruibiao 孫瑞標, Miu Huiping 繆慧頻, and Liu Lijian 劉麗堅. 2007. *Zhonghua Renmin Gongheguo qiye suodeshui fa shishi tiaoli caozuo zhinan* 中華人民共和國企業所得稅法實施條例操作指南 (Guidebook on the "Regulations for the Implementation of the Enterprise Income Tax Law of the People's Republic of China"). Beijing: China Commercial Publishing House.

The Chinese Institute of Certified Public Accountants. 2009. *Shuifa* 稅法 (The Tax Law). Beijing: Economic Science Press.

The Textbook Editorial Committee of the Qualifying Examination of National Certified Taxation Advisor. 2007. *Shuifa* 稅法 (The Tax Law). Beijing: China Taxation Press.

Wu Gaosheng 吳高盛. 2007. *Zhonghua Renmin Gongheguo qiye suodeshui fa shiyi* 中華人民共和國企業所得稅法釋義 (Explanations of the Enterprise Income Tax Law of the People's Republic of China). Beijing: China Taxation Press.

Zhai Jiguang 翟繼光 and Zhang Xiaodong 張曉冬. 2008. *Zuixin shuishou zhengce xiangjie yu shiwu yingyong shouce* 最新稅收政策詳解與實務應用手冊 (Guidebook on the Current Taxation Policies and Practical Implementation). Beijing: Publishing House of Electronics Industry.

Index